300 Most Important Chess Exercises

Study five a week to be a better chessplayer

Thomas Engqvist

BATSFORD

First published in the United Kingdom in 2022 by
B.T. Batsford, an imprint of B.T. Batsford Holdings Limited
43 Great Ormond Street
London
WC1N 3HZ

ISBN: 9781849947510

A CIP catalogue record for this book is available from the
British Library.

27 26 25 24 23 22
10 9 8 7 6 5 4 3 2 1

Reproduction by Rival Colour Ltd, UK
Printed by CPI Mackays, Chatham, UK

This book can be ordered direct from the publisher at
www.batsford.com, or try your local bookshop.

Contents

Introduction

My first two books for Batsford – *300 Most Important Chess Positions* (2018) and *300 Most Important Tactical Chess Positions* (2021) – are manuals for positional and tactical ideas, rather than handbooks, because the overall aim has been to support the solutions with instructive comments. However I felt it my duty to round off with a third book and create a trilogy. One strong argument was the following statement made by the most respected chess instructor Mark Dvoretsky (1947-2016) in his preface to *Dvoretsky's Endgame Manual* (Russell Enterprises 2003):

"A confident retention of theory cannot be accomplished solely by looking at one example: one must also get some practical training with it. For this purpose additional examples [...] will be helpful."

Dvoretsky is highlighting the fact that practical training is the same thing as solving appropriate exercises. Therefore here you will find 300 additional positions of a wide variety. Many of the positions will contain similar positional and tactical ideas which have been published in my two earlier books, so the third volume is an exercise book.

300 Most Important Chess Exercises starts off with 150 opening and middlegame positions to solve and the quota is 75 exercises where you practice positional ideas, and 75 exercises where the focus is on tactics. The other half of the book deals with 75 positional endings and 75 tactical endings. This is the only hint the solver will get. The best training is the one Botvinnik advocates – that the training environment should be as similar as possible to a tournament situation. The methods of analysing from positions with hints or several alternatives to choose from are to my mind questionable because this is too far removed from the harsh reality where you are sitting alone with a ticking clock, while trying to solve a difficult position under pressure. The best practice is to find out on your own the possible candidate moves, just as you would in real life competitive play, and without any outside help. The key method is to learn how to think and how to come up with suggestions, and in that way develop your **own** creativity and only then compare your thoughts with the suggested solution.

The reader will be offered complete solutions to the positions at the end of each section of the book in the style of a manual. The main reason for placing the solutions there is to help the reader resist the temptation to quickly look at the solutions before trying to solve the positions from the diagram, or preferably from a real chessboard. Indeed, the ideal situation is to sit in front of a chessboard equipped with a pencil and paper and write down all the relevant ideas and variations. A clear benefit of such an arrangement is that you can check your analysis again and compare it with the new insights that have been consolidated in your mind after having repeated the positions on a regular basis. The specific time to spend on each position is of minor importance, because that depends on your playing strength and the fact that the main objective is to learn and above all **assimilate** all moves and ideas you can come up with, especially the first time you are engaged on a position. Every time the position is revised your thought processes should be more effective as well as accelerated due to your increasing familiarity with the secrets of the positions.

When you analyse a position for the first time you should make notes of your evaluation, plan, method or variations to enable you to compare these with the solution. Next time, when revising the position, it will be easier to come up with more, since you should have gained an increased overall understanding of the position.

I should mention that it's **not** necessary to have access to my two earlier books because it is possible to start with the exercise book at once to see if the tactical or positional ideas pop up in your mind, regardless of whether you have seen the principal idea before or not. However if you have read my two earlier books thoroughly there is a pretty good chance that you will come up with the right idea. If not, you will learn the ideas in the positions anyway by solving them

one by one as well as consulting the solution. If any new piece of knowledge should turn up while solving the exercises, you ought to revise the positions at a later time to derive the most benefit from them.

A typical exercise published in the endgame section, covering positional ideas, is the following:

Capablanca – Stearns
Simultaneous Exhibition,
Cleveland 1922

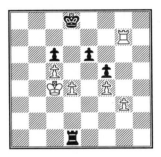

White to move

56 ♔b4!

The idea of sacrificing a pawn in exchange for a penetration into enemy territory clearly parallels Capablanca's famous endgame against Tartakower.

56...♖d3?

56...♖xd4+? 57 ♔a5 followed by ♔b6 and ♔xc6 wins in the same fashion as when Capablanca beat Tartakower. Correct was 56...♖a1! and White's king is unable to penetrate Black's position. Then a draw is the most likely outcome despite the fact that White has an extra pawn.

57 ♔a5 ♖xd4

Cutting off the king with 57...♖b3 fails to 58 ♔a6 followed by 59 ♖b7.

If 58...♔c8 then 59 ♖e7 decides.

58 ♔b6 ♖d7 59 ♖xd7+ ♔xd7 60 ♔b7 Black resigns.

Compare this exercise with the following one which was published as position 258 in *300 Most Important Chess Positions*.

Capablanca – Tartakower
New York 1924

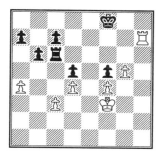

White to move

This classic position is a world famous example demonstrating in the most instructive manner that activity is more important than material in rook endings. White's rook and king are much stronger than their counterparts since the black king is cut off on the last rank. If White activates his king on g6 or f6 White will win since the cooperation between the king, rook and g5-pawn will be too much for Black to handle in the position.

Capablanca played the delicious move **35 ♔g3!!**

The point of the manoeuvre is to walk into the enemy camp on the kingside.

35...♖xc3+ 36 ♔h4 ♖f3?

36...♖c1? loses quickly after 37 ♔h5! (Not 37 g6? ♖h1+ 38 ♔g5 ♖xh7 39 gxh7 ♔g7 40 ♔xf5 c5! and

Black obtains a passed pawn which will secure the draw.) 37...♖h1+ 38 ♔g6 and Black's f-pawn is lost leaving White with two connected passed pawns and an easy win.

The best defence was 36...a6! after which Capablanca would have been forced to find 37 ♔h5 b5 38 ♔g6! ♖c6+ 39 ♔xf5 bxa4 (39...b4 40 a5!) 40 ♖h3 with good winning chances.

37 g6! ♖xf4+ 38 ♔g5 ♖e4 39 ♔f6!

It's more important to get the king to the sixth rank than to capture the f-pawn. Note the perfect harmony between the white pieces. The two pawns deficit doesn't matter when compared to the full activity and cooperation White enjoys on the kingside.

39...♔g8 40 ♖g7+ ♔h8 41 ♖xc7 ♖e8 42 ♔xf5

This is a good moment to capture the f-pawn, as all the black pieces are passive.

42...♖e4 43 ♔f6 ♖f4+ 44 ♔e5 ♖g4 45 g7+ ♔g8

45...♖xg7 46 ♖xg7 ♔xg7 13 ♔xd5 is a simple win.

46 ♖xa7 ♖g1 47 ♔xd5 ♖c1 48 ♔d6 ♖c2 49 d5 ♖c1 50 ♖c7 ♖a1 51 ♔c6 ♖xa4 52 d6 Black resigned.

This flawlessly played ending is one of the reasons Capablanca has the reputation of being one of the strongest rook endgame players. However, he had studied more than a thousand rook endings to achieve this mastery.

Even if you are unfamiliar with the above rook ending between Capablanca and Tartakower it's possible to come up with the idea 56 ♔b4 followed by ♔a5-b6xc6. In the exercise it was possible for Black to draw by cutting off the white king with 56...♖a1!. The most important points of discussion here were the two sides' ways of handling the penetration into Black's camp.

Another example showing how to deal with exercises with or without prior knowledge is the following:

Maczuski – Kolisch
Match, Paris 1864

1 e4 e5 2 ♘f3 ♘c6 3 d4 exd4 4 ♘xd4 ♕h4 5 ♘c3 ♗b4 6 ♕d3 ♘f6 7 ♘xc6 dxc6 8 ♗d2 ♗xc3 9 ♗xc3 ♘xe4 10 ♕d4 ♕e7 11 0-0-0 ♕g5+?

Correct was 11...♘xc3 12 ♕xg7 ♘xa2+ 13 ♔b1 ♖f8 14 ♔xa2 ♗d7 with a slight advantage to Black.

12 f4 ♕xf4+ 13 ♗d2 ♕g4?

13...♕h4 was necessary to avoid mate but Black was clearly lost anyway after 14 ♗d3, when e4 as well as g7 is hanging.

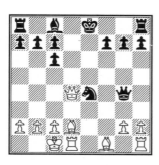

White to move

14 ♕d8+!

Due to the fact that Black's queen was threatened the decisive discoverer was somewhat concealed.

14...♔xd8 15 ♗g5+ ♔e8 16 ♖d8 mate.

Maczuski beat Kolisch with the same discoverer 46 years before the famous miniature game Réti – Tartakower, Vienna 1910.

Compare that game with the following, published as position number 4 in *300 Most Important Tactical Chess Positions*.

Réti – Tartakower
Vienna 1910

1 e4 c6 2 d4 d5 3 ♘c3 dxe4 4 ♘xe4 ♘f6 5 ♕d3 e5?

Black makes a mistake, which was very common before Morphy entered the arena, i.e. opening up the game when White has more pieces in play. Surprisingly, Tartakower commits the same kind of "ancient" error.

6 dxe5 ♕a5+ 7 ♗d2 ♕xe5 8 0-0-0 ♘xe4??

8...♗e7 was necessary.

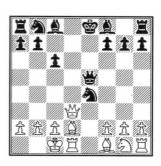

White to move

As a young amateur, Réti managed to beat Tartakower with the most famous discoverer in history.

9 ♕d8+! ♔xd8 10 ♗g5+

Of course the double check 10 ♗a5+?? would be a huge mistake leading nowhere after 10...♔e8 or 10...♔e7.

10...♔c7

10...♔e8 11 ♖d8 mate is the so called Opera mate after the Morphy – Duke of Brunswick and Count Isouard game played at a Paris theatre in 1858:

1 e4 e5 2 ♘f3 d6 3 d4 ♗g4 4 dxe5 ♗xf3 5 ♕xf3 dxe5 6. ♗c4 ♘f6 7 ♕b3 ♕e7 8 ♘c3 c6 9 ♗g5 b5 10 ♘xb5 cxb5 11 ♗xb5+ ♘bd7 12 0-0-0 ♖d8 13 ♖xd7 ♖xd7 14 ♖d1 ♕e6 15 ♗xd7+ ♘xd7 16 ♕b8+! ♘xb8 17 ♖d8 Opera mate.

This game is the most famous of all games and should be learned by heart since it's a very illuminating example of how to play when ahead in development.

11 ♗d8 mate.

Because of the beautiful finish to this game, the mate is called Réti's mate.

One speculation is that Tartakower saw the obvious Opera finale but overlooked the more unusual Réti mate.

What's interesting about the two exercises is that the games took place before the more famous ones. Capablanca carried out his king manoeuvre two years before his famous king walk against Tartakower and Maczuski beat Kolisch 46 years earlier than the same discoverer as the famous Réti – Tartakower game in 1910. An amusing coincidence is that Tartakower was on the losing side on both occasions.

By learning an individual key position, you will be learning an important idea or technique which can be applied in other positions. It is not really the positions or the players that are most important rather it is understanding the ideas that will be beneficial, although sometimes specific positions or famous players can make such ideas easier to remember. The whole concept of whether a specific position is important doesn't necessarily mean that you will encounter it in practical play. What is of more and even vital importance, especially in endgames, is to gain a deeper appreciation of the inner **qualities of the pieces**, their movements, how they cooperate, and their actual value in different positions. One might say, as the ancient Greek historian Herodotus (c. 484 – c. 425 BC) wrote about king Leonidas of Sparta (c. 530-480 B.C.) and his 300 hoplite warriors, after losing a battle against an invading Persian army at the Battle of Thermopylae in 480 B.C., that the names of all 300 deserve to be remembered. Each of the positions deserves continual attention because of their utility value at different levels of play. We shouldn't forget them.

As in my two earlier 300-books, the present volume is intended to stimulate all players regardless of their level. Apart from the fact that even the greatest players sometimes make mistakes or lack important pieces of knowledge, the main thing for every chess player is to keep the important positions fresh in their mind, even though they have already been learned by heart. This pearl of wisdom came from no less a player than Mikhail Tal when he was reading a book of chess combinations by Kurt Richter, despite the fact that he already knew

9

all of them! Knowledge is like a muscle, if we don't exercise it then it withers. The length of time it takes to lose a skill is actually proportional to the time it takes to learn that same skill.

Advanced players may sometimes experience superfluities in the comments but this is mainly due to the fact that all levels of player have to be satisfied. There are auxiliary (small) diagrams attached to the solutions to stimulate spontaneous reading from the book without any need of a computer or a chessboard. I strongly urge the ambitious reader to try to calculate the variations after each diagram to improve their ability to calculate variations, which is one of the cornerstones of chess strength. Additional reasons for auxiliary diagrams are to show turning-points or to highlight other ideas. One way of addressing different levels at the same time is to start with an advanced position and then, as things become clearer, wait for something more basic to turn up. For example, exercise 218 focuses on the endgame of queen against rook. I believe the most important position to concentrate on is where the third-rank defence is involved, because later on a more basic position turns up, known as Philidor's position (1777) and this can be seen in the auxiliary diagram.

Another most important idea to understand is how you can get one of the 300 positions in your own games. For example how did the Swedish chess genius Ulf Andersson achieve such a crushing endgame position against another chess genius, the "ice-cool" Russian Andrei Sokolov, who was rated number three in the world after Kasparov and Karpov in the period 1987/88?

U. Andersson – A. Sokolov
Bilbao 1987

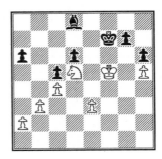

Black to move

The h5-pawn has the same value as Black's two kingside pawns and White's knight is clearly superior to the bishop. White is technically winning and the game concluded...

42...♗h4 43 b4 cxb4 44 ♘xb4 a5 45 ♘d3 ♗d8 46 e4 ♗b6 47 a4

Another ideal position has been reached where all White's pawns are placed on light squares whereas Black's are all placed on dark squares.

47...♔e7 48 ♘f4 ♗d4 49 ♘e6 ♗c3 50 c5

White creates a passed pawn on the e-file.

50...dxc5 51 ♘xc5 ♔d6 52 ♘d3 ♗a1 53 e5+ ♔d5 54 ♘f4+ ♔c4 55 e6 ♗f6 56 ♘g6 ♔c5 Black resigns.

When we know the evaluation of a specific position as well as the technique of how to play it, the next step forward, a deeper understanding of the position, is to figure out **why** and **how** this position arose. By going backwards in the game we have to locate various important clues. For the moment we are mainly curious how White managed to get his king, as well as his h-pawn, so far advanced and how he managed to gain such a clearly superior minor piece with most of the black pawns stuck on dark squares.

White to move

On move 27 Andersson exploited his space advantage on the kingside by the strong move…

27 ♔g4!

White plays actively with the king in order to prepare the pawn-push f4-f5 and f5-f6.

27...♔e8

If 27...g6 then 28 h5 opens the h-file and this is in White's interest, according to the principle of the two weaknesses, since Black's rooks are tied down to the defence of the d6-pawn. By opening up a new avenue the black rooks will have problems catching up, due to the white rooks' ability to swing over to the kingside on the first and second rank. Black cannot do likewise due to his lack of space.

28 f5 exf5+ 29 ♔xf5 ♔f8

29...g6+ 30 ♔g4 h5+ 31 ♔g3 ♔f8 was a better defensive set-up.

30 ♔g4 ♔e8

White has more space whereas Black has no counterplay.

31 ♖f1 ♖d7 32 h5

Now White can play g5-g6 or h5-h6 at an appropriate moment.

32...♗d8 33 ♖fd1 ♗e7 34 ♘c3 ♖cc7 35 ♘d5 ♖b7 36 ♖f1 ♗d8 37 ♖df2 ♔f8 38 g6 h6

Or 38...hxg6 39 hxg6 ♔g8 40 ♔f5.

39 ♖xf7+ ♖xf7 40 gxf7 ♖xf7 41 ♖xf7+ ♔xf7 42 ♔f5

The endgame we saw earlier in the diagram has arisen.

On the 27th move the ambitious and serious player can analyse more deeply and continually ask key questions such as "why did it happen" and "how did it happen" and go further and further backwards in the game. It's possible to find out how this specific pawn structure arose, how White got a space advantage on the kingside, how White was left with two rooks and a knight versus two rooks and a bishop, why Black didn't go for the minority attack and so on and so forth. The underlying key to all important positions is to ask such questions, especially if one's goal is to improve and obtain similar positions in one's own games.

From time to time the complete game is given. There are several reasons for this. If the whole game is available and relevant (as for example in the minority attack) the reader will be able to do the above mentioned research whenever motivated. The idea of giving the whole game is in accordance with the principle that all phases of the game are connected. I was inspired by GM

John Emms' eminent book *The Most Amazing Chess Moves of All Time* (Gambit 2000) where the full games were attached to the solutions of the positions. Actually only a part of the work has been done if one is faced with a position, even though it's important or astonishing. Everything is connected to the position just like the present is connected to the past and the future. This is to my mind the fundamental key to success in chess and especially important when analysing a typical pawn structure such as the minority attack, because a successful minority attack results in a weak pawn on c6, which in many cases will be permanent in all stages of the game.

Before I leave the reader to start solving the 300 exercises, plus a few additional ones buried in the solutions, I want to mention that the sources of all these positions are mainly from my own library where I have a big selection of chess literature, for example the *Informant*, magazines and a lot of chess books. Sometimes I mention the source in my comments to the positions. Many of the positions I have regarded as important ever since I was a junior and have been an important source of knowledge to

me over the years, and if one is thinking from this perspective many years have gone into this book. Some positions are from articles I have written in magazines and newspapers and some of the newer positions are from live tournaments on the Internet. All have been checked by either Komodo, Stockfish or Tablebase depending on the specific position. For evaluations Komodo is number one, for speed and depth in the variations Stockfish has been chosen and Tablebase for endgames with less than seven pieces.

When you have finished reading the book, feel free to contact me at **thomasengqvist@protonmail.com** I would really appreciate your comments and feedback for possible future editions. I'm very grateful for all the responses I received after my first book *300 Most Important Chess Positions* was published in 2018 and some of your feedback was used to improve the book for the second edition published in spring 2021.

Thomas Engqvist
International master
Stockholm, December 2021

Part 1:

75 most important exercises in the Opening and the Middlegame

1

White to move

3

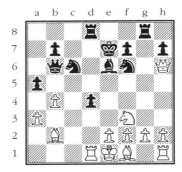

White to move

2

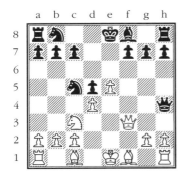

White to move

4

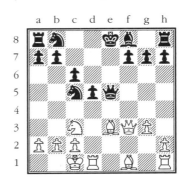

White to move

5

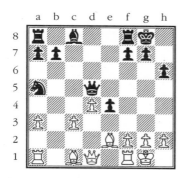

Black to move

6

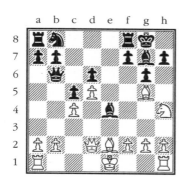

Black to move

7

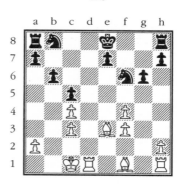

White to move

8

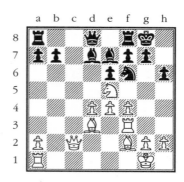

White to move

9

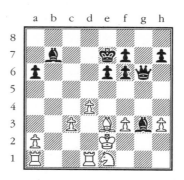

Black to move

10

White to move

11

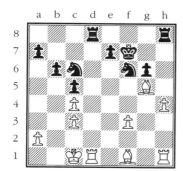

White to move

12

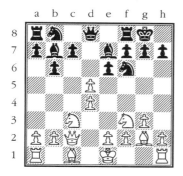

Black to move

13

White to move

14

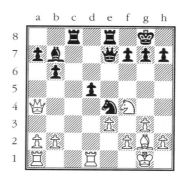

White to move

15

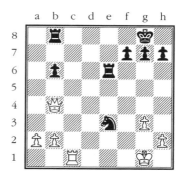

White to move

16

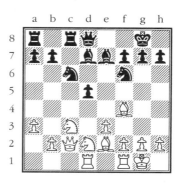

White to move

17

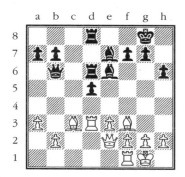

White to move

18

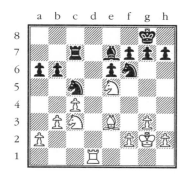

White to move

19

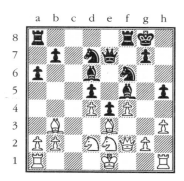

Black to move

20

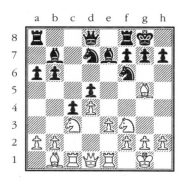

White to move

21

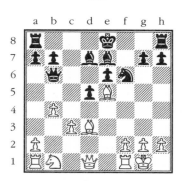

White to move

22

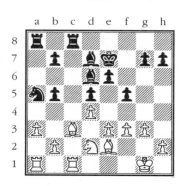

Black to move

23

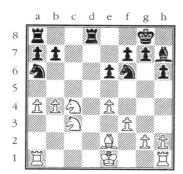

White to move

24

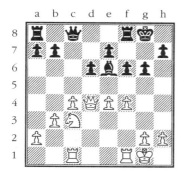

White to move

25

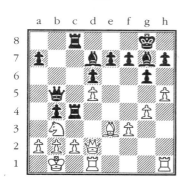

White to move

26

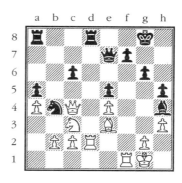

White to move

27

White to move

28

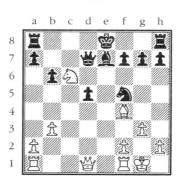

White to move

29

Black to move

30

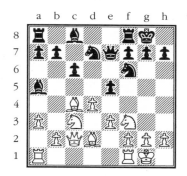

White to move

31

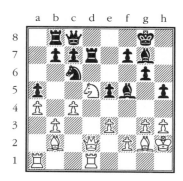

White to move

32

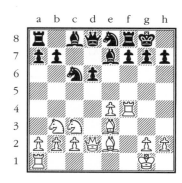

Black to move

33

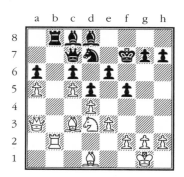

White to move

34

Black to move

35

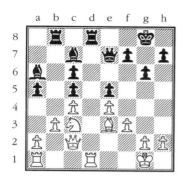

Black to move

36

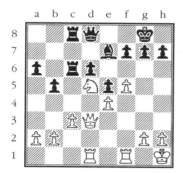

White to move

37

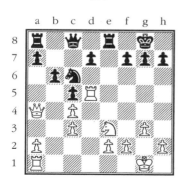

Black to move

38

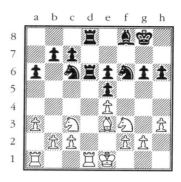

White to move

39

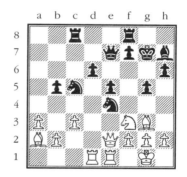

White to move

40

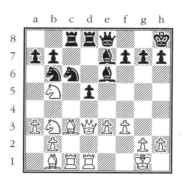

Black to move

41

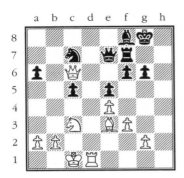

White to move

44

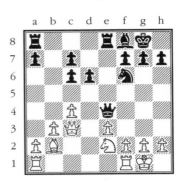

White to move

42

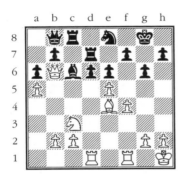

White to move

45

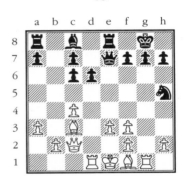

White to move

43

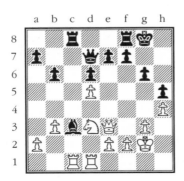

White to move

46

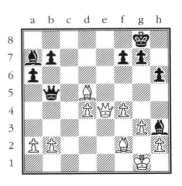

White to move

47

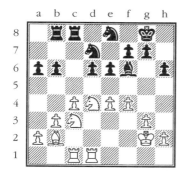

White to move

48

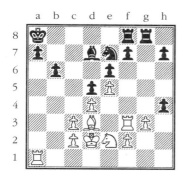

White to move

49

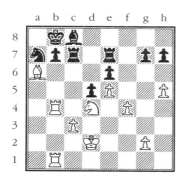

White to move

50

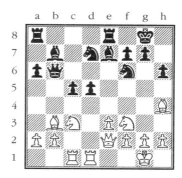

Black to move

51

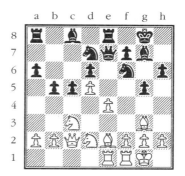

White to move

52

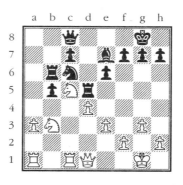

White to move

53

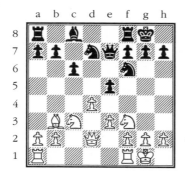

White to move

54

White to move

56

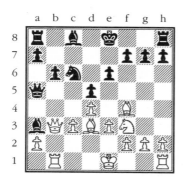

White to move

56

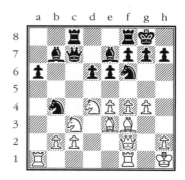

Black to move

57

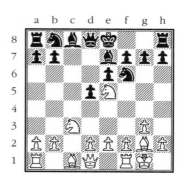

White to move

58

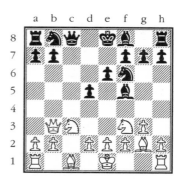

White to move

59

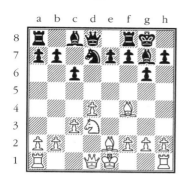

Black to move

60

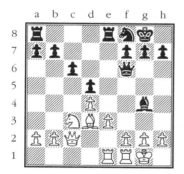

White to move

61

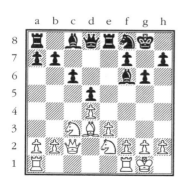

White to move

62

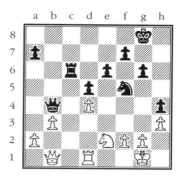

Black to move

63

White to move

64

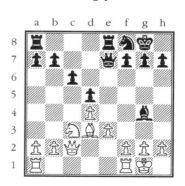

White to move

65

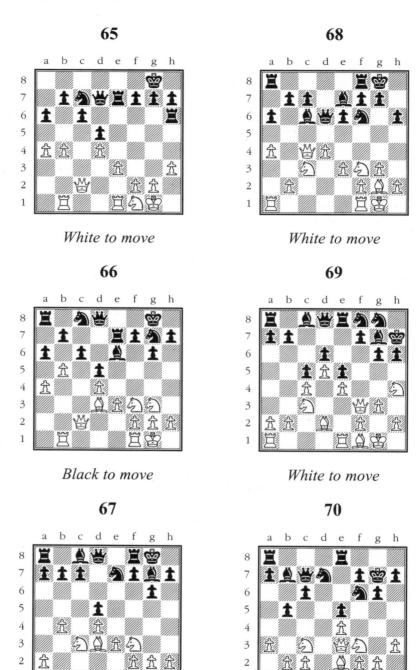

White to move

66

Black to move

67

Black to move

68

White to move

69

White to move

70

Black to move

71

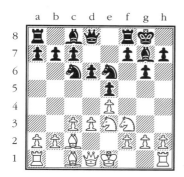

White to move

74

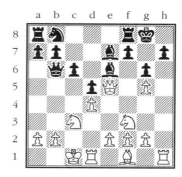

White to move

72

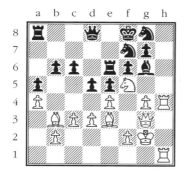

White to move

75

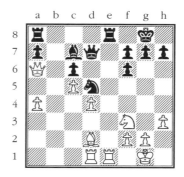

Black to move

73

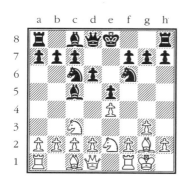

Black to move

Solutions to Exercises 1-75

1

Morphy – Schulten
New York 1857

(1 e4 e5 2 ♘f3 ♘c6 3 ♗b5 ♗c5 4 c3 ♘ge7 5 0-0 0-0 6 d4 exd4 7 cxd4 ♗b6 8 d5 ♘b8 9 d6! cxd6)

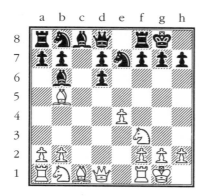

White to move

The American chess genius Paul Morphy (1837-1884) was the first player who really understood the importance of developing the pieces before going all out for an attack.

10 ♗f4

Morphy claimed his 10th move was as an improvement on 10 ♕xd6 which was given in the leading treatises of the day (Hanstein – von der Lasa, in Staunton's "Handbook"). However, this is not true if one consults the computer programs Komodo and Stockfish. It's good to capture the d6-pawn as long as White can maintain pressure on the d-file. What's more is that there is an even better move, suggested by both computers, namely 10 ♘c3!. This is very interesting since Komodo makes good evaluations and Stockfish is good at deep calculations, but they still come up with the same move!

This simple knight move also follows Lasker's principle that a knight should be developed before the bishop. The idea is to prepare ♗f4 next move without allowing the d-file to be closed after ...d5. Morphy played according to the principle of development so his move is understandable, but the computers' choice is the most precise. Even if we do know that development is on the agenda, we must also think carefully which minor piece to move first.

10...♗c7?

Correct was 10...d5! exploiting the fact that White cannot capture on d5 with a piece. After 11 exd5 d6 followed by ...♘g6 and/or ...♗g4 Black would have a fully playable position.

11 ♘c3

The logical follow-up 11 ♗xd6 would most probably lead to the same position by transposition after 11...a6 12 ♗c4 b5 13 ♗b3 ♗b7 14 ♘c3 etc.

11...a6 12 ♗c4 b5 13 ♗b3 ♗b7 14 ♗xd6 ♗xd6?

This exchange only helps White's development. It was better to play 14...♘bc6.

15 ♕xd6 h6?

15...♘bc6! is correct.

16 ♖ad1 ♘c8?

Black plans the neutralisation of the classical bishop but it's more important to neutralise the knight on f3 with 16...♘bc6.

Another problem with the text move is that f5 becomes a really weak square.

17 ♕f4

It's a matter of taste whether one prefers to focus on f7 as in the game or g7 with 17 ♕g3 followed by 18 ♘h4 and 19 ♘f5, because these squares are equally weak when White has so much activity as here.

17...♘b6?

17...♘c6 still ought to have been played. It's pretty clear that Morphy's opponent(s) didn't understand the importance of bringing all their pieces into play.

18 ♘e5

A good move, exploiting the freedom of the knight White has been given, while the f7-pawn is a problem in Black's position which forces him to weaken his position further. But moves such as 18 ♘h4 or 18 ♘d4 followed by 19 ♘f5 were even more devastating.

18...♕f6

Because of the weak pawn push on the 15th move Black doesn't have the natural defensive resource 18...♕e7 due to 19 ♘g6. The other alternatives 18...d5 and 18...♘c4 would lose a pawn.

19 ♕xf6

To exchange or not exchange? It was Morphy's trademark to be pragmatic and terminate an attack if he saw an advantageous simplification leading to a winning endgame. Before Morphy, most players would prefer to continue the attack so here 19 ♕g3 suggests itself, which incidentally is the computer's choice.

19...gxf6 20 ♘g4 ♔g7

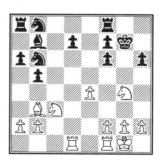

21 ♘xf6

27

This is the point of Morphy's exchange of queens, exploiting the unprotected knight on b6. More precise however was 21 ♘e3! followed by 22 ♘f5+ and Black will slowly be suffocated. This kind of "strangulation play" was not Morphy's cup of tea. We had to wait for players like Schlechter and Tarrasch at the beginning of the 19th century for that kind of "torturous" play.

21...♗c6?

Better was 21...♔xf6 22 ♖d6+ ♔e7 23 ♖xb6 ♗c6 and White's rook is temporarily trapped. Black can catch it by the manoeuvre ...♔d8-c7 but this is just an illusion after 24 ♖c1 due to the manoeuvring point d5.

22 e5

22 ♘h5+! would simultaneously hit all three weaknesses, the king on g7 and the pawns on f7 and h6. 22...♔h7 (22...♔g6 23 ♖d6+! ♔xh5 24 ♗d1+ ♔h4 [Or *24...♔g5 25 f4+ ♔h4 26 ♖xh6 mate*] 25 g3+ ♔g5 [If *25...♔h3 then 26 ♖xh6 mate*] 26 f4 mate) 23 ♖d6 followed by 24 e5 is a tough nut for Black to crack. 23...♘c8 is answered by 24 ♖f6 and the f7-pawn is lost.

22...a5 23 ♖d3

Morphy's plan is to play on the g-file rather than the sixth rank.

23...♖h8 24 ♘cd5 ♘c4 25 ♗xc4 bxc4 26 ♖g3+ ♔f8 27 ♘b6 ♖a7 28 ♖d1 ♗b5 29 ♖d4 ♖c7 30 ♖dg4 Black resigns.

"Winning by force," says Morphy. "This game has certainly no claims to brilliancy, but illustrates the difficulty of a correct defence to the Ruy Lopez game" (A.C.M. 1858).

Maróczy, however, claims the game as one of Morphy's best performances, owing to the iron precision of his moves. Note that one important reason for Black's loss in this game was a reluctance to develop his b8-knight. In essence Black played a piece down right from the start. It seems that Schulten just forgot about this knight after it returned to the stable with the move 8...♘b8.

Don't forget to assimilate games played by Morphy even though he didn't meet the toughest opponents, because his games are nevertheless very instructive. He's one of the most important players in chess history to study in depth and really understand. It's no coincidence that geniuses like Bobby Fischer and Anatoly Karpov regarded him very highly.

One of the best English language books about his play and contributions is *Paul Morphy – A Modern Perspective* by the Austrian GM Valeri Beim.

2

Bernstein – Spielmann
Ostend 1906

(1 d4 d5 2 c4 e6 3 ♘c3 c5 4 cxd5 exd5 5 dxc5 d4 6 ♘a4 ♗xc5? 7 ♘xc5 ♕a5+ 8 ♕d2 ♕xc5 9 b4 ♕b6 10 ♗b2 ♘c6 11 a3 ♗e6 12 ♘f3 ♖d8 13 ♕g5 ♘f6? 14 ♕xg7 ♔e7 15 ♕h6 ♖hg8 16 ♖d1 a5)

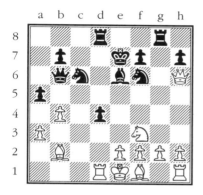

White to move

This hair-raising position has been discussed by several authorities such as Spielmann himself in *The Art of Sacrifice in Chess*, Suetin in *Plan Like A Grandmaster*, Tarrasch in the *Berliner Lokal-Anzeiger* (1883-1945) and Marco in the *Wiener Schachzeitung* (1855-1949) Interestingly, they made the same mistake of overestimating Black's position, probably because of his three-tempi lead in development. However, it's not possible to open the central files, according to Morphy's principles, so White can calmly proceed with...

17 g3!

...followed by ♗g2 and 0-0 and catching up the three tempi he is down on the kingside. Black has no antidote to this simple plan of development. Black's best variation appears to be...

17...axb4 18 ♗g2 ♕a5 19 axb4 ♕xb4+ 20 ♕d2 ♕xd2+ 21 ♖xd2 ♘e4 22 ♖d1

...with a clear advantage to White due to his bishop pair and better pawn structure. Black's initiative evaporates in all relevant variations after...

22...♘c3 23 ♖c1 ♘a4

23...♘a2 is answered by 24 ♖c2 d3 25 ♖d2 ♗c4 26 e3 while 23...b5?, with the idea of ...b5-b4, fails to 24 ♘xd4!.

24 ♗a1 etc.

In the game the incomprehensible 17 ♕d2??

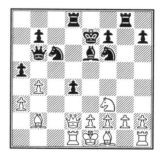

...was followed by 17...♘e4? (17...axb4 should have been played since the reply 18 axb4? would have lost to the devastating 18...♘e4 and then 19...♕xb4+.) 18 ♕c2? (White should have returned the queen to h6, because 18 ♕h6! axb4? [Better is *18...♘c3*] is met by 19 ♕h4+ ♔e8 [*19...♘f6? 20 ♘xd4*] 20 ♕xe4.

29

Despite the loss of a piece Black has sufficient compensation after 20...bxa3 21 ♗a1 ♖g4 22 ♕xh7 etc.) 18...f5 Now Black is completely lost. 19 bxa5 ♕xa5+ 20 ♘d2 ♘e5 21 ♗c1 In a hopeless position White plans the exchange of queens on b4 to reduce the pressure somewhat. 21...♖d6 After this move, one of the best teachers in chess history, Dr Siegbert Tarrasch (1862-1934), makes the following remark: "One of many good moves which Black has in this customary strong position."

The direct way to mate (and one must play for no less in such strong positions) in my opinion was 21...♘g4 with the continuation 22 f3 ♘e3 23 ♕b2 ♕a4 (According to the silicon monster Black could play more precisely with the incredible "family fork" 23...♘f2!!.

First the knight forks two rooks and if the knight is taken both king and queen are forked by the other knight. I've never seen anything like this before. White's best according to the computer is 24 ♕xb7+ [*24 ♔xf2 ♘xd1+*] 24...♖d7 25 ♕b4+ ♕xb4 26 axb4. The main variation goes 26...♘xh1 27 ♘b1 ♘xd1 etc. A funny variation in which all of

White's pieces, as well as two of the enemies', end up on the first rank! Sometimes one can discover the most amazing variations with "brute force".) 24 fxe4 (24 ♕b4+ ♕xb4 25 axb4 ♘c2 mate) mate) 24...♕xd1+ 25 ♔f2 ♘g4+ 26 ♔g1 ♕e1 and ...♕f2 mate".) 22 f3 ♘c3 (Morphy would probably have played 22...d3 23 exd3 ♘c5 24 d4 ♖xd4 25 ♗e2 ♖xg2 and all of Black's six pieces are ready for an attack on the king!) 23 g3 ♖b6 24 ♔f2 ♖c8 25 ♔g1 "Escaping from 25...♘e4+ but overlooking 25...♘xe2+" – Hoffer. White resigns.

To summarise, one must say that it's surprising that so many highly competent chess players, including the player of the white pieces, Bernstein, missed the simple and logical continuation 17 g3, 18 ♗g2 and 19 0-0. However it should also be mentioned that Tarrasch recommended the idea of continuing g3, ♗g2 and 0-0, but only as a follow-up to his rather passive suggestion 14 ♕c1 which he regarded as the best move but which is far inferior to the consequent and correct move 14 ♕xg7. I think this position is very illuminating for the fact that it's not enough to be three tempi ahead in development, unless there is an effective way of opening the central lines against the opponent's king. This was Morphy's most important discovery but surprisingly not fully comprehended by the above mentioned respected players and commentators, who underestimated Black's position and therefore failed to discover the correct continuation.

3

Spielmann – Flamberg
Mannheim 1914

(1 e4 e5 2 ♘c3 ♘f6 3 f4 d5 4 fxe5
♘xe4 5 ♘f3 ♗g4 6 ♕e2 ♘c5 7 d4
♗xf3 8 ♕xf3 ♕h4+)

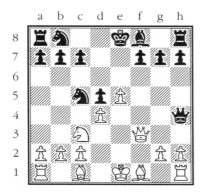

White to move

Paul Morphy's great contribution to chess was that a lead in development is the most important element in an open position. The Austrian GM Rudolf Spielmann (1883-1942) therefore played...

9 g3!

9 ♕f2 ♕xf2+ 10 ♔xf2 ♘e6 11 ♘xd5 c6 12 ♘f4 ♘xd4 13 c3 ♘e6 was perhaps the continuation Flamberg expected.

9...♕xd4 10 ♗e3 ♕xe5

Spielmann recommends in his classic *The Art of Sacrifice in Chess* (*Richtig Opfern!*, 1935) 10...♕b4 but it's actually worse because of 11 ♗b5+ ♘bd7 (11...♘c6 12 0-0-0 0-0-0 13 ♖xd5 ♖xd5 14 ♕xd5 or 11...c6 12 ♖f1 and the f-pawn falls.) 12 ♗xc5 ♗xc5

13 ♗xd7+ ♔xd7 14 ♕xd5+ ♔c8 15 0-0-0 etc.

11 0-0-0 c6 ...

4

Spielmann – Flamberg
Mannheim 1914

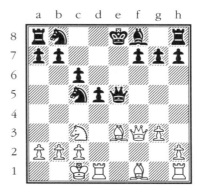

White to move

Spielmann maintained that in the majority of cases a lead of three tempi should almost automatically ensure a won position. Here Black needs three moves to connect his rooks but only two to place his king in safety so White must act fast, in the tradition of Morphy, and open the central files.

12 ♘xd5!

This is the most principled move but it was also possible to accelerate his development by playing 12 ♗h3.

12...cxd5 13 ♖xd5

Stronger was 13 ♗xc5! ♗xc5 14 ♗b5+ ♔f8 15 ♖he1 ♕g5+ 16 ♔b1 ♘c6 17 ♖xd5 ♘d4 18 ♕g2 and White regains his piece with a decisive advantage.

31

13...♕e6?

13...♕e4? was also bad on account of 14 ♗b5+ ♘c6 15 ♗xc5 with the idea 15...♕xf3 16 ♗xc6+ bxc6 17 ♖e1+ ♗e7 18 ♖xe7+ ♔f8 19 ♖xa7+ ♔g8 20 ♖xa8 mate.

The best defence was 13...♕c7 when Spielmann planned 14 ♗f4 (Rather than 14 ♗b5+ ♘c6 15 ♗xc5 ♗xc5 16 ♖xc5 0-0 17 ♗xc6 ♖ac8 [*17...bxc6 18 ♖xc6*] 18 ♗xb7 ♕xc5 19 ♗xc8 ♖xc8 which only wins a pawn.) 14...♕b6 15 ♗xb8! ♗e7! (15...♖xb8 is answered by the devastating continuation 16 ♕f4! ♖c8 17 ♗b5+! ♕xb5 18 ♖e1+ ♗e7 19 ♖xe7+ ♔xe7 20 ♕d6+ ♔e8 21 ♖e5+ ♘e6 22 ♖xb5).

According to Spielmann White's attack is then so strong that there would be no question about the result. Presumably he would have continued 16 ♗e5 0-0 17 ♗c4 so he was indeed right when he preferred to continue the attack instead of being satisfied with winning a pawn.

14 ♗c4 ♕e4? 15 ♗xc5 Black resigns.

After 15...♕xf3 16 ♖e1+ it is mate in three.

5

Osnos – Stein
Leningrad 1963

(1 d4 ♘f6 2 c4 c5 3 d5 d6 4 ♘c3 g6 5 e4 ♗g7 6 ♗e2 0-0 7 ♘f3 a6 8 0-0 e5 9 dxe6 ♗xe6 10 ♗f4)

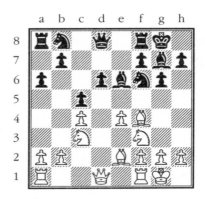

Black to move

A common decision during calculation or when choosing openings or strategies is whether one should be active or passive.

10...♕b6!?

Faithful to his style Stein chooses the most active as well as the more risky move. Compare the move played with the continuation 10...♘e8 11 ♕d2 ♘c6 12 ♖fd1 ♕a5 followed by ...♖ad8 which defends the d6-pawn instead of sacrificing it. This more passive continuation was not inferior to the active continuation in the game.

11 ♗xd6?!

Critical was 11 ♕xd6 ♕xb2 12 ♗d2 ♘c6 13 ♖ab1 ♕xc3! 14 ♗xc3 (14 ♕xf8+ ♗xf8 15 ♗xc3

♘xe4 16 ♗a1 is enough for a slight advantage.) 14...♘xe4 15 ♗xg7 ♘xd6 16 ♗xf8 ♔xf8 17 ♖fd1 ♔e7 and Black must fight for the draw. This was the concrete risk Stein took. 11 ♘a4 ♕c6 12 e5 is not as dangerous as it looks. After 12...♘h5 13 ♗e3 dxe5 Black isn't worse.

11...♖d8 12 ♗xc5

An important continuation is 12 e5 ♘e8 13 ♗xc5 ♕c7 14 ♗d4 (or 14 ♗d6 ♘xd6 15 exd6 ♖xd6 when Black has enough compensation for the pawn deficit due to his bishop pair.) 14...♘c6 15 ♘d5 ♗xd5 16 cxd5 ♖xd5 17 ♗c4 ♖dd8 18 e6 ♘xd4 19 exf7+ ♔h8 20 fxe8♕+ ♖xe8 21 ♖c1 ♖ad8. Black's active pieces secure full compensation for the f-pawn.

12...♕c7 13 ♗d4 ♘xe4

13...♘c6! was the strongest continuation with enough compensation for the two central pawns.

14 ♕c2

White is slightly on top but nevertheless lost the game after 42 moves.

6

C. Bergstroem – L. Karlsson
Stockholm 1984

(1 c4 c5 2 ♘f3 ♘c6 3 ♘c3 e5 4 e3 ♘f6 5 d4 cxd4 6 exd4 e4 7 ♘g5 ♗b4 8 ♗e2 h6 9 ♘h3 d5 10 ♘f4 0-0 11 a3 ♗xc3+ 12 bxc3 ♘a5 13 ♘xd5 ♘xd5 14 cxd5 ♕xd5 15 0-0)

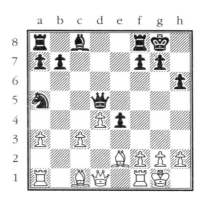

Black to move

In my youth I was impressed by Karlsson's play in this game. Which is the best square for Black to develop his bishop? There are three interesting options.

15...♗d7

Black hopes to be able to exchange the bishop on b5 for the bishop on e2. If this mini-plan succeeds Black has not only split White's bishop pair but has also secured control of the light squares in White's position. 15...♗e6 was also a good move followed perhaps by a future ...♗e6-c4.

16 f3 ♗f5

Now this is the correct square for the bishop, because Black would obviously be happy to centralise his bishop on e4 if an exchange should occur.

17 ♖b1 exf3

Stronger would be to maintain the tension in the centre by playing 17...a6 followed by 18...♖ac8.

18 ♗xf3 ♕d7 19 ♖b2 ♖ac8 20 ♖bf2

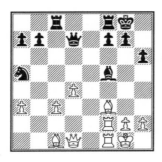

20...♖xc3

Safer was 20...b6 but, being fond of dynamic and risky play, Karlsson prefers to sacrifice the exchange.

21 ♕e1 ♖xc1 22 ♕xc1 ♕xd4

Quite a brave decision considering the fact that White's pieces are very active whereas Black's are hanging and don't coordinate well.

23 ♖d1 ♕b6 24 ♕f4

24...♗e6

Definitely the best square for the bishop, where it not only defends f7 but is also defended by the f7-pawn. It's important to have the pieces anchored when the sea is stormy.

25 ♖d6

It was better to play 25 ♕b4 at once.

25...♕c5 26 ♕b4 ♕xb4 27 axb4

From here on it's interesting to note all the important tempi Black gets for free in return for his knight.

27...♘c4 28 ♖d4 a5!

28...b5 can be met by 29 ♖a2.

29 ♗g4 ♗xg4 30 ♖xg4

30 ♖xc4 ♗e6 31 ♖c7 axb4 32 ♖xb7 b3 33 ♖b2 would end in a draw.

30...♘e5 31 ♖e4 ♘d3 32 ♖f5 a4 33 ♖a5 ♖c8 34 ♔f1 ♘b2

It looks like the knight's only purpose is to defend the pawn on a4 but a hideous trap is contained within this move.

35 b5?? ♘c4

Such a trap makes a stronger impact if one is aware of the fact that b2, b7, g2 or g7 are normally regarded as very bad squares to place a knight. Remember that on an empty board a rook on d4 traps a knight on b2 – but here it proves to be a tricky grasshopper.

36 ♖xa4

Unfortunately for White 36 ♖xc4 ♖xc4 37 ♖a7 will not help. Black plays 37...a3! 38 ♖xa3 (38 ♖xb7 a2 39 ♖a7 ♖c1+) 38...♖b4 39 ♖a5 b6 and remains two pawns up.

36...♘d2+ 37 ♔e2 ♘xe4 38 ♖xe4 ♖c2+ 39 ♔f3 ♔f8 40 h4 ♖c5 41 ♖b4 ♔e7 42 g4 ♔d6 43 ♔e4 ♖e5+ 44 ♔d4 f5 45 gxf5 ♖xf5 46 ♔e3 ♔c5 47 ♖g4 g5 48 hxg5 ♖xg5 White resigns.

7

Carlsen – Van Wely
Tata Steel 2013

(1 c4 g6 2 d4 ♘f6 3 ♘c3 ♗g7 4 e4 d6 5 ♗e2 0-0 6 ♗g5 c5 7 d5 e6 8 ♕d2 exd5 9 exd5 ♕b6 10 ♘f3 ♗f5 11 ♘h4 ♘e4 12 ♘xe4 ♗xe4)

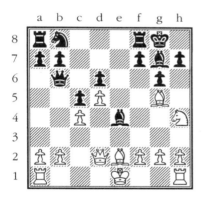

White to move

How does White meet the threat against b2 in the best way?

13 f3!

It's important to understand that the developing move 13 0-0-0?? is a serious mistake and alarm bells should ring when one sees that three pieces are pointing in the king's direction and a fourth can be introduced by the knight manoeuvre ...♘b8-a6-b4. Black's attack will be too strong for White to resist since there aren't enough defending pieces on that sector of the board. The game Zukaev – Tal, USSR Championship 1956, continued 13...♘a6! 14 f3 (14 a3 ♕b3! 15 f3 ♕a2 16 fxe4 ♕a1+ 17 ♔c2 ♕xb2+ 18 ♔d3 ♕b3+) 14...♘b4! 15 fxe4 (15 b3 ♗c3!) 15...♘xa2+ 16 ♔b1 (16 ♔c2? ♕xb2+ 17 ♔d3 ♕b3+) 16...♘c3+ 17 ♔c1 ♘xe4 White's queen is overloaded since it has to defend both b2 and g5 at the same time. Black won with the help of the two extra pawns after the moves 18 ♕c2 ♘xg5.

Note the fast super knight which manoeuvred from b8 to g5 via a6-b4-a2-c3-e4-g5. Such knight manoeuvres can be difficult to predict and that is why one must never underestimate a knight's capability even when it's at home sitting on its original starting square! The lesson to be learned is that one should never forget the concrete nuances of a position, because chess is full of exceptions when there are better moves than pure developing ones.

13...♕xb2?!

The strongest continuation was 13...h6 14 ♗xh6 ♗xh6 15 ♕xh6 ♕xb2 16 ♖c1 ♗c2 with an equal game. 13...♗xb2 was not good due to 14 ♖d1 ♗f5 15 ♘xf5 gxf5 16 0-0 and White has good winning chances thanks to Black's weakened kingside.

14 ♖c1 ♗f5 15 ♘xf5 gxf5 16 ♕xb2 ♗xb2 17 ♖b1!

This natural move was actually a novelty when the game was played. Earlier 17 ♖c2 was seen in a high-level game but Black had no problems after 17...♗e5.

17...♗c3+ 18 ♔d1

White threatens to take on b7 but also ♗e7 is a threat.

18...♖e8 19 ♖xb7 ♘a6 20 a3

Black's knight has to be neutralised!

20...♖ab8

21 ♖xb8

An even stronger continuation was 21 ♖xa7! ♖b1+ 22 ♗c1 ♗b2 23 ♔c2 ♖xc1+ 24 ♖xc1 ♗xc1 (24...♖xe2+ 25 ♔d3) 25 ♔xc1 ♖xe2 26 ♖xa6 ♖xg2 27 ♖xd6 ♖xh2 28 ♖c6 ♔f8 29 d6 ♔e8 30 ♖xc5 ♔d7 31 ♖d5 and White wins the rook ending. The main threat is 32 c5 followed by 33 c6+.

21...♘xb8

If 21...♖xb8 then 22 ♔c2.

22 ♗d3 ♘d7 23 ♔c2

23 ♗xf5? is met by 23...♘e5 24 ♔c2 ♗d4 25 ♗d3 ♖b8.

23...♗d4 24 ♖b1 ♘b6 25 ♗f4 ♗e5 26 ♖e1

A further tactical motif arises, namely the pin on the e-file.

26...♔g7 27 ♗g3! ♖e7 28 f4 ♗f6 29 ♖xe7 ♗xe7 30 ♗e1 h5 31 g3 ♗f6 32 ♔b3 ♔g6 33 h3 Black resigns.

The f5-pawn is pinned by the bishop on d3 so there is nothing to do against g3-g4. A very fine game by Carlsen with many tactical points.

8

Dus-Chotimirsky – Lasker
St. Petersburg 1909

(1 d4 d5 2 ♘f3 ♘f6 3 c4 e6 4 ♘c3 ♗e7 5 ♗f4 0-0 6 e3 ♘bd7 7 ♗d3 c6 8 ♕e2 dxc4 9 ♗xc4 ♕a5 10 0-0 ♘d5 11 ♗g3 ♘xc3 12 bxc3 ♘f6 13 ♗d3 h6 14 ♘e5 ♕d8 15 f4 ♘d5 16 ♖f3 c5 17 e4 ♘f6 18 ♗f2 cxd4 19 cxd4 ♗d7)

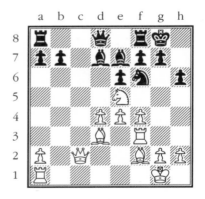

White to move

Sometimes the Pillsbury-knight can be exchanged for a bad bishop. Then the advantage of a strong knight is transformed into other advantages such as the bishop pair and the pawns' desire to attack the kingside. An early example of this idea is the following where Dus-Chotimirsky played the surprising capture (especially in those days before the famous 22 ♘xd7‼ in Fischer – Petrosian, Buenos Aires 1971).

20 ♘xd7!

Lasker, who lost this game, confirms the strength of this creative exchange in the tournament book: "White shows splendid judgment of position by playing for the two bishops; this gives him a lasting superiority." Stockfish chooses this as the best move after thinking 15 moves deep which to a high degree confirms the objective value of the exchange. After all, although the knight is stronger than the bishop, the pieces that remain on the board are even stronger. According to the computer White's advantage is actually around 1.5 pawn(s) at this point.

20...♛xd7 21 h3

This is both a defensive move against ...♘g4 as well as preparation for ♚g1-h2 followed by g2-g4. More circumspect was 21 ♚h1 with the idea 21...♘g4 22 ♝g1.

21...♜ac8 22 ♛e2 ♜c7 23 f5 ♘h7?

Black must stop the threat of e4-e5 followed by f5-f6. 23...exf5 24 ♜xf5 with an absolute centre was apparently not Lasker's cup of tea.

24 e5 exf5

Lasker gives 24...♘g5 25 f6.

25 ♝xf5 ♛d8 26 ♜d1 g6 27 ♝c2 ♛c8 28 ♝b3 ♜c1 29 ♚h2

There was no need for this circumspect move. More aggressive moves were either 29 h4! to take away the knight's only square or an immediate expansion in the centre with 29 d5.

29...♘g5

29...♜xd1 30 ♛xd1 ♘g5 was more precise.

30 ♜fd3 ♜xd1 31 ♜xd1

White's pieces act in perfect harmony. Everything is prepared for the pawn push d4-d5.

31...♝d8 32 h4

32 d5! before h3-h4 would effectively shut the knight out of the game.

32...♘e6 33 d5 ♘f4 34 ♛e4 ♛g4

Lasker comments: "A swindle. Owing to White's two bishops and the strong passed pawn, Black can defend himself only by counterattack."

35 g3

Simpler and best was 35 ♗g3 g5 36 ♗c2 f5 37 exf6 ♖xf6 38 ♕h7+ ♔f8 39 ♖d4! with the idea that 39...gxh4 is answered by 40 ♗xf4 ♖xf4 41 ♕xh6+ and White wins the rook.

35...♗xh4 36 gxh4 ♖c8

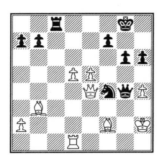

37 ♖d3!

Lasker: "The only, but sufficient, defence against 37...♖c3." Indeed so, 37 ♗e1?? is met by 37...♖c3!! 38 ♗xc3 ♕xh4+ 39 ♔g1 ♘h3+ 40 ♔h2 ♕xe4 41 ♔xh3 ♕f3+ 42 ♔h2 ♕xc3 43 e6 fxe6 44 d6 (44 dxe6 ♔f8) 44...♔f7 45 d7 ♕c7+ 46 ♔h3 ♕d8 and Black should win with precise play. Dus-Chotimirsky must be very careful not to fall into a Lasker swindle!

37...♖c1 38 ♕f3

The pawns cry out to be pushed. 38 e6! was the most crushing move.

38...♕f5 39 ♖d4 g5 40 e6! ♕e5 41 ♖e4 ♕d6 42 e7

The pawn runs home so Lasker resigned. Don't forget the Pillsbury-knight which paradoxically sacrificed its inherent strength for the exchange of a mere bad bishop to make room for the e4-pawn to advance all the way to the dream square e8!

9

Szabó – Euwe
Groningen 1946

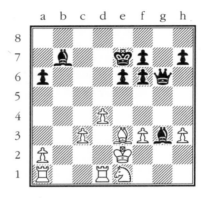

Black to move

29...♗xe1!

A typical advantage when using the full power of the bishop pair, as Steinitz showed in several games (31...♗g5! and 38...♗xe2 in Englisch – Steinitz, London 1883), is that the opponent, paradoxically, must be ready for an exchange to take place at any time. Here Euwe yields his bishop pair to exchange the passive, but important, defensive knight so as then to penetrate White's entire position on the light squares with his queen and unopposed bishop. Furthermore what we are going to witness is the way Euwe hounds Szabó's king over all eight ranks and all eight files, and that in itself is an unbelievable and unforgettable achievement!

30 ♖xe1

If 30 ♔xe1 then 30...♗xf3.

30...♕g2+ 31 ♔d3 ♗xf3

Of course the opposite-coloured bishop only helps Black's attack.

32 a4 ♗e4+ 33 ♔c4 ♕c2

33...♗c2! threatens mate in three by 34...♕d5+ 35 ♔b4 a5+ 36 ♔a3 ♕b3 mate. The only way to avoid short-term mates, under nine moves, is by playing 34 ♖eb1 to cover the important b3-square, but this loses a whole rook by force in three moves.

34 d5

White needs some vacant squares around his king, especially dark squares, but it's not enough.

34...♗xd5+ 35 ♔b4

35...♔d7

Interestingly, just as Spielmann had with the black pieces in his king-hunt against Rubinstein in San Sebastian 1912 (35...h6 with the idea ...♔h7-g6), Euwe has the same human predilection for bringing his king closer to the enemy king (king-to-king), instead of just tightening the net with readily available active pieces: 35...♕b3+ 36 ♔a5 (36 ♔c5 ♕xc3+ 37 ♔b6 ♕b4+ 38 ♔xa6 ♗c4+ 39 ♔a7 ♕a5+ 40 ♔b8

♗d5 and it's mate in two by 41...♕a8+ 42 ♔c7 ♕d8 mate.) 36...♕xc3+ 37 ♔xa6 ♗c4+ 38 ♔b7 ♕a5 39 ♖ed1 White prevents mate in three beginning with 39...♗d5+ but after 39...♗a6+ 40 ♔c6 ♗e2 41 ♗b6 ♗f3+ 42 ♔c7 ♕c3+ 43 ♔b8 ♗xd1 44 ♖xd1 ♕b3 Black wins due to his material preponderance.

36 c4

This pawn sacrifice creates more empty space for the king but it doesn't increase the constrained area where White's king is most vulnerable, since it is already caught in a mating-net by Black's extremely powerful pieces, including the bold king himself.

36...♕xc4+ 37 ♔a5 ♕c3+ 38 ♔xa6

38 ♔b6 ♕c7+ 39 ♔xa6 ♗c4 mate.

38...♗c4+ 39 ♔b7

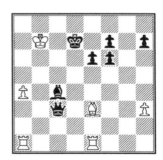

39...♕b3+

The fastest and prettiest way to mate was by a queen manoeuvre along the second rank and g-file to c8: 39...♕b2+! 40 ♗b6 ♕g2+ 41 ♔b8 ♕g8+ 42 ♔a7 ♕c8! and White is powerless against the double threat of 43...♔c6 followed by 44...♕b7 mate or 43...♕a6+

44 ♔b8 ♕xb6+ 45 ♔a8 ♗d5 mate. In this demonstration of the might of her royal majesty, who shows her diagonal, vertical and lateral power in just one variation, lies the key to gaining a deep understanding of how best to exploit the queen's movements to the maximum!

40 ♗b6 ♕f3+ 41 ♔b8

41 ♔a7 is met by 41...♔c8!.

41...♗a6

The human and pragmatic move. Black could once more use the squares on the g-file to decisive effect by playing 41...♕g3+ 42 ♔b7 ♕g2+ 43 ♔b8 ♕g8+ 44 ♔a7 ♕c8! 45 ♖ed1+ ♔c6.

42 ♖ed1+

A symbolic consolation check which justifies White's 34th move.

42...♔e8 White resigns.

In his *The Art of Sacrifice in Chess* (Dover 1995) Spielmann makes the following interesting comment about king-hunt sacrifices: "Nowadays, thanks to highly developed technique, king-hunt sacrifices are rather infrequent.

It must be added, however, that this is not to be explained only by the fact that the modern player is much more careful in attending to the safety of his king; rather have the principles of the modern chess strategy – often no doubt misunderstood! – bred a certain pusillaminity in the conduct of an attack."

10

Spassky – Gheorghiu
Moscow 1971

1 d4 ♘f6 2 c4 g6 3 ♘c3 ♗g7 4 e4 d6 5 f3 c5 6 dxc5 dxc5 7 ♕xd8+ ♔xd8 8 ♗e3 ♘fd7 9 0-0-0 b6 10 f4 ♗xc3 11 bxc3 ♗b7 12 ♘f3 ♔e8 13 e5 ♗xf3 14 gxf3 f5 15 exf6 ♘xf6

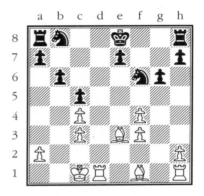

White to move

White has the better development as well as the pair of bishops, so it's logical to look for a continuation which provides more scope for these bishops.

16 f5! ♘c6

Black could have accepted the pawn sacrifice with only a slightly worse position after 16...gxf5 17 ♗h3 e6 18 ♖d6 ♔e7 19 ♖hd1 ♖g8! followed by ...♘bd7.

However not at once 19...♘bd7? because after 20 ♗g5 Black cannot avoid loss of material. 19...♘d5 is strongly met by the exchange sacrifice 20 ♖1xd5 exd5 21 ♖h6 and White smashes through with all his pieces.

17 fxg6

This important exchange of the f-pawn for the h-pawn makes the g6-pawn a positional weakness. White can now prepare a new break with f4-f5 and create a passed pawn on the h-file.

17...hxg6 18 ♗g5

An active and safe square for the dark-squared bishop which now has something to bite on.

18...♔f7 19 h4 ♖ad8 ...

11

Spassky – Gheorghiu
Moscow 1971

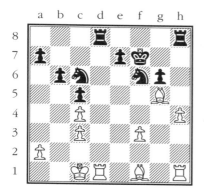

White to move

20 ♖e1!

In principle it's wrong to allow Black to exchange a pair of rooks, since the bishop pair is even more dangerous with two rooks on the board. At least Black should have to work for the exchange as in the game.

20...♖d6! 21 ♖h2

21 ♗h3, to prevent ...♖e6, doesn't really work due to 21...♘a5, since the c4-pawn has lost its natural protection.

21...♘h7 22 ♗d2 ♘f6 23 ♔c2

White shouldn't exaggerate the importance of avoiding an exchange of a pair of rooks because if White prevents this with 23 ♗h3 Black can sacrifice the exchange by 23...♖xh4 24 ♗e6+ ♖xe6 25 ♖xh4 ♖xe1+ 26 ♗xe1 ♘e5 and win another pawn without standing worse.

23...♖e6 24 ♖xe6

If White avoids the exchange of the black rook it will control the semi-open e-file and support a knight on e5.

24...♔xe6

Black has succeeded in carrying out his fundamental plan of exchange.

25 ♗d3 ♔f7 26 ♗f4

White prevents ...♘e5.

26...♘h5

Bernard Cafferty, in his book on Spassky, recommends 26...e6 with the idea ...♘e7-f5.

27 ♗g5 ♘g3

27...♘e5? is answered by 28 ♖e2 winning a pawn after 28...♘c6 29 ♗xg6+! ♔xg6 30 ♖e6+ ♔f5 31 ♖xc6 with a winning position.

28 ♖h3

28 ♖g2! was more active than the text move.

28...♘h5

28...♘f5 followed by ...♘d6 was also good. If 29 h5 then 29...♔e6 and if White continues 30 h6 then Black has 30...♘e5 with mutual chances.

29 f4 ♘f6

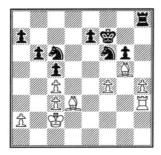

30 ♖g3

30 ♖e3! followed by f4-f5 would have put Black under far greater pressure than the text move, since White not only gets a passed pawn on the h-file but also significant activity for all his pieces in an open position.

30...♖g8

30...♘h7!, with the idea of placing the knight on f8, would have made it hard for White to penetrate Black's position. White can win a pawn after 31 ♗h6 ♘f8 32 ♗xf8 ♔xf8 33 ♖xg6 but if Black replies 33...♘b8 34 ♖g4 ♘d7 35 f5 ♘f6 36 ♖f4 ♖g8 he has sufficient compensation due to White's passive bishop and rook.

31 f5! ♘e5

31...gxf5 32 ♗xf5 ♘d8 followed by ...♘e6 is promptly anticipated by

33 ♖e3 but it was nevertheless a serious option.

32 fxg6+

This is the second time an exchange takes place on the magnet g6 square. White establishes a distant passed pawn on the h-file and in combination with his two bishops this represents a very strong asset for White.

32...♘xg6 33 ♖e3 ♘f8 34 ♗f5

White's rook, bishop pair and rook pawn totally dominate Black's kingside.

34...e6 35 ♗h3

35...♖g6

Black could try 35...♘6h7 36 ♗f4 ♖h8 37 ♔b3 ♘g6 38 ♗xe6+ ♔f6 when White's best move is 39 ♗h6!. The rook has to be protected otherwise ...♖e8 pins the bishop. After the further 39...♘xh4 40 ♗d5 ♘g5 41 ♗xg5+ ♔xg5 42 ♖e7 ♘f5 43 ♖xa7 ♖h3 followed by ...♘d4+ Black has reasonable drawing chances.

36 a4 ♘6h7 37 ♗f4 ♖f6 Black resigns.

12

Karpov – Spassky
USSR 1975

(1 d4 ♘f6 2 c4 e6 3 ♘f3 b6 4 g3
♗b7 5 ♗g2 ♗e7 6 ♘c3 0-0 7 ♕c2
d5 8 cxd5)

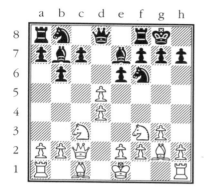

Black to move

In Botvinnik's opinion "the essence of a game of chess is generally exchange. The aim of an exchange is a relative gain of material and positional values." Here Black has to make the very important decision whether to recapture on d5 with the knight or the pawn. According to Karpov it's a matter of taste: "On the one hand, such an exchange is favourable for Black, since with fewer pieces on the board it is easier for him to defend his cramped position. On the other hand, Black has to be prepared for a position with hanging pawns, where a greater number of pieces allows him better chances of fighting for the initiative."

8...♘xd5

Black follows in Tarrasch's footsteps and exchanges a pair of knights to relieve his slightly more cramped position. I believe Capablanca would also have chosen this move but for him it would have been a matter of creating more harmony in the position. Later on it might be possible to exploit the vacant square on f6 by placing the other knight or the bishop there. A player like Alekhine might have chosen the slightly more risky and complicated recapture 8...exd5 which eventually, after a timely ...c7-c5, would probably have led to a position with hanging pawns but with all minor pieces on the board.

9 0-0

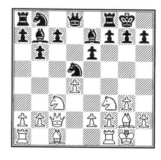

9...♘d7

Other good alternatives were 9...♘a6 10 ♘xd5 exd5 11 ♖d1 and 9...c5 10 ♖d1 (10 ♘xd5 would be less precise due to 10...♕xd5) 10...♘xc3 Slightly worse would have been 9...♘xc3 10 bxc3 (Of course not 10 ♘g5?? because of the intermediate 10...♘xe2+! followed by 11...♗xg2 and Black wins.). Now Black has to play the slightly uncomfortable 10...♕c8 to protect the fianchettoed bishop or the anti-positional move 10...f5, since 10...c5?? would run into the famous trap 11 ♘g5!

with the decisive double threat on h7 and b7 which wins material by force.

10 ♘xd5

If White constructs a classical centre with 10 e4 Black's position would be fine after 10...♘xc3 11 bxc3 c5 12 d5 exd5 13 exd5 ♗xd5 14 ♖d1 ♗e6 15 ♘e5 ♘xe5! 16 ♖xd8 ♖axd8.

10...exd5

10...♗xd5? 11 e4 ♗b7 12 ♖d1 gives White a clear advantage according to Karpov. It's hard not to agree since Black has no effective way of attacking the classical centre and has to reckon with the central pawn push d4-d5 in various situations.

11 ♖d1

The rook will be usefully placed here after Black has played ...c7-c5. If Black chooses a passive set-up with ...c7-c6 the e4-square will be weakened and he will essentially be playing for only one result.

11...♘f6 12 ♘e5 c5 13 dxc5

13...♗xc5

13...bxc5 leads to a position with hanging pawns which is to White's advantage. Not only has a pair of knights been exchanged but all White's pieces will be in excellent positions after 14 ♗g5 followed by 15 ♖ac1 with strong pressure on the hanging pawns.

14 ♘d3

According to Nimzowitsch's famous principles of blockade the knight belongs on d4. With the knight on d3 Black might in the future get the possibility of moving the isolated pawn to d4 with subsequent pressure on the e2-pawn, but that isn't possible now due to the pin on the long light-square diagonal.

14...♗d6

After 14...♖c8 15 ♘xc5 ♖xc5 Karpov comments that "Black's position is only slightly inferior, but on the other hand...for the entire game." 15...bxc5 16 ♗g5 is totally bad.

13

Karpov – Spassky
USSR 1975

White to move

44

15 ♗f4

Karpov comments: "The exchange of black-squared bishops is one of White's best plans, since the isolated pawn becomes even more vulnerable." Nimzowitsch wrote that the true weaknesses of the isolated pawn are the black squares d4, c5 and e5 and the exchange of dark-squared bishops obviously accentuates these dark-square weaknesses.

15...♖e8 16 e3

White needs to protect the e2-pawn after a subsequent ...♖c8 because White wants to reply ♕a4.

16...♘e4 17 ♗xd6 ♕xd6 18 ♘f4

18...♖ac8

Obviously Black has to parry the threat against e4 but Karpov prefers 18...♖ad8 which he thinks is a superior move. This is not confirmed by the computer which clearly prefers the move Spassky played in the game. The problem with Karpov's suggestion is that Black's position is too passive and this is clearly visible after 19 ♖d4 followed by 20 ♖ad1. It's understandable that Spassky goes for the more active continuation

even though it's a piece of cake for Karpov to deal with Black's attempt to muddy the water.

19 ♕a4 ♕e7

Spassky wants to focus on the fact that White's e-pawn is placed on e3 rather than e2 so the knight sacrifice on f2 is always in the air.

14

Karpov – Spassky
USSR 1975

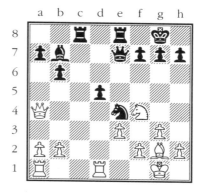

White to move

20 ♕xa7!

Karpov comments: "I thought over this move for quite a long time and convinced myself that I would gain an advantage. White appears to take his queen away from the main theatre of events, but a more careful examination shows that it can soon be exchanged for its black opposite-number, which is situated on the same rank." The continuation 20 ♗xe4 ♕xe4 21 ♖d4 ♕c2 22 ♕xa7 ♕xb2 23 ♖ad1 ♗a8 24 ♘xd5 ♗xd5 25 ♖xd5 wins a pawn but it's not clear whether it would be enough to win the game.

45

20...♘xf2 21 ♘xd5

Of course not 21 ♔xf2?? ♕xe3+ 22 ♔f1 ♖c2 and White is mated in four moves.

21...♗xd5

Black is forced to accept the exchange of queens because the continuation 21...♕e5 22 ♕xb7 ♘xd1 23 ♖xd1 ♖c2 24 ♖f1 ♖f8 25 b4! ♖xa2 26 b5 would give White the luxury of playing with too many pieces.

22 ♕xe7

22...♘xd1

One can understand that Spassky didn't want to enter the line 22...♖xe7 23 ♖xd5 ♘g4 24 ♗h3 ♘xe3 25 ♗xc8 ♘xd5 26 ♖d1 since the bishop is stronger than the knight and White has a pawn majority.

23 ♖c1

A nice move exploiting Black's weak back rank.

23...♖b8

Karpov gives 23...♖a8 24 ♗xd5 ♖xe7 25 ♗xa8 ♖e8 26 ♗c6 ♖d8 27 e4 after which Black's position is quite hopeless.

24 ♕b4

24 ♕d7 ♗xg2 25 ♖c7 ♖f8 leads to a position where White's pieces are slightly entangled.

24...♗xg2 25 ♔xg2 ♘xe3+ 26 ♔g1 ♖e6...

15

Karpov – Spassky
USSR 1975

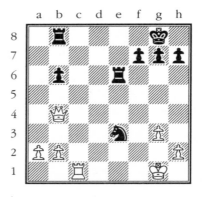

White to move

It's useful to assimilate Karpov's pedagogic comments at this technical stage of the game: "Black's drawing chances are associated with the insecure position of the white king, and if he were able to achieve co-ordination between his forces, it might prove difficult for White to realize his advantage. White therefore begins a forcing variation, the aim of which is to exchange off one of the black rooks. In this case the opponent's chances of resisting will be severely reduced."

27 ♕f4 ♖d8

If 27...♖be8 then 28 ♖c7 ♖f6 29 ♕xe3! and once more Black's weak last rank is exploited.

28 ♕d4 ♖de8

28...♖ee8 29 ♕xb6 ♘d1 would have cut off the white rook and deserved consideration as the last attempt to save a difficult position.

29 ♕d7 ♘g4 30 ♖c8

30...♘f6

The continuation 30...♖e1+ 31 ♔g2 ♖1e2+ is met by 32 ♔h3 (32 ♔f3?? leads to a neat mate after 32...♘xh2+ 33 ♔f4 ♖2e4+ 34 ♔f5 ♖4e5+ 35 ♔f4 g5 mate.) 32...♘f2+ 33 ♔h4 ♖2e4+ 34 g4 ♖xg4+ 35 ♕xg4 and White wins.

31 ♖xe8+ ♖xe8 32 ♕b7 ♖e6 33 ♕b8+ ♘e8 34 a4 g6 35 b4 ♔g7 36 ♕b7 h5 37 ♔g2

Karpov comments: "There is no reason to hurry, and White can strengthen his position to the maximum extent before commencing the advance of his queenside pawns."

37...♔f6 38 h3 ♖d6 39 a5 bxa5 40 bxa5 ♖e6 41 a6 ♘c7 42 a7

Karpov comments: Of course, after 42 ♕xc7 ♖xa6

...Black is lost, but then the game would have dragged out, whereas I wanted to win cleanly." This is certainly true because there is no fortress. Even with the king on h7 and the rook on f5 the position would have been lost due to the possibility of g3-g4 destabilising the rook at the right moment. Note though that such a position would have been drawn with the white pawn on h4 instead of h3.

42...♖e7 43 ♕c6+ ♔e5

43...♔g7 is met by 44 ♕d6 ♔f8 45 ♕d8+.

44 ♔f3 Black resigns.

A rewarding game to study due to the number of important positions which focus on exchanges from different perspectives.

16

Karpov – Spassky
Montreal 1979

(1 d4 ♘f6 2. c4 e6 3 ♘f3 d5 4 ♘c3 ♗e7 5 ♗f4 0-0 6 e3 c5 7 dxc5 ♘c6 8 ♕c2 ♕a5 9 a3 ♗xc5 10 ♖d1 ♗e7 11 ♘d2 ♗d7 12 ♗e2 ♖fc8 13 0-0 ♕d8 14 cxd5 exd5)

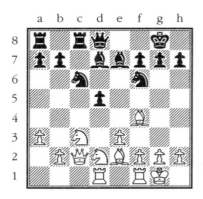

White to move

15 ♘f3! h6

Black wants to rule out the possibility of a knight or a bishop occupying the useful g5-square.

16 ♘e5

Karpov follows the same plan as in the famous game, Botvinnik – Zagoryansky, Sverdlovsk 1943, where Botvinnik played the same knight manoeuvre.

The exchange on c6 will result in weaknesses on the dark d4 and e5 squares which will become important springboards to invade Black's position. Another point of the move is that the light-squared bishop now has access to the f3-square from where it can pressurise the black isolani.

16...♗e6

Nimzowitsch said that "it must always be remembered that the bishop on e6 is attached to the d5-pawn as is a nurse to a suckling child!" This famous statement is also essentially an example of over-protection.

However, from a modern perspective, where activity is regarded as the most important element, the placement of the bishop on a square such as g4 is to be preferred, because the essence of playing with an isolated pawn is activity to compensate for the riskier pawn structure.

17 ♘xc6 ♖xc6

17...bxc6? 18 ♗a6 wins the exchange.

18 ♗f3

After Karpov's clever knight manoeuvre it will be much easier for White to prove that the isolani is more of a static weakness than a dynamic strength.

Firstly White can place the bishop on f3 and secondly the other bishop can use the e5-square to put pressure on the f6-knight. These bishop manoeuvres leave the isolani barely protected rather than over-protected.

18...♕b6 19 ♗e5! ♘e4

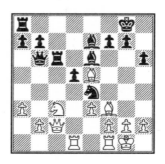

20 ♕e2

The most comfortable square for the queen, while at the same time forcing the following exchange of knights. An interesting alternative was 20 ♗d4 ♗c5 21 ♗xc5 ♖xc5 22 ♗xe4 dxe4 23 ♖d4 (23 ♕xe4? does not lead to any advantage because Black can play 23...♕xb2 24 ♘a4 ♖e5! 25 ♕f4 ♕b5! 26 ♘c3 ♕a5 and Black has survived the one-move threats.) 23...f5 24 ♕d2 with positional pressure along the d-file.

There is no significant gain in the pawn-grab 20 ♗xe4 dxe4 21 ♕xe4 because Black can calmly reply 21...♕xb2. After 22 ♖b1 (22 ♘d5? ♕xa3!) 22...♕xa3 23 ♖xb7 ♖ac8 24 ♘b1 ♕c5 (The only move, since the bishop on e7 must be defended.) 25 ♗d4 ♕d6 26 ♖xa7 the position is dynamically balanced despite the fact that Black is a pawn down. Black's pieces are compactly and harmoniously placed whereas White's are more scattered with pronounced problems in gaining activity for the knight and king's rook.

20...♘xc3 21 ♗xc3 ♖d8

The continuation 21...♗xa3? 22 ♗xg7! ♔xg7 23 bxa3 leads to a position where White doesn't need to play for a second weakness since Black's ruined kingside offers plenty of scope for White's pieces to combine an attack on the isolani with an assault on the exposed king.

22 ♖d3! ♖cd6

If Spassky wasn't interested in the exchange of the dark-squared bishops he could have played 22...♖c7 followed by 23...♖cd7.

17

Karpov – Spassky
Montreal 1979

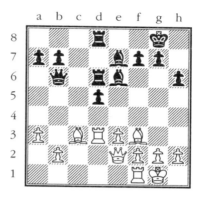

White to move

23 ♖fd1

Interestingly Karpov avoids Spassky's tacit proposal to exchange the dark-squared bishops. A plausible continuation with this logical exchange taking place is 23 ♗b4 ♖6d7 24 ♗xe7 ♖xe7 25 ♖fd1 ♖ed7 26 ♖d4. The exchange in itself is advantageous and besides that features the same pawn structure and constellation of pieces as in the afore-mentioned Botvinnik – Zagoryansky game. The most vital similarity is the fact that the h-pawn is on h6 which means that White can play for the break g4-g5 so as to create a second weaknesses on the kingside. This is exactly what Botvinnik did but compared with the present game his queen was strongly placed on e5, which made this plan easier to carry out. The different placement of the queens is the most significant difference. However, later in the game Karpov puts his queen on h5

49

while keeping his dark-squared bishop on the long diagonal. So maybe this is an improvement of Botvinnik's model game or perhaps a matter of postponing the exchange until later?

23...♖6d7 24 ♖1d2 ♕b5 25 ♕d1

The so-called "Alekhine's gun" which was popularised by Capablanca and Alekhine in their games. The most famous example is that seen in Alekhine – Nimzowitsch, San Remo 1930. The queue of major pieces concentrated on one file is the strongest weapon which exists in chess. On a diagonal only two pieces can exert pressure. However, when it comes to applying pressure on squares it's a different story.

25...b6 26 g3 ♗f8 27 ♗g2 ♗e7 28 ♕h5!

Karpov activates his queen but compared with the Botvinnik game it's more difficult to carry out the important break g4-g5 due to the fact that the dark-squared bishops are on the board!

28...a6

Just in case Spassky pragmatically defends his queen, then Black will

not need to worry about the pawn-push e3-e4.

29 h3 ♕c6 30 ♔h2 ♕b5 31 f4 f6 32 ♕d1

Again Karpov triples on the d-file after Black has made a second concession on the kingside.

32...♕c6 33 g4 g5?

A better defence was to play a waiting move with the king by 33...♔h8 so as not to unnecessarily weaken the kingside. If White isn't patient and wants to win the d5-pawn as quickly as possible, then Black gets counterplay after 34 ♔h1 a5 35 f5 ♗f7 36 e4 ♗d6 37 exd5 ♕c4.

34 ♔h1 a5 35 f5 ♗f7

36 e4!

After very skilful manoeuvring, Karpov has managed to win the isolated pawn. It's normally a hard nut to crack but the key in this game was first to exchange the knights and then attack the defenders, which became additional weaknesses for White to focus on. First the bishop on e6 was attacked and after it had to leave the ideal square e6 (remember Nimzowitsch's famous statement!)

the d7-rook lost an important protector so White was able to exploit his pressure on the d-file and the fact that the d5-pawn was now pinned.

36...♔g7 37 exd5

The most principled move, but an interesting alternative was 37 e5!? fxe5 38 ♗xe5+ ♔g8 leaving White clearly better thanks to his better protected king and more active pieces which can operate on both files and diagonals. Such a continuation is also principled since it attaches importance to the "principal evil", to use an expression by Nimzowitsch, which is the complex of squares surrounding the isolani, rather than the isolani itself, in this case d4 and e5 which arose from the key exchanging manoeuvre ♘d2-f3-e5xc6.

37...♕c7 38 ♖e2

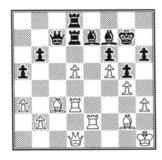

38...b5?

Spassky overlooks the isolani's lust to expand or possibly the 41st move. 38...♕d6 was necessary, as the natural protection with 38...♗d6 weakens the kingside thereby enabling White to invade the e6-square by the Russian exchange sacrifice 39 ♖e6! ♗xe6 (or 39...♗e5

40 ♗xe5 fxe5 41 ♖c6) 40 fxe6 ♖e7 41 ♕f3 ♖f8 42 ♕f5 with an overwhelming position.

39 ♖xe7! ♖xe7 40 d6 ♕c4 41 b3! Black resigns.

18

Henley – Schneider
Elekes Memorial, Hungary 1981

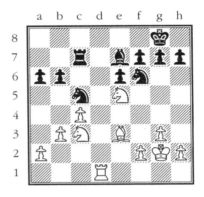

White to move

22 ♘a4!

A creative move, which puts immediate pressure on the most alarming weakness in Black's position, the b6-pawn.

22...♘xa4

The only defence. The alternatives lose a pawn which gives White a three-to-one majority on the queenside: 22...♘fd7? 23 ♘xd7 or 22...♖b7? 23 ♘xc5 bxc5 24 ♘c6 ♗f8 25 ♖d8 ♘d7 26 ♘e7+ ♔h8 27 ♗xc5.

23 bxa4

Even though the pawn structure on the queenside is disrupted the

51

a4-pawn should not be regarded as weak, because there is no way for Black to attack it.

23...♘e4

The b6-pawn cannot be held after 23...♖b7 due to 24 ♖b1 ♗d8 25 a5! b5 26 cxb5 and now 26...♗xa5 is met by 27 bxa6! ♖xb1 28 a7.

24 ♗xb6 ♖c8 25 ♖c1 f6 26 ♘d3 ♘c5 27 ♘xc5

A serious alternative was 27 ♗xc5 ♗xc5 28 f4 followed by the centralisation of the king.

27...♗xc5 28 a5

Note that the b3-pawn is now on a5 where it helps to anchor the bishop. It's interesting to observe that not only is the knight move to a4 associated with pressure on the b6-pawn but also the b3-pawn is now linked to the b6-square.

28...♔f7 29 ♔f3 ♔e7

29...♖c6! 30 ♖b1 ♗f8 wins the c4-pawn but after the forced 31 ♖d1 ♖xc4 32 ♖d7+ ♔g6 33 ♖a7 White wins the a6-pawn. After the further 33...♖a4 34 ♖xa6 ♗b4 35 ♖a8 ♗c3 36 a6 ♗d4 37 ♗xd4 ♖xd4 38 ♖e8 ♖a4 39 ♖xe6 ♖xa2

...an interesting rook ending arises where White's rook protects the pawn from the side. Protection from the side is good when the outside passed pawn is on the second or third rank, because then the rook can help to defend the pawns on the kingside.

A famous example is Karpov – Knaak, Baden-Baden 1992 which should be studied by anyone not familiar with it. Here it's difficult for White to approach the a-pawn with the king because of the weak pawns on the kingside, so Black has good drawing chances.

30 ♔e4 ♖c6 31 ♖b1! ♗xb6? 32 axb6 ♖xc4+ 33 ♔d3 ♖c8 34 a4! ♔d6 35 a5 ♔c6 36 ♖c1+ ♔b7 37 ♖xc8 ♔xc8 38 ♔d4 ♔d8 39 ♔c5 ♔d7 40 h3 g6 41 h4! h6 Black resigns.

19

Bruehl – Philidor
London 1783

(1 e4 e5 2 ♗c4 c6 3 ♕e2 d6 4 c3 f5 5 d3 ♘f6 6 exf5? (Staunton) 6...♗xf5 7 d4 e4 8 ♗g5 d5 9 ♗b3 ♗d6 10 ♘d2 ♘bd7 11 h3 h6 12 ♗e3 ♕e7 13 f4 h5 14 c4 a6 15 cxd5 cxd5 16 ♕f2 0-0 17 ♘e2)

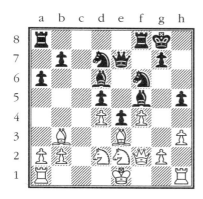

Black to move

Philidor played...

17...b5

...planning ...♘b6 and ...♘c4. The idea of using pawns to help the pieces take up good squares, so called outposts, originates with Philidor. According to the Russians, a knight defended by two pawns inside enemy territory is a "ring", just like Pillsbury's ♘e5 with pawns on d4 and f4. The Russian chess coach Anatoly Terekhin has baptized this important positional idea, or priyome, after Francois-André Danican Philidor (1726-1795) because of this, his most famous game. 17...♖ac8 is answered by 18 0-0 followed by ♖ac1. If the rooks are exchanged the defence will be easier for White. Note that if Black plants a knight on c4 Black's rooks will become stronger than White's and that's why it's important to place the knight on c4 before trading rooks.

18 0-0 ♘b6 19 ♘g3 g6

A modern player would have moved the bishop to one of the five available squares.

20 ♖ac1

It's pointless to place a rook on the c-file since Black will block the file anyway with ...♘c4. It was better to play 20 ♘xf5 gxf5 21 a4.

20...♘c4

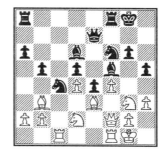

Black attacks the b2-pawn while sometimes an exchange on e3, according to Fischer's or Dus-Chotimirsky's concept, might be good since White loses a good defensive bishop. The c-file is now closed and that means that Black can increase his terrain on the queenside with ...a6-a5-a4 and add more pressure by doubling rooks on the c-file.

21 ♘xf5

Note that 21 ♗xc4 dxc4 not only gives Black a pawn majority but also a very strong outpost on d5 for his other knight. Philidor, who was the first really great chess genius, discovered a very clever concept indeed, and that was one of the reasons he called the pawns the soul of chess. "Pawns are the soul of the game. They alone create attack and defence, the way they are deployed decides the fate of the game."

21...gxf5 22 ♕g3+?

The queen is very exposed on the g-file. More defensive opportunities were possible after 22 ♖fe1 followed by ♕h4 and ♘f1.

22...♕g7

22...♔h7! would have been embarrassing for White's queen because of ...♖g8 next move.

23 ♕xg7+?

23 ♕f2 should have been preferred.

23...♔xg7

The exchange of queens is clearly in Black's favour due to the fact that all his minor pieces and pawns are more actively placed than White's.

24 ♗xc4

Sooner or later the strong knight has to be eliminated since it's hardly possible to play around it or go beyond it.

24...bxc4?

24...dxc4 would have improved Black's position much more. 25...♘d5 could have been played next move, followed by preparing the advance of the queenside pawn majority.

25 g3?

An immediate 25 b3 was more useful.

25...♖ab8?

It was better to place one of the rooks on c8.

26 b3 ♗a3 27 ♖c2 cxb3 28 axb3

Stronger was 28 ♘xb3! and White has a good outpost on c5. However it is not as strong as Black's on c4 because White's outpost is only covered by one pawn.

28...♖fc8 29 ♖xc8 ♖xc8 30 ♖a1 ♗b4?

30...♖c1+! 31 ♖xc1 ♗xc1 32 ♘f1 ♗b2 looks convincing, considering the space Black enjoys and the more active positions of all his pieces.

31 ♖xa6 ♖c3 32 ♔f2 ♖d3 33 ♖a2?!

The best chance to fight for a draw was 33 ♘f1 ♖xb3 34 ♔e2.

33...♗xd2 34 ♖xd2 ♖xb3 35 ♖c2 h4?

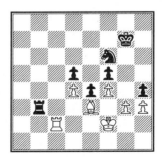

This move looks better than it is. Correct was 35...♔f7.

36 ♖c7+

36 gxh4! ♘h5 37 ♖c7+ ♔f6 38 ♖c6+ ♔e7 39 ♖g6 ♘xf4 40 ♗xf4 ♖f3+ 41 ♔e2 ♖xf4 42 h5 would have led to an equal rook ending. White's rook has very good squares on g6 and g5.

36...♔g6 37 gxh4 ♘h5 38 ♖d7

Staunton's improvement 38 ♖c6+! is still valid today.

38...♘xf4?!

38...♖b2+ 39 ♔f1 ♖h2 was a stronger continuation.

39 ♗xf4 ♖f3+ 40 ♔g2 ♖xf4 41 ♖xd5 ♖f3

If 41...♖xh4 then 42 ♔g3 ♔g5 43 ♖d8!.

42 ♖d8 ♖d3 43 d5 f4 44 d6 ♖d2+ 45 ♔f1 ♔f7 46 h5 e3 47 h6?

47 ♖d7+ ♔e6 48 ♖d8 leads to a draw, for example 48...♖f2+ 49 ♔e1 ♖f3 50 ♖f8 ♔xd6 51 h6 ♖xh3 52 ♖xf4 etc.

47...f3 White resigns.

Don't forget the key to Philidor's victory: ...b5, ...♘b6 and ...♘c4!, Philidor's ring!

20

Pillsbury – Tarrasch
Hastings 1895

(1 d4 d5 2 c4 e6 3 ♘c3 ♘f6 4 ♗g5 ♗e7 5 ♘f3 ♘bd7 6 ♖c1 0-0 7 e3 b6 8 cxd5 exd5 9 ♗d3 ♗b7 10 0-0 c5 11 ♖e1 c4 12 ♗b1 a6)

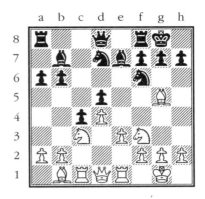

White to move

Probably inspired by Philidor and to a certain extent Labourdonnais, Pillsbury successfully placed a knight on e5, with pawns on d4 and f4, in several games in the Queen's Gambit. Here he plays it for the first time against Tarrasch at Hastings 1895, the tournament which made him immortal.

13 ♘e5!

One of the most famous plans in the Queen's Gambit is Pillsbury's attack beginning with ♘e5, followed by f2-f4 and ♕f3. In this position it's also an effective counter to Black's pawn majority.

13...b5

Black cannot prevent White from setting up a Pillsbury position since 13...♘xe5 14 dxe5 ♘d7 15 ♗xe7 ♕xe7 16 f4 is too awkward.

14 f4 ♖e8

Black plans a reinforcement of the h7-square with ...♘f8 but this set-up is a little passive. More active was either 14...b4, setting the pawn majority in motion, or centralisation with 14...♘e4 which also reveals the main defect of White's set-up, the e4-square.

15 ♕f3 ♘f8 16 ♘e2 ♘e4 17 ♗xe7 ♖xe7

18 ♗xe4!

This thematic exchange was a surprise for Pillsbury's contemporaries but it is better that Black has a pawn on e4 than a strong knight which disturbs White's position more and besides that supports the black queenside pawn majority.

18...dxe4 19 ♕g3!

A good place for the queen to x-ray Black's king.

19...f6 20 ♘g4 ♔h8 21 f5!

The f-pawn shows its teeth by immobilising the black knight while providing a square for the e2-knight as well as the f1-rook on f4.

21...♕d7 22 ♖f1

The position is pretty balanced since White cannot activate the knight on f4 due to the pressure on f5. Pillsbury managed to win a thrilling game and mated Black's king in the 52nd move.

21

Nimzowitsch – Salwe
Karlsbad 1911

(1 e4 e6 2 d4 d5 3 e5 c5 4 c3 ♘c6 5 ♘f3 ♕b6 6 ♗d3 ♗d7?! 7 dxc5! ♗xc5 8 0-0 f6?! 9 b4! ♗e7 10 ♗f4 fxe5 11 ♘xe5 ♘xe5 12 ♗xe5 ♘f6)

White to move

13 ♘d2

White should permanently blockade the d4- and e5-squares. 13 ♕c2? is a one-move-threat which ignores the important central squares. After 13...0-0 14 ♗xf6 ♖xf6 15 ♗xh7+ ♔h8 16 ♗g6 (16 ♗d3 e5) 16...e5! White has won a pawn but Black has liberated his position and is ready to march on in the centre. White would probably lose the game in the long run.

13...0-0 14 ♘f3! ♗d6

14...♗b5 15 ♗d4 ♕a6 16 ♗xb5 ♕xb5 17 ♘g5 wins the e-pawn.

15 ♕e2!

The idea of extending the blockade, by blockading the d4-square with the bishop and the e5-square with the knight, is doomed to fail after 15 ♗d4 ♕c7 16 ♕e2 ♘g4! 17 h3 (17 ♗xh7+ ♔xh7 18 ♘g5+ ♔g6 19 ♕xg4 ♖f4 20 ♕h3 ♔xg5 21 ♗xg7 ♔g6 22 ♕h6+ ♔f7 23 ♕h7 ♔e8 This incredible variation shows what the defending king is capable of if White doesn't control the centre.) 17...e5. Note that Black exploits the mobility of the e-pawn. This is the reason that White should not have lifted the blockade for a second, since the pawn's lust to expand is executed with all its inherent dynamic energy.

15...♖ac8

If 15...♗xe5 then 16 ♘xe5 ♖ac8 17 c4!.

16 ♗d4!

Now is the right moment to extend the blockade to d4 and e5.

16...♕c7 17 ♘e5

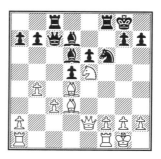

Black is seriously blockaded. Note the bishop on d7 which is suffocated behind its own pawns on e6 and d5. Note also how precisely White had to play to achieve this total blockade in the centre.

17...♗e8 18 ♖ae1

Overprotection is one of the most important strategic concepts discovered by Nimzowitsch.

18...♗xe5 19 ♗xe5 ♕c6 20 ♗d4 ♗d7 21 ♕c2

White initiates a decisive regrouping.

21...♖f7 22 ♖e3 b6 23 ♖g3 ♔h8 24 ♗xh7 e5

Or 24...♘xh7 25 ♕g6 ♔g8 26 ♗xg7 ♘f8 27 ♕h6 ♘h7 28 ♗f6+.

25 ♗g6

A necessary intermediate move. If 25 ♗xe5?? ♘xh7 and Black's queen controls g6.

25...♖e7 26 ♖e1 ♕d6 27 ♗e3 d4

Note the pawn's lust to expand!

28 ♗g5 ♖xc3 29 ♖xc3 dxc3 30 ♕xc3 ♔g8 31 a3 ♔f8 32 ♗h4 ♗e8 33 ♗f5 ♕d4 34 ♕xd4 exd4 35 ♖xe7 ♔xe7 36 ♗d3 ♔d6 37 ♗xf6 gxf6 38 h4 Black resigns.

The main idea was to stop Black's central pawns expanding after 1 e4 e6 2 d4 d5 3 e5. If Black manages to liquidate White's pawns on d4 and e5 with ...c5 and ...f6, White has to replace the pawns with pieces. In the game the bishop replaced the pawn on d4 and the knight the pawn on e5.

The move 7 dxc5! is regarded as one of the deepest moves ever played since it was the starting-point for a new philosophy regarding the treatment of the centre in the French Defence.

22

Janowsky – Capablanca
New York 1916

(1 d4 ♘f6 2 ♘f3 d5 3 c4 c6 4 ♘c3 ♗f5 5 ♕b3 ♕b6 6 ♕xb6 axb6 7 cxd5 ♘xd5 8 ♘xd5 cxd5 9 e3 ♘c6 10 ♗d2

10...♗d7!? An extraordinarily deep move, Capablanca is already preparing Philidor's famous knight manoeuvre ...♘c6-a5, ...b6-b5 and ...♘a5-c4. This is actually what he wrote in his autobiography *My Chess Career.* 11 ♗e2 (11 ♘e5 would have prevented Black's Philidor-plan and was the critical move to challenge Black's set-up.) 11...e6 12 0-0 ♗d6 13 ♖fc1 ♔e7! 14 ♗c3 ♖hc8 15 a3 ♘a5 16 ♘d2 f5 17 g3 b5 18 f3)

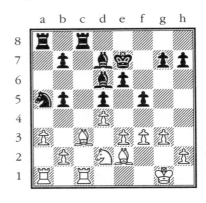

Black to move

18...♘c4!

Capablanca plays according to Philidor's concept. The knight is so well placed on c4, where it attacks four squares in enemy territory, that sooner or later White will be forced to exchange it, and then Black gets rid of his doubled pawn and will enjoy a space advantage on the queenside.

19 ♗xc4?!

19 ♔f2 was the alternative if White can tolerate the bold knight. Otherwise 19 ♘xc4 bxc4 20 e4 was the lesser evil.

19...bxc4

Everything goes according to plan. Black's b5-pawn is now undoubled and he can increase the pressure against the queenside pawns with the key break ...b7-b5-b4.

20 e4 ♔f7 21 e5 ♗e7 22 f4 b5 23 ♔f2 ♖a4 24 ♔e3 ♖ca8 25 ♖ab1 h6

Black's plan is to utilise the greater mobility of his rooks and work with two breaks at the same time, so White has to reckon with both ...b5-b4 and ...g7-g5.

26 ♘f3 g5 27 ♘e1?

The knight was well-placed on f3 so it was correct to benefit from this by playing 27 fxg5 hxg5 28 h4 g4 29 ♘g1 b4 30 axb4 ♗xb4 31 ♗xb4 ♖xb4 32 ♘e2. It would not be a disaster to lose the b2-pawn, due to White's blockading possibilities, so this continuation should definitely have been tried.

27...♖g8 28 ♔f3 gxf4 29 gxf4 ♖aa8 30 ♘g2 ♖g4 31 ♖g1 ♖ag8 32 ♗e1 b4 33 axb4

Worse would have been 33 ♗xb4? ♗a4! 34 ♖bc1 ♗xb4 35 axb4 ♖b8.

33...♗a4 34 ♖a1

34 ♖c1 was necessary to stop the decisive bishop manoeuvre ...♗a4-c2-e4, but White has been outplayed anyway.

34...♗c2 35 ♗g3 ♗e4+ 36 ♔f2 h5

White cannot avoid the loss of material with ...h5-h4 hanging over him.

37 ♖a7 ♗xg2 38 ♖xg2 h4 39 ♗xh4 ♖xg2+ 40 ♔f3 ♖xh2 41 ♗xe7 ♖h3+ 42 ♔f2 ♖b3 43 ♗g5+ ♔g6 44 ♖e7 ♖xb2+ 45 ♔f3 ♖a8 46 ♖xe6+ ♔h7 White resigns.

23

Alekhine – Bogoljubow
Game 5, World Championship,
Wiesbaden 1929

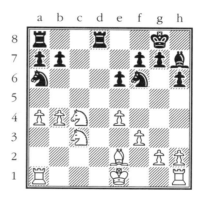

White to move

17 ♘a2!

The only way to retain White's positional advantage. It contains an annoying threat since Black has to calculate how to meet 18 ♘a5 ♖ab8

19 ♘xb7!. If instead 17 b5 then Black solves the problem of his badly placed queenside knight by 17...♘c5. 17 ♖b1 would have given Black promising counterplay with 17...♘d5!, thanks to the pin on the h7-b1 diagonal.

17...♘b8

Black intends the knight manoeuvre ...♘b8-c6-d4.

18 ♔f2

18 b5 ♘bd7 gives the queenside knight prospects of a bright future on the fine c5 square.

18...♘c6 19 ♖hd1 ♘d4 20 ♖ac1 ♔f8

Black's long-term-plan is to get the queen's bishop in play after ...♘e8, ...♗g8, ...f6 and ...e5, but in the meantime White will increase the queenside pressure.

21 ♗f1 ♘e8 22 ♘c3

Alekhine wants all his pieces in play before embarking on an attack with ♘a5.

22...f6 23 ♘a5 ♖ab8?

23...b6 was necessary with a slight advantage to White.

24 ♘b5!

The seemingly passive a2-knight has a lot of energy in store and clinches the game by winning a pawn by force.

24...♘xb5

24...e5 25 ♘xd4 exd4 26 ♘b3 and the pawn is lost.

25 ♖xd8 ♖xd8

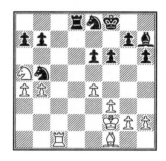

26 ♘xb7!

This intermezzo must have been overlooked by Bogoljubow.

26...♖b8

26...♖d2+ 27 ♔e3 ♘bd6 28 ♔xd2 ♘xb7 29 ♖c8 and 30 ♖a8 would give White two connected passed pawns.

27 ♘c5

This is the point. Black cannot defend against the knight fork on d7 and the capture on b5 so it "is actually a walk-over for White" to use Alekhine's own expression in his annotations to the game. Black resigned on the 48th move.

24

Pachman – Gunnarson
Vrnjacka Banja 1967

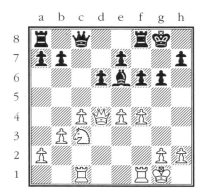

White to move

17 ♘d5

The so called Marco jump is the fundamental drawback of Black's pawn structure. Apart from this idea White can also play for different breaks such as f4-f5, to play on the kingside, or e4-e5 with play in the centre. Also the more unusual c4-c5, focusing on the queenside, is sometimes playable. 17 f5 ♗f7 has the disadvantage that Black can manoeuvre his queen to c5 or e5. 18 ♖f3 (18 ♔h1 ♕c5 19 ♕d2 ♔g7 followed by ....♕e5 also gives Black a solid position.) 18...♕c5.

17...♗xd5 18 ♕xd5+

After 18 exd5 ♕c5 Black can always defend the e7-pawn with his king after an exchange of queens. 18 cxd5 ♕d7 followed by ...♖fc8 makes White's space advantage less pronounced after an exchange of rooks.

18...♔g7 19 c5 dxc5 20 ♖xc5 e6

20...♕b8 is met by 21 ♕d7 followed by ♖c7 but 20...♕d8! would have dealt with these possibilities.

21 ♕c4

21 ♕d6 was also possible.

21...♕e8

21...♕d8!, controlling the d-file, was the best square for the queen although White has a comfortable advantage after 22 e5 with his space advantage and active major pieces.

22 e5

An alternative was 22 ♖c7+ ♖f7 23 ♖d1 making it impossible to capture on c7.

22...f5?

22...fxe5 23 ♖xe5 ♖f6 24 ♖fe1 and Black has problems holding the e6-pawn since 24...♔f7 can be met by 25 ♖c5. 22...♕d8 was the best defence but Black's position remains hard to handle in a practical game after 23 exf6+ ♕xf6 24 ♖e5.

23 ♖d1

The open files belong to White and the win is only a matter of time.

23...♖f7 24 ♖d6 ♖d8!? 25 ♖c7!

White avoids 25 ♕xe6 ♕xe6 26 ♖xe6 ♖d1+ and 25 ♖xe6 ♖d1+ 26 ♔f2 ♕d7 with counterplay in both variations. White should not give up his files unnecessarily.

25...♖fd7 26 ♖dxd7+ ♖xd7 27 ♕b5 Black resigns.

25

Jansa – Bilek
1968

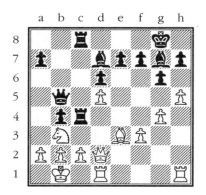

White to move

1 ♘a1!

White plays according to Steinitz' principle of economic defence. Steinitz – Golmayo, Havana 1889, comes to mind where Steinitz played 12 ♘e1 to strengthen the most vulnerable points, the pawns on c2 and g2. Similarly the text move defends the key point c2 which in itself protects the king's position. The original English player Michael Basman once stated that a knight in the corner stands well because all it can do is improve its position! Other moves would have been worse:

(a) 1 ♖c1? The rook is needed in the attack on the black king. Black replies 1...a5 2 hxg6 fxg6 3 ♕h2 h5! 4 ♘d2 (4 gxh5? ♗f5 5 ♘a1 a4 followed by ...b3 and Black's attack is far more dangerous than White's.) 4...♕xd5! 5 ♘xc4 (5 gxh5 ♗e6! 6 b3 ♖c3) 5...♕xc4 6 ♕d2 hxg4 7 fxg4 ♗e6 8 b3 ♕xg4 and Black is slightly better.

(b) 1 hxg6? would have been strongly met by the intermediate move 1...♖xc2! and after 2 gxf7+ ♔xf7 3 ♕xc2 ♖xc2 4 ♔xc2 ♕e2+ 5 ♗d2 ♗a4 the game would be over.

(c) 1 ♗d4? ♖xc2! 2 ♕f4 (2 ♕xc2? ♖xc2 3 ♔xc2 ♕e2+) 2...f6! and Black is clearly better.

(d) 1 ♖h2? ♖xc2! 2 ♕xc2 ♖xc2 3 ♖xc2 gxh5! and Black wins.

(e) 1 ♘d4? ♕xd5 2 ♕h2 ♗e5 3 f4 ♗xd4 4 hxg6 h5! 5 gxf7+ ♕xf7! 6 ♖xd4 (6 ♗xd4 ♗xg4) 6...♖xd4 7 ♗xd4 ♕d5 8 ♕g1 (8 ♕xh5 ♕xd4) 8...♗xg4 and Black has excellent winning chances with an extra pawn, more active pieces and a bishop of opposite colour.

1...e6?

Stronger was 1...a5!. Direct attacks like 2 ♕h2 (If 2 hxg6 fxg6 3 ♕h2 then 3...h5 4 gxh5 ♗f5 5 ♖d2 a4 followed by the decisive break ...b4-b3.) don't work due to the surprise move 2...g5!! 3 ♗xg5 a4 when White's cornered knight looks forever doomed, especially if Black plays ...a4-a3 and White answers b2-b3.

**2 hxg6 hxg6 3 ♕h2 exd5 4 ♕h7+
♔f8 5 ♗h6 ♗xh6 6 ♕xh6+ ♔e8
7 ♕h8+ ♔e7 8 ♕h4+ f6 9 ♖he1+
♔d8 10 ♕xf6+** and White wins.

26

Karpov – Spassky
Game 9, Candidates match,
Leningrad 1974

(1 e4 c5 2 ♘f3 e6 3 d4 cxd4
4 ♘xd4 ♘f6 5 ♘c3 d6 6 ♗e2 ♗e7
7 0-0 0-0 8 f4 ♘c6 9 ♗e3 ♗d7
10 ♘b3! a5 11 a4 ♘b4 12 ♗f3 ♗c6
13 ♘d4 g6 14 ♖f2 e5 15 ♘xc6 bxc6
16 fxe5 dxe5 17 ♕f1 ♕c8 18 h3
♘d7 19 ♗g4! h5 20 ♗xd7 ♕xd7
21 ♕c4 ♗h4 22 ♖d2 ♕e7 23 ♖f1
♖fd8)

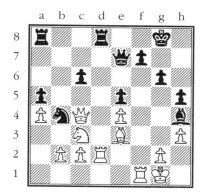

White to move

24 ♘b1!!

According to the Russian school,
when you don't know what to do an
effective plan is to check which of
your pieces is the worst placed and
then improve it. The knight did
nothing constructive on c3, and it
stood in the way of the pawn on c2,
but now it can manoeuvre to f3

where it has far greater prospects.
This kind of manoeuvre has been
seen before, the most famous game
being Lasker – Pillsbury, Paris 1900,
where Lasker practically won a
pawn by force after playing the
brilliant manoeuvre 22 ♘b1-d2-f3
and then jumping further into
Black's position. If you have access
to this game you should have a look
at it.

24...♕b7 25 ♔h2!

Also the position of the king can
be improved!

25...♔g7 26 c3 ♘a6

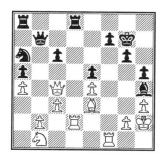

27 ♖e2!

White evacuates the d2-square for
the knight while avoiding a rook
exchange.

**27...♖f8 28 ♘d2 ♗d8 29 ♘f3 f6
30 ♖d2 ♗e7 31 ♕e6 ♖ad8 32 ♖xd8
♗xd8 33 ♖d1 ♘b8 34 ♗c5 ♖h8
35 ♖xd8 Black resigns**.

Black loses after 35...♖xd8
36 ♗e7. Note that the manoeuvre of
the white knight was decisive since
it forced Black to weaken his
position by 29...f6, which in turn
allowed the white queen to
manoeuvre to the heart of Black's

position, the e6-square. The Czechoslovakian-born German GM Vlastimil Hort has said that this ninth game of the match was the most impressive one. Hort was impressed by Karpov's ability to exploit weaknesses with the help of just pieces and without needing pawn breaks. This is not as easy as it looks.

26a

Zherebukh – Shirov
FIDE World Cup 2021

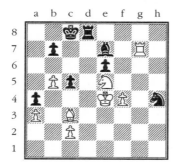

Black to move

When I watched the World Cup live I was very impressed by Shirov's knight manoeuvre in the following position.

43...♘f5 44 ♖h7 ♘d6+ 45 ♔f3

45 ♔e3 was actually more precise in order to avoid the knight check on d4 which comes later in the variation.

45...♘xb5 46 ♖xe7 ♘xc3 47 ♖xe6

Here the passed f-pawn looks very dangerous and the white pieces

cooperate very well. How is the f-pawn to be stopped? White threatens the simple pawn march to f7 followed by ♖e8. Now look at Black's knight!

47...♘b5 48 ♔g4?

This natural move is a mistake and should have been replaced by 48 ♘c4.

48...♘xa3 49 f5 ♘xc2 50 f6 ♘d4 51 ♖e7 a3

52 ♘c4

The point of Black's play is that 52 f7 a2 53 ♖e8 is answered by 53...♘e6!!. What an incredible knight! It's doing everything in Shirov's hands.

52...a2 53 ♖e1 ♘c2 White resigns.

This is one of the most incredible knight manoeuvres I've ever seen. Remember, it travelled from h4-f5-d6-b5-c3-b5-a3-c2-d4-c2. Five of these moves were gained with tempo thanks to threats on the king, rook and bishop, not to mention the fact that the knight liquidated all the pawns on the queenside and still managed to control the f-pawn.

27

Vukić – Karpov
Bugojno 1978

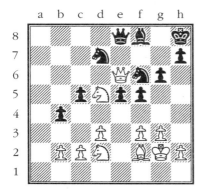

White to move

33 ♕c6?

White overlooked that 33 ♘c7!!
wins a pawn by force after
33...♕xe6 (33...♕d8 34 ♘a6! and
there is nothing Black can do to
prevent 35 ♘b3 winning the pawn
on c5.) 34 ♘xe6 ♗e7 35 ♘b3 and
the c5-pawn falls.

**33...♘xd5 34 ♕xd5 ♘b6 35 ♕b7
♕e6 36 ♕a6 ♕d6 37 ♘b3 ♘d7
38 ♕b7 ♗e7 39 ♘a5 ♕e6 40 ♘c4
♔g7 41 ♔f1 g5! 42 ♔g2 h5 43 h3
♔h6 44 ♘e3 f4! 45 ♕d5?**

45 ♘d5 would keep alive some
winning chances. After the text
move it's a draw.

**45...♕xd5 46 ♘xd5 fxg3! 47 ♗xg3
♗f8 48 ♔f2 ♔g6 49 ♔e2 ♔f5 50 c3
bxc3 51 bxc3 ♔e6 52 ♘e3 ♗g7
53 ♗e1 ♘f8 54 ♗d2 ♘g6 55 ♘f1
♘f4+ 56 ♗xf4 exf4 57 ♘d2 Draw**

28

Mamedyarov – Karjakin
Gashimov Memorial 2016

(1 ♘f3 ♘f6 2 c4 b6 3 d4 e6 4 g3
♗a6 5 b3 ♗b4+ 6 ♗d2 ♗e7 7 ♘c3
c6 8 e4 d5 9 exd5 cxd5 10 ♘e5 ♗b7
10 ♗g2 ♘c6 11 0-0 ♘xd4 12 ♗f4
♘f5 13 cxd5 ♘xd5 14 ♘xd5 ♗xd5
16 ♘c6 ♕d7 17 ♗xd5 exd5)

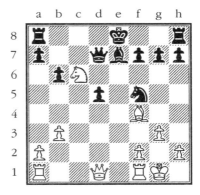

White to move

18 ♘b8! ♕b7

18...♕d8? 19 ♕d3 and Black has
problems with the weaknesses on d5
and c6.

19 ♕d3 ♘d6

Another idea is 19...g6 20 ♕b5+
♔f8 followed by ...♔g7.

20 ♘a6!

White has completed a very beautiful and rare V-manoeuvre which is most common in the endgame of knight and bishop versus a lone king. It's very unusual that a knight resembles a billiard ball. Here it bounces against both sides of the board, first b8 and then a6. Less original would have been 20 ♗xd6 ♗xd6 21 ♕b5+ ♔f8 22 ♘c6 ♗c5 23 ♘e5 ♖d8 24 ♖ac1 a6 25 ♕d3 h5 followed by 26...♖h6 and Black has no problems.

20...0-0 21 ♘b4 d4 22 ♕xd4 ♘f5 23 ♕d5

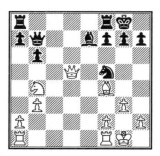

23...♕xd5

If Black avoids the exchange of queens by 23...♕c8? White can return his knight to the c6-square by 24 ♘c6!, thereby completing a c6-b8-a6-b4-c6 manoeuvre in the shape of a cut diamond. This is incredibly rare and proof of Mamedyarov's high creative ability because this manoeuvre was in no way forced.

24 ♘xd5 ♗c5 25 ♖ad1 ♖fd8 26 ♗c7 ♖e8 27 ♗f4 ♖ed8 28 ♗c7 ♖e8 29 ♗f4

Here the players agreed a draw in a completely equal position. This was a so-called "correct" game in which neither of the players

made a mistake. However, due to Mamedyarov's highly original play this short draw is well worth knowing and studying. Naturally we will be vigilant and keep an eye on what Mamedyarov's knights have in store in the future!

29

Miezis – Volkov
Stockholm 2020

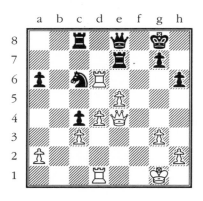

Black to move

26...♘a7!

A very elegant knight manoeuvre in the style of Kramnik, who also likes to exploit squares on the edge of the board. Both the a7- and b5-squares are pretty unusual springboards for the knight but the reason is that the c3-pawn is a tactical weakness which Black wants to exploit.

27 ♖xa6 ♘b5 28 ♖c1

In this position one might say that Black plays with three major pieces against two, since the c1-rook is occupied with defending the c3-pawn. Here we see one fundamental drawback of having three pawns versus a knight. White doesn't have enough activity to maintain the balance in the position.

28...♔h8?

Here there is an illuminating variation showing the fragile defence of the white king: 28...♕h5! 29 ♕d5+ ♖f7 30 ♕xb5??. Black then has three winning moves: 30...♕g5, 30...♕f3 and 30...♕e2.

29 a4 ♘c7 30 ♖c6 ♘e6 31 ♖xc8 ♕xc8 32 h4

White has managed to take away the b5- and the g5-squares from Black's versatile knight.

32...♘c7 33 ♖f1

White cannot expand his classical centre since 33 d5! is met by the decisive 33...♕h3! and all White's weak pawns are in jeopardy.

33...♕d8!

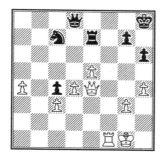

The d5-square is now in Black's possession. The position remains balanced since Black didn't exploit his chances on the 28th move, although in practice White's position is more difficult to play. It cannot have been easy for Miezis to make the correct decision with little time on the clock, so it's perfectly understandable that his position collapses. Black has three pieces

against Black's two and White's passers are under full control.

34 a5?

There is a narrow, relatively forced variation to draw. With little time or inclination to calculate, White could calmly play 34 ♖b1 ♘d5 35 ♕f3 and the game is mutually balanced after a further 36 ♖b5, which forces the knight to temporarily abandon the strong blockading square on d5. The relatively forced variation requires precise calculation to the end: 34 ♕g6 ♘d5 35 ♖f7! ♖xf7 36 ♕xf7 ♘xc3 37 ♕xc4 ♕xd4+ 38 ♕xd4 ♘e2+ 39 ♔f2 ♘xd4 40 ♔e3 ♘b3 41 ♔e4 ♘c5 42 ♔f5 ♘xa4 43 e6 ♔g8 44 ♔g6 ♔f8 45 e7+ ♔xe7 46 ♔xg7.

This variation clearly shows Miezis' precarious situation and it's not easy to go right into the jungle of variations and correctly evaluate all the different stepping-stones.

34...♘d5 35 ♖f3

35...♖a7

A cooler way to win the a-pawn was 35...♔g8 36 a6 ♖e6 37 a7 ♖a6 but I guess a lot of time would have been required to find and play such a variation.

36 ♕e2?

This is also a position where it's easy to go wrong. White has to be active and play 36 e6!. It's such an amazing variation that extra diagrams are required so the true chess lover doesn't miss what shouldn't be missed. 36...♖xa5 (36...♘f6 37 ♕e5) 37 ♖f7 ♖a1+ 38 ♔h2 ♖a2+ 39 ♔h3 ♘f6 40 ♕g6 ♕g8 41 e7 ♖a8

42 h5!! Amazingly this is the only move to win and at first sight it can be difficult to understand why it's so important to protect the queen with a pawn. Let's continue the variation. A waiting move like 42...♖b8 (42...♘d5 43 ♔h4!!

...is another incredible move and besides it's the only move which wins. Black is in zugzwang. Unbelievable but true: any moves by

the rook or the knight lose. 43...♘xc3 [If *43...♖b8 44 ♕d6* with treble threats on d5, b8 and f8 or *43...♖c8 44 ♕f5*] 44 ♕c6 ♖b8 45 ♕d6!! with double threats on b8 and f8.) is met by 43 ♖xf6 gxf6 44 d5!!. Here one can really talk about "the pawn's lust to expand" to use Nimzowitsch's famous words or Philidor's that "the pawns are the soul of the game." 44...♕xg6 (44...♕xd5 45 ♕xh6+ ♔g8 46 ♕g6+ ♔h8 47 e8♕+ ♖xe8 48 ♕xe8+ ♔g7 49 ♕g6+ and the f6-pawn falls as well.) 45 hxg6 ♔g7 46 d6 and the d-pawn promotes on d8 thanks to the g6-pawn which controls the important f7-square. It's really beautiful! 46...♔xg6 47 d7 ♔f7 48 d8♕ etc.

36...♕c8 37 ♕f1?

Logical was 37 ♕a2? but here this error was due to time pressure.

37...♔g8 38 ♕a1 ♕c6

Volkov misses yet another good chance to activate his queen with 38...♕g4.

39 ♕a3

When I visited this game for the second time during the Rilton Cup

2019/20 this was the precise position. I was surprised at what had happened, since I thought that White had played a dynamic game which should have been rewarded with more than this position. It is not necessary to analyse the check on f8 because Black can play the pragmatic...

39...♖a8

...and be happy because White cannot conjure up anything dangerous.

40 ♔h2 h5

Volkov overlooks a strong queen move for the third time in the game. 40...♕g6 followed by 41...♕e4 would have been devastating for White's position.

41 ♕d6

Miezis has seen the strong queen move and decides to reluctantly concede to an exchange of queens, but the reality is that Black's queen is far stronger than White's.

41...♕xd6 42 exd6 ♖xa5 43 d7 ♖a8 44 ♖f5 ♘f6 45 ♖c5 ♘xd7 46 ♖xc4 ♖a2+ 47 ♔g1 ♘f6 48 ♖c8+ ♔f7 49 ♖c7+ ♔g6 50 c4 ♖c2 51 c5 ♖d2 White resigns.

30

Botvinnik – Euwe
World Championship Tournament,
The Hague/Moscow 1948

(1 d4 d5 2 c4 e6 3 ♘f3 ♘f6 4 ♘c3 c6 5 e3 ♘bd7 6 ♗d3 ♗b4 7 a3 ♗a5 8 ♕c2 ♕e7 9 ♗d2 dxc4 10 ♗xc4 e5 11 0-0 0-0)

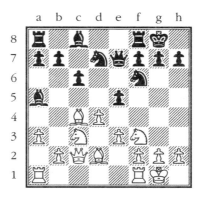

White to move

12 ♗a2!!

According to the Russian GM Vladimir Simagin (1919-1968) this retreating move is winning for White because there are no satisfactory replies for Black. Although it's a prophylactic idea of the highest order it is somewhat of an exaggeration to say that it's winning, despite being a very cunning and strong move. Black's main strategic plan is the ...e5-e4 advance but at the moment 12...e4 isn't possible due to the tactical resource 13 ♘xe4, as Black's bishop is unprotected. In the game Botvinnik played 12 ♖ae1 and commented that it was "a cunning move, since it is not easy for Black to find a satisfactory reply." However, in reality this set-up is rather routine, since White is placing his rooks in the manner of Morphy. The plan is to support the advance of the e- and f-pawns but it isn't new as Alekhine demonstrated in his game against Bogoljubow in Budapest 1921. 12...♗c7! Black prepares ...e5-e4 which White obviously has to prevent. 13 ♘e4 ♘xe4 14 ♕xe4 a5! This move prevents White from playing ♗d2-b4. Black position is fine, though Botvinnik nevertheless won after only 32 moves.

12...♗xc3

The best defence according to the computer. Alternatives were:

(a) 12...a6, preparing 13...♗c7, looks logical, albeit slow. White can play the useful 13 h3 and after 13...♗c7 decide whether to play 14 ♖ae1 in the style of Morphy and Alekhine or continue with normal development by 14 ♖ad1 followed by 15 ♖fe1. White is clearly better in both cases.

(b) According to Dvoretsky in *Positional Play* Black's only reasonable move appears to be 12...♗c7 but after 13 ♘b5 ♗b6 14 ♗b4 c5 15 dxc5 ♗xc5 16 ♖fd1 White's position is overwhelming.

(c) 12...♗d8 is simplest and best met by 13 ♖ad1 with a superior position.

13 ♗xc3 exd4 14 ♘xd4 ♕e4 15 ♕xe4 ♘xe4 16 ♗e1.

As we will learn from Alekhine – Bogoljubow, Budapest 1921, exercise 53, this is clearly an advantageous position for White because he has the possibility of setting up a strong central structure with f2-f3 and e3-e4. White has the bishop pair which will dominate the board thanks to the open centre.

It should be mentioned that the prophylactic move 12 ♗a2!! made a deep impression on Mark Dvoretsky, because it taught him to sense the power and beauty of quiet positional moves.

31

Polugaevsky – Lutikov
USSR Championship, Kharkov 1967

(1 c4 e5 2 ♘c3 ♘c6 3 g3 g6 4 ♗g2 ♗g7 5 e3 d6 6 ♘ge2 ♘f6 7 d4 0-0 8 0-0 ♗d7 9 h3 a6 10 b3 ♖b8 11 a4 a5 12 ♗b2 ♖e8 13 ♕d2 h5 14 dxe5 dxe5 15 ♖fd1 ♕c8 16 ♔h2 ♖d8 17 ♘d5 ♗f5 18 ♘ec3 ♖d7 19 ♘xf6+ ♗xf6 20 ♘d5 ♗g7)

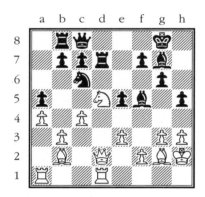

White to move

21 ♗c3!

White plans to set up a battery on the long dark diagonal with ♕b2 and then follow it up with an overprotection of the d5-knight by doubling rooks on the d-file. After this White can consider the central breakthrough f2-f4.

21...♕d8

The queen is better placed on f8 in order to protect the bishop on g7 and prepare the development of the rook to d8.

22 ♕b2 ♗e6 23 f4?

23 ♖d2 followed by 24 ♖ad1 was more logical as it accentuates the

activity of his pieces and retains options such as a timely ♘f4.

23...f6?

Black plays too passively: 23...h4! 24 g4 ♘b4! would have given Black counterplay. The idea is to meet 25 ♗xe5 ♗xe5 26 ♕xe5 with 26...♗xd5 27 cxd5 ♘c2 28 ♖ac1 ♖e7 and the e3-pawn falls.

24 ♖d2 ♔h7 25 ♖f1

25 ♖ad1! was the right place for the rook.

25...♕h8

26 fxe5

The computer suggests the ingenious pawn break 26 g4!! hxg4 27 hxg4 followed by ♔g3 so as to exploit the uncomfortable "married couple" on the h-file.

26...♘xe5 27 ♘f4 ♖xd2 28 ♕xd2 ♖d8 29 ♕e2 ♕e8 30 ♗xa5 b6 31 ♗c3 f5 32 e4!

A very strong and decisive central breakthrough.

32...h4 33 gxh4 ♗c8 34 exf5 ♗xf5 35 ♖e1 ♕d7 36 h5!

36 ♗xe5 would be met by 36...♖e8.

36...♘d3

Despair!

37 hxg6+ ♗xg6 38 ♘xg6 ♘xe1 39 ♕h5+ ♔h6 40 ♗e4 Black resigns.

32

Geller – Andersson
London 1982

1 e4 c5 2 ♘f3 d6 3 d4 cxd4 4 ♘xd4 ♘f6 5 ♘c3 e6 6 ♗e2 ♗e7 7 0-0 0-0 8 f4 ♘c6 9 ♗e3 e5 (The Modern Scheveningen) 10 ♘b3 exf4 11 ♖xf4 ♘e8 12 ♕d2

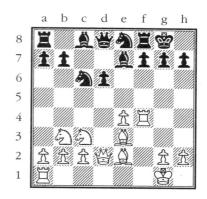

Black to move

12...♗f6

Andersson's ingenious idea is to put the bishop on e5 and follow with ...♘e8-f6. The centralised bishop will exert pressure on h2 and on the c3-knight, which makes the e4-pawn a target for Black's knight on e8. Note that it's cleverer to have the bishop on e5 rather than the knight because the c6-knight is busy marking the b3-knight so it cannot reach the dream d4 square.

13 罩f2

In the game Mortensen – Tisdall, Gausdal 1982, White preferred a more centralised strategy with the rooks by 13 罩ff1 桌e5 14 ②d4 ②f6 15 h3 ②xd4 16 桌xd4 桌e6 17 罩ad1 罩c8 with equal play.

13...桌e5

The bishop is like a rock on e5!

14 桌g5 ②f6 15 罩af1?

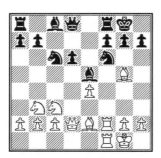

Geller overlooks a tactical idea. Correct was 15 桌f3 to defend the e4-pawn.

15...桌xc3! 16 豐xc3 ②xe4 17 桌xd8 ②xc3 18 bxc3 ②xd8 19 罩d1 桌e6 20 罩xd6 罩c8

Andersson has transformed the active bishop on e5 to a superior pawn structure. He went on to win the game after 49 moves:

21 罩d3 罩e8 22 罩e3 當f8 23 桌b5 罩e7 24 罩d2 罩ec7 25 桌e2 a6 26 桌f3 當e7 27 罩dd3 g6 28 ②d4 當f6 29 ②xe6 ②xe6 30 桌g4 當e7 31 桌xe6 fxe6 32 罩h3 h5 33 罩hg3 罩g8 34 當f2 罩c5 35 當e2

35 罩d4 罩gc8 36 罩xg6 罩xc3 also loses a pawn.

35...罩a5 36 當d2 罩xa2 37 罩d4 罩a5 38 c4 罩c5 39 罩b3 罩b8 40 罩g3 g5 41 罩gd3 當f6 42 h3 罩bc8 43 罩f3+ 當e7 44 罩b3 b5 45 cxb5 罩xc2+ 46 當d3 罩xg2 47 罩e4 罩d8+ 48 當c4 罩c2+ 49 當b4 罩b8 White resigns.

33

Steinitz – Chigorin
World Championship Havana (20)
1892

1 ②f3 d5 2 d4 ②f6 3 e3 e6 4 c4 桌e7 5 ②c3 ②bd7 6 c5 c6 7 b4 0-0 8 桌b2 豐c7 9 桌e2 ②e8 10 0-0 f5 11 豐c2 ②ef6 12 a4 ②e4 13 b5 罩f6 14 a5 ②xc3 15 桌xc3 a6 16 bxa6 bxa6 17 罩fb1 罩f8 18 罩b2 桌b7 19 罩ab1 罩fb8 20 ②e1 桌c8 21 ②d3 罩xb2 22 罩xb2 桌f6 23 豐a4 當f7 24 豐a3 桌d8 25 桌d1 罩b8

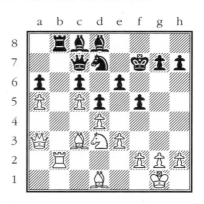

White to move

26 罩b6!

Staunton's famous positional exchange sacrifice 29...罩c4 against Saint-Amant in the 21st unofficial world championship game (Paris 1843) can be regarded as the original archetype of the so called "Russian exchange". It bears a striking resemblance to Petrosian's 30...♖c4!! against Spassky, in the 27th world championship game (Moscow 1969) which suggested to Raymond Keene that they be called "astrally related" in his book *Howard Staunton - the English world chess champion* (B.C.M. 1975). Nearly fifty years after Staunton's positional discovery Steinitz managed to exploit the outpost on b6 with an exchange sacrifice and upset the static values of the pieces from a positional and long-term perspective.

26...♘xb6

Otherwise the pressure on the a6- and the c6-pawn would be unbearable after moves such as ♗d1-e2 and ♘d3-b4.

27 cxb6!

By recapturing away from the centre White secures the a3-f8 diagonal as well as the c5-square.

27...♕b7 28 ♘e5+

Note that the knight is stronger than the rook so the normal values of the pieces are not valid here, which is a fact Steinitz was fully aware of since he wrote in *The Modern Chess Instructor* that a rook is a little stronger than a knight and two pawns. According to another authority, Staunton's "Handbook", the knight is worth 3.05 and the rook 5.48, which signifies an enormous difference in mobility. In this position it's clearly seen that the knight is a monster whereas the rook is pretty useless and below its normal strength. This marked difference in mobility is the main reason why a long-term concept like the positional exchange sacrifice works.

28...♔g8 29 ♗a4 ♕e7

After 29...♗e7 30 ♗b4 or 29...♗d7 30 ♕d6 White benefits from the dark-squared a3-f8 diagonal.

30 ♗b4 ♕f6 31 ♕c3 h6 32 ♗d6 ♖xb6

This move proves the rook's true value!

33 axb6 ♗xb6 34 ♕xc6 ♕d8 35 ♗c5 ♗c7 36 ♘g6 ♔h7 37 ♗e7 ♗d7 38 ♗xd8 ♗xc6 39 ♗xc6 ♗xd8 40 ♘f8+ ♔g8 41 ♘xe6 Black resigns.

The exchange sacrifice wasn't the order of the day in the 19th century. We had to await a further development of classical conceptions of strategy. It was Alekhine and especially players who represented the Russian school, who placed the emphasis on dynamic chess and made the exchange sacrifice an accepted and consistent weapon in their games.

34

Selezniev – Alekhine
Triberg 1921

1 d4 ♘f6 2 ♘f3 b6 3 g3 ♗b7 4 ♗g2 d6 5 0-0 ♘bd7 6 ♗f4 h6 7 ♘c3 c5 8 d5 b5 9 ♘e1 a6 10 a4 b4 11 ♘e4 ♘xe4 12 ♗xe4 g6 13 c4 bxc3 14 bxc3 ♗g7 15 ♖b1 ♖b8 16 c4 0-0 17 ♕c2 a5! (Note how Black is preparing the following exchange sacrifice.) 18 ♘f3 ♕c7 19 ♗d2 ♗a6 20 ♗d3

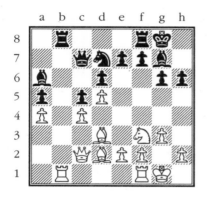

Black to play

20...♖b4!!

Alekhine writes that the exchange sacrifice is "absolutely correct. The strong passed pawn thus resulting, supported by the bishop on g7, and the possibilities of attack on White's c4-pawn are, on the whole, worth more than the exchange." Apart from Staunton and Steinitz, who were too far ahead of their time to be properly understood by their contemporaries, Alekhine was one of the forerunners of the "Russian exchange sacrifice" before Botvinnik and Petrosian used this brilliant concept repeatedly in their heydays.

In his book *The Development of Chess Style* (1978) Euwe writes that "very long-range sacrifices of the exchange seem to occur more frequently in Russia than anywhere else." What is interesting though is that here Alekhine, like Steinitz and Staunton, carried it out on the queenside but one square further back if compared with Steinitz's ♖b6 and one rank further to the side if compared with Staunton's ...♖c4. Obviously it matters how deep the rook is penetrating the position and how much impact it has on the small central area of the board.

21 ♗xb4

If the enemy rook is left untouched Black can follow up with ...♖fb8 and ...♖b2.

21...cxb4

The b-file is now closed, which limits the value of the white rooks and at the same time secures Black control of the strong c5-square for his pieces.

22 ♘d2 ♘c5

It was more logical to maintain the pressure on c4 by 22...♖c8 followed by a possible 23...♘b6. The text move focuses on the a4-pawn and plans 23...♕d7.

23 ♘b3! ♘d7

23...♘xa4? is answered by the strong 24 ♕a2! ♘c3 25 ♕xa5 ♕xa5 26 ♘xa5 ♘xb1 27 ♖xb1 ♖b8 28 ♘c6 and White wins the b4-pawn.

24 c5

White utilises the time to rid himself of his weak pawn.

24...♗xd3

25 exd3

The strongest recapture according to Alekhine. Against 25 ♕xd3 Black would have retorted 25...♘xc5. Alekhine had actually planned the inferior 25...dxc5 in the belief that the passed pawns would decide the game, but it's not so simple after 26 ♕a6 when White is even slightly on top.

25...dxc5 26 ♖fe1 ♘e5?

Simpler was 26...♗f6, because the f3-square is easy to control and the knight needs to protect the c5-pawn.

27 ♖e3 ♖c8?

It was better to admit the mistake and return with the knight. The point is that after 27...♘d7 28 ♖xe7 Black continues 28...♕d6 and the d5-pawn falls.

28 ♖c1 ♕d7?

28...♘d7 was still preferable.

29 d4?

Here White missed the very strong 29 ♕e2! ♕xd5 30 d4 ♘d7 31 dxc5 with good winning chances.

29...♘g4 30 ♖e4?

Necessary was 30 ♖ee1 c4 31 ♘c5 ♕xd5 32 ♕xc4 with mutual chances.

30...c4 31 ♘c5 ♕f5!

This is the reason e4 was a fatal square for the rook, because now White is unable to capture on c4 due to the pressure on f2.

32 ♕e2

What is Black's strongest continuation?

32...b3?

Alekhine attached two exclamation marks to his move but the strongest continuation was the harder-to-find 32...♘xf2!! 33 ♕xf2 ♕xd5. Despite the fact that Black has only three pawns against White's rook the pawns turn out to be stronger. This is clearly evident after the further 34.♖ce1 c3! when Black plans either 35...f5, 35...c2 or 35...b3. What dynamic pawns!

33 ♖xg4

Alekhine claims that Black has the advantage after 33 ♕xg4 b2 34 ♖b1 ♕xg4 35 ♖xg4 c3 36 ♘d3 ♖c4 37 ♘xb2! ♖b4! 38 ♖e4 ♔f8?

(38...cxb2 was correct with enough compensation for the exchange.) but he overlooked 39 d6!! with the idea 39...exd6? 40 ♖be1 ♗xd4 41 ♘d3 and White wins.

33...b2 34 ♕xb2 ♕xg4 35 ♖xc4 h5 36 ♕c2?

The correct defence was 36 h4, intending to meet 36...g5 with 37 hxg5 h4 38 ♕b3 ♗xd4 39 ♕d3 with equal play.

36...h4 37 ♕d3 ♖d8! 38 f3 ♕h5 39 ♕e4 hxg3 40 hxg3 ♕g5 41 ♔g2?

41 ♔f2! ♕d2+ 42 ♕e2 with the idea 42...♗xd4+ 43 ♔f1 was a better defence.

41...♕d2+ 42 ♔h3 ♗f6!

Alekhine: "In order to occupy the h-file with the rook: the only means of securing the win."

43 ♖c2 ♕h6+ 44 ♔g2 ♔g7 45 g4

45 f4!.

45...♖h8 46 ♔f2!

46...♖b8

Alekhine gives this move two exclams and it's good enough, but

46...♕h1! would have focused directly on the king and made more use of the rook's dynamic capability on the h-file (h2 or perhaps later on h1). However Alekhine's focus is first to liquidate the pawn on d4, which is the central heart of White's position, by manoeuvring the rook to the outpost on b4.

47 ♔e2 ♖b4

Note that this is the same square where the earlier exchange sacrifice took place. It's pretty clear that Alekhine plays artistically rather than using brute force to checkmate the opposing king or win an abundance of material. It's all about colours and exploiting the vital black squares.

48 ♖d2 ♕h2+ 49 ♔e3

If 49 ♔d3 then 49...♕g1!.

49...♕g1+ 50 ♔e2 ♗xd4

Not only have the flanks fallen apart but also the centre, thereby leaving White in a completely resignable position.

51 ♘d3 ♖b1

Alekhine gives 51...♗c3! 52 ♘xb4 ♕g2+ as immediately decisive.

76

52 ♘c1! ♝c3

Unnecessarily prolonging the game when Black could have won in short order by relatively easy means after 52...♕f2+ 53 ♔d3 ♕f1+! 54 ♘e2 (54 ♔xd4 ♖b4+) 54...♖b3+ 55 ♔xd4 (55 ♔c4 ♖b4+ 56 ♔d3 ♕b1+ 57 ♖c2 ♕d1+ 58 ♖d2 ♕b3+ 59 ♘c3 ♝xc3!) 55...♕a1+! 56 ♔c5 ♕a3+ etc.

53 ♕xb1 ♕g2+ 54 ♔d3 ♕xd2+ 55 ♔c4 ♕d4+ 56 ♔b3

56...♝a1!

It was this nice bishop manoeuvre that attracted Alekhine when playing 52...♝c3.

57 ♔a3

57 ♔a2? leads to the amusing 57...♕xa4 mate.

57...♕c5+ 58 ♔a2 ♝f6

There is no way to defend the d5-pawn due to the sad placement of the knight.

59 g5 ♕xd5+ 60 ♘b3 ♕xg5 61 ♕e1 ♕g2+ 62 ♕d2 ♕xf3 63 ♕xa5 g5 64 ♕e1 ♕c3 65 ♕xc3 ♝xc3 66 a5

66...♝xa5!

The main track of the exchange sacrifice is still visible, especially the play on the dark squares on the queenside where White's pieces have been enticed and stranded.

67 ♘xa5 g4 68 ♘c4 g3 69 ♘d2 ♔g6 70 ♔b2 ♔f5 71 ♘f3 ♔f4 72 ♘g1 ♔e3 73 ♔c2 ♔f2 74 ♘h3+ ♔f1 White resigns.

Alekhine: A very difficult and interesting game in all its phases.

35

Liublinsky – Botvinnik
Moscow Championship 1943

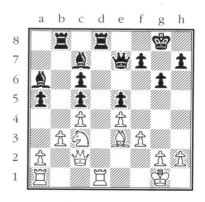

Black to move

25...♖d4!

Botvinnik's splendid positional sacrifice is displayed in the central area of the chessboard.

He makes the following instructive comment on his successful Russian exchange sacrifice: "This sacrifice could not be delayed. It is possible only if Black retains one rook for the attack. After the exchange sacrifice Black's pawn chain is repaired, he obtains a passed pawn, the closed nature of the position deprives the white rooks of any activity, and what tells is no longer the material, but the positional advantage."

26 ♘e2

If White wants to accept the offer then 26 ♗xd4 should have been played, even though it would have given Black the bishop pair. After 26...cxd4 27 ♘a4 (or 27 ♘e2 followed by ♘c1-d3) 27...c5 28 ♘b2 the knight would have been much better placed on d3, where it effectively blockades the d4-pawn, compared with the future prospects of the bishop as seen in the game.

26...♗c8 27 ♘xd4

It was still possible to continue 27 ♗xd4 cxd4 28 ♘c1 c5 29 ♘d3 with an ideally placed knight on the d3 square.

27...cxd4 28 ♗f2

White should have played 28 ♗d2 because here it can support the two pawn breaks b3-b4 and f3-f4.

28...c5

Botvinnik: "White is completely without counterplay and is obliged to await the development of events."

29 ♖f1 f5 30 ♗g3 ♗d7 31 ♖ae1

Botvinnik: "Of course, the exchange 31 exf5 gxf5 was dangerous, since in the end Black would have created two connected passed pawns in the centre. But now he gains the opportunity to restrict the enemy pieces still further and to launch an attack on the kingside."

31...f4 32 ♗f2 g5 33 g4

Botvinnik: "A vain attempt to forestall the opponent's assault, although to allow 33...g4 would have been even worse. Now the black pieces are free to take up their most active positions."

33...fxg3 34 ♗xg3 ♗h3 35 ♖f2 h5

Black is utilising Steinitz' method, which is applicable when playing with the bishop pair, and therefore restricts the action of the white bishop. It would have been harder to limit a knight's radius of action on d3.

36 ♖d2?

A cleverer move was 36 ♕d3! because 36...h4? can be met by 37 ♗xe5! ♗xe5 38 f4 ♗xf4 39 ♕xh3, even though Black would have full compensation after

39...♕e5. This was White's best practical chance to hold the game.

36...h4 37 ♗f2 ♖f8 38 ♖d3 ♖f4 39 ♔h1 ♔h7 40 ♖g1 ♗d8 41 ♕e2 ♕f7

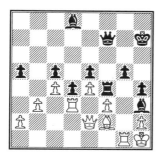

42 ♕d1

Botvinnik: "As was shown by home analysis (the game was adjourned) after 42 ♗e1 g4 43 fxg4 ♗xg4 44 ♖xg4 ♖xg4 45 ♕xg4 ♕f1+ 46 ♕g1 ♕xd3 47 ♕g4 ♕f1+ 48 ♕g1 ♕e2 the e4-pawn would have also been lost."

42...♕h5 43 ♗e3

Otherwise Black will decide the game with 43...g4.

43...♕xf3+

An alternative win was 43...dxe3 44 ♖xd8 ♕xf3+ 45 ♕xf3 ♖xf3 46 ♖dd1 g4 followed by a king march to f4.

44 ♕xf3 ♖xf3 45 ♗xg5 ♖xd3 46 ♗xd8 ♖e3 47 ♗b6 ♖xe4 48 ♗xc5 ♖e2 49 ♖d1 ♗g4 50 h3 ♗xh3 51 b4 ♗f5 52 ♗d6 d3 53 bxa5 h3

This is a good practical model game showing how a rook and two

bishops can outperform two rooks and bishop when having a significant advantage in space.

36

Fischer – Gadia
Mar del Plata 1960

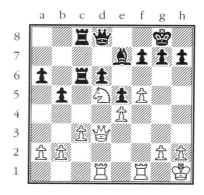

White to move

The move that one chooses to play in this particular position reveals whether you prefer tactical or positional play. Here Fischer played the amazing...

21 ♖a1!!

The idea is surprisingly to initiate play on the queenside. The mini-plan in itself isn't unusual since it's very common in the Spanish game to make a pawn-push to a4. However, it's unusual to first develop the rook to d1 and then go back to a1, especially when there are tempting possibilities on the kingside. To me this move is a clear sign of genius that Fischer valued the pawn break a2-a4 higher than the "obvious" f5-f6 which probably would have been played by most players, no matter what their level. 21 b4, followed by ♖a1 and a4, according to Nimzowitsch's concept that a weakness should be blockaded before it is attacked, was also playable.

It's interesting and revealing (Fischer's favourite player by the way was Capablanca) that Fischer didn't play the natural attacking continuation 21 f6 ♗xf6 22 ♖xf6! gxf6 23.♖f1 ♔h8 24 ♕h3. Black's strongest defence would then have been 24...♕g8 25 ♘e7 ♕g5 26 ♘xc6! (26 ♘xc8 f5!) 26...♖xc6 27 ♕d7 ♖c4 28 ♕xf7 ♖c8 but after 29 g3! Black would most likely succumb in a rook ending a pawn down, since the f6-pawn will fall.

Fischer might very well have seen this variation and opted for the clearer and safer text-move.

21...f6?

Black doesn't want to have to deal with the f5-f6-possibility and weakens the classic a2-g8 diagonal and seventh rank, as well as making his bishop even worse. Better was 21...♗f6.

22 a4 ♖b8?

22...bxa4 23.♖xa4 a5 was a better try but of course Black is clearly lost.

23 ♘xe7+ Black resigns.

The rook falls after 23...♕xe7 24 ♕d5+. After the game Bronstein asked Fischer how come he had thought of that rook move. Fischer replied: "Tal moves his rooks back and forth, why can't I do the same?"

37

Benko – Keres
Piatigorsky Cup, Los Angeles 1963

Black to move

White's last move was the knight transfer from g2 to e3 so the Black's reply must have come as an unpleasant surprise for Benko.

18...♖xe3!

"A fully justified sacrifice" according to the tournament book and indeed so. Black eliminates the knight, which in the future might have been very strong on one of the squares d5 or f5. Now the game is transformed in such a way that Black has the upper hand, not least psychologically.

19 fxe3 ♕e8 20 ♕c2?!

20 ♔f2? ♕e4! followed by ...♘e5 would have been very unpleasant for White. A plausible continuation might have been 21 ♕d1 ♘e5 22 ♖xe5. The only way to remove the monstrous knight but after 22...♕xe5 White's disrupted kingside would be a serious problem with major pieces on the board, as

well as the isolated pawns which would be difficult to defend. Best was 20 ♖d3 ♘e5 21 ♖d5 ♘g4 22 ♖d3! since 22...♘xe3? wouldn't work on account of 23 ♕xd7.

20...♕xe3+ 21 ♔h1 ♘e5

Thanks to the exchange sacrifice Black has a very nice outpost on e5, since the pawn move to f4 is no longer possible. This beautifully placed knight is reminiscent of the fifth game between Botvinnik and Petrosian in their world title match 1963. In that game Petrosian laid the foundations for winning the game by placing a so-called "eternal knight" on e4.

22 ♖f1 ♖e8 23 ♖f4 f6 24 ♕e4?

24 ♖d1 was better but Black has full compensation since the rooks don't have much play.

24...♘g6

White was hoping for 24...♕xc3? 25 ♖xd7! when he would be back in the game.

25 ♕xe3 ♖xe3 26 ♖xd7

26 ♖f2 ♘e5 and the monster is back on its ideal square. 26 ♖f3 ♖xe2 27 ♖xd7 ♘e5 28 ♖d8+ ♔f7

29 ♖f1 ♖xa2 and White loses in the long run. The super knight controls the important squares d7 as well as f3 so it's hard for White to double his rooks on the seventh rank.

26...♘xf4 27 gxf4 ♖xe2 28 ♖xa7 ♖f2 29 ♖b7 ♖xf4 30 ♖xb6 ♖xc4 31 ♖b3 ♔f7

Black wins the rook ending easily due to his more active position as well as the possibility of creating two connected passed pawns on the kingside. The remaining moves were:

32 ♔g2 g5 33 ♔f3 ♔e6 34 ♖a3 h5 35 ♔e2 ♖h4 36 ♖a6+ ♔e5 37 a4 c4 38 ♖c6 ♖xh2+ 39 ♔e3 ♖h3+ 40 ♔d2 ♖d3+ 41 ♔c2 h4 42 ♖xc4 ♖d8 White resigns.

38

Rozentalis – Ehlvest
Koszalin 1998

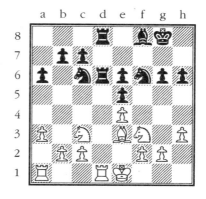

White to move

18 ♖ac1!

A nice prophylactic move which prepares the doubling of the rooks

81

on the d-file. An immediate 18 ♖d2 would have been less sophisticated due to 18...♖xd2 19 ♘xd2 ♘d4 and the c2-pawn would be unprotected.

18...b5 19 ♖d2 g5

19...♖xd2 20 ♘xd2 ♘d4 21 ♘e2, followed by c2-c3, was another point of placing the rook on c1.

20 ♖cd1 g4

There was no reason to swap off all four rooks commencing with 20...♖xd2, since Black is saddled with the worse pawn structure as well as the worse bishop. It's also wrong psychologically since one of his goals is the doubling of rooks.

21 hxg4 ♘xg4

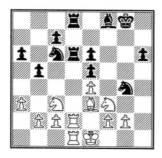

Black's pawn structure looks clearly worse with three pawn islands versus White's two, but in this position it doesn't really matter because of his firm control of the central squares, especially d4 and d5.

22 ♔e2 ♔f7 23 ♖d3

White plays with the rooks in the same spirit as Black and retains the option of recapturing with the c2-pawn.

23...♗e7 24 ♘b1 ♘xe3

24...♖g8!? would have forced White to think about the g-pawn.

25 fxe3

Now White too has good control of the centre. The problem with the black position is the idle bishop.

25...♖g8 26 ♔f2 ♖gd8 27 ♘bd2!

Believe it or not this knight is actually on its way to d7 with devastating effect!

27...♖xd3 28 cxd3 ♗d6

Of course not the suicidal continuation 28...♖xd3? 29 ♖c1 ♖d6 30 ♖xc6 ♖xc6 31 ♘xe5+.

29 ♖c1 ♘e7 30 ♘b3 c6 31 ♘c5 ♖a8

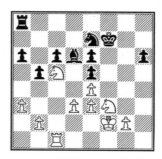

32 ♘d7

White wins either the pawn on e5 or, if Black defends it with the knight, the pawn on c6.

32...♔e8 33 ♘fxe5 ♔d8 34 d4 ♖a7 35 ♘c5

35 ♘f8 was equally good as the text move but optically more devastating and humiliating since White would use the opponent's square on the last rank as if he were

playing a game of billiards on a rectangular table with a ball and a cue.

35...♗xe5 36 dxe5

An instructive and unusual position showing that tripled pawns in the centre can indeed be strong.

36...♘g6 37 ♘xe6+ ♔d7 38 ♘c5+ ♔e7 39 ♘d3 ♖c7 40 ♖h1 c5 41 ♖xh6 ♖c6 42 e6! Black resigns.

39

Kramnik – Harikrishna
Gashimov Memorial 2017

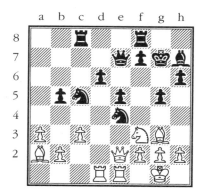

White to move

White has a difficult positional problem to solve because Black is planning ...f7-f5-f4 to shut the bishop out of the game. Kramnik doesn't want to lose in the style of Winter – Capablanca, Hastings 1919, which is the most famous fundamental model game how to exploit a buried bishop on g3.

24 ♖d5!?

I followed the game live and when I saw this and the following move I couldn't believe my eyes. It made me think about when Spassky played

the famous move 16...♘c6!? (position 148 in *300 Most Important Chess Positions*), despite the fact that there was a white pawn on d5, in a game against Averbakh in the USSR Championship 1956. In that game Spassky, just like Kramnik, was positionally outplayed but managed to turn the tables by changing the character of the game. The same thing is happening here because Kramnik realises that something drastic has to be done to avoid being crushed by the Indian steamroller.

24...f5 25 ♖xe5!?

Quite an amazing sacrifice!

25...dxe5 26 ♗xe5+

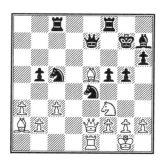

The two raking bishops exploit the weaknesses on the classical and long diagonal. Apart from these bishops, working on adjacent diagonals, White will get three pawns. Not such a bad deal for the sacrificed reserve rook!

26...♘f6

The knight on c5 was superfluous, so now it can be placed on e4 while the f6-knight concentrates on defending the king, thereby creating more harmony in Black's position. 26...♔g6 could also have been played but I think most humans would go for the natural text move. A plausible continuation is 27 ♗d4 (27 ♕xb5? g4 loses more material.) 27...♗g8 28 ♘e5+ ♔h7 29 ♗b1 ♕d6 30 ♕xb5 ♖ce8 31 f3 ♖xe5 32 fxe4 ♖b8 33 ♗xe5 ♕xe5 34 ♕e2 ♘xe4 and Black is winning thanks to his strong central position and active pieces.

27 ♕xb5 ♘ce4 28 ♗d4 ♖fd8 29 h3 ♖b8 30 ♕e2 ♗g8?

Correct was over-protection of the most important strategic point e4 by 30...♖e8.

31 ♗b1 ♕b7 32 b4 ♖e8 33 c4 ♕c6?

The first major turning point since the incredible rook sacrifice. Correct was the double attack on the c4- and a3-pawn weaknesses by 33...♕a6 with good winning chances.

34 ♕b2

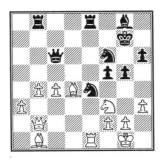

34...♖bd8?

Note that 34...♗xc4? doesn't work on account of 35 ♘e5 ♕e6 36 ♗xe4! (But not 36 ♘xc4? ♕xc4 37 ♗xe4 ♕e6!! with a decisive counter-pin. The reserve rook is

gone, remember) Best was to step off the long diagonal with 34...♔h7. The long dark diagonal is generally more dangerous since the white battery controls four squares in enemy territory.

35 c5

Probably a pragmatic choice but the strongest was 35 b5! exploiting the fact that 35...♕xc4 leads to a lost queen ending after the forced 36 ♗xe4 ♖xd4 37 ♘xd4 ♖xe4 38 ♘xf5+ ♔g6 39 ♘e7+ ♔f7 40 ♖xe4 ♕xe4 41 ♘xg8 ♘xg8 42 b6 ♘e7 (42...♕b7 43 ♕b3+ ♔f8 44 a4 ♘e7 45 a5 ♘d5 46 ♕g3!) 43 b7 ♘c6 44 b8♕ ♘xb8 45 ♕xb8.

35...♕e6 36 b5 ♔f8??

The losing move. The only continuation to stay in the game was 36...♕b3 37 ♕a1 ♔g6 with mutual chances.

37 c6 g4 38 hxg4 fxg4 39 ♗xe4 gxf3

Or 39...♘xe4 40 ♖xe4! ♕xe4 41 ♗g7+ ♔e7 42 ♕f6 mate.

40 ♗xf6 ♖d6 41 ♗g7+ ♔f7 42 ♗e5 Black resigns.

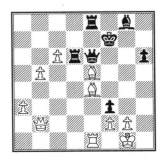

The end position is certainly a triumph for the bishop pair! Thanks to his psychological and tactical acuity, Kramnik managed to overcome the difficult positional problem of his queenside bishop and transform it into a super-bishop which even helped to decide the game in his favour. The price he played was the sacrifice of his reserve rook and in a way he played a handicap game without his a1-rook, as they sometimes did during the romantic period when handicap games were the order of the day to compensate for differences in skill. Today the psychological and pragmatic way of playing chess is even more important, because this kind of play doesn't concern computer programs so much, since a psychological player will focus on his opponent's fear or discomfort rather than striving to find the theoretically best move.

40

Steinitz – Burn
Hastings 1895

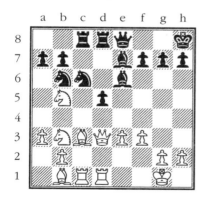

Black to move

25...♕g8!

This idea is one of the original defensive manoeuvres which illustrates why Burn had the reputation of being a very strong defensive player. Black's queen is certainly passive but he didn't need to weaken his position with any pawn move as his other pieces, placed in the centre and on the queenside, are ready to attack. After a very exciting game the final result was a draw. However it should be remembered that even if such a defensive strategy is risky against very active and accurate play by White, it's worth remembering because such a manoeuvre can be playable in other positions. Normally one should avoid placing the queen on a passive square but on this particular occasion it worked since it was part of a deep defensive plan where all the black pieces worked in harmony. A position where a queen placement on g8 or g1 can be playable is in the Hedgehog system after for example 1 c4 c5 2 ♘f3 ♘f6 3 ♘c3 e6 4 d4 cxd4 5 ♘xd4 a6 6 e3 b6 7 ♗e2 ♗b7 8 0-0 ♗e7 9 f3 0-0 10 e4 ♕c7 11 ♗e3 d6 12 ♖c1 ♘bd7 13 ♕d2 ♖fe8 14 ♖fd1 ♖ac8 15 ♗f1 ♕b8 16 ♕f2 ♗d8 17 ♔h1 ♗c7 18 ♕g1. Here the queen has the defensive function of protecting h2 after a possible ...d6-d5.

41

Spassky – Korchnoi
Candidates match, Kiev 1968

In the following position Spassky found a quiet "creeping" move which only slightly changes the piece formation in White's favour but nevertheless represents a very important redeployment

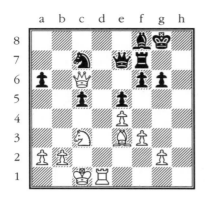

White to move

26 ♕b6!

26 ♘d5 ♕e6 would have been weaker.

26...♔g7 27 ♘d5 ♕e6 28 ♗xc5

This is the point with White's "creeper" since the c5-pawn could not be taken with the queen on c6. Now the queen is defended by the bishop.

28...♗xc5 29 ♕xc5 ♘b5 30 ♕e3 ♕c6+ 31 ♔b1 ♘d4 32 ♖c1 ♕b5 33 ♘c7 ♕e2 34 ♘e6+ ♔h7

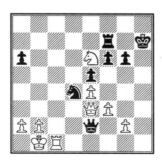

35 ♕h6+! Black resigns.

A pretty finish! White carried out beautiful manoeuvres with his queen. First the gradual one to b6 and then the longer queen moves to h6 via e3. Geometrically the queen manoeuvre b6-e3-h6 represents an upside down pyramid and is very aesthetic.

42

Dolmatov – Plaskett
Groningen 1978

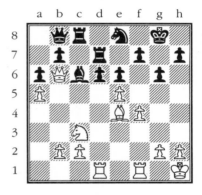

White to move

The question we should ask ourselves is what Black wants to do if it were his turn to move. Well, he wants to exchange bishops on e4 followed by ...d5 and perhaps also play ...♕c7. Therefore White made the clever move...

26 ♕b4!! ♕c7?!

The deep idea behind Dolmatov's move was after 26...♗xe4 27 ♘xe4 d5 to play the superb and unexpected pawn break 28 c4!! with the idea that 28...♖xc4? is answered by 29 ♕xc4 dxc4 30 ♖xd7 and White wins.

27 ♗xc6 ♕xc6 28 ♘a4!

Thanks to the queen move to b4 White's knight can now go to b6.

28...♘c7?

28...♖dd8 was correct.

29 c4! dxe5 30 ♘b6 ♖xd1 31 ♖xd1 ♖e8 32 fxe5 ♔g7 33 ♕d6 ♖b8 34 ♕xc6 bxc6 35 ♖d7 ♘e8 36 g4 g5 37 b4 ♔g6 38 ♖e7 ♖d8 39 b5 cxb5 40 cxb5 axb5 41 a6 b4 42 a7 Black resigns.

43

Andersson – Partos
Interzonal, Biel 1985

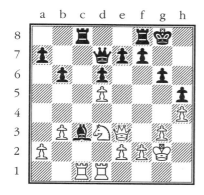

White to move

20 ♕e4!!

This beautiful move cooperates with the knight because of the possibility of ♘f4 and ♘xg6. In this way the value of the queen and the knight increases. Another possibility is ♘b4, especially if it cannot be taken by the bishop. 20 ♖c2 would not have been so effective with the queen on e3 due to 20...♗d4, but this tactical possibility is now removed.

20...♖c7 21 ♘f4!

White attacks the vulnerable g6 square.

21...♗e5

Black's best defence was 21...♗c5!, which would have been met by 22 ♘e6! fxe6 23 ♖xc3 ♖f6 (23...♖xc3?? 24 ♕xg6+ ♔h8 25 ♕xh5+ ♔g7 26 ♖d4 exd5 27 ♖g4+ ♕xg4 28 ♕xg4+ ♔h7 29 ♕h5+ ♔g7 30 ♕g5+ and White wins the e7- or d5-pawn.) 24 ♖xc5 dxc5 25 f3 with a slight advantage to White.

22 ♘d3 ♗c3 23 ♘f4 ♗e5 24 ♖xc7 ♕xc7 25 ♘d3 ♕c2 26 ♖c1

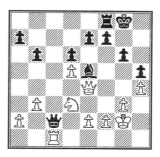

26...♕xa2?

Black could put up stronger resistance by 26...♕d2 27 ♖c7 ♗f6 28 ♘b4 a5 29 ♘c6 ♕xa2 (29...♖e8 30 a4 is too passive for Black.) 30 ♘xe7+ ♗xe7 31 ♕xe7 a4! 32 ♕xd6 axb3 33 ♕xb6 b2 34 ♖b7 ♕xd5+ 35 f3 with drawing chances.

27 ♘xe5 dxe5 28 ♕xe5 ♕xb3 29 ♖c7 e6 30 d6 a5 31 ♕d4!

This centralising move behind the pawn makes the passer more effective!

31...e5 32 ♕xe5 ♖d8 33 d7 Black resigns.

44

Karlsson – Moberg
Swedish Team Championship
2015/16

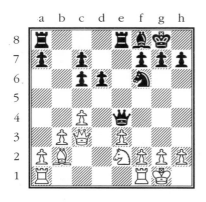

White to move

White is a little better with the more stabilised pawn structure and positional pressure along the long dark diagonal. In such situations it can be difficult to know whether one should play aggressively and embrace Steinitz's attacking principle, which means that one should attack the weakest point in the enemy position, or whether one should continue the activation of the pieces as much as possible before embarking on an attack. Karlsson played the logical...

17 ♕a5!

White immediately attacks the weak c7 point and f6-knight as well as controlling the fifth rank. The player who has the advantage should attack immediately otherwise he risks losing the advantage he has already gained. This principle is also applicable regarding the initiative when we are working with threats on several points. Compare this with an

attack which always aims at the weakest point or sector of the board. 17 ♘g3 ♕e5 would make it easier for Black to defend since White is unable to activate his queen as in the game.

17...♕c2

The pawn sacrifice 17...♕e7 18 ♗xf6 ♕xf6 19 ♕xc7 ♖ec8 was perhaps the best pragmatic solution for Black to handle White's initiative.

18 ♗xf6

Even stronger was 18 ♘d4! ♕e4 (18...♕xb2 19 ♖fb1 and Black's queen is trapped, but Black has a counter threat: 19...♖e5 20 ♕b4 c5 21 ♕b7 ♕c3 22 ♘b5 ♕a5 23 ♕xa8 and White has won the exchange.) 19 ♕xc7 with an active game and an extra pawn.

18...♕xe2 19 ♗c3 ♖ec8?

Black had to accept playing a pawn down after 19...c5 20 ♕xc7 a5! and focus on pursuing the minority attack with ...a4.

20 ♕f5!

This strong queen move along the fifth rank takes away two important white squares from the black queen.

20...h5!

20...g6 21 ♕f6 and mate next move.

21 h3! Black resigns.

He could have saved his queen with the forced 21....h4 22 ♖fe1 g6 23 ♕e4! ♕h5 but after 24 ♕xc6 White nevertheless wins in the long run due to his superior position and extra pawn. Understandably Moberg was not attracted to that option and terminated the game.

45

Urkedal – I. Sokolov
Xtracon Chess Open 2017

(1 d4 ♘f6 2 c4 e6 3 ♘c3 ♗b4 4 ♕c2 ♘c6 5 ♘f3 0-0 6 ♗d2 d6 7 a3 ♗xc3 8 ♗xc3 ♖e8 9 ♖d1 ♕e7 10 e3 e5 11 d5 e4? 12 dxc6 exf3 13 gxf3 bxc6 14 ♖g1 ♘h5? (14...c5 and...♗b7 was the correct way to continue.)

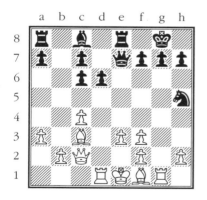

White to move

15 ♕e4!

This strong centralisation of the queen enhances White's more active

position. The queen move has several ideas. It threatens not only the c6-pawn but also the exchange of queens followed by ♖g5-a5 with strong positional pressure. White can make a gradual manoeuvre with the queen to d4 as well, so there are plenty of options and this practically forces Black to swap off the queens.

15...♖b8?

A better try was 15...♕xe4 16 fxe4 ♖xe4 17 ♗e2 ♖h4 but if White finds 18 ♖d4! ♖h3 19 ♗a5 it's not pleasant to be Black.

16 ♗e2?

White should have played 16 ♖g5! g6 17 ♕xe7 ♖xe7 18 ♖a5 with domination over the whole board. This was the cleanest way to win.

16...♗e6?

Black could have defended with 16...g6 and sacrificed the a-pawn after 17 ♕d4 (If 17 ♖g5 then 17...f5 and White's rook is cut off from the queenside.) 17...f6 18 ♕xa7 ♗e6 and White still has to find good moves to win the game.

17 f4 ♘f6?

Necessary was 17...f5 18 ♕xc6 ♘f6.

18 ♖xg7+! ♔f8

After 18...♔xg7 19 ♕g2+ ♔f8 20 ♕g5 the game would be over for Black.

19 ♕g2 Black resigns.

The double threat of 20 ♖g8+ and 20 ♕g5 cannot be prevented without material loss. Geometrically the queen manoeuvre to the kingside from the queenside via the centre was very beautiful. This is how to use the full force of the strongest piece on the board!

26...♕f1+ 27 ♗g1 ♗g4 28 ♕g2

White has parried the deadly threat of 28...♗xd4 29 ♕xd4 ♕f3+! 30 ♗xf3 ♗xf3 mate. Sometimes it's easy to overlook king moves as Flohr did in this famous episode. 20 years after this game Flohr visited Switzerland and when he encountered Grob he told him: "You know, the game I lost to you 20 years ago – it was a win for me!" However, Grob couldn't even remember the position!

46

Flohr – Grob
Match, Switzerland 1933

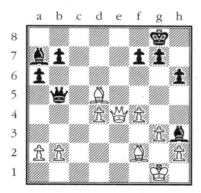

White to move

Black's last move was 30...♕b5 and Flohr resigned. A few years after this game Flohr gave an exhibition in Russia. A schoolboy asked him why he had resigned his game against Grob. "Why" said Flohr, "because I was lost." The schoolboy asked quietly whether he had considered...

26 ♔h1

...when White is slightly on top after

47

Karpov – Gheorghiu
Moscow 1977

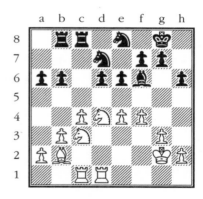

White to move

21 ♔f3!

White overprotects the e4-pawn and liberates the c3-knight for other duties.

21...♖b7

Gulko recommends 21...♔f8 bringing the king to e7. It works tactically since 22 e5? doesn't work on account of 22...dxe5 23 ♘xe6+ ♔e7. However the problem is

22 ♗a3 when Black's king is uncomfortably placed, especially in conjunction with e4-e5. It's easier for White to activate his king to a useful square than it is for Black and this is one of the advantages of enjoying a space advantage without the light-squared bishop and the queen on the board.

22 ♗a3 ♖bc7

Black wants to break with ...b6-b5.

23 ♘ce2 ♘c5 24 ♖d2 g6 25 ♘c2

Karpov plans to increase the harmony in his position by manoeuvring his knight to e3.

25...♗g7

The alternative was to become active on the queenside with 25...b5.

26 ♘e3 f5 27 exf5 gxf5 28 h3 h5 29 ♖g1 ♖f7

29...♔f7 is answered by 30 g4 hxg4+ 31 hxg4 fxg4+ 32 ♖xg4 followed by f4-f5 at an appropriate moment with a clear advantage.

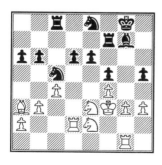

30 g4!

It looks scary to open up the position in front of the white king

but Black has no way of increasing the pressure on the f4-pawn. The main function of the king is actually to overprotect the f4-pawn so White is actually playing with an extra piece in the central area of the board.

30...hxg4+ 31 hxg4 fxg4+ 32 ♖xg4

The f-pawn is now firmly protected so the e2-knight is free to manoeuvre to the kingside and prepare the important break f4-f5 to penetrate Black's position.

32...♔f8 33 ♘g3

Another continuation was to exploit the fact that the other over-protector is free to manoeuvre as well and can be activated along the sixth rank by 33 ♖g6, attacking Black's small pawn centre. The e6-pawn in particular is weak, since the natural protector on f7 is gone.

33...a5 34 ♖g6

34...♔e7

34...♗e5 would probably have been met by the tactical opportunity 35 ♘gf5!. The over-protector(s) can work wonders, but Black nevertheless has good drawing chances after 35...♘g7 36 fxe5 ♘xf5 37 ♔e2. The king is no longer well placed on f3 and therefore changes its position to a safe square on the e-file where it still protects the knight. Apart from players like Petrosian and Seirawan, Karpov too has on several occasions demonstrated great skill in showing how to play with the king. 37...♘e7 38 ♖f6 dxe5 39 ♘g4 ♖xf6 40 ♘xf6 ♔f7 41 ♘d7 ♘xd7 42 ♖xd7 ♖e8 etc.

35 f5 ♖f6?

It was better to parry the threat of 36 ♗xc5, followed by 37 ♖xe6+, by playing 35...♔d7.

36 ♖xf6 ♘xf6?

The bishop becomes a target on g7 so better was 36...♗xf6.

37 ♖e2!

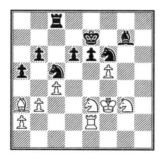

37...♖f8?

This loses by force. Relatively best was 37...♘fd7 38 ♘d5+ ♔f7 39 fxe6+ ♘xe6 40 ♘f5 which loses the pawn on d6 but after 40...♗e5 41 ♗xd6 ♘d4+ 42 ♘xd4 ♗xd6 Black still has some hopes for a draw, because all the pawns are placed on the same side of the board.

38 ♗xc5 bxc5 39 fxe6 ♔xe6

Black has no good discovered check with his knight as White responds with a knight check himself!

40 ♘ef5+ Black resigns.

What stands out in this game is how well placed the king was on f3 even though Black at times had a rook on the f-file targeting it, but nothing ever materialised since White had too many pieces on the kingside. The lesson to be learned is that sometimes it's possible to play with an active king despite the fact that there are many pieces on the board. It's all about the concrete nuances of the position. If one wants to focus on learning how to play with an active king then good teachers are the Chinese players, who generally understand this better than western players – for example GM Wang Hao.

48

Morozevich – Lputian
Sochi 2007

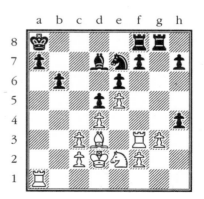

White to move

25 罝h1!

The creation of manoeuvring space (vacant squares) is sometimes more important than the pawn itself that is situated there. 25 gxh4 makes room for Black's pieces. 25...罝g4 26 罝h1 h6 27 ②g3 White's idea is to manoeuvre the knight to f6 but Black has enough manoeuvring space to stop this idea. 27...②g8 28 ②h5 f5! 29 exf6 奧e8.

25...hxg3

The drawback with 25...罝g4 is that it's in White's interest to exchange the queen's rook, since all White's pieces are more active than Black's remaining ones. 26 罝xh4 罝xh4 27 gxh4 h6 28 ②f4 ②g8 29 ②g6 and White wins the pawn on f7.

26 ②xg3 罝h8

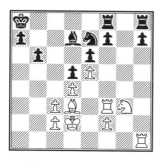

27 ②h5!

The manoeuvring space is more important than taking the pawn on h7. 27 罝xh7 罝xh7 28 奧xh7 奧b5 and Black has counter-chances with his a-pawn.

27...②g8 28 罝g1

White has a lot of vacant squares to choose from so sometimes there

are alternative ways to exploit them. 28 罝h4 followed by 29 罝hf4 was also strong.

28...f5 29 罝g7

29 exf6? 奧e8! and Black is back in the game. It's all about manoeuvring space rather than taking a pawn.

29...奧c8 30 ②f4 ②h6

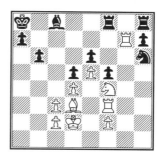

31 c4

31 罝h3 ②f7 32 c4! dxc4 33 奧xc4 ②d8 34 罝a3! was also good. Note that the pawn on h7 isn't the most important. More important is the manoeuvring space on the third rank because it will result in the win of a more important pawn on a7 after 34...堂b8 35 罝gxa7!, on b6 after 35...a5 36 罝b3 or on e6 after 35...罝f7 36 罝xf7 ②xf7 37 ②xe6. It's all about manoeuvring space!

31...dxc4 32 奧xc4 罝d8 33 c3 ②g4 34 堂e2

White obviously keeps his beautiful and strong centre intact.

34...罝he8 35 罝h3 罝d7 36 罝xd7 奧xd7 37 罝xh7 b5 38 奧b3 奧c8 39 f3 a5 40 fxg4 Black resigns.

The domination of Black's knight decides the game.

It's certainly worthwhile not to forget about Morozevich's idea to create empty squares out of nothing because it will turn up again in practical chess as well as later in this book, so beware!

49

Kosteniuk – P. Cramling
Match, Nalchik 2008

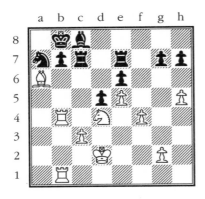

White to move

A fundamental example showing how to play against two weaknesses is the following:

28 ♖b6!

Alexandra Kosteniuk writes in her book *Diary of a Chess Queen*: "The position on the board is a classic example of playing against two weaknesses. Black doesn't have the resources to defend her weak pawns." The French pawn (Yes! surprisingly Pia Cramling played the French instead of her beloved Sicilian.) on e6 has become a fixed weakness due to the pressure on the sixth rank and the strong knight on d4. Despite the fact that the b7-pawn is over-protected it constitutes a weakness because Black cannot play the important defensive manoeuvre ...♗d7 followed by ...♞c8. Also the knight on a7 constitutes a weakness because it is unable to move to c6.

28...h6 29 g3 ♖e8 30 ♖d6 ♖ee7

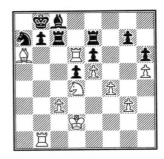

31 ♗f1!

Kosteniuk: "I was very proud of this bishop transfer during the game." It's interesting to compare the bishops because their respective mobility is clearly visible and not only that of the rooks and knights. When the attacking player has more space it often implies more manoeuvrability, which is underlined by the fact that the bishop manoeuvres undisturbed from a6-f1-h3-e6. The f1 and h3 squares are like the edges of a pool table. A very beautiful redeployment and who wouldn't be proud to find and play such a long and decisive bishop manoeuvre?

31...♗d7 32 ♗h3 ♞c8 33 ♗xe6!

Kosteniuk: "It's no secret that in such overwhelming positions, one often finds the winning combination." The heroic bishop exploits the awkward position of the black rooks.

33...♘xd6 34 exd6 ♗xe6 35 dxe7 ♗d7

35...♖xe7 is answered by one of the fundamental tricks in chess: "the fork" 36 ♘c6+ or "the pin" 36 ♖e1.

36 ♘f5 Black resigns.

Kosteniuk concludes the game by exploiting the overloaded bishop and after 36...♗e8 37 g4 Black's position is hopeless.

50

Szabó – Petrosian
Candidates Tournament,
Zürich 1953

(1 d4 ♘f6 2 c4 e6 3 ♘c3 d5 4 ♗g5 ♗e7 5 e3 0-0 6 ♘f3 h6 7 ♗h4 b6 8 ♗d3 ♗b7 9 0-0 ♘bd7 10 ♖c1 c5 11 ♕e2 a6 12 cxd5 exd5 13 dxc5 bxc5 14 ♖fd1 ♖e8 15 ♗c2 ♕b6 16 ♗b3)

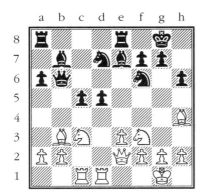

Black to move

White has chosen a typical plan when playing against hanging pawns – to provoke one of them to advance.

16...c4!

However, this is quite a good option as Capablanca showed a long time ago. In the classic game Bernstein – Capablanca, Moscow 1914, Capablanca made a similar move which he has described in detail in *My Chess Career*. The important point of Capablanca's revolutionary move is that the e7-bishop becomes an active piece. Another important point is that the b2-pawn becomes a tactical weakness which Black can attack along the b-file. A third important issue is that if White blockades the d5-pawn by placing his knight on d4 the attack on the d-file is temporarily stopped. In addition to these arguments Nimzowitsch wrote in his classic *My System* that a move such as ...c4 makes the hanging pawns relatively secure, because after this move Black has only one weakness instead of two.

17 ♗a4

17 ♗c2 is more precise because on a4 the bishop might later be exposed to an attack by ...♘d7-c5.

17...♗c6

Preferable was 17...♖ed8 with the idea of 18...♘c5.

18 ♗xc6

There was no reason to exchange Black's bad bishop which will be further blockaded by ♘d4 but White reasons that the d5-pawn will be weaker after the exchange. More to the point was 18 ♗c2 when White remains slightly more comfortable due to the weak d4 and f5 points.

18...♕xc6 19 b3!

A good move which completely rules out the knight manoeuvre ...♘c5-d3 but has the drawback of increasing the power of Black's bishop.

19...♖ac8

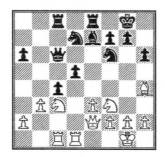

20 ♘a4?

This move only helps Black to improve the placing of his queen on a more commanding post. It would be more logical to utilise the weak d4 square and play 20 ♘d4 ♕b6 21 ♕f3 when Black must decide how to defend the d5-pawn. The position is about equal after the most active continuation 21...♗a3 22 ♖c2 ♕a5.

20...♕b5 21 ♘c3 ♕a5 22 ♗xf6 ♘xf6 23 bxc4 dxc4 24 ♘d2

Better was 24 ♖d4 ♕b4 25 ♘e5 ♖c5 26 f4 with about equal play. But not 26 ♖xc4? ♕a3! and several pieces are hanging.

24...♖c6 25 ♘xc4?

It was Szabó's style to take unnecessary risks. Here the risks involve the unstable knights. There were several solid options available such as 25 g3 or 25 ♖c2 with mutual chances.

25...♕c7 26 ♘a4 ♖c8

With the help of Alekhine's gun Black has created a triple pin along the c-file. White must play very precisely so as not to lose material.

27 ♖d4 ♘e8

27...♘h7! followed by ...♘f8-e6 and ...♗f6 was more precise.

28 e4??

The only defence was 28 ♕d1 ♘d6 29 ♘ab6 ♖xb6 30 ♘xb6 ♕xc1 31 ♘xc8 ♕xc8 32 g3 with balanced play.

28...♗f6 29 e5 ♗xe5 30 ♖e4 ♘f6 31 ♘ab6

If 31 ♖xe5 ♖xc4 32 ♖xc4 ♕xc4 33 ♕d1 (33 ♕xc4 ♖xc4) 33...♕xa4 Black wins with the help of a back-rank motif.

31...♖xb6 32 ♖xe5 ♖c6

32...♕xc4 takes advantage of the back-rank after 33 ♖xc4 ♖b1+.

33 ♖e7 ♖xc4 34 ♖e1

If 34 ♖xc7 then 34...♖xc1+ 35 ♖xc1 ♖xc1+.

34...♕c6 35 h3 ♖c1 36 ♖xc1 ♕xc1+ 37 ♔h2 ♕c4 38 ♕f3 ♕xa2 39 ♖a7 ♕d5 White resigns.

51

Najdorf – Fischer
Piatigorsky Cup, Santa Monica 1966

(1 d4 ♘f6 2 c4 g6 3 ♘c3 ♗g7 4 e4
d6 5 ♗e2 0-0 6 ♗g5 c5 7 d5 e6
8 ♘f3 h6 9 ♗h4 exd5 10 cxd5 g5
11 ♗g3 b5 12 ♘d2 a6 13 0-0 ♖e8
14 ♕c2 ♕e7 15 ♖ae1 ♘bd7)

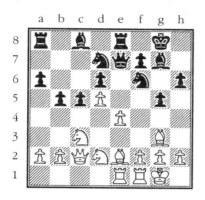

White to move

16 a4!

The other natural break 16 f4 is
met by 16...gxf4 17 ♖xf4 ♘e5 and
Black is relatively okay.

16...b4

A positional mistake would be
16...bxa4 17 ♘c4! ♘e5 18 ♗xe5
dxe5 19.♘xa4 with a winning
positional advantage for White.
White has a protected passed pawn
and can attack the weak pawns on c5
and a6. Black has a very bad bishop
on g7. Fischer wasn't fond of
closing the diagonal of his favourite
piece.

17 ♘d1 ♘e5

After 17...♘xe4? 18 ♗d3 f5
19 ♗xe4 fxe4 20 ♖xe4 White is
positionally winning.

18 ♘e3

White has two knights controlling
c4 but Black has only one.

18...♘g6 19 ♘ec4

19...♘f4

19...♖d8 is strongly met by
20 ♘a5 ♗d7 21 ♘dc4 ♗e8 22 ♗d1
and White is prepared for the central
break e4-e5 running over Black's
position.

20 ♗xf4 gxf4 21 e5! dxe5 22 ♗f3 ♕f8

22...♘d7? is met by 23 d6.

23 ♘xe5 ♗b7 24 ♘dc4 ♖ad8

Not 24...♘xd5? 25 ♘d7.

25 ♘c6 ♖xe1 26 ♖xe1 ♖e8 27 ♖d1 ♖c8 28 h3 ♘e8 29 ♘6a5 ♖b8 30 ♕f5 ♘d6 31 ♘xd6 Black resigns.

Note that it wasn't only the c4
square that was exploited by 16 a4!
but also the weak pawns on c5 and
a6.

Here Fischer had a taste of
his own medicine because it's
interesting to compare 16 a4! with
Fischer – Gadia, exercise 36.

52

Andersson – Miralles
Cannes 1989

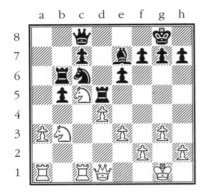

White to move

27 a4! bxa4

27...b4 28 a5 is only to White's advantage because the distant passed a-pawn will be more dangerous than the blockaded enemy passer.

28 ♘xa4

The structural advantage for White with this exchange of pawns is that Black is now saddled with two pawn islands, where the c7-pawn in particular is a permanent weakness.

28...♖a6 29 ♕c2 ♗d6 30 ♘c3 ♘b4 31 ♕e2 ♖g5

Black has problems achieving harmony between his pieces which are scattered around the board without any clear purpose.

32 ♖xa6 ♘xa6 33 ♘e4 ♖d5 34 ♖a1 ♘b8 35 ♘c3 ♖g5 36 ♘e4 ♖d5 37 ♘c3 ♖g5 38 ♕c4 ♕b7 39 ♖b1 ♕c6 40 ♘c5 ♘d7 41 ♘xd7! ♕xd7

Or 41...♕xc4 42 ♖b8+ ♗f8 43 ♖xf8 mate.

42 ♘e4 Black resigns,

Because of the double threat on g5 and d6 followed by ♖b8+.

53

Alekhine – Bogoljubow
Budapest 1921

(1 d4 ♘f6 2 ♘f3 e6 3 c4 ♗b4+ 4 ♗d2 ♗xd2+ 5 ♕xd2 d5 6 e3 0-0 7 ♘c3 ♘bd7 8 ♗d3 c6 9 0-0 dxc4 10 ♗xc4 e5 11 ♗b3 ♕e7)

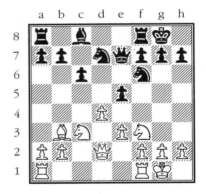

White to move

12 e4!

This strong pawn move in the centre not only prevents Black from playing ...e5-e4 but also prepares a future attack with the e- and f-pawn after the inevitable release of the tension in the centre. If that should be the case one might call this kind of pawn play an attack of the three musketeers (= d+e+f-pawn)!

12...exd4 13 ♘xd4 ♘c5

Of course not 13...♘xe4? due to the deadly pin 14 ♕e3.

14 ♗c2 ♖d8 15 ♖ad1 ♗g4 16 f3 ♘e6 17 ♕f2 ♘xd4 18 ♖xd4 ♗e6 19 ♖fd1

19 ♖xd8+ looks tempting since 19...♕xd8 (19...♖xd8 fails to 20 ♕xa7 with a clear advantage.) looks awkward but after 20 ♖d1 ♕b6 White has only helped Black to exchange queens, which suits him more than his opponent.

19...b6?!

Black defends his a-pawn but more active was 19...a5 followed by ...b5 and ...b4 attacking the knight. Black has a pawn majority on the queenside and should activate it. Just as White is attacking Black's pieces on e6 and f6 Black should do likewise on the other flank and strive for a dynamic balance.

20 h3

Everything is prepared for the advance of the e- and f-pawn now that the g4-square is defended. White's harmonious piece formation gives him real prospects of an attack in the centre and on the kingside.

20...c5?!

Black weakens the d5-square without getting anything in return. 20...b5 was the correct way of mobilising the queenside majority.

21 ♖4d2 ♖xd2

It was perhaps better to take measures against the advance of the e- and f-pawn by 21...♘e8 22 f4 f6 but Black has a difficult position after 23 ♘d5 (or 23 ♗a4!) 23...♗xd5 24 exd5.

22 ♕xd2 c4?

Black's plan to activate the queenside majority is too slow compared with White's attack. The c-pawn has only managed to weaken the d5-square and now the d4-square as well.

23 f4 g6

23...♕c5+ 24 ♔h1! is very strong but if White prefers an endgame then 24 ♕f2 ♕xf2+ 25 ♔xf2 also leads to an overwhelming advantage.

24 ♕d4

Alekhine's centralisation of the queen provokes Black into an exchange of queens. White's tactical idea is that he threatens to win the c4-pawn by 25 f5. However an immediate 24 g4! should have been played, according to plan, so as not to be distracted by the c-pawn which is less important.

24...♖c8?

It was better to play 24...♖f8 with the idea 25 f5 ♗c8.

25 g4

White threatens both f4-f5 and e4-e5 and Black has no antidote to the menacing pawns.

25...♗xg4 26 hxg4 ♘xg4 27 ♔g2! h5 28 ♘d5 ♕h4 29 ♖h1 ♕d8 30 ♗d1!

Black resigns.

Alekhine: "An instructive game from the strategic point of view."

So don't forget this typical plan how to play with a central majority and a majority on the kingside. It can be reinforced by thoroughly understanding this model game.

It's also a good structure with queens off the board. For example Petrosian – Portisch, Santa Monica 1966 began 1 d4 d5 2 c4 e6 3 ♘c3 ♗e7 4 ♘f3 ♘f6 5 ♗g5 0-0 6 ♖c1 ♘bd7 7 e3 c6 8 ♗d3 dxc4 9 ♗xc4

♘d5 10 ♗xe7 ♕xe7 11 ♘e4 (Alekhine's continuation in the Orthodox Queen's Gambit) 11...♘5f6 12 ♘xf6+ ♕xf6 13 0-0 e5 14 e4 exd4 15 ♕xd4 ♕xd4 16 ♘xd4.

White is slightly better but in this type of position it is White who plays for two results rather than Black who lacks dynamic counter measures. The Slovenian GM Enver Bukic (1937-2017), who was famed for his splendid technique and patience, had several victories to his credit utilising Alekhine's ingenious idea. Some of his games can be found in Chess Informant's *Yugoslav Chess Triumphs* (Belgrade 1976) and Chessbase's *Mega Database*.

54

Réti – Rubinstein
Karlsbad 1923

(1 ♘f3 d5 2 g3 ♘f6 3 ♗g2 g6 4 c4 d4 5 d3 ♗g7 6 b4! 0-0 7 ♘bd2 c5 8 ♘b3! cxb4 9 ♗b2 (9 a3!) 9...♘c6?! (9...♖e8!) 10 ♘bxd4 ♘xd4 11 ♗xd4 b6 12 a3 ♗b7 13 ♗b2 bxa3 14 ♖xa3 ♕c7 15 ♕a1 ♘e8 16 ♗xg7 ♘xg7 17 0-0 ♘e6 18 ♖b1 ♗c6)

100

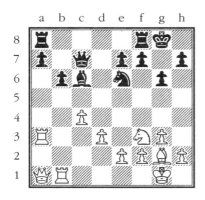

White to play

19 d4!

Réti plays according to "the hypermodern paradox" a term which was coined by the American GM Reuben Fine (1914-93) in his classic book *The World's Great Chess Games* (Dover 1983).

He defines it as follows: "if you occupy the centre immediately, the pawns soon become weakened, and the opponent will then be able to occupy it. This means though that it is not occupation that is bad; it is in many cases *immediate occupation*."

Incidentally Stockfish 11 comes up with the same move if it's allowed to think at least 20 moves deep!

19...♗e4 20 ♖d1 a5 21 d5!

Obviously "the hypermodern paradox" has a lot of inherent dynamism, because, in the spirit of Philidor, the well-developed pieces are its servants from behind the d-pawn.

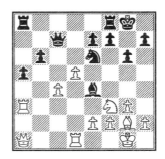

21...♘c5

21...♘d8? is too passive because after 22 ♘h4 White has the very beautiful intermediate move 22...♗xg2 23 d6!! showing the full impact of "the hypermodern paradox". It creates two empty squares on d5 and f6 and the white knight wants to occupy one of these. After 23...exd6 24 ♘xg2 ♕xc4? 25 ♘f4 White has the deadly threat 26 ♘d5. Black's best is 25...♖e8 but after 26 h4! (26 ♘d5 ♖xe2) White has excellent winning chances.

22.♘d4 ♗xg2 23 ♔xg2 ♖fd8?

Black thereby only helps White to plant the knight on c6 with a gain of tempo. A better defensive move was 23...♘d7 when 24 ♘c6 can be met by 24...♘b8 25 ♘e5 ♘d7.

24 ♘c6

24 ♘b5! is the computer's preference.

24...♖d6

24...♖e8! should have been played, calmly preparing ...♘c5-d7-b8 to challenge the strong knight on c6.

25 ♖e3 ♖e8

25...♖xc6 26 dxc6 ♕xc6+ 27 f3 would have led to a stable advantage for White but was perhaps Black's best chance to stay alive in the game.

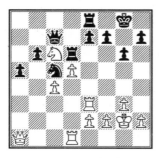

26 ♕e5?!

26 ♕b2, with the idea 27 ♖b1 or 26 ♖b1 followed by 27 ♕b2, was more accurate and would sooner or later have forced the exchange sacrifice on c6. Réti's idea with the queen centralisation is to provoke the weakening ...f6, but it turns out that Black gets a good square for his king on f7. Compare this variation with the game continuation: 26...♖xc6 27 ♕b5 ♖c8 28 dxc6 and Black cannot defend e7 in a convenient way. He would like to have his king on f7 but there is neither time nor space for that.

26...f6 27 ♕b2 e5?

This was an interesting moment for 27...♖xc6 because 28 ♕b5! ♖c8 29 dxc6 ♔f7! followed by ...♕xc6 would lead to a position which might be defendable in a practical game.

28 ♕b5

White makes the capture on c6 less appealing.

28...♔f7 29 ♖b1 ♘d7 30 f3

Réti's intention is to prevent ...e5-e4 when White's rook is placed on d3.

30...♖c8 31 ♖d3 e4

White is preparing the completion of the hypermodern paradox with e2-e4 so Black's move is a desperate try to disturb White.

32 fxe4 ♘e5?

It was better to play a waiting game one pawn down with 32...h5 followed by ...♖c8-e8 and ...♔f7-g7.

33 ♕xb6!

This exchange sacrifice is the best, simplest and the most aesthetic continuation to decide the game.

33...♘xc6 34 c5!

This intermediate move is the point.

34...♖d7 35 dxc6 ♖xd3 36 ♕xc7+ ♖xc7 37 exd3 ♖xc6 38 ♖b7+ ♔e8

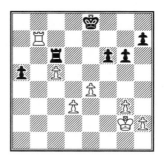

39 d4!

"The hypermodern paradox" is played out for the second time, or perhaps the third time if 32 fxe4 is included in the concept.

39...♖a6 40 ♖b6!

This move demands precise calculation due to the subsequent transition to a pawn ending.

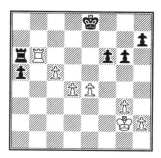

40...♖a8

The following variation leads to a pretty mate with two queens: 40...♖xb6 41 cxb6 ♔d8 42 e5 fxe5 43 dxe5 a4 44 b7 ♔c7 45 e6 a3 46 e7 a2 47 e8♕ a1♕ 48 b8♕ mate.

41 ♖xf6 a4 42 ♖f2 a3 43 ♖a2 ♔d7 44 d5 g5 45 ♔f3 ♖a4 46 ♔e3 h5 47 h4 gxh4 48 gxh4 ♔e7 49 ♔f4 ♔d7 50 ♔f5 Black resigns.

Fine calls this game "One of the earliest triumphs of the hypermodernism". This classic game has influenced modern chess. For example Stein – Rodriguez Gonzales, Havana 1968 was played according to the plan outlined in Réti – Rubinstein as I have written about in detail in my book *Stein – move by move* (Everyman Chess 2015).

55

Botvinnik – Denker
USSR – USA Match 1945

(1 d4 d5 2 ♘f3 ♘f6 3 c4 c6 4 cxd5 cxd5 5 ♘c3 ♘c6 6 ♗f4 ♕a5 7 e3 ♘e4 8 ♕b3 e6 9 ♗d3 ♗b4 10 ♖c1 ♘xc3 11 bxc3 ♗a3 12 ♖b1 b6)

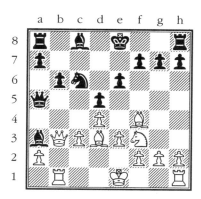

White to play

13 e4!

The right moment for this important pawn break in the centre. White has to forestall 13...♗a6 which was on Black's agenda. Another possibility was the tempting 13 ♗b5 which would have been answered by 13...♗d7 but this loses control of the e4-square and misplaces the bishop, which belongs on d3.

13...dxe4 14 ♗b5

In his annotations to the game, Botvinnik writes that "White is by no means obliged to agree to the routine continuation 14 ♗xe4 ♗b7, after which he would be obliged to parry the threat of 15...♘xd4."

As a matter of fact after 15 0-0 (15 ♘d2 fails to 15...♘xd4!

16 cxd4 ♗xe4 since the knight is pinned.) 15...0-0 (15...♘xd4? 16 ♘xd4 ♗xe4 is suicidal due to 17 ♖be1! ♗d5 18 c4 ♗b7 19 ♘b5! and White wins material.) 16 ♕c2 g6 17 c4 White is clearly better due to his more harmonious position. The hanging pawns are a strength rather than a weakness and they want to move forward!

14...♗d7 15 ♘d2

15...a6?

The lesser evil was 15...0-0 16 ♗e3 (It's too early for 16 ♘c4?? on account of 16...♘xd4 17 ♘xa5 ♘xb3 18 ♖xb3 ♗xb5 19 ♖xb5 bxa5 20 ♖xa5 ♗b2 with good winning chances.) 16...ac8 17 ♘c4 ♘xd4 18 ♗xd4 ♕xb5 19 ♘xa3 ♕g5 20 0-0 e5 21 ♗e3 ♕g6. Black can fight on with two pawns for the knight and some play on the light squares.

16 ♗xc6 ♗xc6 17 ♘c4 ♕f5 18 ♗d6

Even more crushing was 18 ♕xa3 ♕xf4 19 ♖xb6 ♗d5 20 ♘e5! with the idea of 21 c4 trapping the bishop.

18...e3 19 ♘xe3 ♕xb1+ 20 ♕xb1 ♗xd6 21 ♕xb6 ♔d7 22 ♕b3

White has won material and can go home and win in a technical manner.

22...♖ab8 23 ♕c2 ♖b5 24 0-0 ♖h5 25 h3 ♖b8 26 c4

The isolated pawn couple have been transformed into hanging pawns.

26...g6 27 ♘g4 ♖f5 28 ♘e5+! ♗xe5 29 dxe5 ♖xe5 30 ♕d2+ Black resigns.

After 30...♔e7 31 ♖d1 White wins more material.

56

Michel – Ståhlberg
Mar del Plata 1947

(1 e4 c5 2 ♘f3 e6 3 d4 cxd4 4 ♘xd4 ♘f6 5 ♘c3 d6 6 ♗e2 a6 7 f4 ♗e7 8 ♗f3 ♕c7 9 0-0 ♘c6 10 ♔h1 ♗e7 11 ♘b3 ♖c8 12 ♕e1 b5 13 a3 0-0 14 ♗e3 b4 15 axb4 ♘xb4 16 ♕f2 ♗c6 17 ♘d4 ♗b7 18 g4)

Black to move

18...d5!

The best answer to an attack on the wing is to counter-strike in the centre! This is absolutely true in the majority of cases. It's all about the centre before going for an attack, and that is why, as was discovered by Steinitz and eventually proven empirically, it's so important to conquer or at least *solidify* the centre before starting an operation on the flank. The prototype of this idea appeared in the game Dubois – Steinitz, London 1862.

19 e5 ♘e4 20 ♗xe4

20 ♘xe4? dxe4 21 ♗g2 ♗c5 would give Black strong pressure on the c-file, practically forcing 22 c3 ♘d3 23 ♕d2 ♖fd8 with an overwhelming position.

20...dxe4 21 h4?

This pawn storm is too aggressive. It would be better to improve the placement of the king by 21 ♔g1 with only a slight advantage for Black.

21...♕d8?

Correct was the more active and centralising 21...♕c4! with the same idea as in the game.

22 g5??

The pawn on h4 wasn't important so White should have replied

22 ♖fd1 with mutual chances. 22...♗xh4? would then be bad because of 23 ♕h2 with the double threat of g4-g5 trapping the bishop and the discoverer ♘d4xe6.

22...♕xd4! White resigns.

After 23 ♗xd4 e3+ Black is a piece up.

57

Smyslov – Darga
Interzonal, Amsterdam 1964

(1 ♘f3 ♘f6 2 g3 d5 3 ♗g2 ♗g4 4 c4 c6 5 cxd5 cxd5 6 ♘e5 ♗c8 7 0-0 e6 8 ♘c3 ♗e7)

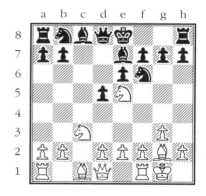

White to move

9 d4

If Black's light-squared bishop is situated behind the pawn chain it's more effective to place the pawn on d4 and prepare a future central break with e2-e4.

9...0-0 10 ♗f4 ♗d7 11 ♕b3! ♕b6?

11...♗c6 is better.

12 ♕xb6 axb6 13 ♘xd7 ♘bxd7 14 ♖fc1

14 e4 is not effective due to the creation of a vacant square on d5 for Black, which can be immediately exploited after 14...dxe4 15 ♘xe4 ♘d5.

14...♖fc8 15 a3 ♖c6 16 ♗d2!

The bishop wasn't doing much on f4 but here it can be exchanged on b4 after the preparatory move ♘c3-a2.

16...♖d8 17 e3!

White improves his position slowly but surely. He hopes to generate the pawn push to e4 under more favourable circumstances.

17...♘e8?

18 e4!

Smyslov displays perfect timing for this important central pawn break. It serves the two important purposes: to activate the two bishops and at the same time exploit Black's passive pieces.

18...dxe4 19 ♗xe4 ♖c4 20 ♘b5 ♖xc1+ 21 ♖xc1 ♘c5 22 dxc5 ♖xd2 23 cxb6 ♖xb2 24 a4! ♔f8 25 ♖c8 Black resigns.

A very instructive game showing that timing of a central pawn break is crucial.

58

Smyslov – Bronstein
USSR 1973

(1 ♘f3 ♘f6 2 g3 d5 3 ♗g2 ♗f5 4 c4 c6 5 cxd5 cxd5 6 ♕b3 ♕c8 7 ♘c3 e6)

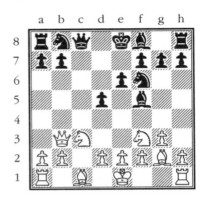

White to move

8 d3!

When Black's light-squared bishop is placed on f5 it's more effective to place the d-pawn on d3 rather than d4. This is a dangerous dynamic plan for Black to meet.

8...♘c6 9 ♗f4 ♗e7 10 0-0

10 ♖c1 would have gained a tempo on the queenside.

10...0-0 11 ♖ac1

Slowly but surely White prepares the opening of the centre by e2-e4, in order to create life out of this seemingly dead variation.

11...♕d7 12 ♘e5

White opens the diagonal for the g2-bishop.

12...♘xe5 13 ♗xe5 ♗g6 14 e4! ♖ad8

106

Or 14...dxe4 15 dxe4 &ad8 16 &fd1.

15 exd5 exd5 16 &xf6 &xf6 17 &xd5 &e5

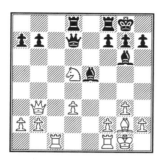

Bronstein has sacrificed a pawn for the bishop pair but White is simply too active and has a clear advantage.

18 d4! &b8

18...&xd4 is met by 19 &cd1 &e5 20 &f6+.

19 &fe1 &fe8 20 &xe8+ &xe8

By forcing the exchange of rooks Black's chances of drawing become more difficult.

21 &e3 &xd4 22 &xb7 h5 23 &c8 &e5 24 &c4 &e1+ 25 &f1 &h7 26 &xb8 &d3 27 &d2 &e2 28 &f3 Black resigns.

59

Har-Zvi – Speelman
Altensteig 1994

(1 e4 c6 2 d4 d5 3 &d2 dxe4 4 &xe4 &d7 5 &f3 &gf6 6 &xf6+ &xf6 7 &e5 &d7 8 &d3 g6 9 c3 &g7 10 &e2 0-0 11 &f4)

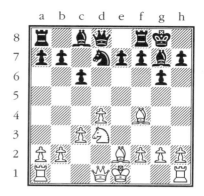

Black to move

11...&a5!?

Speelman's choice is interesting since the liberating move ...e7-e5 is hard to stop, but it's not the strongest. 11...e5! would have equalised at once after 12 dxe5 (But not 12 &xe5 &xe5 13 dxe5 &a5! and White cannot hold the pawn on e5 after 14 &d4?! &e8 15 b4 &c7 etc.) 12...&e7. Surprisingly this simple liberating centralised pawn break has not yet been played. At least not according to *Mega Database 2021*, so a TN (theoretical novelty) is in store.

12 0-0 e5 13 b4 &c7 14 &g3

White has a slight advantage.

14...&d8 15 &b3 c5!?

A very creative move by Speelman but unfortunately it's too optimistic. The game nevertheless ended in a draw after the following moves.

16 bxc5 b6 17 cxb6 axb6 18 &f3 &a5 19 &fe1 &e8 20 &ad1 &a6 21 &b4 &c4 22 &b1 h5 23 dxe5 &xe5 24 &d5 &xd5 25 &xd5 &c5 26 &h1 &e6 27 &xe5 &xe5 28 &xe5 Draw

60

Pillsbury – Showalter
USA Championship 1898

(1 d4 d5 2 c4 e6 3 ♘c3 ♘f6 4 ♗g5
♗e7 5 e3 ♘bd7 6 ♘f3 0-0 7 cxd5
exd5 8 ♗d3 c6 9 ♕c2 ♖e8 10 0-0
♘f8 11 ♘e5 ♘g4 12 ♗xe7 ♕xe7
13 ♘xg4 ♗xg4 14 ♖ae1 ♕f6)

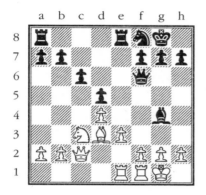

White to move

The minority attack is one of the
most important motifs in chess and
can take place on the queenside or
the kingside. However, in practice
it's more common on the queenside
to avoid exposing the king.

Interestingly the minority attack
has been subjected to more
detailed analyses than the majority
attack, quantitatively as well as
qualitatively, because the analyses
and methods are more general.

Obviously one should be familiar
with the history of the minority
attack and the first official game
where we can see the embryo of this
idea is the move introduced by
Pillsbury...

15 a4

Better was 15 f4 with the idea
f4-f5 and h2-h3 trapping the bishop.

15...♖e7

Pillsbury's idea after 15...a5 was
probably to play 16 ♖b1 followed by
b2-b4 with pressure on the b7-pawn.
However, this kind of minority
attack seems less reliable since
Black can develop his rook on a8
and place the bishop on c8 and in
that way defend the weakness on b7
economically. White has to play a4-
a5 followed by ♘c5 to increase the
pressure on b7 but if Black has a
knight on e6 it's hard to see how
White can proceed with the attack.

16 b4

After a transposition of the moves
a2-a4 and b2-b4 we now return to a
normal minority attack and therefore
this game should be regarded as the
first embryo or prototype.

**16...♖ae8 17 b5 ♕g5 18 f4 ♕f6
19 ♕d2 ♗f5**

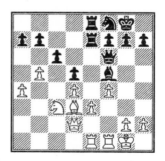

20 a5

Pillsbury has the ambitious plan of
creating pawn weaknesses on the
queenside and in the centre (the d5-
pawn) by a further a5-a6 to crack
Black's diagonal of pawns so they

fall like dominos. 20 ♗xf5 ♕xf5 21 bxc6 bxc6 22 ♘a2 followed by ♘b4 was correct and in the spirit of the minority attack. From b4 the knight not only attacks the c6-pawn but can also manoeuvre to the ideal square d3.

20...♕g6 21 ♗xf5 ♕xf5

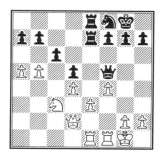

22 a6

This is the type of minority attack Pillsbury was interested in and we can attribute this double pawn break to him. 22 bxc6 bxc6 23 ♘a2 followed by ♘b4 was still a valid option. The position is balanced due to White's pawn weakness on e3.

22...cxb5 23 ♘xb5 ♕d7 24 axb7 a6

Not 24...♕xb5? 25 ♖b1.

25 ♘c3 ♕xb7 26 ♖b1 ♕c6 27 ♖fc1 ♕d6

27...♖xe3? loses to 28 ♘e4!.

28 ♘d1

White's ambitious plan of a5-a6 has succeeded but due to the weak pawn on e3, which has to be economically defended by the knight, the position is equal.

However, Pillsbury managed to win the game after imprecise play by his opponent.

28...♘g6 29 g3 h5 30 ♕e2 h4 31 ♕h5 hxg3 32 hxg3 ♘f8 33 ♖c5 ♖d8 34 ♖bc1 g6 35 ♕f3 ♘e6 36 ♖c8 ♔g7 37 ♖xd8 ♘xd8 38 ♖c5

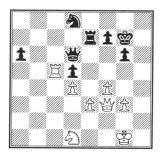

38...♘e6?

38...♖d7 39 ♘c3 ♘e6 40 ♖xd5 ♕c6 was a better continuation.

39 ♕xd5 ♕b6 40 ♖c1 ♕b4 41 ♘f2 ♕d2?

41...♕a3 is better.

42 ♕e5+ f6 43 ♕xf6+! ♔xf6 44 ♘e4+ ♔f5 45 ♘xd2 g5 46 d5 gxf4 47 gxf4 ♘xf4 48 exf4 ♔xf4 49 ♖c5 ♖d7 50 ♘c4 ♔e4 51 d6 ♔d4 52 ♖c7 ♖d8 53 d7 ♔d5 54 ♖c8 Black resigns.

When studying the minority attack I recommend looking at complete games because it is linked to all phases.

Already the exchange 7 cxd5 exd5 prepares the attack which starts with the key move 16 b4. When the position has been clarified on the queenside (28 ♘d1), White will profit from the weaknesses.

109

61

Steinitz – Lee
London 1899

1 d4 d5 2 c4 e6 3 ♘c3 ♘f6 4 ♗g5
♗e7 5 e3 0-0 6 ♗xf6 ♗xf6 7 cxd5
exd5 8 ♕b3 c6 9 ♗d3 ♖e8 10 ♘ge2
♘d7 11 ♕c2 ♘f8 12 0-0 g6

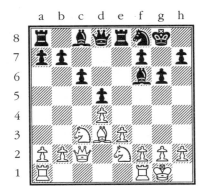

White to move

13 b4

Here this move represents the transitional stage between the opening and the middlegame, because White plans an attack on the c6-pawn with b4-b5 in order to isolate it after b5xc6 ...b7xc6. This game can be regarded as the prototype where a true minority attack was employed. However note that Steinitz lost a tempo by forcing the natural move 8...c6 with 8 ♕b3 and then placed the queen on the right square at move eleven. Steinitz was ahead of his time since according to the Tarrasch school a pawn minority should not advance against a majority. The Hungarian chess journalist Leopold Hoffer, annotator for the tournament book of London 1899, wrote that "the plan of attacking on the left wing,

practically four pawns with two should not succeed."

This clever idea was later taken up by other prominent players such as Capablanca in the world championship match against Lasker in 1921. Capablanca and Alekhine both used the minority attack in their match in 1927. Flohr and Botvinnik played it regularly in the 30s. If you haven't seen the idea before, it might seem strange to attack where Black is stronger but White has an advantage in the semi-open c-file which he wants to exploit. Note that White didn't need to prepare the move with ♖a1-b1 since the exchange on f6 already has taken place to deflect the bishop from the a3-f8 diagonal.

13...a6

It's normally a good idea to get rid of the a-pawns for Black since otherwise the a7-pawn might turn out to be a second weakness after Black has been saddled with a weakness on c6.

14 a4 ♗e7

Hoffer wrote "Black might have played 14...b6 stopping 15 b5, because of 15...c5 and establishing a passed pawn." However White is clearly better after 16 dxc5 bxc5 17 ♖ad1 with strong pressure on the hanging pawns so the variation chosen by Hoffer, to prove his statement, was wrong. However, one move earlier at move 15 Black should have played the stronger 15...axb5 16 axb5 ♖xa1 17 ♖xa1 c5 18 dxc5 bxc5 19 ♖d1 which would have led to a position in a state of dynamic equilibrium so he wasn't altogether wrong by suggesting 14...b6.

15 b5 axb5 16 axb5 ♖xa1 17 ♖xa1

The drawback to exchanging the a-pawns is that White gains control of the a-file but nothing is for free in chess, not even getting rid of the a-pawns!

17...f5?

This is too ambitious because it will not be easy for Black to play a minority attack himself with ...f5-f4 or to manoeuvre the knight to e4, due to White's attack on the queenside. Better was 17...♘e6.

18 ♖a8 ♘d7 19 ♘a4 ♘b6

Black would like to play 19...♘f6 but it doesn't work on account of 20 bxc6 bxc6 21 ♕xc6 ♗d7 22 ♖xd8 ♗xc6 23 ♖xe8+ ♗xe8 24 ♘ac3 and White plays an ending with an extra pawn.

20 ♘xb6 ♕xb6

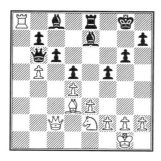

21 ♘c3?

Steinitz misses the tactical breakthrough 21 g4!! which would have exploited Black's weakened kingside. The pawn is taboo because

after 21...fxg4? White plays 22 ♗xg6 hxg6 23 ♕xg6+ ♔f8 24 ♘f4 ♗h4 25 ♕h7 and White mates or wins the queen. I'm pretty sure that from the 1860s Steinitz would have seen this tactical opportunity but by now he was probably too focused on the queenside.

21...♗d7 22 ♕a2 ♖xa8 23 ♕xa8+ ♗d8?

23...♗f8 was the correct place for the bishop.

24 ♘a4 ♕c7 25 b6?

Apparently Steinitz wasn't happy with the extra pawn after the forced 25 ♘c5 ♕c8 26 ♕xb7 ♕xb7 27 ♘xb7 ♗b6 28 bxc6 ♗xc6 29 ♘c5. Normally one has to be prepared to play technical endings a pawn up after a successful minority attack.

25...♕c8 26 ♕a7 f4!

This is the only move to stir the pot. Interestingly Black manages to counter tactically with his own minority attack. This pawn-push is the most logical way to counter White's minority attack but in general it's rare to play the pawn to f4 due to the resulting exposure of his king, especially when there is a bunch of major pieces on the board.

27 ♘c5?

27 exf4 ♗f6 28 ♘c5 ♗xd4 29 ♘b3 was Steinitz's last chance to secure a full point.

27...fxe3 28 ♘xb7

If 28 fxe3 then 28...♗g5.

28...exf2+ 29 ♔f1 ♗f5 30 ♗xf5 ♕xf5 31 ♘xd8 ♕d3+ 32 ♔xf2 ♕d2+ 33 ♔f3 ♕d3+ 34 ♔g4 ♕f5+ 35 ♔g3 ♕d3+ 36 ♔h4 ♕xd4+ 37 g4 ♕f6+ 38 ♔g3 ♕e5+ Draw

White cannot escape the queen checks. This wasn't a typical minority attack game since the exchange on c6 never took place. However, the manoeuvre ♘a4-c5 is typical since that is White's strongpoint. Black never took advantage of his strongpoint on e4 and that helped Steinitz to carry out the clever exchange on f6 without even waiting for Black to waste a tempo on ...h6. It's a pity that this was Steinitz's last tournament because he had discovered an important method to combat the Queen's Gambit Declined and brought to life the exchange of the c-pawn for an e-pawn.

62

Lasker – Capablanca
World Championship, Havana 1921

(1 d4 d5 2 c4 e6 3 ♘c3 ♘f6 4 ♗g5 ♗e7 5 e3 0-0 6 ♘f3 ♘bd7 7 ♕c2 c5 8 ♖d1 ♕a5 9 ♗d3 h6 10 ♗h4 cxd4 11 exd4 dxc4 12 ♗xc4 ♘b6 13 ♗b3 ♗d7 14 0-0 ♖ac8 15 ♘e5 ♗b5 16 ♖fe1 ♘bd5 17 ♗xd5 ♘xd5

18 ♗xe7 ♘xe7 19 ♕b3 ♗c6 20 ♘xc6 bxc6 21 ♖e5 ♕b6 22 ♕c2 ♖fd8 23 ♘e2 ♖d5! 24 ♖xd5 cxd5 25 ♕d2 ♘f5 26 b3 h5 27 h3 h4 28 ♕d3 ♖c6 29 ♔f1 g6 30 ♕b1 ♕b4 31 ♔g1)

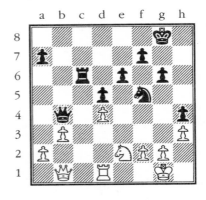

Black to move

31...a5!

In *Chess From Morphy to Botwinnik – A Century of Chess Evolution* (Dover 1977) Imre König wrote that "Capablanca revived the Minority Attack as Black in the tenth game of the World Championship Match against Lasker, in 1921. He demonstrated with great skill that, contrary to accepted theory, a majority of pawns can be successfully assailed, provided the attacker has an advantage in space for the mobility of the supporting pieces."

32 ♕b2 a4 33 ♕d2 ♕xd2 34 ♖xd2 axb3 35 axb3

The minority attack has been successful and Black has two weaknesses on which to focus as well as potential ones on the kingside.

35...♖b6! 36 ♖d3

112

36 ♖b2 ♖b4 loses a pawn.

36...♖a6

For the moment Black cannot win any of the pawns so he should penetrate White's position on the back two ranks with his only major piece.

37 g4 hxg3 38 fxg3 ♖a2 39 ♘c3 ♖c2 40 ♘d1

White must defend against 40...♘xd4 but more active was 40 ♘b5 followed by g3-g4.

40...♘e7 41 ♘c3 ♖c1+ 42 ♔f2 ♘c6 43 ♘d1

43...♖b1

Lasker had a devilish trap if Capablanca had continued 43...♘b4 44 ♖d2 ♖b1 45 ♘b2 ♖xb2?. The

knight would have been trapped on b2 after 46 ♖xb2 ♘d3+ 47 ♔e3 ♘xb2 48 ♔d2 and the pawn ending would have resulted in a draw.

44 ♔e2?

44 ♔e1 ♘a5 45 ♔d2 ♖xb3 46 ♖xb3 ♘xb3+ 47 ♔c3 was a better chance to stay in the game.

44...♖xb3! 45 ♔e3

If 45 ♖xb3? then 45...♘xd4+.

45...♖b4 46 ♘c3 ♘e7 47 ♘e2 ♘f5+ 48 ♔f2 g5 49 g4 ♘d6 50 ♘g1 ♘e4+ 51 ♔f1 ♖b1+ 52 ♔g2 ♖b2+

53 ♔f1

53 ♔f3? ♖f2+ 54 ♔e3 f5 would leave White in zugzwang. White loses his rook after 55 ♖d1 f4+ 56 ♔d3 ♖b2 57 ♘f3 ♘f2+ 58 ♔c3 ♘xd1+.

53...♖f2+ 54 ♔e1 ♖a2 55 ♔f1 ♔g7 56 ♖e3 ♔g6 57 ♖d3 f6!

The key to win is to transfer the king to d6 followed by ...e6-e5 to create a passed pawn in the centre.

58 ♖e3 ♔f7 59 ♖d3 ♔e7 60 ♖e3 ♔d6 61 ♖d3 ♖f2+ 62 ♔e1 ♖g2 63 ♔f1 ♖a2 64 ♖e3 e5!

The decisive central breakthrough!

65 ♖d3 exd4 66 ♖xd4 ♔c5 67 ♖d1 d4 68 ♖c1+ ♔d5 White resigns.

A very important game to assimilate since it does show Capablanca's technical ability in how to exploit tiny advantages such as having fewer pawn islands than the opponent, in this case two versus three. The key method to worsen White's pawn structure was the minority attack, because after the attack had been carried out Black had only one pawn island against White's three.

63

Capablanca – Alekhine
Game 25, World Championship,
Buenos Aires 1927

(1 d4 d5 2 c4 e6 3 ♘c3 ♘f6 4 ♗g5 ♘bd7 5 e3 ♗e7 6 ♘f3 0-0 7 ♖c1 a6 8 cxd5 exd5 9 ♗d3 c6 10 ♕c2 ♖e8 11 0-0 ♘f8 12 ♖fe1 [Imre König writes that this "seemingly insignificant move" is "in reality a typical conception of Capablanca, who thus retains the option of attacking in the centre, should Black initiate any attack on the king's wing". This placement of the rook was later adopted by Flohr and Karpov.] 12...♗e6?! [*12...♘e4* or *12...♗g4* followed by *...♗h5-g6* was the right way to handle the position.] 13 ♘a4 ♘6d7 14 ♗xe7 ♕xe7 15 ♘c5 ♘xc5 16 ♕xc5 ♕c7 17 b4 ♘d7 18 ♕c2 h6 19 a4 ♕d6 20 ♖b1 ♖ec8 21 ♖ec1 ♗g4 22 ♘d2 ♖c7 23 ♘b3 ♗h5 24 ♘c5 ♘xc5 25 ♕xc5 ♕f6)

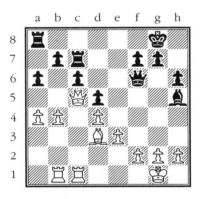

White to move

26 b5?!

This is slightly premature due to the fact that White's useful bishop will be exchanged. It was better to play 26 ♖a1, according to Alekhine's recommendation, before contemplating b4-b5 and answer 26...♗g6 with 27 ♗f1 or 27 ♗e2. On either of these squares the bishop could be used both for the attack on the queenside, by controlling the f1-a6 diagonal, and defence of the kingside. Black's bishop would essentially not do anything useful on the h7-b1 diagonal, because it would not be able to help the defence on the queenside. The control of the e4-square would be small consolation, since a bishop on f1 would easily neutralise any pressure on g2.

114

26...axb5 27 axb5 ♗g6!

Of course it's in Black's interest to exchange off his inferior bishop. It's surprising that Capablanca allowed this as he had a very deep formula regarding which pieces to keep and which to exchange.

28 ♗xg6 ♕xg6 29 ♖a1 ♖ac8

White's only chance to win is if Black captures on b5 as happened in Flohr – Euwe, Amsterdam 1932, exercise 64.

30 b6 ♖d7 31 ♖a7 ♔h7 32 ♖ca1 f5 33 ♕c2 ♖e7 34 g3 ♖ce8 35 ♖a8 ♖e4 36 ♖xe8 ♖xe8 37 ♖a7 ♖b8 38 h4 h5 39 ♔g2 ♕e6 40 ♕d3 ♔g6 41 ♔h2 Draw

64

Flohr – Euwe
Amsterdam 1932

(1 d4 d5 2 c4 e6 3 cxd5 exd5 4 ♘c3 ♘f6 5 ♗g5 ♗e7 6 e3 c6 7 ♗d3 ♘bd7 8 ♘f3 0-0 9 ♕c2 ♖e8 10 0-0 ♘f8 11 ♘e5 ♘g4 12 ♗xe7 ♕xe7 13 ♘xg4 ♗xg4)

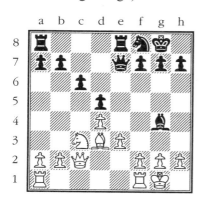

White to move

14 ♖fe1

Perhaps inspired by Capablanca's 12th move in exercise 63, the great technician Salo Flohr (1908-1983) plays a more sophisticated move than Pillsbury's 14 ♖ae1. Flohr plans a regrouping of his knight to f1 to secure his kingside against a potential attack.

14...♖ad8 15 ♘e2 ♖d6

15...♗xe2 would spoil White's strong knight manoeuvre, but on the other hand when Black's bishop disappears from the board it will be harder to attack the kingside with one piece less. The white bishop could actually replace the knight on f1 if it should be necessary to cover some light squares near the king, as was discussed in exercise 63. The advantage of having a bishop on f1, compared with a knight, which is purely defensive on that square, is that the bishop could still participate in the minority attack on the queenside by covering the important squares c4, b5 and a6. On principle Black should therefore avoid such an exchange.

16 ♘g3 ♖h6

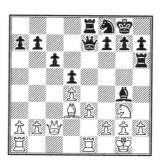

Black prefers to attack with pieces but it will not be so easy to implement in practice, so possibly the pawn push 16...h5!? was a better try to first provoke some weaknesses on the kingside.

17 &f5

White's idea is to continue the policy of exchanging potential attacking pieces before embarking on a minority attack. A typical variation, which shows the black bishop's potential, is the following: 17 ♖ab1 ♕h4 18 ♘f1 ♘e6 19 f3 (19 b4?? &f3! 20 gxf3 ♘g5 and Black's attack is decisive.) 19...&h5 (19...&xf3 20 gxf3 ♘g5 21 ♔g2 ♕h3+ 22 ♔h1 ♘xf3 23 ♖e2 and White wins.) 20 ♕f2 and White stands a little better with his safe kingside.

17...♕g5 18 &xg4 ♕xg4 19 h3!

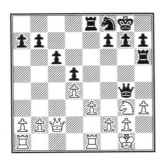

Note that this natural pawn-push is not a one-dimensional move as we will see later in the comments to move 24 and 41.

19...♕d7 20 b4

Now, when the kingside is secured from an attack, White begins his own minority attack on the queenside.

20...♘e6 21 ♖ab1 ♘c7

21...♘g5 forces White to consider the consequences of a knight sacrifice on h3 and is simplest met by 22 ♕f5.

22 a4 a6 23 ♘f1 ♖e7

65

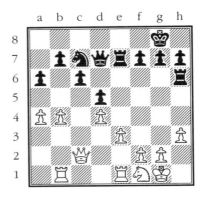

White to move

24 ♘h2!!

The strong multi-purpose 19th move makes way for a very beautiful manoeuvre where the vacant h2 square is exploited to the fullest. White plans 25 ♘g4 embarrassing the rook on h6. The unimaginative knight manoeuvre 24 ♘d2 ♖ee6 25 ♘f3 would not work at all, due to 25...♖eg6 and Black is even winning, for example 26 ♔f1 ♖xg2!. If Black has no light-squared bishop to sacrifice on the board the rook will do!

24...♖he6 25 ♘f3 f6

Now Black cannot attack the kingside so this is the right moment to manoeuvre the knight to the queenside.

26 ♘d2 ♖e8 27 ♘b3 ♖6e7
28 ♘c5 ♕c8 29 ♖ec1 ♖d8 30 ♘d3
♕b8 31 ♘f4

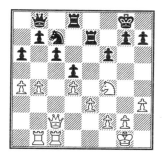

31...♘e6?

For unknown reasons Black suddenly allows the minority attack. Black could have supported his own minority attack by 31...♖f8 followed by ...g7-g5 and ...f6-f5-f4. Obviously there would have been risks involved, because of the weakening of the kingside and the e5 square, but above all it's an active continuation. In the game Black was doomed to passivity without any counterplay whatsoever. It was Kasparov who said "I used to attack because it was the only thing I knew. Now I attack because I know it works best." He's certainly right from a psychological point of view, especially if he is referring to an attack on the king, which he probably does. Many players, unless they play the Sicilian Defence, where you actually get used to attacks, feel uncomfortable when their kingside is under fire.

32 ♘xe6 ♖xe6 33 b5 axb5 34 axb5 cxb5?

This is normally bad policy when defending against the minority attack. Black gets two weaknesses on b7 and d5 instead of one as after 34...♕c7 35 bxc6 bxc6.

35 ♖xb5 b6 36 ♕b3

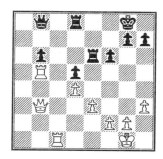

36...♕d6

36...♕b7 holds on to the pawns a little longer, but the c-file as well as the seventh or the eighth rank cannot be held, so Black is forced to give up material sooner or later anyway. An illustrative variation, if Black insists on not giving up one of his pawns, is 37 ♖bc5! ♖d7 38 ♖c8+ ♔f7 39 ♕d1! g6 40 ♕f3! ♔g7 (40...♖e8 41 ♖xe8 ♔xe8 42 ♕xf6) 41 h4! h5 (41...b5 42 h5) 42 ♕g3 ♖ee7 (White was threatening 43 ♖1c7.) 43 ♖1c2! (43 ♖b8 ♖c7 44 ♖xc7 ♕xc7 45 ♕xc7 ♖xc7 46 ♖xb6 wins one pawn at least, but White is after the king since he has already penetrated to the eighth rank!) 43...b5 44 ♖b8 ♕a6 45 ♖cc8 ♕e6 46 ♕f4! ♕f5 47 ♖g8+ ♔f7 48 ♕h6 ♔e6 49 ♖gf8! The f6-pawn proves to be the weakest point in Black's "new" residence. 49...♖b7 (49...♖d6 50 ♖fe8! ♖dd7 51 ♖b6+ ♖d6 52 ♕f8) 50 ♕h8 ♖xb8 51 ♖xb8 ♕b1+ 52 ♔h2 ♔f5 53 ♖f8 ♖e6 54 ♕h6! ♖e4 55 ♕g5+ and it's mate in five moves. These variations clearly show that the main aim of a minority attack, or a queenside attack by other means, is not only a matter of winning a pawn. A higher aim is to invade behind the enemy lines, with the help of the major pieces.

37 ♖b1

White wins a pawn.

37...♖d7 38 ♖xb6 ♕xb6 39 ♕xb6 ♖xb6 40 ♖xb6

White has an extra pawn, the more active rook and Black has a weak pawn on d5. This is a typical ending after a successful minority attack.

40...♔f7 41 ♔h2

Here we see another point of the strong 19th move.

41...♔e7 42.♔g3 ♖a7 43 ♔f4 g6?

Black unnecessarily weakens f6 which makes it easier for White to win the rook ending. 43...h5 should have been played.

44 g4! ♖a2

If Black is passive with the rook, let's say with 44...♖c7, then 45 h4 followed by g4-g5 will decide. White will get two connected passed pawns in the centre if the pawns are

exchanged. Otherwise White gains access to the e5-square for his king.

45 ♖b7+ ♔e6 46 ♔g3 White resigns.

The h-pawn is lost after 46...h5 47 gxh5 gxh5 48 ♖h7.

66

H. Kramer – Fichtl
Vimperk 1949

(1 d4 d5 2 c4 e6 3 ♘c3 ♘f6 4 ♗g5 ♗e7 5 e3 0-0 6 ♘f3 ♘bd7 7 ♖c1 a6 8 cxd5 exd5 9 ♗d3 c6 10 ♕c2 ♖e8 11 0-0 g6 12 ♖b1 ♘b6 13 ♘e2 ♘h5 14 ♗xe7 ♖xe7 15 b4 ♘g7 16 ♘g3 ♗e6 17 a4 ♘c8 18 b5)

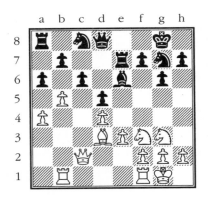

Black to move

18...cxb5

18...axb5? 19 axb5 ♖c7 20 bxc6 bxc6 would lead to a concluded minority attack where White would dictate terms for a long time to come.

19 axb5 a5

This is a very interesting but more unusual method to meet the minority attack. Euwe/Kramer recommend first 19...♖c7 to take control of the c-file and only then 20...a5. Black has no problems after 20 ♕d2 a5 21 b6 (21 ♖a1 b6 22 ♘e5 ♘e7) 21...♖c6 with mutual chances.

20 ♖fc1

White controls the c-file but Black has enough compensation due to the dangerous passed pawn.

Here Black should have played...

20...♘b6

The knight blockades the hostile b-pawn, supports the a-pawn and controls the c4-square.

Euwe and Kramer have written that "It seems by no means impossible that this scheme – the creation of a passed a-pawn combined with pressure against White's c4 – may be instrumental in banishing the dread of the minority attack, or at least considerably reducing it."

Unfortunately 20...♘d6? was played in the game and Kramer in his turn missed the fact that 21 b6! would have led to a clearly better game for White.

67

Petrosian – Krogius
USSR Championship, Tbilisi 1959

(1 d4 ♘f6 2 ♘f3 g6 3 c4 ♗g7 4 ♘c3 d5 5 ♗g5 ♘e4 6 cxd5 ♘xg5 7 ♘xg5 e6 8 ♘f3 exd5 9 e3 0-0 10 ♗d3 ♘c6 11 0-0 ♘e7 12 b4)

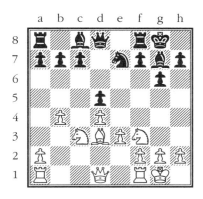

Black to move

12...♗f5?!

Normally it's pointless to exchange the light-squared bishops if Black cannot exploit the c4-square with a knight to block the c-file and in that way combat the minority attack. The normal move was 12...c6 but it seems that Krogius' plan was to avoid moving the pawn on c7 and keep the pawn wall united according to Steinitz' rule. However the minority attack will work nevertheless because sooner or later Black will have to play ...c7-c6 anyway, due to the strong pressure on the d5-pawn and the c-file.

13 ♗xf5 ♘xf5 14 b5

Interestingly Petrosian isn't interested in forcing events with 14 ♕b3, practically forcing 14...c6, as Steinitz was anxious to do. White's choice in the game gives Black more options. The questions Krogius needs to ask himself are related to the placements of the c- and a-pawns.

14...♕d6

14...a6 would have been most simply answered by 15 a4. On the other hand 15 bxa6 ♖xa6 16 ♕b3 ♖a5, with the idea 17 ♕xb7, gives Black counterplay after 17...c5.

15 ♕b3 ♘e7

Black still postpones the crucial 15...c6.

16 ♖fc1

16...♔h8?

Black's king was perfectly placed on g8. He probably plans his own minority attack with ...f5-f4 but this plan has few chances of success. Black should have taken care of his queenside, so better was 16...♖fc8.

17 ♖c2 h6

This unnecessary defensive move, which aims to prevent ♘g5 in conjunction with e3-e4, only proves that it was necessary to admit his mistake and go back with 17...♔g8.

One cannot go against the requirements of the position and Krogius' psychological game goes too far this time.

18 ♖ac1 c6

19 ♘a4!

The immediate routine capture 19 bxc6 bxc6 followed by 20 ♘a4 gives the opponent breathing space with 20...♖ab8.

19...♖ab8 20 g3!?

More active was 20 ♘c5. The move played is characteristic of Petrosian's prophylactic style. The move itself is useful and prophylactic, and according to the "no hurry" principle, to show that one is complete master of the situation. It's useful to give the king a square on g2 before opening any lines. This would be prophylactic because it prevents the minority attack ...f7-f5-f4 even before Black has put his pawn on f5! Such a move has a strong psychological impact on the opponent because it means additional pressure, which in turn increases the chances of mistakes.

20...♔h7 21 ♘c5 ♖fd8

21...b6 22 ♘d3 cxb5 23 ♕xb5 ♖fc8 24 ♖xc8 ♖xc8 25 ♖xc8 ♘xc8 26 ♕e8 leads to a win for White, for example 26...♕c7 (or 26...♕e6

27 ♕xe6 fxe6 28 ♘f4) 27 ♘fe5 ♘d6 28 ♕c6 ♕xc6 29 ♘xc6 ♘b5 30 a4 ♘c3 31 ♘xa7 ♖xa4 32 ♘b5 and White wins the d5-pawn by force.

22 bxc6 bxc6 23 ♕a4 ♕f6 24 ♔g2

Also here Petrosian chooses a useful move rather than the active 24 ♘e5.

24...♖a8

Black defends the a7-pawn but loses the c6-pawn instead.

25 ♘b7 ♖e8 26 ♘a5

The c6-pawn's destiny is sealed.

26...g5

Better late than never, Black tries to do something on the kingside.

27 h3

Another typical Petrosian-move showing that his opponent must dance to his tune. 27 ♘xc6 was winning too but the problem is where to place the knight after 27...g4 since all five reasonable knight moves are winning!

27...♕f5 28 ♘xc6 ♕e4 29 ♖c5

White wants to exchange queens by ♕c2.

29...f5 30 ♕c2

A beautiful symbolic line-up on the c-file where White has already broken through.

30...♘xc6 31 ♖xc6 f4

Black's thematic attack comes when White's pieces are already on their ideal locations!

32 exf4 gxf4 33 g4 ♗xd4 34 ♕d2

34 ♖c7+ ♔g7 35 ♕c6 followed by 36 ♕d7 would prolong the harassment on the c-file initiated by the minority attack.

34...♗g7 35 ♖e1 ♕a4 36 ♕xd5 ♖xe1 37 ♘xe1 ♖f8 38 ♘f3 ♔h8 39 ♖c7 a6 40 ♕b7 ♖g8 41 ♘h4 Black resigns.

68

Shankland – Karjakin
FIDE World Cup, Sochi 2021

(1 c4 ♘f6 2 g3 e6 3 ♗g2 d5 4 d4 ♗e7 5 ♘f3 0-0 6 0-0 dxc4 7 ♕c2 a6 8 a4 ♗d7 9 ♕xc4 ♗c6 10 ♗g5 ♘bd7 11 ♘c3 h6 12 ♗xf6 ♘xf6 13 e3 ♕d6)

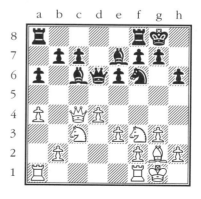

White to move

In the following instructive recent example Shankland shows that sometimes it's possible just to threaten a minority attack to force a weakening of the opponent's pawn structure.

14 ♖fb1

White threatens to play b4-b5 with the bishop on c6 as a target rather than a pawn which is the normal target in the minority attack.

14...a5

Black prevents this idea very easily and White even has a hole on b4 now, so what's the justification for Shankland's idea? He wanted to provoke the a6-pawn to a5 and make the important pawn break ...c7-c5 less palatable because it would weaken the b5-square. It's better to play ...c5 with the a-pawn on a7 or a6 but not on a5. After the further...

15 ♕e2 ♗xf3 16 ♗xf3 c6

...the king's rook had fulfilled its purpose of changing Black's pawn structure to a more passive one so the move...

17 ♖d1

...suggests itself. Later in the game Shankland doubled rooks on d3 and

d1 and overprotected the d4-pawn in the spirit of Nimzowitsch. He then went on to win a fine game after 45 moves.

69

Gligorić – Klein
London 1951

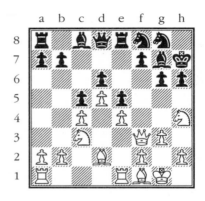

White to move

15 a3

Here Black has failed to play the normal as well as crucial break ...f7-f5. Now it will be easier for White to concentrate on opening the queenside. Black's central structure can be difficult to crack since the key to this lies in the seemingly indestructible d6-pawn. It is instructive to study how Gligorić solves this intricate but typical positional problem when dealing with the particular blocked pawn structure. After 15 ♕xf7?? ♘f6 there is no return to the white camp for the queen.

15...♖e7 16 b4 b6

16...cxb4? 17 axb4 is useless since there is no way to exploit the fact that the c4-pawn is weak.

17 ♖ab1 ♗d7 18 bxc5

18...bxc5

Normally 18...dxc5 is to be preferred if it's possible to place a knight on d6. If White plays the routine move 19 a4 (19 d6? ♖e6 20 ♕xf7 ♖xd6 21 ♘d5 is only in Black's interest after 21...♘f6 with adequate counterplay.) with the continuation 19...♘f6 20 a5 ♘e8 21 ♖b2 ♘d6 Black has achieved his goal. But White has achieved his goal as well due to the strong pressure he exerts on the queenside after 22 ♖a1.

19 ♕d3

White needs the queen on the queenside to exploit the open file where Black has his weaknesses.

19...♗e8 20 ♖b2 ♖b8 21 ♖eb1 ♖b6

Black's idea is that if White exchanges on b6 he will have some counterplay along the a-file. 21...♖xb2 22 ♖xb2 helps White to double on the b-file with ♕b1. This is White's dream position since the main idea with 15 a3 was to open the b-file and then exploit it.

22 ♖xb6

22 a4!? was also an option.

22...axb6 23 ♕c2 ♖a7 24 ♕b3 ♖a6

Here the black rook is both passive and active at the same time.

25 ♘b5 ♘e7

25...♗xb5 26 cxb5 (26 ♕xb5 ♖xa3 27 ♕xb6 gives White possibilities of applying pressure on d6 but Black has defensive resources after 27...♗f6) 26...♖a7 27 a4 followed by a4-a5 at the right moment gives White the advantage.

26 ♗h3

White prevents the defensive move ...♘c8 and practically forces Black to exchange his good bishop.

26...♗d7 27 ♗xd7 ♕xd7 28 ♘g2

White's knight is no longer needed to prevent ...f5, since Black is busy defending his queenside and cannot create any counterplay on the other flank.

28...♘c8

28...f5 29 f3 g5 30 ♘e3 f4 31 ♘f5! ♘xf5 32 exf5 only leads to weaknesses on the kingside.

29 ♘e3 h5 30 ♘d1 ♗f6

30...♗h6 could be considered.

31 ♔g2 ♔g7 32 ♘e3 ♘h7 33 h4!

The rook-pawn dominates both the bishop and the knight.

33...♔g8 34 a4!

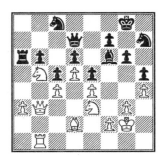

White's plan is to break with a4-a5 and then to penetrate along the b-file.

34...&g7 35 ♘c3 ♘a7?

Black wants to prevent the queen penetrating to b5 but better was 35...♖a5 and let the knight defend the two main weaknesses in Black's position.

36 a5! ♘c8

36...bxa5 is answered by 37 ♕b8+ ♘c8 38 ♖b7 or 36...♖xa5 37 ♕xb6.

37 ♘a4! bxa5 38 ♕b5 ♕xb5

Or 38...♖a7 39 ♕xd7 ♖xd7 40 ♖b8 ♖d8 41 ♘b6 etc.

39 cxb5 ♖a7 40 b6 ♘xb6

40...♖b7 is met by 41 ♘c4.

41 ♖xb6 &f8 42 ♘c4 ♘f6 43 f3 ♘d7 44 ♖c6 ♔g7 45 ♘xd6! Black resigns.

The heart of Black's central pawn structure has at last fallen. An instructive model game, showing how to break through the central structure c5-d6-e5 with a3 followed by b4, with a subsequent decisive penetration on the b-file.

70

Radovici – Stein
Bucharest 1961

(1 e4 d6 2 d4 g6 3 ♘c3 &g7
4 &e3 c6 5 ♕d2 ♕a5 6 ♘f3 ♘d7
7 &e2 ♘gf6 8 0-0 0-0 9 h3 ♖e8
10 a3 ♕c7 11 ♖ad1 b5 12 ♖fe1 &b7
13 &h6 e5 14 &xg7 ♔xg7 15 dxe5
dxe5 16 ♕e3)

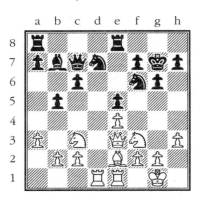

Black to move

16...a6

Black plans to set his qualitative pawn majority in motion by ...c5 and ...b4 with the objective of attacking the e4-pawn. 16...a5 would not give Black so many options to play with his pawns on the queenside after 17 b4.

17 ♖d2 c5 18 ♖ed1

18 ♘d5 produces no results after 18...&xd5! 19 exd5 c4 since White's passed pawn isn't dangerous. If White doesn't push his pawn to d6 then Black can make use of the d6 and c5 squares to manoeuvre his pieces.

18...b4 19 axb4 cxb4 20 ♘d5 &xd5!

In this position it's correct to keep the knight pair rather than the bishop and the knight.

21 exd5 ♕d6 22 c4 ♘c5

Now we can see why it was so important to exchange the bishop since Black has very strong dark-square control. Note also White's bad bishop and that Black's pawn majority on the a- and b-files is more difficult to stop than the pawns on c4 and d5 which are effectively blocked.

23 ♖e1 ♘fe4 24 ♖dd1 a5 25 ♗d3 ♘f6 26 ♘d2 a4 27 ♗e4 h5 28 f3 h4

To use a famous expression from Hans Kmoch's *Pawn Power in Chess* (McKay 1959) we have a case of serious "monochromy" on the kingside. For some unclear reasons his nomenclature hasn't been

accepted in the chess world. It's difficult to find a better word to describe a complex of dark squares that is weak.

29 ♗c2 b3 30 ♗b1 ♘fd7 31 ♘e4?!

It's technically incorrect to help Black get rid of his superfluous knight so more precise was 31 ♕f2.

31...♘xe4 32 fxe4?

32 ♕xe4 was the right recapture.

32...♖ec8 33 ♗d3 ♕c5 34 ♔f2 f5 35 ♔e2 f4 36 ♕xc5 ♘xc5 37 ♖a1 ♔f6 White resigns.

71

Steinitz – Chigorin
Game 4, World Championship,
Havana 1892

(1 e4 e5 2 ♘f3 ♘c6 3 ♗b5 ♘f6 4 d3 d6 5 c3 g6 6 ♘bd2 ♗g7 7 ♘f1 0-0 8 ♗a4 ♘d7 9 ♘e3 ♘c5 10 ♗c2 ♘e6)

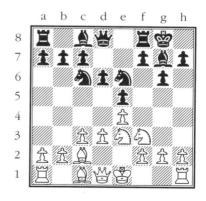

White to play

11 h4!

Nowadays this is standard procedure with a stabilised situation in the centre. The plan to attack the kingside, by striving to open a file, was first developed by Steinitz with the black pieces in his game versus Dubois in London 1862. It is Steinitz' most important attacking idea.

11...♘e7?!

Black wants to respond to the flank attack with a reaction in the centre but White is too strong there.

This is the main idea of starting a flank attack with a closed central structure. 11...h5 or 11...♘f4 would have made it harder for White to open the h-file and was a better practical choice.

12 h5

Now the game is like a self-playing piano.

12...d5 13 hxg6

13...fxg6

Black weakens the classical a2-g8 diagonal but it was hardly better to open the h-file with 13...hxg6 because after 14 ♘g4! dxe4 15 dxe4 ♛xd1+ 16 ♗xd1 f6 17 ♗b3, despite

the fact that the queens are off the board, White has a small but enduring advantage with his more active minor and major pieces.

Incidentally, Réti writes in his classic *Modern Ideas in Chess* (Dover 1960) that Steinitz would probably have played 14 ♕e2 since it is part of his strategy to avoid the exchange of queens. After the further 14...♘f4 15 ♕f1 followed by 16 ♗d2 and 17 0-0-0 White would have the slightly better chances.

14 exd5 ♘xd5 15 ♘xd5 ♛xd5 16 ♗b3 ♛c6 17 ♕e2 ♗d7 18 ♗e3 ♔h8

One can understand Black's reluctance to place his king on the classical diagonal but, as the game shows, it is no better placed in the corner. It would be better to start an immediate counterattack with 18...a5!.

19 0-0-0 ♜ae8

20 ♕f1

Komodo prefers 20 ♕d2!. The plan is to continue either with 23 d4 or 23 ♗h6, depending on Black's reply. Steinitz's move is slightly passive and it was only because of

Chigorin's poor defence that it turned out to be a really good one.

20...a5?

More resilient was 20...h5! which could have been met by 21 ♗c2 with the idea 22 d4.

21 d4! exd4 22 ♘xd4 ♗xd4 23 ♖xd4 ♘xd4?

Chigorin makes a mistake in a lost position and gives Steinitz the opportunity to show off.

24 ♖xh7+! ♔xh7 25 ♕h1+ ♔g7 26 ♗h6+

The spontaneous 26 ♕h6+ leads to a fast mate too after 26...♔f6 27 ♕h4+ ♔g7 28 ♗h6+ and 29 ♗xf8 mate.

26...♔f6   27   ♕h4+   ♔e5 28 ♕xd4+ Black resigns.

White mates next move, either with the queen on f4 or the pawn on g4. Which mate would you prefer?

In my opinion this is one of the best classical games showing how to attack with a safe position in the centre. So embrace this fundamental and very important idea and learn the game by heart!

72

Capablanca – Marshall
New York 1909

(1 e4 e5 2 ♘f3 ♘c6 3 ♗b5 d6 4 c3 ♗g4 5 d3 ♗e7 6 ♘bd2 ♘f6 7 0-0 0-0 8 ♖e1 h6 9 ♘f1 ♘h7 10 ♘e3 ♗h5 11 g4 ♗g6 12 ♘f5 h5 13 h3 hxg4 14 hxg4 ♗g5 15 ♘xg5 ♘xg5 16 ♔g2 d5 17 ♕e2 ♖e8 18 ♖h1 ♖e6 19 ♕e3 f6 20 ♗a4 ♘e7 21 ♗b3 c6 22 ♕g3 a5 23 a4 ♘f7 24 ♗e3 b6 25 ♖h4 ♔f8 26 ♖ah1 ♘g8)

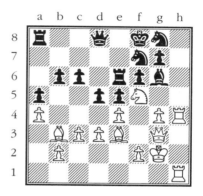

White to move

27 ♕f3!

White's pieces harmonise optimally with each other. The rooks control the only open file, the bishops exercise pressure on the key diagonals and the knight is placed on the "optimal attacking square for the knight" according to Kasparov. Meanwhile the queen cooperates with the bishop on b3 to break down the central point on d5. Compare the activity and the coordination of every white piece with the equivalent black piece. It's not so strange that the black position soon collapses!

27...♗xf5

27...dxe4 28 dxe4 ♖e8 29 ♕h3 followed by ♖h8 wins according to Reinfeld and that is indeed confirmed by Komodo10.

28 gxf5 ♖d6 29 ♕h5 ♖a7 30 ♕g6!

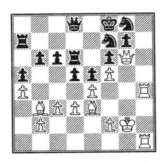

30...♘fh6

30...♘e7 31 ♖h8+ ♘xh8 (31...♘g8 32 ♖1h7 ♘xh8 33 ♖xh8 gives Black one extra tempo but it doesn't change the result.) 32 ♖xh8+ ♘g8 33 ♕h7 ♔f7 34 ♗xb6 and White wins according to Capablanca, however the computer suggests the even stronger 34 ♗d1! which forces mate in eleven moves.

31 ♖xh6 gxh6 32 ♗xh6+ ♔e7

If 32...♘xh6 then 33 ♖xh6.

33 ♕h7+ ♔e8 34 ♕xg8+ ♔d7 35 ♕h7+ ♕e7 36 ♗f8 ♕xh7 37 ♖xh7+ ♔e8 38 ♖xa7 Black resigns.

Capablanca comments that this is one of his best games. It looks so easy when he wins like this. Such games are typical for his style. His opponents seem helpless when he manages to coordinate all his pieces.

Harmony or cooperation is the key in attacking play. It's not enough to count the number of pieces that are attacking in comparison with those defending, the relative level of activity must also be taken into account.

73

Augustin – Nunn
European Team Championship
1977

(1 e4 e5 2 ♘c3 ♘f6 3 g3 ♗c5
4 ♗g2 d6 5 ♘ge2 ♘c6 6 0-0)

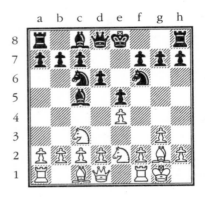

Black to move

6...h5!

A strong and typical move when White has played g2-g3 followed by a fianchetto of his bishop, as well as ♘ge2 and 0-0. Black's strong control of the d4-square and powerful bishop on the Italian diagonal are also good signs for advancing the h-pawn two steps.

7 d3

7 h3 is answered by 7...h4 8 g4 ♘xg4! 9 hxg4 ♗xg4 and Black has compensation thanks to his attacking

chances. One plausible variation is 10 ♔h2 h3 11 ♗h1 ♕h4 12 f3 ♗e6 followed by queenside castling and Black has more activity as well as two pawns for the sacrificed knight. 7 h4 weakens g4 and is answered by 7...♗g4 followed by ...♘d4, ...♕d7 and ...0-0-0 with strong pressure on several relevant diagonals.

7...h4 8 ♗g5 hxg3 9 ♘xg3

9 hxg3 weakens g4 and is most simply exploited by 9...♗g4 followed by ...♕d7.

9...♘d4 10 ♘h5 ♘e6 11 ♘xg7+ ♘xg7 12 ♘d5

12...♘xd5!?

The English GM John Nunn is famous for his enterprising attacking play and was feared by many during his heyday, especially when he had the white pieces. Together with Murray Chandler and Nigel Short he developed the so-called English attack against the Sicilian Defence. Here he sacrifices his queen for a strong offensive.

13 ♗xd8 ♘f4 14 ♗g5 ♘ge6 15 ♗xf4 ♘xf4 16 ♔h1 ♗e6 17 ♗f3 ♖h4 18 ♖g1 ♔e7 19 ♖g2 ♘xg2 20 ♗xg2 ♖ah8

21 ♕d2?!

Drawing the married couple nearer to each other with 21 ♕g1, in the spirit of Steinitz – Burn, Hastings 1895, was the best defence, although Black retains good winning chances with 21...♖f4 22 ♖f1 ♗g4 etc.

21...♖xh2+ 22 ♔g1 ♖2h4 23 ♖e1 ♖g8 24 ♖e3 ♗xe3 25 ♕xe3 ♗h3 26 ♔f1 ♗xg2+ 27 ♔e2 c5 28 ♕d2 b6 29 ♕c3 ♖f4 30 ♕a3 a5 31 ♕b3 ♗h3 32 f3 ♖g2+ 33 ♔e3 ♗g4! White resigns.

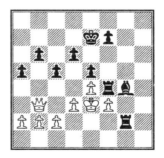

A nice finish, it's mate after 34 fxg4 ♖gf2 and ...♖4f3.

74

L. Karlsson – Glimbrandt
Swedish Grand Prix 1992

(1 d4 ♘f6 2 c4 g6 3 ♘c3 d5 4 ♗g5 ♘e4 5 cxd5 ♘xg5 6 h4 e6 7 hxg5

exd5 8 ♕d2 c6 9 ♘f3 ♗e7 10 ♕f4 ♕b6 11 0-0-0 ♗e6 12 ♕e5 0-0)

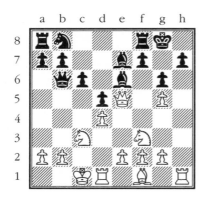

White to move

13 g4!

Much stronger than 13 ♕h2 h5 14 gxh6 ♘d7 and White's attack has lost its momentum.

13...♘d7

13...♗xg4? loses to 14 ♕xe7.

14 ♕h2 h5 15 gxh5 ♔g7 16 ♗h3

If 16 hxg6 then 16...♖h8.

16...c5 17 ♗xe6 fxe6 18 hxg6

Such doubled pawns are indeed a very particular kind of monster for Black's king to deal with.

18...♖h8 19 ♕f4 ♖af8 20 ♕g4

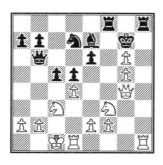

White's nice queen manoeuvre to the light g4 square has created all kinds of threats, e.g. 21 ♘xd5, 21 ♖h7 and 21 ♖h6.

20...cxd4 21 ♘xd4 ♘c5 22 ♖xh8! ♖xh8 23 ♘xd5!

The e6-pawn is the key to Black's defence and is liquidated in stylish fashion.

23...exd5 24 ♘f5+ ♔xg6 25 ♘xe7+ ♔f7 26 ♘xd5 ♕c6 27 ♕f4+ ♔g7 28 ♕e5+ ♔f7

29 g6+!

A very beautiful example of the dynamism inherent in the doubled g-pawns.

The last g-pawn sacrifice exploited the perfect coordination between White's queen and knight.

Now 29...♔xg6 could be met by the fork 30 ♘e7+ but even stronger would have been 30 ♖g1+ ♔f7 31 ♕e7 mate. 29...♕xg6 is met by 30 ♕e7+ ♔g8 31 ♘f6+, 29...♔g8 by 30 ♘e7+ while 29...♔f8, the politest way to finish the game, allows the beautiful 30 ♕xh8 mate.

Black resigns.

75

Nepomniachtchi – Carlsen
World Rapid Championship 2016

(1 e4 c6 2 ♘c3 d5 3 ♘f3 dxe4
4 ♘xe4 ♘f6 5 ♘xf6+ exf6 6 d4 ♗d6
7 ♗e2 0-0 8 0-0 ♖e8 9 c4 ♘d7
10 ♗d3 ♘f8 11 h3 ♘g6 12 ♕c2
♕a5 13 c5 ♗b8 14 ♗d2 ♕d8
15 ♖fe1 ♗e6 16 ♗c4 ♘f8 17 ♖ad1
♗c7 18 ♕b3 ♗xc4 19 ♕xc4 ♕d7
20 b4 ♘g6 21 a4 ♘e7 22 b5 ♘d5
23 bxc6 bxc6 24 ♕a6)

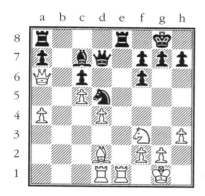

Black to move

24...g5!

This pawn-push is typical for
Black's system as Korchnoi has
shown in a couple of games. Note
that White's pawn majority is
conveniently blockaded by the
c6-pawn and the knight.

25 ♘h2 ♗xh2+!

A beautiful exchange in the spirit
of Capablanca. The feeling when
playing through this game is that
Carlsen honours both the positional
ideas of Korchnoi and Capablanca!

26 ♔xh2 ♔g7!

The elevation concept is also part
of Capablanca's arsenal of ideas.

27 ♔g1 ♖xe1+ 28 ♖xe1 ♖b8

Black has squares of infiltration on
the b-file but White has none on the
e-file. The snare is slowly tightened.

29 ♕d3 ♖b2

Control of the seventh rank (from
Black's point of view) is a
very important concept which
Nimzowitsch discussed in detail in
My System.

30 a5 h6

Black secures the kingside but
...f5-f4 is not yet necessary since it
weakens the kingside. The f-pawn's
primary task is to protect the king on
the seventh rank and the black
squares surrounding it.

31 ♗c1?

A better defence is 31 ♖b1 but it's
in Black's interest to exchange
rooks, since queen and knight are
stronger than queen and bishop in
this position. This is one of the
concepts Capablanca is famous for
and today such an ending is dubbed
a "Capablanca ending."

31...♖a2 32 ♗d2 ♕b7

Black's threat to penetrate to the seventh rank is heavier than White's lack of threats on the e-file.

33 ♖e8 ♕b2 34 ♗e1!

The bishop has found its correct location from a defensive point of view. The weaknesses on f2 and a5 are simultaneously defended and the rook on e8 protects the bishop.

34...♘f4

The versatile knight hits White's position at exactly the right moment.

35 ♕a6

35 ♕f5 ♖a1! 36 ♕c8 ♘g6! 37 ♕xc6 ♕xd4 would have led to the same position as in the game.

35...♕xd4 36 ♕c8 ♘g6

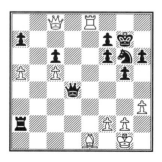

With the knight close to the king it's never mate! Note the mobility from attack to defence. White's bishop is no more than an extra in a movie.

37 ♕xc6 ♖a1

Black concentrates on pinning the defender, the bishop on e1, because otherwise the f2- and a5-pawns are too well protected.

38 ♕e4

38 ♖e3 ♕b4 and Black wins the pawn on a5.

38...♕xc5 39 ♔h2

White's dream is to activate the bishop on c3, followed by a swindle in the spirit of Marshall.

39...h5

The pawn storm in the spirit of Korchnoi starts to take real shape.

40 ♕e3 ♕c6

41 ♗c3

41 ♕c3 was objectively better, although after 41...♕d6+ Black would provoke the weakness 42 g3 from which he can profit in the sequence 42...♕d1 43 ♕d2 ♕a4 44 ♕e3 ♖a3 45 ♕e4 ♕d7 followed by

...h5-h4. With the queen on e4 Black doesn't gain anything by playing ...♘d7-e5 due to ♕e4-a8 but after 46 ♕e2 ♘e5 (46...h4 is not so good due to 47 ♖e3) is strong as it forces White to sacrifice the exchange, thereby leaving Black with an easy win.

41...♖a4 42 f3 ♖a2 43 ♔h1 ♖c2

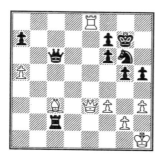

44 ♗e1

In a bad position there are only bad moves. The more active 44 ♗d4 would succumb to 44...♖c1+ 45 ♔h2 ♖d1! and White's pieces are hanging and his king is too exposed.

44...♕b5

Black has discovered the weak point on g2.

45 ♗g3

45 ♖d8 ♖e2 46 ♕g1 ♘f4 and the g2-pawn falls.

45...h4 46 ♗h2 ♕b1+ 47 ♗g1 ♕f1 White resigns.

There is no defence to cover g2.

Part 2:

75 most important tactical exercises in the Opening and the Middlegame

76

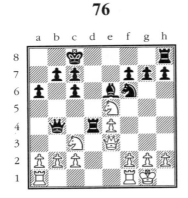

White to move

77

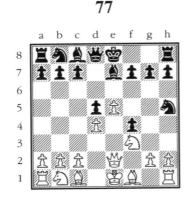

(after 6...d7-d5) White to move

78

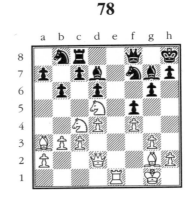

White to move

79

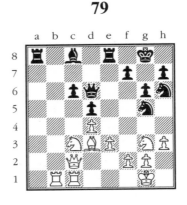

White to move

80

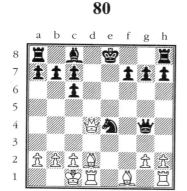

White to move

81

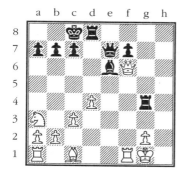

Black to move

82

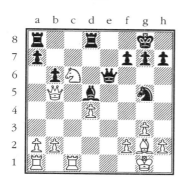

Black to move

83

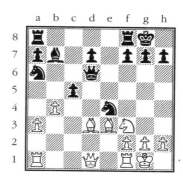

White to move

84

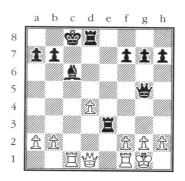

White to move

85

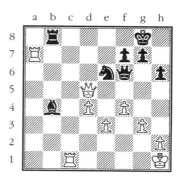

White to move

86

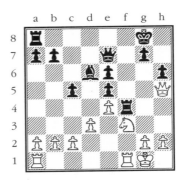

White to move

87

Black to move

88

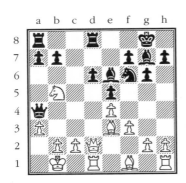

White to move

89

White to move

90

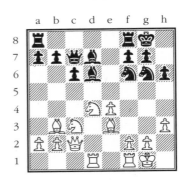

White to move

91

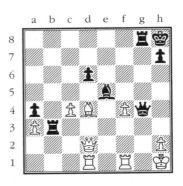

Black to move

92

Black to move

93

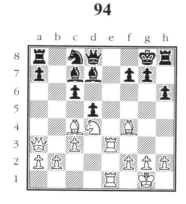

White to move

94

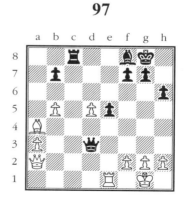

White to move

95

White to move

96

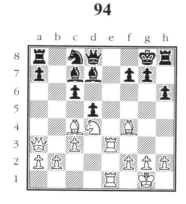

White to move

97

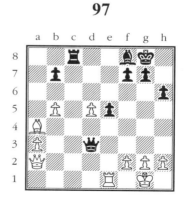

Black to move

98

Black to move

99

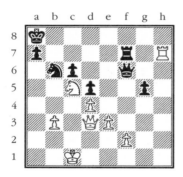

White to move

100

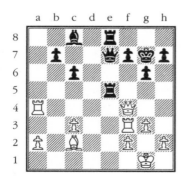

Black to move

101

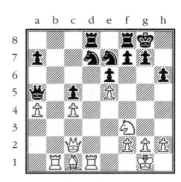

Black to move

102

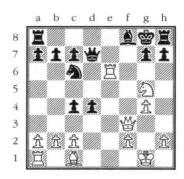

White to move

103

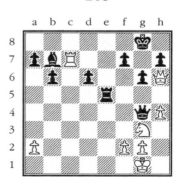

Black to move

104

White to move

105

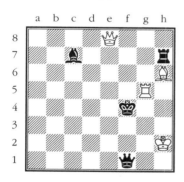

White to move

106

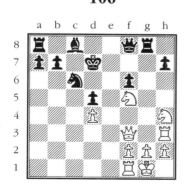

White to move

107

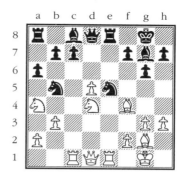

White to move

108

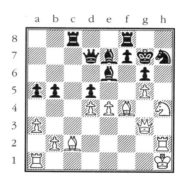

White to move

109

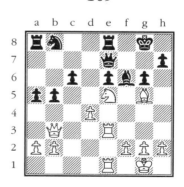

White to move

110

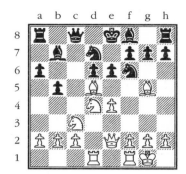

White to move

113

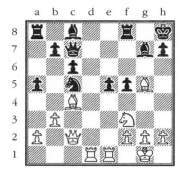

White to move

111

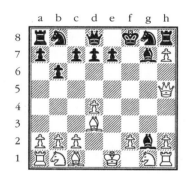

White to move

114

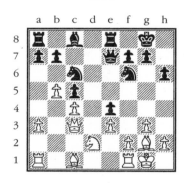

Black to move

112

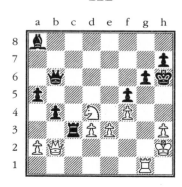

White to move

115

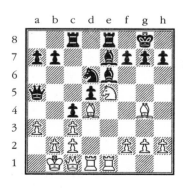

White to move

116

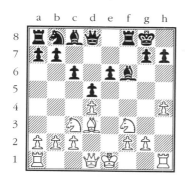

White to move

117

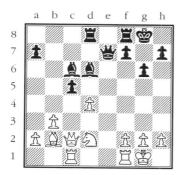

Black to move

118

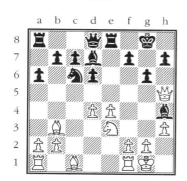

White to move

119

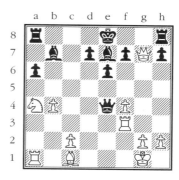

Black to move

120

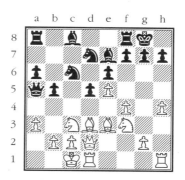

White to move

121

White to move

122

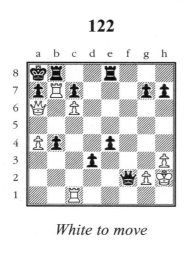

White to move

123

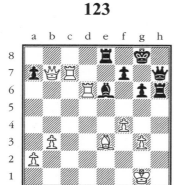

White to move

124

White to move

125

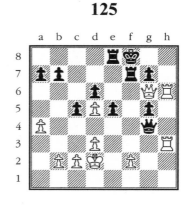

White to move

126

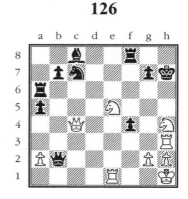

White to move

127

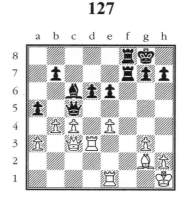

Black to move

128

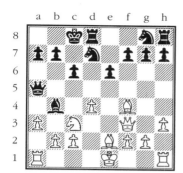

White to move

131

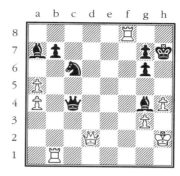

White to move

129

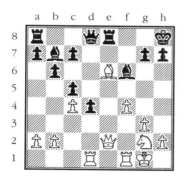

Black to move

132

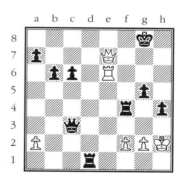

Black to move

130

White to move

133

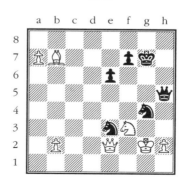

White to move

134

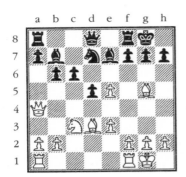

White to move

137

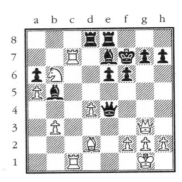

White to move

135

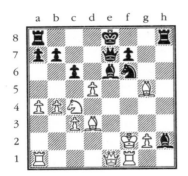

White to move

138

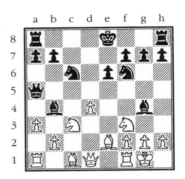

White to move

136

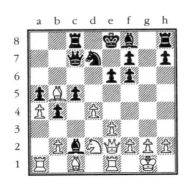

White to move

139

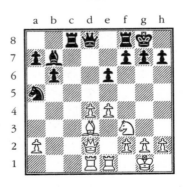

White to move

140

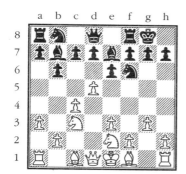

Black to move

141

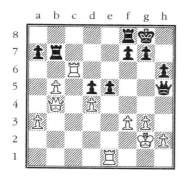

Black to move

142

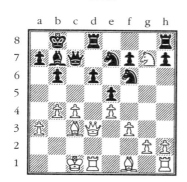

Black to move

143

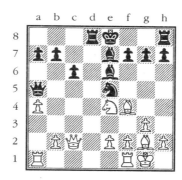

White to move

144

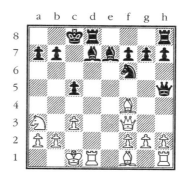

White to move

145

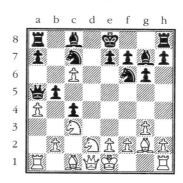

White to move

146

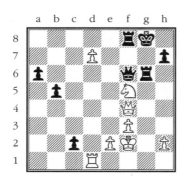

White to move

147

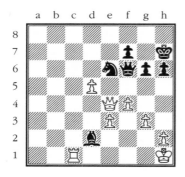

White to move

148

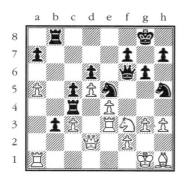

Black to move

149

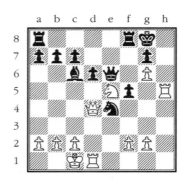

Black to move

150

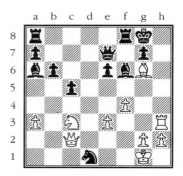

White to move

Solutions to Exercises 76-150

76

Bogoljubow – H. Müller
Triberg 1934

1 e4 e5 2 ♘f3 ♘c6 3 ♗b5 a6
4 ♗xc6 dxc6 5 ♘c3 ♗c5 6 d3 ♕e7
7 ♗e3 ♘f6 8 ♗xc5 ♕xc5 9 ♕d2
♗g4 10 d4 ♕b4 11 ♘xe5 0-0-0
12 0-0 ♖xd4 13 ♕e3 ♗e6

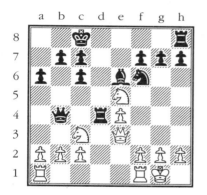

White to move

There is the motif of a pawn fork if
the c3-knight moves with tempo and
it's indeed possible in this position.
Bogoljubow played the beautiful:

14 ♘d5!! ♕c5?

14...♘xd5 15 exd5 ♖xd5 16 ♕a7,
taking advantage of the fact that
Black's king isn't placed on b8, is
another point of the combination.
Here we are dealing with another
theme, namely the skewer, since the
only way to prevent mate on a8 is by
the elimination of the knight. After
16...♖xe5 17 ♕a8+ ♔d7 18 ♕xh8

♕g4 19 f3! (19 ♕xh7 ♗d5 20 f3
♖e2 21 ♖f2 ♕d4 22 ♕f5+ ♔d8
23 ♖af1 ♖xf2 24 ♖xf2 ♕xb2
unnecessarily gives Black some
counterplay.) 19...♕g6 20 ♖f2!
White wins due to his extra material
and Black's exposed king.

14...♗xd5 runs into the pawn fork
15 c3. The best defence is to allow
the pawn fork with 14...cxd5 15 c3
and then continue 15...♕xb2
(15...♕b6 16 cxd4 dxe4 or 15...♕d6
16 cxd4 dxe4 are the options if
Black wants to keep queens on the
board and play with a healthier pawn
structure.) 16 ♕xd4 ♕b6 17 ♕xb6
cxb6 18 exd5 ♘xd5 after which
White must show good technique to
win the ending and exploit the slight
material advantage of rook against
bishop and pawn.

15 ♕xd4!! Black resigns.

White will deliver a knight fork
after 15...♕xd4 16 ♘e7+ ♔d8
17 ♘exc6+ bxc6 18 ♘xc6+ ♔d7
19 ♘xd4. It's unusual that two
knights help each other in such a
way as to produce a fork and that
makes it a rather spectacular gem!

147

77

Budrich – Ahues
Germany 1953

(1 e4 e5 2 f4 exf4 3 ♘f3 ♘f6 4 e5 ♘h5 5 ♕e2 ♗e7 6 d4 d5?? The king is too exposed on e8 so correct was 6...0-0 and only then either 7...d5 or 7...d6.)

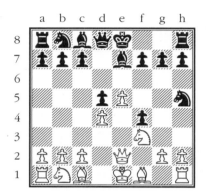

White to move

7 exd6 ♕xd6 8 ♕b5+ ♘c6 9 ♕xh5

Many players have problems seeing long queen moves and Botvinnik confessed that this was one of his weaknesses.

9...♘xd4 10 ♘xd4 ♕xd4

White is obviously winning but still managed to lose the game. The simplest now would have been...

11 ♘c3!

...followed by ♗d2 and 0-0-0 and placing the king in safety.

If you have managed to analyse the variation this far and also made a correct evaluation, you have done a good job!

78

Keres – Z. Nilsson
Stockholm 1960

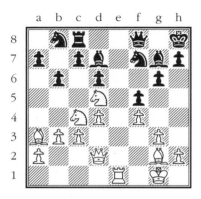

White to move

25 ♘e5!

With the help of a pin along the a3-f8 diagonal White creates the threat of a fork by playing 26 ♘e7 with a double attack on c8 and g6.

25...♗e8?

A mistake in a difficult position. 25...c5 would have prevented 26 ♘e7? due to 26...dxe5 27 ♘xc8 exd4 28 ♘xa7 dxc3 29 ♕d5 h5! and Black has created a rather chaotic position.

However 26 ♘xf7+ ♕xf7, to be followed by the simple penetration 27 ♖e7 and 28 ♗b2, would have sufficed for a winning advantage.

26 ♘xg6+!

Perhaps Zandor Nilsson was hoping for three pieces in exchange for the queen after 26 ♘e7 dxe5 27 ♘xg6+ hxg6 28 ♗xf8 ♗xf8, but even this variation wouldn't have been enough due to White's two extra pawns and central dominance after 29 fxe5.

26...hxg6 27 ♘e7 ♘h6 28 ♘xc8 Black resigns.

What a bold knight!

79

Kludacz – Pavlovskaya
Hasselbacken Open (Women),
Stockholm 2001

(1 d4 d5 2 c4 e6 3 ♘c3 ♘f6 4 cxd5 exd5 5 ♗g5 ♗e7 6 ♕c2 c6 7 e3 0-0 8 ♗d3 ♘bd7 9 ♘ge2 ♖e8 10 0-0 ♘f8 11 ♖ab1 ♘g4 12 ♗xe7 ♕xe7 13 h3 ♘h6 14 b4 a6 15 a4 g6 16 ♘g3 ♘e6 17 b5 axb5 18 axb5 ♘g5 19 bxc6 bxc6 20 ♖fc1 ♕d6)

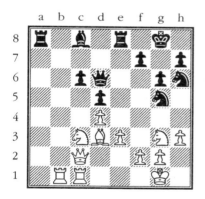

White to move

This position is a good example of tactics after a minority attack has taken place.

21 h4!

Kludacz overlooked this tactical opportunity and played the weaker 21 e4? which led to a lost position and the game after 21...♗xh3 22 gxh3 ♘xh3+ 23 ♔g2 ♘f4+ 24 ♔f3 ♕f6 25 e5 ♕g5 26 ♘ce2 ♕g4+ 27 ♔e3 ♘g2+ 28 ♔d2 ♕g5+ 29 ♔c3 c5 30 ♖b5 ♖a3+ 31 ♖b3 cxd4+ 32 ♔b2 ♖xb3+ 33 ♕xb3 ♕xe5 34 ♖c5 ♘f4 35 ♘xf4 ♕xf4 36 ♕xd5 ♕d2+ 37 ♗c2 d3 38 ♘e4 ♕b4+ 39 ♗b3 ♕xe4 White resigns.

21...♘e6

Presumably Kludacz missed the following knight sacrifice...

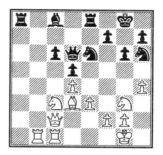

22 ♘ce4!! dxe4 23 ♘xe4

White exploits the tactical weaknesses on f6 and c6. Black has no effective defence.

23...♕c7

If 23...♕e7 then 24 ♕xc6.

24 ♘f6+ ♔f8

White doesn't need to cash in on e8 but can exploit the pin on the c-file.

25 d5!

Now Black's position collapses and White wins.

80

Maczuski – Kolisch
Match, Paris 1864

(1 e4 e5 2 ♘f3 ♘c6 3 d4 exd4
4 ♘xd4 ♕h4 5 ♘c3 ♗b4 6 ♕d3
♘f6 7 ♘xc6 dxc6 8 ♗d2 ♗xc3
9 ♗xc3 ♘xe4 10 ♕d4! ♕e7!
11 0-0-0 ♕g5? (Correct was
11...♘xc3 12 ♕xg7 ♘xa2+ 13 ♔b1
♖f8 14 ♔xa2 ♗d7 with a slight
advantage to Black.) 12 f4! ♕xf4+
13 ♗d2 ♕g4? (Necessary was
13...♕h4 to avoid mate by the
beautiful discoverer but Black was
clearly lost anyway after 14 ♗d3
when e4 as well as g7 is hanging.).

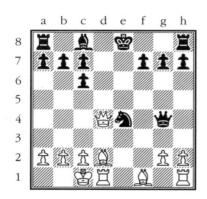

White to move

14 ♕d8+!

Due to the fact that Black's
queen was threatened the decisive
discoverer was slightly hidden.

**14...♔xd8 15 ♗g5+ ♔e8 16 ♖d8
mate.**

Maczuski beat Kolisch with the
same discoverer 46 years before the
famous miniature game Réti –
Tartakower, Vienna 1910.

81

Raubitschek – Capablanca
New York 1906

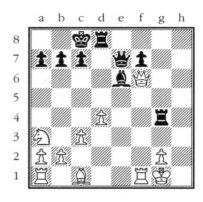

Black to move

Capablanca has sacrificed his
knight on f6 and must play
vigorously on the g-file and the long
light-squared h1-a8 diagonal.

23...♖dg8!

23...♗d5? is a mistake due to
24 ♕f5+ ♗e6 25 ♕e5, because now,
with the queen on e5, White's rook
isn't overloaded on f2 as we'll see in
the game. 25...♗d5 (25...♖dg8
26 ♖f2) 26 ♖f2.

24 ♖f2?

None of the alternatives help:

(a) 24 ♕xe7? ♖xg2+ 25 ♔h1
♗d5! 26 ♕e5 ♖2g4+ 27 ♕xd5 ♖h4
mate.

(b) 24 ♕f3 ♖g3 25 ♕e2 (25 ♕e4
f5 26 ♖xf5 ♖xg2+ 27 ♕xg2 ♖xg2+
28 ♔xg2 ♗xf5) 25...♗d5 26 ♖f2
♕h4 27 ♗f4 ♖h3 and mate follows.

(c) 24 ♕f2!

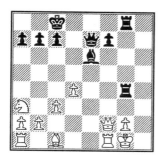

The best defence but it doesn't help after 24...♕d7! (24...♗d5 25 ♕f5+ ♗e6 26 ♕f2 only repeats the position.) Black wins by force as the following long variation proves: 25 ♗f4 ♗d5 26 g3 ♖h4 27 ♕e3 ♕h3 28 ♔f2 ♖xf4+! 29 ♕xf4 ♖e8 30 ♕e5 (The only way to avoid mate.) 30...♕g2+ 31 ♔e3 ♖xe5+ 32 dxe5 ♕xb2 33 ♖ad1 ♕xc3+ (Black picks up a bunch of pawns just as effectively as a vacuum-cleaner.) 34 ♖d3 ♕xe5+ 35 ♔d2 ♕b2+ 36 ♔e3 ♗xa2 and Black eventually wins with his queenside pawns.

24...♖xg2+

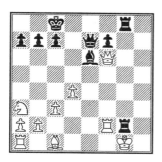

25 ♔f1

25 ♔h1 ♖g1+ 26 ♔h2 ♕xf6 27 ♖xf6 ♖8g2 mate or 25 ♖xg2 ♖xg2+ 26 ♔xg2 ♕xf6 etc.

25...♗c4+ 26 ♘xc4 ♖g1 mate.

82

Hübner – Timman
Bugojno 1978

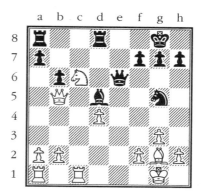

Black to move

A good method when familiarising yourself with a position is to ask yourself what motifs are there for a combination? Here one can ascertain three motifs: (1) After the removal of the light-squared bishops White will be weak on the light squares on the kingside. (2) The possibility to attack with the queen and knight. (3) The unprotected queen on b5.

19...♗xg2! 20 ♘xd8

20 ♔xg2 ♕h3+ 21 ♔h1 ♘f3 wins as does 20 ♕xg5 ♗xc6.

20...♕e4!

This quiet move can be difficult to spot since it's easy to focus on mating variations, but now what it's all about is the unprotected white queen.

21 h3

21 ♕xg5 ♗h3 22 f3 ♕e2! and White can't prevent mate on g2.

21...♘f3+! White resigns.

151

22 ♔xg2 is met by 22...♘xd4+.

21...♗xh3 22 ♕c6 ♘f3+ 23 ♔h1 ♗f5 also won but it is a more complicated variation.

The theme of the combination was the discovered check resulting in the win of the enemy queen.

83

Benjamin – Shabalov
USA Championship 2021

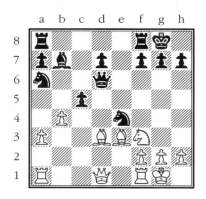

White to move

In the U.S. Senior Championship 2021 Benjamin missed a decisive tactical opportunity based on the discoverer and hanging pieces. Benjamin played...

19 ♗xe4?

Correct was to put more pressure on the e4-knight by 19 ♘g5! and exploit the hanging queen on d6 if the knight moves or is defended by a pawn.

(a) 19...♘xg5 is answered by the discoverer 20 ♗xh7+. A very instructive position and even more instructive because Benjamin missed it. So even at GM-level we are dealing with fundamental tricks

only a couple of moves ahead. Essentially this position is the same as Réti – Tartakower, Vienna 1910 (or Maczuski –Kolisch, Paris 1864) so by learning to x-ray the position and locate the pressure on the d-file and the hanging piece(s) it's possible to see more advanced combinations containing a simple tactical trick.

(b) 19...f5 is also answered by a discoverer but on the classical diagonal after 20 ♘xe4 followed by 21 ♗c4+. Note that the tricky 20...♕g6 is met by 21 ♘g3 and the f-pawn is unable to fork White due to the pin.

(c) A defence with the rook 19...♖ae8 fails to 20 ♗xe4 ♕xd1 and now the intermediate move 21 ♗xh7+ ♔h8 22 ♖fxd1. If Black tries to regain the piece by 22...f6 White wins material after 23 ♗g6.

(d) 19...♕e7 is met by 20 ♘xe4 and the bishop on b7 is overloaded since it also has to protect the knight on a6.

In these variations we can see four tactical tricks work at the same time: discoverer, pin, overloading and fork. A fifth tactical device was the intermediate move which sometimes is easy to miss in the calculation of variations.

19...♕xd1 20 ♖fxd1 ♗xe4 21 bxc5?

White could still play for a win by destroying the harmony in Black's position after 21 ♖d6 ♗c6 22 bxc5 followed by ♘d4 with a clear advantage. After the exchange of knight and bishop White's rooks and bishop will be a stronger combination than Black's rooks and knight.

21...♖fc8

White ran out of steam and the game ended in a draw after 44 moves.

84

Rubinstein – Lasker
St Petersburg 1909

(1 d4 d5 2 ♘f3 ♘f6 3 c4 e6 4 ♗g5 c5 5 cxd5 exd5 6 ♘c3 cxd4 7 ♘xd4 ♘c6 8 e3 ♗e7 9 ♗b5 ♗d7 10 ♗xf6 ♗xf6 11 ♘xd5 ♗xd4 12 exd4 ♕g5 13 ♗xc6 ♗xc6 14 ♘e3 0-0-0 15 0-0 ♖he8 16 ♖c1 ♖xe3)

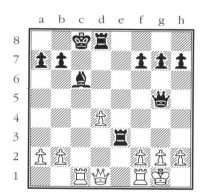

White to move

17 ♖xc6+

This exchange sacrifice is mandatory due to 17 fxe3?? ♕xg2 mate.

17...bxc6 18 ♕c1!

This move is one of the most famous pinning and winning moves ever played. 18 fxe3? ♕xe3+ 19 ♔h1 ♕xd4 20 ♕c2 would have led to a position with mutual chances where the most likely result would have been a draw.

18...♖xd4

An interesting defensive continuation was 18...♕d5!? 19 fxe3 ♖e8 followed by ...f5 and ♔b7. Black could then decide whether the best place for the g-pawn is on g6, setting up a pawn wave, or on g5, playing for activity.

19 fxe3!

Stronger than 19 ♕xc6+ ♔b8 20 ♖c1 ♖d8 21 ♕c7+ ♔a8 22 fxe3 ♕xe3+ 23 ♔h1.

19...♖d7?

Stronger was 19...♖d6! 20 ♖xf7 ♕h5 driving the enemy rook away from the seventh rank. After the text move White penetrates the position with devastating effect.

20 ♕xc6+ ♔d8 21 ♖f4!

A very strong defensive as well as attacking move. The e3-pawn is defended and White now threatens to utilise the rook along the fourth rank, especially the e4 and c4 squares in combination with queen checks.

21...f5

Black controls the important e4 square. The cold-blooded line 21...♖d1+ 22 ♔f2 ♕a5! (22...♖d2+? 23 ♔e1 ♕xg2? 24 ♖d4+! fails

153

to 24...♖xd4 25 ♕xg2), allowing the checks 23 ♕a8+ ♔e7 24 ♖e4+ ♔f6 25 ♕c6+ ♔g5, reaches a rook ending with good winning chances for White after 26 b4 ♕d5 27 h4+ ♔h5 28 ♕xd5+ ♖xd5 29 ♖d4!.

22 ♕c5 ♕e7

22...♖d1+ 23 ♔f2 ♖d2+? 24 ♔e1 ♕xg2 still doesn't work due to the double attack 25 ♕a5+.

23 ♕xe7+ ♔xe7

23...♖xe7? 24 ♖xf5 ♖xe3 25 ♖f8+ ♔e7 (25...♔c7 26 ♖f7+) 26 ♖a8 and White gets two connected passed pawns on the queenside.

24 ♖xf5 ♖d1+ 25 ♔f2!

Activity of both king and rook is the key in rook endings. 25 ♖f1 is met by 25...♖d2!

25...♖d2+ 26 ♔f3 ♖xb2 27 ♖a5 ♖b7 28 ♖a6!

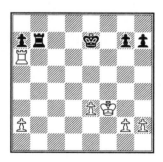

This famous (and important) rook ending is technically winning for White. White not only has an extra pawn but also the far more active rook and king.

28...♔f8 29 e4 ♖c7 30 h4!

White seizes space on the kingside before advancing with the passed pawn.

30...♔f7 31 g4 ♔f8 32 ♔f4 ♔e7

Black can only wait while avoiding weaknesses.

33 h5

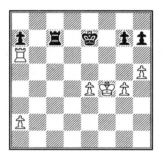

It's important to realise that White cannot win with just his e-pawn. It's of vital importance to provoke another weakness on the kingside, in accordance with the principle of two weaknesses.

33...h6

A waiting strategy also loses: 33...♖b7 34 g5 ♖c7 35 e5 ♖b7 36 ♔f5 ♖c7 37 g6 h6 38 a4 ♖b7 39 ♖e6+! ♔d7 (39...♔f8 40 ♖c6 ♔e7 41 ♖c8 and Black cannot prevent 42 ♖g8.) 40 ♖f6!! ♔e8 (40...gxf6 41 g7 ♖b8 42 exf6) 41 ♖f7! ♖xf7+ 42 gxf7+ ♔xf7 43 e6+ ♔e7 44 ♔e5! and White wins.

34 ♔f5 ♔f7 35 e5 ♖b7 36 ♖d6 ♔e7 37 ♖a6 ♔f7 38 ♖d6 ♔f8

38...♖c7 is met by the pseudo-sacrifice 39 ♖d7+! ♖xd7 40 e6+ ♔e7 41 exd7 ♔xd7 42 ♔g6 and White wins.

39 ♖c6 ♔f7 40 a3! Black resigns.

White avoids a possible ...♖b7-b4 and places Black in zugzwang. A possible continuation was 40...♔f8 (or 40...♖e7 41 e6+ ♔g8 42 ♔g6 ♖e8 43 e7! followed by 44 ♖d6 and 45 ♖d6.) 41 ♔g6 ♖b3 42 ♖c8+ ♔e7 43 ♔xg7 ♖xa3 44 ♔xh6. It's understandable that Lasker didn't want to endure this massacre.

85

Petrosian – Veresov
USSR Championship 1947

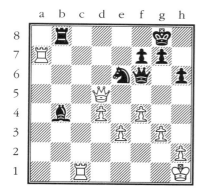

White to move

The most uncomfortable move for Black to meet was...

33 ♖b1!

...as it would have pinned Black's bishop and secured a clear advantage.

In the game the inferior 33 ♖a8? was played. The rook exchange makes it easier for Black to defend his position. Petrosian was only 16 years of age at the time the game was played and his play had yet to mature to reach the level he

achieved in the 1950s and especially the 1960s, when he remained one of the top players in the world.

After 33...♖xa8 34 ♕xa8+ instead of 34...♔h7? Black should have played 34...♗f8! with only a slight advantage to White. It would not have been easy for White to fulfil his dream plan and advance the pawns to d5 followed by e4-e5 and d5-d6. An immediate 35 d5? would have failed to 35...♕b2 and if then 36 ♖c8 Black could have profited from White's exposed king and played for a draw with 36...♕f2.

33...♘f8 34 ♔g2

Black has serious problems with the coordination of his pieces.

86

Onoprienko – Jaracz
Milada Boleslav 1994

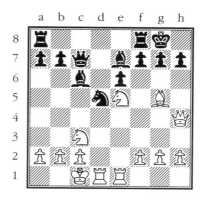

White to move

14 ♗xe7 ♘xe7

14...♕xe7 15 ♕xe7 ♘xe7 16 ♘xc6 ♘xc6 17 ♖d7 leads to a comfortable endgame for White where Black can only hope for a draw.

15 ♖d7

Vasyukov's idea from 1972 isn't so easy to discover if you aren't familiar with it.

15...♗xd7

15...♘g6 16 ♖xc7 ♘xh4 17 ♘xc6 bxc6 18 ♖xc6 ♘xg2 19 ♖e4 is clear advantage for White according to Vasyukov.

16 ♕xe7 ♖ad8 17 ♖e3!

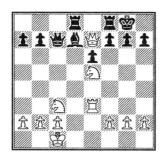

Black is completely paralysed.

17...b6?

Black plans to liberate his position with ...♕c7-c5 but this is easily stopped. Komodo's improvement is 17...h6. One plausible variation demonstrating that White has enough compensation is 18 b4 (18 f4? ♕b6 shows why it's important to keep the b6-square for the queen.) 18...a6 19 a3 b5 20 ♔b2 ♔h7 21 ♘xf7 ♖de8 22 ♕d6 ♕xd6 23 ♘xd6 etc.

18 b4! a6 19 f4

White is preparing to move the rook to g3 or d3.

19...♕c8 20 ♘e4! ♗a4 21 ♖c3 ♕a8 22 ♘f6+ ♔h8 23 ♕xf7! ♗xc2 24 ♕g8+! Black resigns.

87

David – J. Balogh
Budapest 1948

(1 ♘f3 d5 2 g3 ♗f5 3 ♗g2 ♘d7 4 c4 c6 5 cxd5 cxd5 6 ♕b3? [6 0-0])

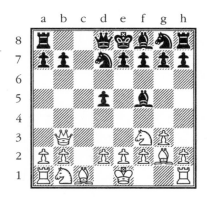

Black to play

6...♘c5!

Black exploits a tactical finesse which White has overlooked.

7 ♕b5+

Correct was the retreat 7 ♕d1!.

7...♗d7! 8 ♕xc5??

8 ♕b4 would have led to an equal game whereas now White has completely forgotten that the c1-bishop is unprotected.

8...♖c8 Black resigns.

Black's last move represents a "relative skewer" because only the pieces on the c-file are involved and not the king. White's queen cannot move due to the back rank mate. Be careful of skewers because they are like reversed pins. Imagine that the queen and the bishop on c1 change places. This is a "pin" which would also be a lost position for White because of 9...b6 next move.

Boleslavsky has created a positional gem to learn from!

20...♕h4 21 ♕e2 ♗f8 22 ♕f1 ♖ac8 23 g3 ♕g5 24 h4 ♕h6 25 g4 g5 26 hxg5 ♕xg5 27 ♖h5 ♕g6 28 g5 h6 29 ♖xh6 ♕xg5 30 ♖h5 White resigns.

This is a perfect model game demonstrating how to win with a superior knight against a bad bishop. A similar example in this collection of positional ideas is Fischer – Gadia, Mar del Plata 1960, exercise 36.

88

Boleslavsky – Lisitsin
USSR Championship 1956

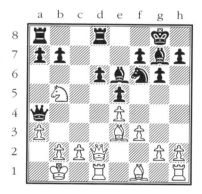

White to move

It seems that Boleslavsky was so focused on long-term positional ideas that he went for...

15 c4

This is a good positional move but he missed the simple tactical shot 15 ♘c7! ♖ac8 (15...♕c6 is necessary but after 16 ♘xa8 White is the exchange up.) 16 ♗b5 and the queen is trapped.

15...♗xc4 16 ♘c3 ♕b3 17 ♗xc4 ♕xc4 18 ♗g5 ♕e6 19 ♗xf6 ♕xf6 20 ♘d5

89

Hort – Beni
Chess Olympiad, Varna 1962

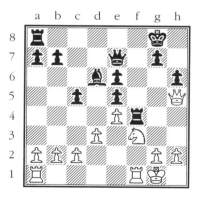

White to move

Can White take the e5-pawn? Yes!

18 ♘xe5! ♖h4 19 ♕g6 ♗xe5 20 g3

White traps Black's rook. White won after...

20...♕g5 21 ♕xg5 hxg5 22 gxh4 ♗xb2 23 ♖ab1 ♗d4+ 24 ♔g2

This is actually an attacking move, because White's king is heading for g6!

24...gxh4 25 ♖xb7 a5 26 ♔h3 ♖d8 27 ♔xh4 ♗f6+ 28 ♔h5 c4 29 ♔g6 cxd3 30 cxd3 ♗e5 31 ♖e7 Black resigns.

90

Toshkov – Russek Libni
Saint John 1988

(1 d4 e6 2 c4 d5 3 ♘c3 ♘f6 4 ♘f3 c6 5 e3 ♘bd7 6 ♗d3 ♗d6 7 0-0 0-0 8 e4 dxc4 9 ♗xc4 e5 10 h3 h6 11 ♕c2 ♕c7 12 ♗e3 exd4 13 ♘xd4 ♘e5 14 ♗b3 ♘g6 15 ♖ad1 ♗d7? [Correct was *15...♖e8*.])

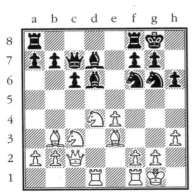

White to move

16 e5!!

Such a move can easily be missed, especially if one isn't familiar with

it. White uses his pawn majority in a tactical way and exploits Black's last move which has taken away a retreat square for the g6-knight.

16...♘xe5

16...♗xe5 17 ♕xg6 is a typical pin of the f7-pawn when one is in control of the classical a2-g8 diagonal. Many games are won because of this diagonal so always keep an eye on it!

17 f4

This is the point; Black has no way of retreat because the bishop has unfortunately blocked the d7 square.

17...♘eg4 18 hxg4 ♘xg4 19 ♗c1

Two pawns are obviously not enough when White's pieces are so well placed. White won after the further moves...

19...♖ad8 20 ♘e4 ♗c8 21 g3 ♕a5 22 ♔g2

The discoverer 22 ♘xc6! was a simpler and faster win because the bishop on d6 is hanging.

22...♖fe8 23 ♘xc6 bxc6 24 ♘xd6 ♖xd6 25 ♖xd6 ♗f5 26 ♕c4 ♗e4+ 27 ♔g1 ♕h5

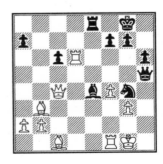

28 ♕xf7+!

The control of the classical diagonal decides the game.

28...♛xf7 29 ♗xf7+ ♚xf7 30 ♖e1
♘f6 31 ♖d4 ♖e7 32 g4 c5 33 ♖a4
♖d7 34 g5 ♗c6 35 ♖a6 ♗b7
36 ♖xa7 ♘g4 37 a4 h5 38 f5 h4
39 ♗f4 **Black resigns.**

91

Varjoma – Lundquist
Sweden 1980

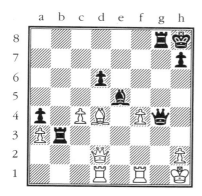

Black to move

1...♖d3!

Black exploits the overloaded
queen which has to cover g2 as well
as d1.

2 ♗xe5+

2 fxe5 is met by 2...♛e4+ and
2 ♕c2 doesn't work on account of
2...♖xd1 because both of White's
major pieces are overloaded. The
queen must cover the g2 square and
the rook has to control the f3 square
to avoid mate.

2...dxe5 3 ♕b2

It seems that White has solved the
tactical problem because 3...♖xd1?
is met by 4 ♕xe5+. However, Black
has the nasty reply...

3...♛f3+! White resigns.

It turns out that the f1-rook is
overloaded. After 4 ♖xf3 ♖xd1+ it's
mate next move.

92

Prasad – Speelman
Interzonal, Subotica 1987

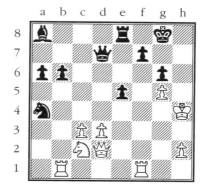

Black to move

29...♘xc3!!

The strongest move in the
position, bringing the knight into
play via d5 or e4.

30 ♕xc3

30 ♖xb6 ♘d5 gains an important
tempo by threatening not only the
rook but also ...♚g7 followed by
...♖h8+ which is deadly now that the
knight is centralised.

For example:

(a) 31 ♖xa6 ♚g7 32 ♖xa8 ♖xa8
33 ♚g3 ♖a2 wins since Black's
pieces are too active and White's
king too exposed.

(b) 31 ♖bf6 31...♘xf6 32 gxf6
♚h7 followed by the central

breakthrough 33...e4 is crushing with the king on h4.

30...♗g2

The queen was overloaded and had to hand over the vacant and unprotected g2 square to his opponent. A high price to pay to get rid of the bold knight. Black threatens mate in one.

31 ♔g3

Helping the black rook into play by 31 d4 exd4 32 ♘xd4 ♖e4+ would of course be disastrous.

31...♕h3+ 32 ♔f2 ♗xf1

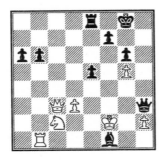

33 ♘e3

Or 33 ♖xf1 ♖c8 34 ♕d2 ♖xc2! 35 ♕xc2 ♕xh2+. A skewer with a king and a piece involved on the same file or rank is called an "absolute skewer".

33...♕xh2+ 34 ♔xf1 ♕h1+

One more "absolute skewer"!

35 ♔f2 ♕xb1 36 ♘g4 ♕a2+ 37 ♔g3 ♕e6!

This is a good pragmatic solution to give back some of the material and not start unnecessary complications. After all, a queen and an anchored knight is a mighty attacking duo.

38 ♘f6+ ♔g7 White resigns.

93

Esipenko – Carlsen
FIDE World Cup, 2021

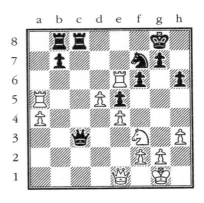

White to move

36 ♖e8+!

I am sure many of you saw the solution immediately because you knew there were some tactics hidden in the position. However, in practical chess it's very easy to miss this simple combination. Nigel Short missed it when he annotated the game, Carlsen missed it when he moved the queen from c4 to snatch the pawn on c3. Esipenko missed it as well, perhaps trusting that the world champion wouldn't fall into such a cheapo! Esipenko played 36 ♕xc3 ♖xc3 37 ♖b5 with a winning position and won after 64 moves.

36...♖xe8

Or 36...♔h7 37 ♕xc3 ♖xc3 38 ♖xb8.

37 ♕xc3

And White wins. It seems that Capablanca missed a similar tactical shot against Euwe at Amsterdam 1931, exercise 143.

93a

Winsnes – Engqvist
Alingsås 2019

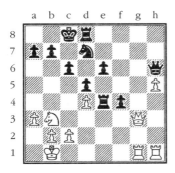

Black to move

In this position I anticipated that White would play the queen to g6 but instead followed...

30 ♕g7?

My opponent IM Richard Winsnes told me immediately after the game that he had seen the tactical idea...

30...♖e1+!

...after he had made his move and had to keep a poker face while I was thinking. I didn't notice anything and it was only after the game when my opponent told me that I had overlooked a move to win the queen that I realised what I had missed. I managed to win the game anyway but I was very disappointed that I hadn't been tactically alert for this standard combination which I had seen so many times before when solving tactical positions.

My own explanation for 30...♖h8? was that I expected a queen move to g6 and didn't adapt to the new circumstance that the queen was only defended by the rook on g7 and forgot about this finesse entirely. So here we are again. Despite the fact that we (= all chessplayers on Earth) know this combination we still miss it. My opponent missed it and I missed it. This is not a coincidence.

The key is **always to be alert for combinational ideas** even when we don't expect them. One needs to develop a sixth sense for them so that we can see them before they appear on the board!

94

Leonhardt – Tarrasch
Hamburg 1910

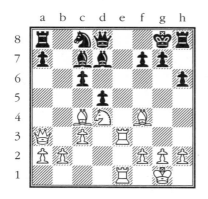

White to move

A classic example of a lateral combination is the following:

19 ♗xc7 ♕xc7 20 ♖e8+! ♗xe8 21 ♖xe8+ ♔h7 22 ♗d3+ f5

Black is desperate. After the natural 22...g6 23 ♖xh8+ ♔xh8 24 ♕f8+ ♔h7 White has the possibility of bringing his last piece into the attack by 25 ♘f5!.

If you have seen the variation 25...♕e5 (or 25...f6 26 ♕xh6+ ♔g8 27 ♕xg6+ ♔f8 28 ♕xf6+) 26 ♕xf7+ ♔h8 27 ♕f8+ ♔h7 28 ♕xh6+ (The computer suggests the super move 28 h4!!) 28...♔g8 29 ♕xg6+ and assessed it as winning, that is obviously enough to be convinced that the variation is decisive for White.

23 ♖xh8+ ♔xh8 24 ♕f8+ ♔h7 25 ♗xf5+ g6

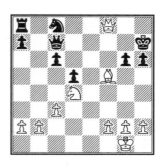

26 ♗xg6+! Black resigns.

Leonhardt ends the game with a nice magnet sacrifice. Tarrasch resigned because he loses his queen after 26...♔xg6 27 ♕f5+ ♔g7 28 ♘e6+.

95

Capablanca – Steiner
Living chess exhibition,
Los Angeles 1933

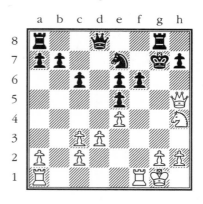

White to move

17 ♖xf6!!

This magnet sacrifice forces the black king out to the f-file where it will be attacked by White's three remaining pieces.

17...♗xf6 18 ♖f1+ ♘f5 19 ♘xf5!

The knight sacrifice is more precise than 19 exf5 ♔e7 20 ♕xh7+ ♔d6 21 fxe6.

19...exf5 20 ♖xf5+ ♔e7 21 ♕f7+ ♔d6 22 ♖f6+ ♔c5

22...♕xf6 23 ♕xf6+ ♔d7 24 ♕xe5 is hopeless for Black in the long run. He is not only three pawns down but has no targets and too many weaknesses in his own position such as his king and three vulnerable pawns.

23 ♕xb7! ♕b6 24 ♖xc6+! ♕xc6 25 ♕b4 mate.

A nice finish! Only the married couple remains of the pieces. The others were exchanged or sacrificed for a higher aim than their own lives.

96

Kasparian – Manvelian
Yerevan 1936

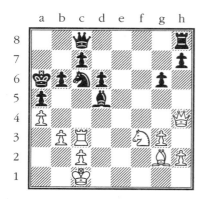

White to move

1 ♖xc6!! ♗xc6

The tricky defence 1...g5, to deflect the queen from the fourth rank, doesn't help either after 2 ♕d4! ♗xc6 3 ♕c4+ etc.

2 ♕c4+ ♔b7

The best defence was 2...♔a7 3 ♕xc6 ♕b7 but after 4 ♕d7 followed by ♘f3-e1 it wouldn't be possible for Black to hold the game.

3 ♕xc6+!! ♔xc6 4 ♘e5+ ♔c5 5 ♘d3+ ♔d4 6 ♔d2! ♕e6 7 c3 mate.

A very nice conclusion where the king and the c-pawn also made their contribution to checkmating the opposing king.

97

Alekhine – Bogoljubow
Game 13, World Championship, Berlin 1929

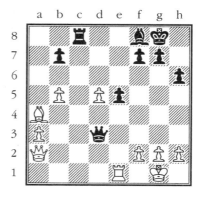

Black to move

Alekhine was in severe time trouble and missed an elementary double threat.

31...♕e4! 32 ♕d2

The only way to defend both hanging pieces would have been with a queen on d1 while 32 ♖xe4 would be met by 32...♗c1+.

32...♕xa4 33 d6 ♕d4 34 ♕xd4 exd4 White resigns.

98

Z. Nilsson – Geller
Sweden – USSR Match 1954

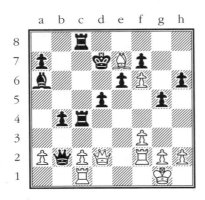

Black to move

It seems that the c2-pawn is adequately defended but it's the back rank which is the real problem.

22...♖xc2!!

A pretty way to exploit the back rank, because it will become weak after the recapture on c2.

23 ♕xc2

23 ♖xc2 ♕b1+! and it's mate because the black bishop controls f1.

23...♕xc1+! White resigns.

Such x-ray moves can easily be missed when calculating variations

so it's important to develop a habit of seeing such awkward moves.

99

Katalymov – Kolpakov
Kazakhstan – Turkmenistan 1975

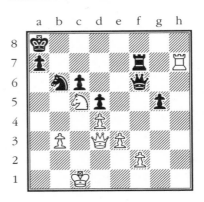

White to move

33 ♕g6! Black resigns.

Black loses at least one rook because 33...♕xg6 fails to 34 ♖h8+ followed by mate. Note that the black pieces' control of the four squares g8, f8, e8 and c8 cannot prevent the bold rook, with the help of the knight, from mating the king in the corner.

33 ♕g6 is a nice diversionary move because it upsets the coordination of Black's major pieces. On f6 the queen controls the important dark squares h8 and f8. When White places his queen on the light square g6 everything collapses because of the weak back rank. It's all about colours!

Another nice idea in the position is that 33...♖f8 can of course be met by the simple 34 ♕xf6 ♖xf6 35 ♖h8+ followed by mate; but the prettier 34 ♖h8 wins as well after for instance 34...♕xh8 35 ♕xc6+ followed by mate on a white square in two different ways.

100

Netto – Abente
Paraguay 1983

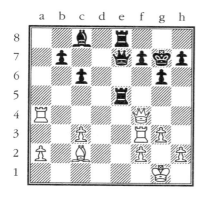

Black to move

Despite the fact that White has a loophole on g2 Black can force a back rank mate.

1...♖e1+ 2 ♔g2 ♖g1+!! 3 ♔xg1 ♕e1+ 4 ♔g2 ♕f1+! 5 ♔xf1 ♗h3+

This rocket move from the rear of Black's position forces the king into a mating net.

6.♔g1 ♖e1 mate.

A back rank mate has been constructed in the most beautiful way but it demanded four pieces, and three of them were major pieces.

101

A. Sokolov – Yusupov
Candidates match, Riga 1986

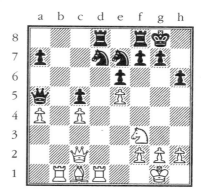

Black to move

In situations where the minor pieces on the queenside are not fully developed it can be worthwhile to check whether there is some continuation to profit from the potentially vulnerable back rank.

19...♘xe5!!

A very nice way of opening up the position and exploiting the fact that the bishop is still on its original square.

20 ♘xe5

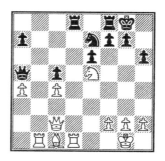

165

20...♕c3

This is the point; White's queen is overloaded due to the vulnerable first rank.

21 ♕e2

If 21 ♕xc3? then 21...♖xd1+.

21...♕xe5!

Black exploits the overloaded queen one more time and remains with an extra pawn as well as the initiative. He won after...

22 ♗e3 ♘f5 23 ♕f3 ♖xd1+ 24 ♖xd1 ♘d4 25 ♗xd4 cxd4 26 ♕d3 ♖d8 27 g3 ♕c5 28 f4 ♕b4 29 ♖a1 a5 30 h4 h5 31 ♖b1 ♕xa4 32 ♖b5 g6 33 ♔g2 ♕a2+ 34 ♔f3 a4 35 ♖b6 ♔g7 36 ♖b1 ♔g8 37 ♖b6 ♕a1 38 ♔e2 a3 39 ♖a6 ♕b2+ 40 ♕d2 d3+ White resigns.

102

Maróczy – Vidmar
Ljubljana 1922

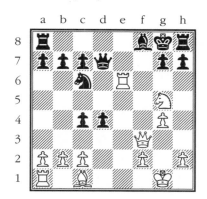

White to move

17 ♖e7!! Black resigns.

A stunning move after which the only way to cover the f7-square is 17...♕xe7, but then the beautiful diagonal move 18 ♕d5+ mates next move.

103

Maedler – Uhlmann
East German Championship 1963

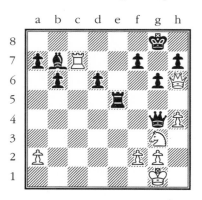

Black to move

White has just played the suicidal 27 ♖c7?? allowing the beautiful finish

27...♖e1+ 28 ♔h2 ♖h1+!! Black resigns.

29 ♔xh1 (The knight is overloaded so 29 ♘xh1 can be met by 29...♕xg2 mate.) 29...♕h3+ (The g2-pawn is pinned with the king on h1.) 30 ♔g1 ♕xg2 mate.

This is a typical example which shows that most of the time three pieces are enough to checkmate.

The general formula is: one piece to sacrifice and two to mate.

104

Hulak – Hort
Wijk aan Zee 1983

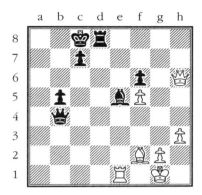

White to move

33 ♖xe5?

In the tournament book an exclamation mark is attached to this move but as a matter of fact it isn't the best. It was better to centralise the queen with 33 ♕e3 with only a slight advantage for Black.

33...fxe5??

Correct was 33...♖d1+ 34 ♔h2 ♕d6! with a pin and good winning chances for Black.

34 ♕a6+ Black resigns.

The queen's long arm leads to a forced mate.

After 34...♔d7 White mates by 35 ♕e6. After 34...♔b8 White has the well-known manoeuvre leading to the famous Damiano's mate. White plays 35 ♗a7+ ♔a8 36 ♗b6+ ♔b8 37 ♕a7+ ♔c8 38 ♕xc7 mate.

105

D. Gurgenidze
The end of a study 1986

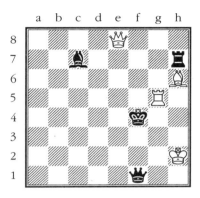

White to move

1 ♕e3+! ♔xe3+

Black captures the queen with check but after...

2 ♖g3+

...it's a double check so Black's king must move, but wherever it moves White is stalemated due to the two pins and the king's lack of squares. To create a stalemate with the help of pins and checks is rare in practice but still useful to know. Chess is truly inexhaustible!

106

Capablanca – Michelsen
Simultaneous exhibition,
New York 1910

(1 e4 c5 2 b4 cxb4 3 a3 e6 4 axb4 ♗xb4 5 c3 ♗e7 6 ♘f3 ♘f6 7 e5 ♘d5 8 c4 ♘f4 9 d4 ♗b4+ 10 ♗d2 ♕e7 11 ♗xb4 ♕xb4+ 12 ♘bd2 ♕c3 13 ♖b1! (The dormant rook is now

activated.) 13...♘d3+ 14 ♗xd3
♕xd3 15 ♖b3! ♕g6 16 0-0 f5
17 exf6 gxf8 18 ♘h4! ♕h6 19 ♖h3!
♖g8 20 ♘e4! d5 21 cxd5 exd5
22 ♘d6+ ♔d7 23 ♘df5 ♕f8 24 ♕f3
♘c6)

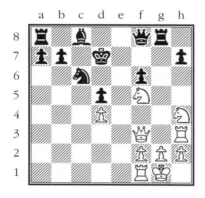

White to move

This is one of many positions
which have convinced me of
Capablanca's great genius. When I
studied the game for the first time I
tried to guess Capablanca's moves
before I played them out on the
board. The whole game is just
amazing from beginning to end.

25 ♘g6!!

Capablanca's tactical ideas have
a lot to do with harmony on
a very high level. Here he wants
to establish a more effective
cooperation between the active rook
and White's queen. I expected first
25 ♕xd5+ but why help the
king move from a bad square?
Capablanca's move order is more
profound, principled, stronger and
more aesthetically appealing. There
is no reason to help the king hide on
c7 and then on b8, when this escape
can be prevented.

25...♕f7

25...hxg6 is most effectively met
by 26 ♖h7+! ♔d8. If the king goes
to the e-file White checks on e1.
27 ♕xd5+ This is the point. When
Capablanca takes on d5 it's with
immediately devastating effect. Note
that 27 ♕f4? fails to 27...♗d7 when
the rook has lost control of the
c7-square.

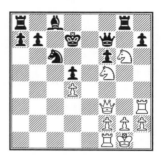

26 ♖xh7!!

26 ♘h6 ♕xg6 27 ♘xg8
(27 ♕xd5+?? loses to 27...♗c7)
27...♕xg8 28 ♕f5+ ♔c7 29 ♕f4+
♔d7 30 ♖e1 also wins but of course
Capablanca's move is the most
logical.

26...♕xh7 27 ♕xd5+ ♔c7

Or 27...♔e8 28 ♖e1+.

28 ♕d6+ ♔b6 29 ♖b1+ ♔a6
30 ♕a3+ ♘a5 31 ♕d3+ Black
resigns.

It's mate in two moves.

What's most extraordinary is that
this game was played in a
simultaneous exhibition! One can
understand why such brilliant games
have contributed to Capablanca
being regarded as the greatest
simultaneous player of his time,
perhaps of all time.

107

Smyslov – Lilienthal
Moscow Championship 1942

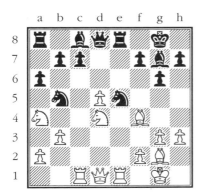

White to move

19 ♘e6!

A typical combinational as well as positional idea to remember. The idea is to activate the g2-bishop and split Black's bishop pair in the process, or disrupt his pawn structure on the kingside.

19...♗xe6

After 19...fxe6 20 ♗xe5 exd5 21 ♕xd5+ Black loses material. 19...♘f3+ 20 ♕xf3 fxe6 21 dxe6 is also to White's advantage.

20 dxe6 ♖xe6 21 ♘c5 ♕xd1

21...♖d6 22 ♕e2 ♘d4 (22...♘d3 23 ♘xd3 ♖xd3 24 ♗xb7) 23 ♕e4 f5 24 ♕e3 and Black's knights are unstable.

22 ♖exd1 ♖d6 23 ♘xb7 ♖xd1+ 24 ♖xd1 ♖b8 25 a4 ♘c3 26 ♖d2

White has a positionally won game. He can combine an attack on Black's weak queenside pawns as well his unstable knights.

White's bishops are too strong in this position.

26...♖e8 27 ♘c5 a5 28 ♖c2! ♘d1 29 ♗d2 ♗f8 30 ♘e4 ♖b8 31 ♗xa5 ♖xb3 32 ♗xc7 ♘d3 33 ♗f1 ♘1b2 34 a5 f5 35 ♘d2 ♖a3 36 ♘c4 ♘xc4 37 ♖xc4 ♖a1 38 ♗b6 ♘e5 39 ♖c3 ♗b4 40 ♖c8+ ♔f7 41 ♔g2 Black resigns.

108

Short – Fenton
SCCU Under-14 Championship, England 1975

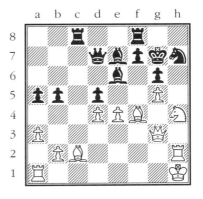

White to move

Nigel Short was only ten years old when he produced this spectacular finish against Paul Fenton.

37 ♘f5+!!

White accomplishes a lot with this move; it opens the h-file, activates the bishop on c2 and does away with the g6-pawn which frees the way for his own g-pawn.

37...gxf5

37...♗xf5 38 exf5 is crushing.

38 ♕h4

There are other wins but this is the most effective.

38...♖h8 39 ♕h6+ ♔g8 40 g6! Black resigns.

White's last move was the only move to win and for Black the only move to lose. There is no defence to 41 gxh7+ and 40...fxg6 is mate in two. Note that 40 ♗e5?? would have lost to 40...♗f8 41 ♕h5 ♖xc2! 42 ♖xc2 fxe4 43 ♗xh8 ♗g4 44 ♕h4 ♔xh8 followed by ....♗g4-f3+.

109

Andersson – Huss
Biel 1977

White to move

In practical chess a common problem is whether one should play pragmatic chess as, for example, Andersson and Karpov or try to find the optimal solution like Rubinstein or Kasparov. In the end everything is a matter of personality or how much energy or time you have on the clock.

19 ♗xf6

Andersson chooses a pragmatic solution but it's possible that a player like Kasparov would have chosen the more spectacular 19 ♘xg6!.

(a) 19...hxg6 20 ♖xe6 a4 21 ♕d3! (This is more devastating than the prosaic 21 ♖xe7+ axb3 22 ♖xe8+ ♔f7 23 ♗h6! g5 24 axb3) 21...♕xe6 22 ♕xg6+ which is where Andersson might have stopped calculating.

(b) However, White also wins after 19...♕f7 20 ♗xf6! (20 ♖xe6 ♖xe6 21 ♖xe6 is equally effective but one must see that 21...♗xg5 is met by the decisive 22 ♘e5!.) 20...hxg6 21 ♗e5 ♘d7 22 ♖f3 ♕e7 23 ♕c2 ♘xe5 24 ♖xe5 and the g6-pawn soon falls.

Apart from the two above-mentioned moves there are a couple of others which also win:

(a) 19 ♘g4 a4 20 ♕xe6+ ♕xe6 21 ♘xf6+ ♕xf6 (21...♔f7 22 ♘xe8) 22 ♖xe8+ ♕f8 23 ♗h6.

(b) 19 ♘xc6 ♕f7 (19...♘xc6 20 ♖xe6 a4 21 ♕d5! ♘b4 22 ♖xe7+ ♘xd5 23 ♖xe8+ ♖xe8 24 ♖xe8+ ♔f7 25 ♖e1 ♗xg5 26 ♖e5) 20 ♖xe6 ♖xe6 21 ♖xe6 ♘xc6 (21...♗xg5 22 ♘e5!) 22 ♗xf6.

19...♕xf6 20 ♘g4 ♕g5 21 ♖xe6 ♖xe6 22 ♕xe6+ Black resigns.

Otherwise he would have to look forward to a slow and painful mate in nine moves.

So which player were you when you solved this position with many wins? Were you the pragmatic-like Andersson or did you calculate some of the other moves in an effort to find out which was the best? There is no right or wrong, only taste and to a certain extent practicality.

110

A. Panchenko – Psakhis
USSR 1978

(1 e4 c5 2 ♘f3 b6 3 d4 cxd4 4 ♘xd4 ♗b7 5 ♘c3 d6 (5...a6!) 6 ♗g5 ♘d7 7 ♗c4 a6 8 ♕e2 b5 9 ♗d5! ♕c8 10 0-0 ♘gf6 11 ♖ad1 e6? (11...b4!)

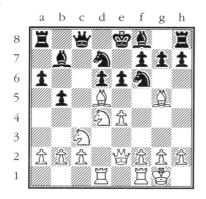

White to move

I remember when I bought my first *Chess Informant* as a junior. It was number 25, and I was so impressed with the way IM Panchenko outplayed Psakhis in the most artistic fashion.

12 ♘xe6! fxe6 13 ♗xe6

This was one of the first games that taught me that the pawn couple e6-f7 is the key to breaking the Sicilian Defence and it is especially the e6-pawn that is the heart of Black's position. Later on I learned from Koblencs (Tal's trainer) in the book *Study Chess with Tal* (Batsford 2013) that the advantage of having a bishop on e6, compared to a knight, is that the king cannot attack it with ...♔e8-f7 so it's harder for the king to castle artificially by escaping to g8. The super bishop on e6 obviously gives White ample compensation for the sacrificed d4-knight.

13...♕c5

White was threatening the decisive breakthrough 14 e5 so the queen had to move away from c8. Remember Morphy's concept of how to play when ahead in development!

14 ♘d5

Of course, the activation of the c3-knight to d5 is the main reason the e6-pawn is so valuable. This is the positional foundation for the sacrifice so it's not solely a matter of winning two pawns and placing the black king in jeopardy. Note also

171

that the queenside rook might be deployed on the third rank to exploit the position of Black's queen. There are so many strong side effects on the queenside despite the fact that the sacrifice took place in the heart of Black's position!

14...♗xd5 15 exd5 0-0-0

Black has escaped from the highly dangerous e-file but White is ready to launch an offensive on the queenside with his more active pieces and the available pawn breaks against the vulnerable b5-pawn.

16 ♖d3!

The attack continues with this rather elementary but strong rook-lift.

16...♔b7 17 ♖c3 ♕d4 18 a4!

A pretty move which endeavours to unlock the door on b5 which is the key to Black's defence. If White manages to eliminate the pawn on b5, the f1-a6 diagonal together with the open files will be decisive.

18...♕e5

18...bxa4 can be met by 19 ♖c6! ♘b8 20 ♖c4 ♕b6 21 ♖a1 ♘fd7

22 ♖axa4 and White's five attacking pieces are too much for Black's defence to handle without losing a huge amount of material.

If 18...♕xa4 then the best is to exchange off the Trojan bishop. After 19 ♗xd7 ♖xd7 20 ♗xf6 gxf6 White penetrates with 21 ♕e6 and Black cannot avoid material loss. For example 21...b4 22 ♖c6 ♖g7 23 ♕c8+ ♔a7 24 ♖c7+ ♖xc7 25 ♕xc7+ ♔a8 26 ♕d8+ ♔b7 27 ♕xf6 and the rook is lost.

19 ♗e3

Most of White's pieces are now pointing in the direction of the black king.

19...♘c5 20 axb5 a5

Black avoids the opening of lines as much as possible but it doesn't help after White's next strong move.

21 b6!

The b5-square is vacated for the queen.

21...♗e7

Yudovich's recommendation of 21...♕h5 intends to meet 22 ♕b5 with 22...♕e8. But stronger is 22 ♕c4 followed by ♖c3-a3, ♖f1-a1 and b2-b4.

22 ♖a1

The pedantic solution is 22 f4 ♕h5 23 g4 ♕e8, with total control of the centre, and only then 24 ♖a1.

22...♖a8

22...♘xe6 loses by force after 23 ♖xa5 ♖a8 24 ♖ca3 ♖xa5 25 ♖xa5 ♘c5 (25...♖a8 26 ♖xa8 ♔xa8 27 ♕a6+) 26 ♖a7+ ♔b8 27 b4!! A nice decoy to force the queen away from the e-file so that White can then penetrate after eliminating the knight with his bishop. This is actually the only move to win. 27...♕b2 28 h3 ♕b1+ 29 ♔h2 ♕xb4 30 ♗xc5 ♕xc5 31 ♕a6! (31 ♕xe7 ♕xb6 32 ♖a3 ♖e8 33 ♕xg7 ♕d4 34 ♖f3 also wins.) 31...♕xd5 32 ♖xe7 ♕a8 33 ♕c4 ♖c8 34 ♖c7 ♖g8 35 ♖a7 and Black loses material.

22...♘xd5 is also hopeless, e.g. 23 ♗xd5+ ♕xd5 24 ♗xc5 dxc5 25 ♖d3! ♕f7 26 ♖xa5 ♖xd3 27 ♕xd3 ♖d8 28 ♖a7+ ♔c6 29 ♕xd8.

23 ♕b5 ♖a6

Black allows a pretty finish rather than suffer the consequences of 23...♘xd5 24 ♖xc5 dxc5 25 ♕d7+ ♔xb6 26 ♗xd5 ♕c7 27 ♕a4 ♖hd8 (The best defence otherwise White plays 28 b4!.) 28 ♕b3+ ♔a6 29 ♗f4 ♗d6 30 ♕c4+ ♔b6 31 ♗xd6 ♖xd6. (The queen has to protect the b7-square.) 32 ♗xa8 and White wins due to his material preponderance.

24 ♕c6+ ♔b8 25 ♕c7+ ♔a8 26 b7+! ♘xb7 27 ♕c8+ **Black resigns.**

The finish is nice not only because of the back rank mate with the queen sacrifice but also because the dark-squared bishop on e3 was vital to create this mate.

111

Roederer – Nefzer
Lauda 1988

(1 e4 b6 2 d4 ♗b7 3 ♗d3 [The natural move, but another one which altogether avoids complications is the solid 3 f3.] 3...f5? 4 exf5! ♗xg2 5 ♕h5+ g6 6 fxg6 ♗g7 [Of course not 6...♘f6?? 7 gxh7+! ♘xh5 8 ♗g6 mate.] 7 gxh7+ ♔f8)

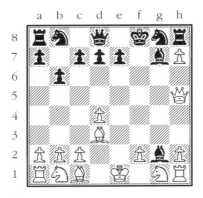

White to move

This position can arise just by playing natural moves, so it's important for White to know how to play this sharp position.

8 ♘f3!

One shouldn't capture the knight on g8 in this variation due to the fact that the h7-pawn is terribly strong and prevents Black's rook from being activated. 8 hxg8♕+? ♔xg8 9 ♕g4 ♗xh1 10 ♘e2 gives White a small advantage, but compare it with the main variation which leads to good chances of a checkmate.

8...♘f6

8...♗xh1? 9 ♘e5! ♗xe5 10 dxe5 and White mates in 12 moves after the best defence.

9 ♕g6

9...♗xh1?

It's fascinating to see that it's always bad to capture the rook in this variation. The continuation 9...♗xf3 10 ♖g1 ♖xh7 11 ♕g3 ♗e4 12 ♗xe4 ♘xe4 13 ♕f3+ is the point. (Black must pay the price that he has played 1...b6 but now has no bishop to cover the long white diagonal.) 13...♔g8 14.♕xe4 was the toughest defence but White is still winning due to Black's insecure king.

10 ♗h6!

Much stronger than 10 ♘e5? ♕e8.

10...♖xh7

10...♘e8 11 ♕f5+! ♘f6 12 ♗xg7+ ♔xg7 13 ♕g6+ ♔f8 14 ♕h6+ ♔f7 15 ♘g5+ ♔e8 16 ♗g6 mate.

11 ♘g5 ♗xh6 12 ♘xh7+ ♘xh7 13 ♕xh6+ ♔f7 14 ♕xh7+ ♔e6 15 ♕h6+ ♔d5 16 ♘c3+ ♔xd4 **Black resigns.**

Otherwise Black would be mated on e3.

112

Akopian – Kruppa
Minsk 1990

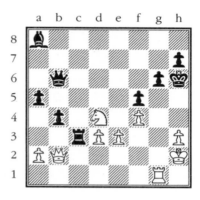

White to move

37 ♘xf5+!

Immediately decisive since the black king is stuck on the h-file.

37...gxf5 38 ♕f2 ♖c2

The natural defensive move 38...♕f6 doesn't work on account of 39 ♖g5. Note the importance of the f4-pawn. Without this it would be a different story. After 39...♕xg5 White wins further material with 40 fxg5+ ♔xg5 41 ♕f4+ ♔g6 42 ♕d6+ ♔h5 43 ♕e7!.

39 ♕xc2 ♕xe3 40 ♕b2!

White decides on the long dark diagonal.

40...♕xf4+

A nicer conclusion of the game would have been 40...♔h5 (40...♕e7 41 ♕f2!) 41 ♖g5+ ♔h4

42 ♖g4+! Here the king and the h3-pawn also contribute to the mate. All White's pieces are coordinating to make this sacrifice possible. 42...♔h5 (42...fxg4 43 ♕f6+ ♔h5 44 ♕g5 mate) 43 ♖h4+! ♔g6 44 ♖h6+! ♔f7 45 ♖xh7+ ♔e6 46 ♖h6+ ♔d7 47 ♕g7+ ♕e7 48 ♕d4+ and Black cannot avoid further material loss.

41 ♖g3 Black resigns.

After 41...♔h5 White wins by 2 ♕e2+.

113

Winants – Gooris
Chess Olympiad, Novi Sad 1990

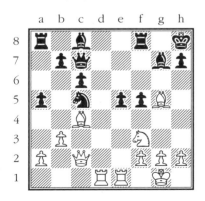

White to move

1 ♘xe5!

The computer prefers the move order 1 ♖xe5!! ♗xe5 2 ♘xe5 ♕xe5 3 ♗c1 etc.

1...♗xe5

The best defence was 1...♘e6 but after 2 ♗c1! Black's position is close to resignation. White has several strong mini-plans to improve his position and one of them is ♗b2 followed by the rook-lift ♖d1-d3-g3 or h3 when Black's position collapses.

2 ♖xe5 ♕xe5 3 ♗c1!

It's always beautiful to see decisive retreating moves although it's obvious the bishop wants to go to the long dark diagonal, when the enemy queen is in front of its own king.

3...♕e7 4 ♕c3+!

The most precise but 4 ♗b2+ also wins too: 4...♖f6 5 ♗xf6+ (5 ♕c3? ♘e4) 5...♕xf6 6 ♖d8+! ♔g7 (6...♕xd8? 7 ♕c3+) 7 ♖g8+ ♔h6

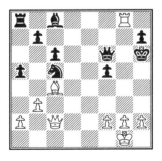

8 g4!! This incredible move is the only way to win. (8 ♕d2+? would have been met by 8...f4 so it's vital to get rid of the f-pawn by threatening g4-g5+ winning the

queen.) 8...♘e4 (The tactical idea is that 8...fxg4 is met by 9 ♕d2+ ♔h5 10 ♗f7+! ♔h4 11 ♖g6!! hxg6 12 ♕h6 mate. A very beautiful finish!) 9 ♕d3! ♕a1+ 10 ♔g2 ♕h1+ 11 ♔xh1 ♘xf2+ 12 ♔g2 ♘xd3 13 ♗xd3 fxg4 (There is no time for 13...b6 and 14...♗b7 due to 14 g5+ ♔h5 15 ♔g3 and White must sacrifice his bishop anyway by 15...♗a6 to prevent mate on e2.) 14 ♗f5 and White wins the endgame arising after 14...♗xf5 15 ♖xa8.

4...♖f6

If 4...♕g7 then 5 ♗b2.

5 ♕xf6+!! ♕xf6 6 ♖d8+! ♕f8

Two variations leading to mate are 6...♔g7 7 ♖g8 mate and 6...♕xd8 7 ♗b2+ ♕f6 8 ♗xf6 mate.

7 ♗b2 mate.

114

Kasparov – Anand
PCA World Championship,
New York 1995

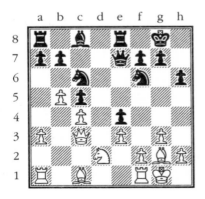

Black to move

15...♘e5!

It's absolutely best to sacrifice a pawn for activity. 15...♘b8 or 15...♘d8 are worse and passive options. Both retreats are answered by 16 ♗b2 with a comfortable edge for White.

16 ♘xe4 ♘f3+?

This was the first move Anand calculated and he was satisfied with the variations. His second option was 16...♗h3! but he didn't dig deeper since he didn't want to spend another 10-15 minutes calculating. This is actually the clever point of the sacrifice. Black uses tactical means to secure the exchange of the light-squared bishops. After 17 ♗xh3 (The tactical point is that 17 ♘xf6+ ♕xf6 18 ♗xh3 is answered by the discoverer 18...♘f3+ winning the queen.) 17...♘xe4 Black has more than enough compensation with two active knights in the centre. 18 ♕c2 ♘f3+ 19 ♔g2 ♕f6

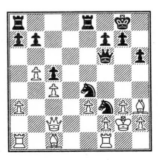

White's bishop pair has clearly not the same value as the knight pair. This is a position Anand certainly would have liked and incidentally such an episode exemplifies the drawback with a so called pragmatic decision. The pragmatic method, so popular today, saves time but loses precision.

17 ♗xf3 ♘xe4 18 ♗xe4 ♕xe4 19 f3 ♕e7 20 e4 ♗e6 21 ♗e3 Draw.

115

Caruana – Duda
Grand Chess Tour, Paris 2019

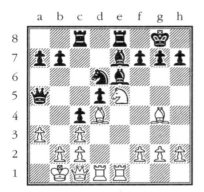

White to move

In this rapid game Caruana activated the queen with 19 ♕f4 and won convincingly after 45 moves. However, it was surprising that he missed the rather elementary...

19 ♘xf7!

...which didn't lead to such complicated variations since it's only a matter of analysing captures and threats.

19...♗xg4

19...♗xf7 20 ♖xe7 ♖xe7 21 ♕g5 and Black cannot defend the double threat on g7 and e7.

20 ♘xd6 ♗xd6

Or 20...♗xd1 21 ♘xc8.

21 ♕g5

Black cannot defend g7 and g4 with a queen move to d7. Even if this was a rapid game it's probably not an excuse to miss this tactical shot. Maybe it was because he trusted the calculating ability of his opponent who he did not know so well on this occasion?

116

Capablanca – Davis
Simultaneous exhibition,
Chicago 1910

(1 d4 d5 2 ♘c3 ♘f6 3 ♗g5 e6 4 e4
♗e7 5 ♗xf6 ♗xf6 6 ♘f3 0-0 7 ♗d3
c6 8 e5 ♗e7 9 h4 f5 10 exf6 ♗xf6)

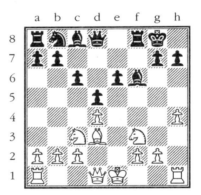

White to move

11 ♗xh7+?

It seems incredible but in this position the Greek gift sacrifice (or the classical bishop sacrifice) only leads to a draw. The chief reason is the strong bishop on f6 which covers the g7-pawn.

11...♔xh7 12 ♘g5+ ♔g8

Worse continuations were either 12...♔h6 13 ♕d3 ♗xg5 14 hxg5+ ♔xg5 15 ♖h7 or 12...♔g6? 13 ♕d3+.

13 ♕h5 ♗xg5??

13...♖e8 should have been played. The pawn on g7 is defended so White has no more than a draw by perpetual. 14 ♕f7+ ♔h8 15 ♘e2 looks dangerous for Black due to the threat of ♘e2-f4-g6 mate but this is easily parried by Black's knight after 15...♘d7 16 ♘f4 ♘f8, so the position is still equal because White can always draw by perpetual.

14 hxg5

White now has three attacking units, the queen, rook and g-pawn.

14...♖e8 15 g6 ♔f8 16 ♕h8+ ♔e7 17 ♕xg7+ ♔d6 18 ♕e5+ ♔d7 19 ♖h7+ ♖e7 20 0-0-0 ♕g8 21 ♖xe7+ ♔xe7 22 ♕g5+ ♔d7

Or 22...♔e8 23 ♖h1 ♘d7 24 ♖h7 (24 g7 ♔f7) 24...♕f8 25 g7.

23 ♖h1 ♔c7 24 g7 Black resigns.

117

Nimzowitsch – Tarrasch
St Petersburg 1914

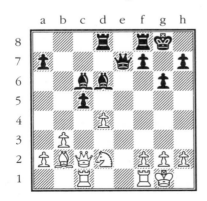

Black to move

25 years after the famous game Lasker – Bauer, Amsterdam 1889, where the double bishop sacrifice was first introduced in chess history, the Nimzowitsch – Tarrasch game featured this sacrifice again in St Petersburg 1914.

19...♗xh2+!

Interestingly 19...♗xg2! would also have worked. After 20 ♔xg2 ♕g5+ 21 ♔h1 ♕f4 22 ♘f3 ♕xf3+ 23 ♔g1 Black can sacrifice the other bishop too and win in the same manner as in the main variation. The cold-blooded 23...cxd4! leads to a position where White cannot prevent the bishop sacrifice on h2 . After, for example, 24 ♕c6 ♗xh2+ 25 ♔xh2 ♖d5 Black wins without any problems.

20 ♔xh2 ♕h4+ 21 ♔g1 ♗xg2! 22 f3

If White accepts the second gift with 22 ♔xg2 Black plays 22...♕g4+ 23 ♔h1 ♖d5 24 ♕xc5 ♖h5+ 25 ♕xh5 ♕xh5+ 26 ♔g2 ♕g5+ and wins in approximately the same manner as Lasker did against Bauer. 22 f4 ♕g3 threatens the deadly discoverer 34...♗e4+.

22...♖fe8!

178

Very good and instructive play at the same time! Tarrasch plays in the spirit of Morphy and introduces all pieces to the attack. The immediate threat is 23...♖e2 followed by mate on h1.

23 ♘e4 ♕h1+ 24 ♔f2 ♗xf1 25 d5

25 ♖xf1 is met by 25...♕h2+.

25...f5 26 ♕c3 ♕g2+ 27 ♔e3 ♖xe4+ 28 fxe4 f4+

A faster finish was 28...♕g3+ 29 ♔d2 ♕f2+ 30 ♔d1 ♕e2 mate.

29 ♔xf4 ♖f8+ 30 ♔e5 ♕h2+ 31 ♔e6 ♖e8+ 32 ♔d7

32 ♔f6 ♕h4 mate.

32...♗b5 mate.

118

Lind – T. Olsson
Malmo open 1976

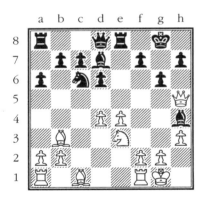

White to move

1 ♗xf7+!

Bishop sacrifices on f7 are very common and can also be regarded as magnet combinations when the king accepts the sacrifice.

1...♔g7

1...♔xf7 2 ♕xh7+ ♔e6 (2...♔f6 3 ♘d5+ ♔e6 4 ♘f4+ ♔f6 5 ♕xg6+ ♔e7 6 ♕g7 mate.) 3 d5+ ♔f6 (3...♔e5 4 dxc6) 4 ♘g4+ ♗xg4 5 ♕xh4+ ♔g7 6 ♕h6+ wins.

2 ♕h6+!!

This queen sacrifice is the nicest move in the combination. It paves the way for a deadly discoverer by the knight.

2...♔xf7

2...♔xh6 3 ♘f5+ ♔h5 4 ♘g7 is a very nice mate.

3 ♕xh7+ ♔f8 4 ♘f5! Black resigns.

Black cannot avoid being mated after three moves due to the undeveloped bishop on c1 being ready for the deadly final blow.

119

Benjamin – P. Cramling
Stockholm 1990

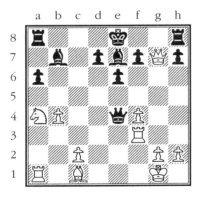

Black to move

Here Cramling missed the beautiful killer move...

16...♗f6!!

In the actual game 16...♖f8 was played and was good enough to play for a win. Cramling did indeed achieve this after 30 moves.

17 ♕xf6 ♖g8

White cannot defend against the rook sacrifice on g2 so it's necessary to defend the f3-rook with the queen and limit the damage on the kingside.

18 ♕c3 ♖c8 19 ♘c5 ♕xf3 20 ♕xf3 ♗xf3 21 g3 d6

Black wins due to her lead in material. What is amazing about the missed combination by Cramling is that she managed to play a similar combination against Ulybin 15 years later and win.

120

Muzychuk – Tan
Women's World Championship
2013

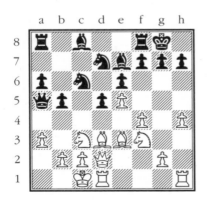

White to move

14 ♗xh7+!

The Greek gift is not often seen in high-level chess and if it is it's normally complicated. Here the position is out of the box due to the queen placement on d2, rather than d1 or e2, so accurate calculation is necessary before executing the bishop sacrifice.

14...♔xh7 15 ♕d3+

The computer prefers 15 ♘g5+ ♔g8 16 ♕e2 despite the fact that White is a tempo down compared with the normal pattern of the Greek gift, as we saw in Capablanca – Davis, exercise 116. However in this position it has no relevance because White is winning anyway. The only way to stop the queen from occupying the vacant square h5 is by 16...g6 but then White increases the power of his kingside rook with 17 h5. After the further 17...♗xg5 18 hxg6 fxg6 19 ♕g4 White's attack is overwhelming thanks to the pressure on the h- and g-files as well as on the e6-pawn, the heart of Black's position.

15...♔g8 16 ♘g5 f5

If 16...g6 then 17 h5 and White's attack plays itself.

17 ♘xd5! b4

17...exd5? 18 ♕xd5+ ♔h8 19 ♕f3 is curtains for Black.

18 ♘xe7+ ♘xe7 19 ♗d2?

Correct was the penetrating 19 ♕d6!.

19...♖b8?

It's a mystery why Black avoided the natural 19...♘d5. Black would not have had any problems after

20 ♕e2 (20 ♘xe6?? ♘xe5) 20...♖a7 21 ♕h5 ♘7f6 22 exf6 gxf6 with mutual chances.

20 ♕d6 ♕c5

21 ♗xb4

Another win was by 21 ♕xe6+ ♔h8 22 ♗xb4 ♖xb4 23 axb4 ♕xb4 24 ♘f7+ with the idea 24...♔h7 25 ♖d6! ♕xf4+ 26 ♔b1 ♖xf7 27 ♕xf7 ♕xe5 28 ♖e6.

21...♕xd6 22 ♗xd6 ♘g6 23 ♘xe6 ♖e8 24 ♗xb8 ♖xe6 25 g3

Black has two knights for a rook but White has four extra pawns.

25...♗b7 26 ♖h2 ♘c5 27 ♖d8+ ♔h7 28 ♗d6 ♘e4 29 h5 ♘h8 30 h6!

The h6-pawn is taboo due to the strong rook on d8.

30...♘f7 31 ♖d7 ♖xd6 32 ♖xf7 Black resigns.

Anyone interested in this 400-year-old idea, and I guess we all are, can specialise on this theme in the book *Sacking the Citadel* by Jon Edwards (Russell Enterprises, 2011). He takes you on a journey through the history, theory and practice of the classic bishop sacrifice.

121

Grischuk – Karjakin
FIDE Grand Prix, Baku 2014

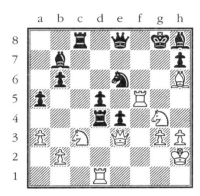

White to move

Grischuk missed a very beautiful instant win by...

32 ♗f8!!

The threat is 33 ♘h6 mate.

In the game followed 32 ♖df1 ♖d3 33 ♕xb6 ♕c6 (Black defends against the threat 34 ♕xe6+ ♕xe6 35 ♖f8+ and mate next move.) 34 ♕f2 ♕e8 35 ♘f6+? (This move throws away the win. Correct was the mobilisation of the other knight with 35 ♘b5!. The immediate threat is 36 ♘d6 and the knight is clearly taboo due to mate in three moves on f8.) 35...♗xf6 36 ♖xf6 ♖f3! 37 ♖xf3 exf3 38 ♕xf3 ♕g6 and the game ended in a draw after the further moves 39 ♖f2 ♗c6 40 ♕f6 d4 41 ♘b1 ♗d5 42 ♘d2 ♕xf6 43 ♖xf6 ♖c2 44 b4 axb4 45 axb4 ♖b2 46 g4 ♖xb4 47 ♔g3.

32...♕xf8

Black's best defence. 32...♘xf8 is met by 33 ♘h6+ ♔g7 34 ♖df1! with the deadly threat of 35 ♕g5+ followed by 26 ♖f7+.

33 ♘h6+ ♕xh6 34 ♕xh6

White wins easily. Black's bishop pair is unable to defend against the powerful queen. Why did the mighty Grischuk miss this short (only two squares) beautiful bishop manoeuvre from h6-f8? Because it's outside the box and not part of a typical pattern. This is the reason we must learn rare patterns or exceptions to the rule.

122

Capablanca – Raubitschek
New York 1906

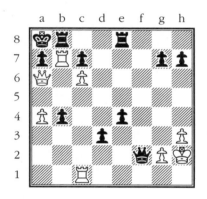

White to move

30 ♖f1! ♕d4?

30...♕e3 avoids a quick mate but if White finds the precise 34th move the game is still lost after 31 ♖f5 (Note that the threat is 32 ♖xa7+! ♕xa7 33 ♖a5 and not 32 ♖a5? because of the perpetual check after 32...♕f4+ and 33...♕c1+ etc.) 31...♖bc8 32 ♖xb4 ♖b8 33 ♖b7 ♖bc8 34 a5!! It's important to control the b6-square. 34...g5 35 ♖b1! White must also control the first rank to avoid perpetual check.

35...♖b8 36 ♖fb5 ♖xb5 37 ♕xb5 Black has no defence since 37...♕b6 (Or 37...♕f4+ 38 ♔h1 and Black has run out of checks.) loses the queen, which was the reason for the strong 34th move. Nor does the clever queen sacrifice 30...♕b6 help to save the game after. 31 ♖xb6 ♖xb6 32 ♕c4 b3 33 ♕f7 ♖c8 34 ♕d7 ♖bb8 (Or 34...♔b8 35 ♕xc8+! ♔xc8 36 ♖f8 mate.) 35 ♖b1 with the threat of 36 ♖xb3. The pawns are not as menacing as they look. After the further 35...♖d8 36 ♕xc7 d2 (36...e3 37 ♖xb3) 37 ♕f4!, for example, 37...d1♕ 38 ♖xd1 ♖xd1 39 c7 is mate in three. (Note the amusing trap 39 ♕xe4? ♖d4!! 40 ♕xd4 (40 ♕f3 ♖f4!!) 40...b2 41 ♕d5 b1♕ 42 c7+ ♕b7 43 cxb8♕+ ♔xb8 and Black has drawing chances in the queen ending.

31 ♖f5! e3 Black resigns.

White mates in three moves. The main variation is 32 ♖xa7+! ♕xa7 33 ♖a5 ♕xa6 34 ♖xa6 mate.

123

Capablanca – Redding
New York 1915

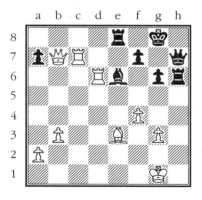

White to move

29 ♖xe6! Black resigns.

When asked what he would have done if Black had played 29...♖xe6, Capablanca astonished the audience by immediately replying that he would force checkmate in ten moves, commencing with 30 ♕b8+ ♔g7 31 ♗d4+ ♖f6 32 ♗xf6+. However according to the computer it's mate in nine moves if, after 32...♔xf6 33 ♕d8+ ♔f5 the move 34 ♕g5+! is played instead of the centralising (human) move 34 ♕d5+ which Capablanca had probably calculated.

124

Turapov – Serper
Uzbekistan Rapid Championship
1994

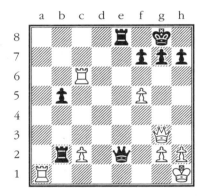

White to move

White missed the incredible move...

1 ♖e6!!

In the game 1 f6? was played and after 1...g6 Black was slightly better.

1...♖xe6

The point is that 1...fxe6 fails to 2 f6 g6 3 ♕c7. The queen's long arm can easily be missed even if you are on the winning side.

2 fxe6 fxe6 3 ♖a8+ ♔f7 4 ♖a7+ ♔f6 5 ♕f4+ ♔g6 6 h4!

And Black is soon checkmated.

125

D. Hersvik – Saevareid
Gausdal 2003

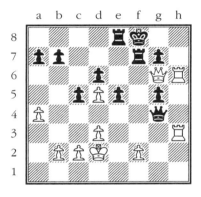

White to move

1 ♖f3!!

The idea of this amazing move is either to lure the queen away from the e6-square or to lure the rook away from the f7-square because then the rook on e8 will be lost. If White fails to find this spectacular rook sacrifice there is another win by quieter and simpler means by playing 1 ♕xd6+ ♖fe7 2 ♖h8+ (But not 2 ♖f6+? ♔g8 when White has problems with his two unprotected rooks and loses momentum in the position.) 2...♔f7 3 ♕xc5 etc. Wrong is 1 ♖h8+? ♔e7 2 ♖xe8+ ♔xe8 3 ♕e6+?? ♕xe6 4 dxe6 ♖xf2+ and Black wins. Of course 4...♖e7?? 5 ♖h8 mate should be avoided.

1...♕xf3

The other capture 1...♖xf3 is met by 2 ♖h8+ ♔e7 3 ♕xe8+ ♔f6 4 ♖f8 mate. Or 1...♕d7 2 ♖h8+ and the f7-rook is hanging.

2 ♖h8+ ♔e7 3 ♕e6+ ♔d8 4 ♕xe8+ ♔c7 5 ♕d8 mate.

126

Loyd – Moore
Elisabeth, New Jersey, 1876

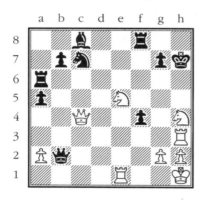

White to move

White can mate in three moves but incredibly the first move is not a check.

24 ♕e6!! Black resigns.

If Black captures the queen it's mate in two after 24...♖xe6 or 24...♘xe6 by 25 ♘hg6+ ♔g8 26 ♖h8 mate and after 24...♗xe6 by 25 ♘f5+ ♔g8 26 ♘e7 mate. There are prosaic mates in six moves with 24 ♘f5+ and in eight with 1 ♘hg6+ but Loyd's queen sacrifice in the heart of Black's position is not only the fastest but also the most beautiful way to decide the game. The move is quiet (no check) and the queen can be taken in three different ways on

the intersection square e6. Such mathematical and geometrical components are typical of Loyd's famous problems but here he managed to find a problem move in a game!

127

Rubinstein – Spielmann
San Sebastian 1912

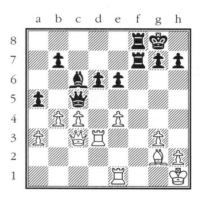

Black to move

25...♗xe4!!

Presumably Spielmann didn't want to play the automatic 25...axb4 due to 26 ♕xb4. Then the combination 26...♗xe4 would not end in a classic king-hunt, since White has the intermediate move 27 ♕xc5 when 27...♖f1+ isn't mate due to 28 ♕g1! (The queen's long arm!) In his classic book *The Art of Sacrifice in Chess* (Dover 1995) Spielmann admits that his sacrifice was largely based on intuition:

"The crowning point of this complicated sacrifice lies in the fact that through the sacrifice of a whole rook the hostile king is forced into the open. It is therefore a king-hunt sacrifice. I could not calculate the combination more exactly, and I had to rely entirely on my conviction that favourable variations would occur as a matter of course. And events proved me to be right."

26 ♖xe4??

Despite the fact that Black is attacking with all his three major pieces White can save himself by playing 26 ♗xe4 (Spielmann analyses 26 ♖f3 axb4 27 axb4 ♕c6 28 b5 (28 ♖xe4? ♕xe4 29 ♖xf7 ♕b1+) 28...♖xf3! 29 ♕xf3! ♗xf3 30 bxc6 ♗xg2+ but much better is 30...♗xc6 31 ♗xc6 bxc6 32 ♖xe6 ♖f1+ 33 ♔g2 ♖d1 when Black not only has an extra pawn but also the more active rook, which normally is a decisive advantage in rook endings with several pawns distributed over the board.) 26...♖f1+ 27 ♖xf1 ♖xf1+ 28 ♔g2 ♖g1+ 29 ♔f3 ♕h5+ and now:

(a) The English GM Neil McDonald analyses exclusively 30 ♔e3? ♕xh2 in *Rudolf Spielmann – The Master of Invention* (Everyman 2006) which according to the computer is a win. Spielmann too restricts himself to 30 ♔e3? ♕xh2 in his analyses from 1935.

(b) 30 ♔f4!! The computer evaluates this position as completely equal (0.00). For example:

(b1) 30...e5+ 31 ♔e3 ♕xh2 32 ♗d5+ ♔f8 33 ♔e4!! ♕e2+ 34 ♖e3 ♕g4+ 35 ♔d3 ♕d1+ 36 ♔e4 (36 ♕d2? ♕b1+ and Black wins the queen.) 36...♕g4+ is a draw by perpetual.

(b2) 30...g5+ 31 ♔e3 (31 ♔xg2 bxc6 32 ♖xe6 ♖f6 33 ♖e7 with some slight drawing chances.) 31...♕xh2 32 ♕f6! ♖e1+ 33 ♔d4 ♕b2+ 34 ♖c3 ♕d2+ 35 ♖d3 is a draw by perpetual.

26...♖f1+ 27 ♗xf1 ♖xf1+ 28 ♔g2 ♕f2+ 29 ♔h3 ♖h1!

This was Spielmann's stepping stone in his calculation and here he made the intuitive assessment that the seriously exposed king must succumb to an attack. 29...♕f5+? would be a mistake due to 30 ♖g4! when Black cannot win with best play.

30 ♖f3

The best defence but it's not enough.

30...♕xh2+ 31 ♔g4 ♕h5+ 32 ♔f4 ♕h6+ 33 ♔g4

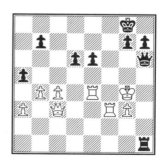

33...g5!!

Due to the mating threat on h5 White must sacrifice one of his rooks.

34 ♖xe6

The weaker defence 34 ♖f8+ ♔xf8 35 ♔f3 is met by 35...♕h5+ 36 ♖g4 ♖f1+ 37 ♔e2 ♕h3 38 ♕d2 ♕g2+ 39 ♔d3 ♖f2! with the idea 40 ♕xg5 ♕f1+ and it's mate in five.

34...♕xe6+ 35 ♖f5

McDonald calls this a "terminal pin". 35 ♔xg5 h6+ 36 ♔f4 axb4 37 axb4 h5

And now:

(a) 38 c5 is met by 38...♖e1 and due to the threat of 39...♕g4 mate White has to sacrifice the queen for the rook.

(b) If the king runs once more into the lion's mouth with 38 ♔g5 White will not be mated but lose his queen after 38...♕g4+ 39 ♔f6 (39 ♔h6 leads to a complete destruction of the white army after 39...h4) and now the deadly decoy 39...♖f1!! 40 ♖xf1 ♕g7+ leads to the win of the queen with the help of a skewer along the dark-squared diagonal.

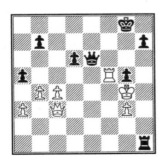

35...h6

Black plans a short king march to g6 but even more beautiful as well as more effective was the queen

manoeuvre from e4 to e8 by playing 35...♕e4+! 36 ♔xg5 h6+ 37 ♔f6 (37 ♔g6 ♕e8+ and mate on f7.) 37...♕e8!!. Black has no defence against mate on f7. Such backward queen moves are sometimes hard to find even when on the attacking side.

36 ♕d3 ♔g7 37 ♔f3

Spielmann gives 37 ♕d5 h5+ 38 ♔f3 ♖f1+ etc.

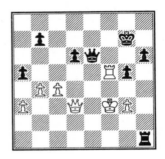

37...♖f1+

The pragmatic continuation. The best and most creative move was 37...♖h2! planning 38...g4+ 39 ♔xg4 ♖f2 followed by 40...♔g6.

38 ♕xf1

If 38 ♔g4 then 38...h5+! 39 ♔xg5 ♕h6+ 40 ♔h4 ♖h1 mate.

38...♕xf5+ 39 ♔g2 ♕xf1+ 40 ♔xf1 axb4 41 axb4 ♔f6 42 ♔f2 h5 White resigns.

A very nice win by Spielmann considering the fact that his opponent Akiba Rubinstein (1880-1961) was at his height during the years 1907-1912 and a serious candidate to play a world title match against Emanuel Lasker, if it weren't for WWI.

128

Canal – Amateur

Simultaneous exhibition,
Budapest 1934

(1 e4 d5 2 exd5 ♕xd5 3 ♘c3 ♕a5
4 d4 c6 5 ♘f3 ♗g4 6 ♗f4 e6 7 h3
♗xf3 8 ♕xf3 ♗b4 9 ♗e2 ♘d7 10 a3
0-0-0?? A serious error. 10...♗xc3+
should have been played.)

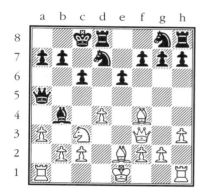

White to move

White has a forced win by
sacrificing both his rooks as well as
his queen to produce a beautiful
mate with the bishops.

**11 axb4! ♕xa1+ 12 ♔d2 ♕xh1
13 ♕xc6+! bxc6 14 ♗a6 mate.**

This mate is common on the
queenside and is called Boden's
mate because Samuel Boden (1826-
1882) was one of the first players in
chess history to carry out this
beautiful mate with a pair of bishops
in the game Schulder – Boden,
London 1853.

The first known game with this
kind of mate however was Horwitz –
Popert, Hamburg 1844.

129

Euwe – Keres

Match, Holland 1939/40

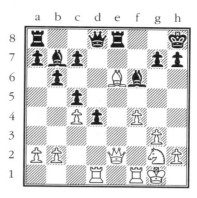

Black to move

Black can win in different ways
due to the strong pin on White's
bishop and the powerful extra pawn
on d4.

Keres chooses a tactical solution.

22...d3!!

The positional way was 22...♕d6
23 f5 g6 24 ♕d3 gxf5 25 ♗xf5 ♗g5
and Black is winning.

**23 ♖xd3 ♕xd3!! 24 ♕xd3 ♗d4+
25 ♖f2**

25 ♔h1 ♖xe6 and White has no
defence against the doubling of
rooks followed by an incursion on
the e2-square.

25...♖xe6 26 ♔f1 ♖ae8

26...♗xf2 27 ♔xf2 ♖ae8 also won
but Keres' move is more effective
since it exploits the harmony
between the rooks and the bishop.
Black plans to manoeuvre the bishop
to h3 via e4 and f5.

187

27 f5 ℤe5 28 f6

If 28 ℤf4 then 28...ℤe2.

28...gxf6 29 ℤd2 ♗c8!

Black plans mate with ...♗h3 and ...ℤe1.

30 ♘f4 ℤe3! 31 ♕b1

Or 31 ♕c2 ℤe1+ 32 ♔g2 ℤg1+ 33 ♔f3 ℤe3+ 34 ♔f2 ℤc3+.

31...ℤf3+ 32 ♔g2 ℤxf4! 33 gxf4 ℤg8+ 34 ♔f3 ♗g4+ White resigns.

The queen would have been lost after 35....♗f5+ if White's king enters the g-file. After 35 ♔e4 it's mate in three moves by 35...ℤe8+ 36 ♔d5 ♗f3+ 36 ♕e4 ♗xe4 mate.

130

Miles – Timman
Las Palmas 1977

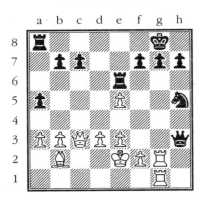

White to move

Black has managed to neutralise the pressure on the g-file and along the long dark-squared diagonal.

22 ♕xc7?

Miles is tempted by a combination but surprisingly it only leads to a draw. Correct was 22 ♕d4! after

which White has a very strong position in the centre whereas the black knight on the edge of the board only has a defensive function.

22...ℤc6 23 ℤxg7+

This is Miles' clever idea. 23 ♕xb7 would have been answered by ℤac8.

23...♘xg7 24 ℤxg7+ ♔xg7 25 e6+

The long diagonal is opened with a gain of tempo. White has two pieces and a pawn to attack Black's king but it's not enough to win.

25...♔h6!

The only square to escape from mate.

26 ♕f4+ ♔h5! 27 ♕xf7+ ♔g4!

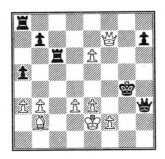

Unbelievably there is no mate in sight.

28 ♕g7+

28 f3+?? would have allowed the black king to escape to h1 after 28...♔g3 29 ♗e5+ ♔g2 30 ♕g7+ ♔h1.

28...♔f5 29 ♕e5+ ♔g6 30 ♕g7+ ♔f5 31 ♕f6+ ♔g4 32 ♕f4+ Draw.

Miles put a lot of time and effort into 32 ♗e5 but after this Black would have won by 32...♕h5! followed by ...♔h3+.

131

Popov – Novopashin
USSR 1979

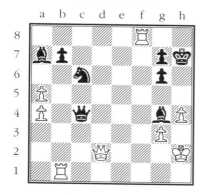

White to move

1 ♕h6+!! Black resigns.

It's a vertical mate upon 1...♔xh6 2 ♖h8 mate and a horizontal one after 1...gxh6 2 ♖xb7+ etc. Black's pieces are not cooperating well because the d7, e7 and f7 squares are controlled only once by Black's defending pieces. Mate is therefore inevitable.

132

Vyzmanavin – Tukmakov
Simferopol 1986

(1 d4 ♘f6 2 c4 g6 3 ♘c3 d5 4 ♗g5 ♘e4 5 ♗f4 ♘xc3 6 bxc3 dxc4 7 e3 ♗e6 8 ♖b1 b6 9 ♘f3 ♗g7 10 ♘g5 ♗d5 11 e4 h6 12 exd5 hxg5 13 ♗e5 ♗xe5 14 dxe5 ♘d7 15 e6 ♘e5 16 ♗xc4 ♘xc4 17 ♕a4+ ♔f8 18 ♕xc4 ♖h4 19 ♕d3 ♕d6 20 exf7 ♖d8 21 ♖d1 ♕e5+ 22 ♔f1 ♕e4 23 ♕d2 ♖f4 24 h4 gxh4 25 ♔g1 g5 26 ♖h3 c6 27 c4 ♕xc4 28 ♕b2 ♔xf7 29 ♖c3 ♖xd5 30 ♖e1 ♕d4 31 ♕e2 ♕xc3 32 ♕xe7+ ♔g8 33 ♖e6 ♖d1+ 34 ♔h2)

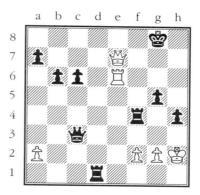

Black to move

34...♕h3+!!

A pretty move along White's third rank which forces mate next move with one of the rooks. One wonders if Carlsen had seen any of these predecessors before he played a similar queen sacrifice in game 4 of the rapid tiebreak against Karjakin in the World Championship in New York 2016. It was actually this kind of beautiful queen sacrifice that decided the match in Carlsen's favour.

133

Engqvist – Pyhälä
Sweden – Finland match, 1994

White to move

46 ♔h1??

Here I made the mistake of not moving out of range from the g4-knight with 46 ♔g1 followed by 47 a8♕ with an easy win. Instead, after the text move, I found myself at the mercy of the strong Finnish tactician Pyhälä's incredibly well coordinated knights.

46...♕b5!!

47 ♗a6

47 ♕xe3 ♘xe3 48 a8♕ ♕xb2 49 ♘g1 ♘g4 50 ♘f3 ♘e3 would also have led to a peculiar draw by repetition of moves. 47 ♕xb5 ♘f2+ 48 ♔g1 ♘h3+ 49 ♔h1 ♘f2+ is a draw by perpetual check in the same fashion as in the game.

47...♕xe2

47...♕xa6 48 ♕xa6 ♘f2+ with perpetual check also works.

48 ♗xe2 ♘f2+ 49 ♔g1 ♘h3+ 50 ♔h1 Draw.

I had to accept that my king couldn't escape the bold knight's checks. It's hard to forget such knights when something like this happens to you in real life!

134

Timman – Brobakken
Politiken Cup 2015

(1 d4 ♘f6 2 c4 e6 3 ♘f3 d5 4 ♘c3 c6 5 ♗g5 ♗e7 6 e3 0-0 7 ♗d3 ♘bd7 8 0-0 b6 9 cxd5 exd5 10 ♕a4 ♗b7 11 ♘e5 ♘xe5 12 dxe5 ♘d7?? [*12...♘h5* was necessary]).

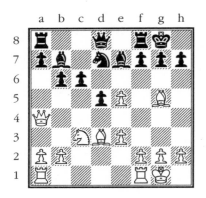

White to move

13 ♕h4! Black resigns.

The queen's long arm had a devastating effect in this miniature game. It's undeniably a beautiful queen manoeuvre from d1-a4-h4 and it clinches the game with the double threat on h7 and e7. It's easy to underestimate or overlook the significance of the newly opened fourth rank after the exchange on e5 if one is not alert or maybe just suffering from fatigue.

135

Planinc – Lutikov
Yugoslavia – USSR, Skopje 1969

(1 e4 ♘c6 2 d4 e5 3 dxe5 ♘xe5 4 ♘f3 ♕f6 5 ♘xe5 ♕xe5 6 ♗d3 ♗b4+ 7 ♘d2 ♘f6 8 0-0 d6 9 ♘c4

♕e7 10 c3 ♗c5 11 b4 ♗b6 12 a4
♗g4 13 ♕e1 c6 14 ♗g5 h6 15 ♗h4
♗c7 16 f4 g5 17 fxg5 hxg5 18 ♗xg5
d5 19 exd5 ♗xh2+ 20 ♔f2 ♗e6)

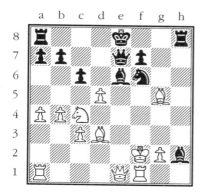

White to move

In this hair-raising position GM
Albin Planinc (1944-2008), known
for his originality, played a most
unexpected move.

21 ♔e2!!

"Unbelievable coolness!" as GMs
Mohr and Mikhalchishin comment
on the move in the biography
*Forgotten Genius – The Life and
Games of Grandmaster Albin
Planinc* (Thinkers Publishing 2021).
It turns out that Black's discoverers
(including a double check) are
completely harmless. Planinc was a
player whose play exhibited a lot of
imagination and creativity, so it's
not surprising that now and then
he found such an incredible
move! Satisfying enough for White
was the prosaic continuation 21 dxe6
♘g4+ 22 ♔e2 ♕xg5 23 exf7+ ♔f8
24 ♖f5 followed by 25 ♔d2. White
is two pawns up. If Black replies
24...♕h6 White has 25 ♔d1 and
♔c2. Another winning continuation
is 21 ♗xf6 ♕xf6+ 22 ♔e2 ♕g5

23 dxe6 fxe6 24 ♔d1 0-0-0
25 ♕xe6+ ♔b8 26 ♔c2 ♕xg2+
27 ♕e2. Considering these very
solid options it's even more
astonishing that he went for the
incredible move 21 ♔e2!!.

21...♗f5+

21...♗xd5+ 22 ♔d1! and the
f6-knight is lost, but not 22 ♔d2?
♘e4+.

**22 ♔d1! ♗xd3 23 ♗xf6 ♕xe1+
24 ♖xe1+ ♔f8 25 ♗xh8 ♗xc4
26 ♖h1 ♗b3+ 27 ♔c1 ♗d6 28 ♗f6
♔e8 29 ♖h8+ ♗f8 30 ♗g7 Black
resigns.**

136

Bogoljubow – Kmoch
San Remo 1930

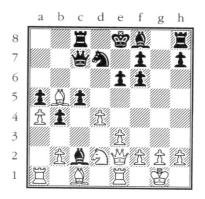

White to move

Here Black's king remains on e8
and Black has a hanging bishop on
c2 so the question is whether
White can exploit these motifs.
Bogoljubow found two excellent
pawn breaks...

19 d5! exd5

19...♗g6 is better from a short-term perspective but after 20 e4 followed by ♘c4 Black will be suffering the whole time until his inevitable defeat.

20 e4! d4

Black clearly wants to prevent White from opening lines but to no avail after...

21 e5!

Bogoljubow is playing in the spirit of Morphy, where the main aim is to open lines against the enemy king and exploit his superior piece activity.

21...fxe5 22 ♘f3

This double attack, the heart of all tactics, is decisive.

22...♗d6

If Black saves the bishop with 22...♗f5 then 23 ♘xe5 crashes through the centre.

23 ♕xc2 c4 24 ♕f5 Black resigns.

137

Alekhine – Sultan Khan
Berne 1932

(1 e4 c6 2 d4 d5 3 exd5 cxd5 4 c4 ♘f6 5 ♘c3 ♘c6 6 ♘f3 ♗g4 7 cxd5 ♘xd5 8 ♗b5 a6 9 ♗xc6+ bxc6 10 ♕a4 ♘xc3 11 ♕xc6+ ♗d7 12 ♕xc3 ♖c8 13 ♕e3 ♗b5 14 a4 ♗c4 15 b3 ♗d5 16 0-0 ♕b6 17 ♗d2 e6 18 ♖fc1 ♖b8 19 ♘e5 f6 20 ♘c6 ♖a8 21 ♘a5 ♔f7 22 ♘c4 ♕b7 23 ♕g3 ♗e7 24 a5 ♖ad8 25 ♘b6 ♗c6 26 ♖c4 ♖he8 27 ♖ac1 ♗b5 28 ♖c7 ♕e4)

White to move

Here White successfully attacks the strongpoint d5.

29 d5

Alekhine repeated this idea in several games.

29...♔g8

According to Alekhine Black's best practical chance was 29...exd5 30 ♖e1 ♗e2 (30...♕f5 31 ♖b7 followed by 32 ♕c7 is devastating.) 31 ♘a4! d4 32 ♘c5 ♕c2 (32...♕g4 33 ♕xg4 ♗xg4 34 ♘xa6 and White should win with his two queenside passed pawns.) 33 ♖xe2 ♕d1+ 34 ♖e1 ♕xd2 35 ♔f1! "and Black would be defenceless against the many threats. The remaining moves would probably be 35...♔g8 36 ♘e6 g6 37 ♘xd8 ♕xe1+ 38 ♔xe1 ♗d6+ 39 ♔d2 ♗xg3 40 hxg3 ♖xd8 41 ♖c6 ♖d5 42 b4 after which Black would have to resign."

30 ♖e1

30 d6! would have continued the attack on Black's strongpoints and was more in line with the earlier

play. 30...♗f8 (30...♖xd6 31 ♖xe7)
31 d7 ♖e7 32 ♖c8 and White wins
material.

**30...♕f5? 31 ♗b4! ♖d7 32 ♖xd7
♗xd7 33 ♗xe7 exd5**

Or 33...♖xe7 34 ♘xd7 ♖xd7
35 ♕b8+.

34 ♕d6 Black resigns.

138

Alekhine – Podgorny
Prague 1943

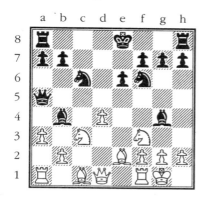

White to move

11 d5!

Alekhine's opponent probably
felt discombobulated after this
surprising move, which attacks a
strongpoint. It's connected to a
strategy which was used by the
Alexander the Great (356 BC – 323
BC). He often used to attack the
strongest point instead of the
weakest as advocated by Steinitz.
The point of Alexander the Great's
reversed strategy was that a great
reward was expected for the attacker
who succeeded. He reasoned that the

general and his advisors had
stationed their forces behind the
strongest point. If a swift attack
succeeded in this area the battle
would be decided. This may be
worth thinking about in chess too
since there may be exceptions to the
rule based on Steinitz's famous
attacking principles. Alekhine had
just advanced his pawn to d5 despite
the fact that Black is stronger there.
Black has the possibility of castling
queenside or placing a rook on d8
and can also exchange on c3 to make
the d5-point even weaker, so it
seems contradictory to attack this
square but look what happened in
the game...

11...exd5

(a) 11...0-0-0 12 axb4! ♕xa1
13 ♕b3 and White wins.

(b) 11...♖d8 12 ♕b3 ♗xc3
13 dxc6 also wins.

(c) 11...♘xd5 12.♘xd5 exd5
13 ♘d4! (More precise than 13 axb4
which also wins.) 13...♗xe2
14 ♕xe2+ ♔f8 15 ♘f5 ♗e7 16 b4
♕c7 17 ♗b2 f6 18 ♖fe1 and White
wins.

12 axb4! ♕xa1 13 ♘d2

Another winning continuation
competing with Alekhine's move
was 13 b5 ♗xf3 14 bxc6 bxc6
15 ♗xf3 0-0 16 ♘e2 and White has
a positional advantage which
compensates for the two pawns
deficit.

13...♗xe2 14 ♕xe2+ ♘e7

14...♔f8 15 ♘b3 ♕a6 16 b5 ♕b6
17 ♘a4 and White wins a piece.

15 ♖e1

Black has problems with the king and the queen. White could have played on with queens on the board by 15 ♕b5+ ♘d7 16 ♖e1 but apparently Alekhine prefers a more simplifying approach.

15...0-0 16 ♘b3

Naturally not 16 ♕xe7?? ♖fe8 and Black wins.

16...♕a6 17 ♕xa6 bxa6 18 ♖xe7

The endgame is technically winning with knight and bishop versus rook.

18...♖ab8 19 b5

19 ♘a2 was more precise because the a7-pawn will not run away.

19...axb5 20 ♖xa7 b4 21 ♘e2 ♖fc8 22 f3 ♖a8 23 ♖xa8 ♖xa8 24 ♔f2 ♘d7 25 ♘f4 ♘b6 26 ♔e3 ♖c8 27 ♔d3 g5 28 ♘h5 Black resigns.

An instructive example showing how Alexander the Great's strategy can be applied with success. By the way, Igor Zaitsev has written a book entitled *Attacking the Strongpoint* for anyone interested in specialising

in this rather deep strategy. Zaitsev came to the conclusion in the mid-1960s "that a well-planned breakthrough of a strongpoint is one of the basic active instruments of strategy".

139

Polugaevsky – Tal
USSR Championship 1969

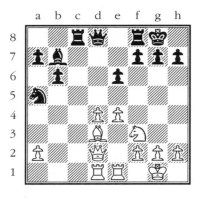

White to move

Here we see Alexander the Great's idea repeated but in another form.

16 d5!

White has a so-called neo-classical centre where it's sometimes clever to sacrifice the d4-pawn by pushing it to d5, despite the fact that Black has a strong hold on d5. The pawn-push is tactical because it's a pawn sacrifice but at the same time it's positional since it has a long-term effect.

16...exd5 17 e5!

Black's bishop and queen have a significantly lower activity because the d5-pawn is in the way. At the same time White's bishop has become strong and the e5-pawn is to be reckoned with in the forthcoming kingside attack. The game continued...

17...♘c4 18 ♕f4 ♘b2 19 ♗xh7+

The Greek gift.

19...♔xh7 20 ♘g5+

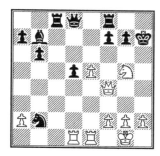

20...♔g6

The only move. 20...♔g8 would lose on the spot after 21 ♕h4 ♖e8 22 ♕h7+ ♔f8 23 e6! fxe6 24 ♕h8+ ♔e7 25 ♕xg7+ ♔d6 26 ♘f7+ and Black's queen is lost. Polugaevsky, who annotates this game in his classic *Grandmaster Preparation* (Pergamon 1981), writes: "The first impression is that nothing comes out of White's attack, but he has at his disposal a prepared move of terrible strength."

21 h4!!

"This is the point of the combination", writes Polugaevsky. It's an elegant but typical quiet move when playing the Greek gift sacrifice. White's immediate threat is 22 h5+ ♔xh5 23 g4+ followed by mate in a couple of moves.

21...♖c4

22 h5+?

Stronger was 22 ♖d4! ♖xd4 23 ♕xd4 because 23...♘c4 would lead to a forced mate after 24 ♕d3+ ♔h5 25 ♕h7+ ♔g4 26 f3+ ♔g3 27 ♕f5 ♗c8 28 e6 ♗xe6 29 ♖xe6 etc., but not 29 ♘xe6?? ♕xh4 and Black would win.

22...♔h6

22...♔xh5? leads to mate in four moves after the sequence 23 g4+ ♔g6 24 ♕f5+ ♔h6 25 ♘xf7+ ♖xf7 26 ♕h5 mate.

23 ♘xf7+ ♔h7 24 ♕f5+ ♔g8 25 e6

The e-pawn is certainly to be reckoned with!

25...♕f6

On 25...♕e7 the piquant 26 h6!, with the threat 27 h7 mate, is devastating.

26 ♕xf6 gxf6 27 ♖d2 ♖c6!

Worse is 27...♘a4 28 ♘d6 ♗c6 29 e7 ♖e8 30 ♘xe8 ♗xe8 31 ♖xd5.

28 ♖xb2

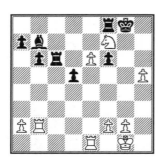

28...♖e8

A lesser evil was 28...♗c8 which could have been answered by 29 ♘h6+! ♔h8 30 e7 ♖e8 31 ♖d2 ♔h7 32 ♘f7 ♔g7 33 ♘d8 ♖c7 34 ♘e6+ ♗xe6 35 ♖xe6 ♖exe7 36 ♖xe7+ ♖xe7 37 ♖xd5 with good winning chances in the rook ending due to the fact that White has possibilities of creating two passed pawns on the kingside.

Black can win one pawn back with 37...♖e1+ (37...♖e4 38 g3! ♖a4 39 ♔g2 ♔h6 40 ♔f3 ♖a3+ 41 ♔g4 ♖xa2 42 f4 ♖a5 43 ♖d6 ♔g7 44 ♔h4 and White wins.) 38 ♔h2 ♖e2 39 f4 ♖xa2 but after 40 ♔h3 White's position looks very promising indeed.

29 ♘h6+ ♔h7 30 ♘f5 ♖exe6 31 ♖xe6 ♖xe6 32 ♖c2 ♖c6 33 ♖e2 ♗c8 34 ♖e7+ ♔h8?

Black loses an important tempo. 34...♔g8 should have been played. A possible line is 35 ♘h4 f5 36 ♖xa7 d4 37 ♔f1 f4 38 ♘g6 ♖c1+ 39 ♔e2 ♗g4+ 40 f3 ♗xh5 41 ♘xf4 ♗f7 and it's not completely over due to Black's passed pawn.

35 ♘h4 f5 36 ♘g6+ ♔g8 37 ♖xa7 Black resigns.

140

Taylor – Yoos
Chicago 1990

(1 d4 ♘f6 2 c4 e6 3 ♘c3 ♗b4 4 e3 b6 5 ♘e2 ♗b7 6 a3 ♗e7 7 d5 0-0 8 g3)

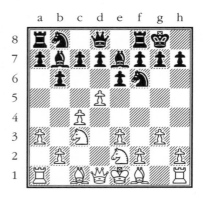

Black to move

8...b5!

This flank move weakens the white pawn centre in hypermodern style and came as a complete surprise for Taylor, athough it had been played before in Leningrad 1939 between Reshevsky and Kan.

9 ♗g2!?

The best move according to Taylor. White sacrifices the c4-pawn to catch up in development. 9 cxb5? ♘xd5 10 e4 ♘xc3 11 ♘xc3 ♗f6 was the continuation in the game from 1939 where Black got the slightly better position. The game ended in a draw after 31 moves. Other interesting options were 11...a6!? or 11...f5!?

Gyimesi – Dinstuhl, Budapest 1994, continued 9 b3 bxc4 10 bxc4

♘a6 11 ♗g2 ♘c5 and Black secured the c5-square for his knight. The game ended in a draw after 43 moves.

9 ♘f4 leads to equal play after 9...bxc4 10 ♗xc4 exd5 11 ♘cxd5 c6 12 ♘xe7+ ♕xe7 13 0-0. White has the bishop pair as compensation for Black's strong pawns on the c- and d-files.

9...bxc4 10 0-0 exd5 11 ♘xd5 c6 12 ♘xe7+ ♕xe7

13 b3!

This is the main idea of Taylor's pawn sacrifice to get enough play for the pawn deficit.

13...cxb3 14 ♕xb3 ♗a6 15 ♖e1 d5 16 ♗b2

White has enough compensation for the pawn and he managed to win the game after 51 moves. This was a triumph for Taylor after the cold shower on the eighth move. He writes in his book *Pawn Sacrifice - Winning at Chess the Adventurous Way* (Everyman 2008) that Reshevsky must have been surprised too but he managed to draw. The main difference was that Taylor played with calculated risk when he opted for 9 ♗g2 and confused his opponent.

141

Gunina – P. Cramling
Women's World Championship
2015

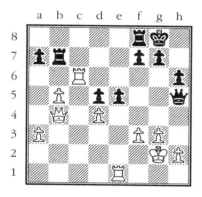

Black to play

32...e4! 33 fxe4 dxe4?

The correct follow-up was the highly original pawn break 33...f5!! opening up the f-file against White's king. 34 exf5 (34 exd5 f4 as well as 34 e5 f4 lead to a dangerous attack for Black.) 34...♕xf5 and Black secures the draw by penetrating either on f3 or f2. A telling variation is 35 ♕b2 ♖xb5! 36 ♕xb5 ♕f3+ 37 ♔h3 ♕h5+ (Note the devilish trap 37...♖f5? 38 ♖xh6!! and White wins after 38...gxh6 39 ♕e8+ ♖f8 40 ♕g6+) 38 ♔g2 ♕f3+ with perpetual check.

34 ♖xe4 ♖d8

34...♖xb5? doesn't work on account of 35 ♕xf8+! ♔h7 (35...♔xf8?? 36 ♖c8 mate.) 36 ♖c2 ♕d5 37 ♖ce2 f5 38 ♕e7 fxe4 39 ♕xe4+ ♕xe4+ 40 ♖xe4 and White has an extra passed pawn in the rook ending.

35 ♖c5 ♕d1

36 d5?

Maybe White was thinking that a major piece should remain behind a passed pawn but this is not really valid here due to White's exposed king. The beautiful gradual manoeuvring move 36 ♕c4!, planning ♖c5-c8, would have secured a slight advantage due to White's extra pawn. It's interesting that first Black had the chance to break through on the f-file and then White on the c-file, so it's like a mirror image of Black's play. Sometimes chess is a very geometric game!

36...♖bd7 37 ♕d4

37 ♖d4 is met by perpetual check, for example 37...♕e2+ 38 ♔g1 (38 ♔h3?? ♕f1+) 38...♕e3+.

37...♕b3!

Here the queen is very strongly placed since it destroys the harmony in White's position. Moreover it contains a double threat against the vulnerable d5 and a3 squares.

38 ♖e5 ♕xa3

The players continued their fight until the 117th move when they finally agreed to split the point.

142

Hillarp-Persson – Short
Xtracon Chess Open 2017

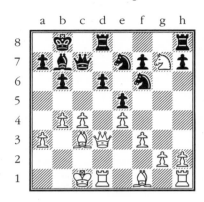

Black to play

20...d5!!

Black attacks White's strongpoint on d5 by opening up the position in front of White's king.

21 exd5 ♘fxd5 22 cxd5 ♘xd5 23 ♕c4

Here Short missed the super move...

23...♕e7!

It's irrelevant that the white knight comes to f5 with a tempo since the big problem for White isn't only the knight on g7 but rather the fact that three white pieces are placed on the c-file. In the game 23...♘xc3? was played with the continuation 24 ♕xc7+ ♔xc7 25 ♖d2 ♔b8! Short displays a very nice feel for the security of his king! 26 ♘f5 e4 The game was equal but in the time scramble Short won after 37 moves.

24 ♔b2

24 ♘f5 is met by 24...♕e6.

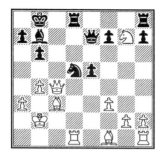

24...♘e3!

Maybe Short analysed the advantageous variation 24...♖c8? 25 ♖xd5 ♖xc4 26 ♖xe5!! ♕c7 27 ♘e8! so much that he missed the strong 24th move!

25 ♖xd8+ ♖xd8 26 ♕b3 ♗d5 27 ♕a4 f6 28 ♗d2 ♘xf1 29 ♖xf1 ♕xg7 30 ♖f2 ♕e7

This variation is undoubtedly not easy to find, especially with little time on the clock, but the main thing is to exploit the exposed position of the king, which is clearly a telling factor in Black's favour.

143

Capablanca – Euwe
Amsterdam 1931

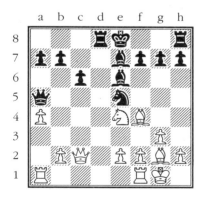

White to play

16 b4!

The pawn push to b4 and then b5 is known as the minority attack. However, sometimes the pawn push b2-b4 can work for tactical reasons as in this instructive example.

16...♗xb4

16...♕c7 was the best defence but then White has his minority attack for free. 17 b5 0-0 Now Pillsbury's idea 18 a5 followed by 19 a6 is stronger than the immediate capture on c6. After the practically forced 18...a6 19 bxa6 bxa6 20 ♘c5 ♗c8 21 ♕c3 f6 22 ♖fc1 followed by 23 ♖ab1 and 24 ♖b6 the positional pressure on Black's position is unbearable.

17 ♕b2

This is the tactical point. White exerts pressure on the pieces which are not defended by any pawns.

17...f6

18 ♗xe5

In the game 18 ♖fb1? was played and Euwe replied 18...0-0. Capablanca must have overlooked that 19 ♕xb4?? wasn't a threat due to the tactical resource 19...♖d1+.

199

White could have retained a large advantage by playing 18 ♖ab1 instead.

18...fxe5 19 ♖ab1

The right rook! White is positionally winning, since the b7-pawn will eventually fall. For example: 19...♖d4 (If 19...♗e7 then 20 ♕xb7.) 20 e3 ♖c4 21 ♘g5

White's attack on the king is too strong, so the price of not losing the b7-pawn will lead to other unsolvable problems instead.

144

Kramnik – J. Polgar
Rapidplay, Paris 1994

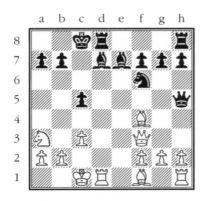

White to play

Kramnik must have regretted he didn't notice the incredible pawn push...

13 g4!!

In the game 13 ♘b5 ♗xb5 14 ♗xb5 ♕xf3 15 gxf3 ♘d5 16 ♗g3 ♘b6 17 ♗d3 g6 was played with a slight advantage to White thanks to his possession of the bishop pair in an open position.

The game ended in a draw after 55 moves.

13...♕xg4

13...♘xg4 relieves the tension between the queens and makes possible the decisive move 14 ♗a6!. It's mate in two or else mate one move earlier after 14...bxa6 15 ♕a8 mate. 13...♗xg4 runs into Boden's famous mate with the pair of bishops (and rook) after the queen sacrifice 14 ♕c6+! bxc6 15 ♗a6 mate. 13...♕g6 is met by 14 ♗g2! (14 ♗a6? ♕e4!) 14...♗c6 15 ♘b5!! ♗d6 (15...♗xb5 16 ♕xb7 mate 15...♗xf3 16 ♘xa7 mate) 16 ♘xa7+ ♔c7 17 ♖xd6! ♗xf3 18 ♖xf6+ ♔d7 19 ♖xg6 fxg6 20 ♗xf3 ♖hf8 21 ♖d1+ ♔e8 22 ♖e1+ ♔d7 23 ♗g5 and White wins.

14 ♘b5!! ♗xb5

14...♕xf3 15 ♘xa7 mate.

15 ♗h3 ♗d7 16 ♗xg4 ♗xg4 17 ♕e3!

White wins due to his material superiority.

145

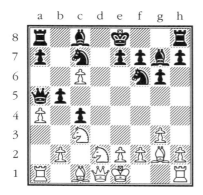

White to move

11 b4!

White plays for fast development so he can exploit the strong c6-pawn and give it more support. Black's king hasn't yet castled so White has several strong motifs to open new lines.

11...cxb3

Worse is 11...♕xb4 12 ♘xb5 ♘xb5 13 axb5 ♕xb5 14 c7 ♘d5 15 ♖b1 ♕d7 16 ♘xc4 and White is winning. One plausible variation is 16...♘xc7 17 0-0 0-0-0 18 ♗xa8 ♘xa8 19 ♕xd7 ♗xd7 20 ♗a3 ♗e6 21 ♖fc1 ♗f6 22 ♖b7 and Black's position falls apart.

11...♕b6 doesn't help either after 12 0-0 (Of course not 12 axb5?? ♘g4 and Black wins.) 12...a6 13 axb5 axb5 14 ♖xa8 ♘xa8 15 ♘db1! 0-0 16 ♘a3 ♗a6 17 ♗f4 with a positional win for White. The c6-pawn is strong and healthy and

Black is chained to the defence of the b5-pawn.

12 ♗b2

This is the idea. White wants to recapture the b3-pawn with the knight in order to increase the attack on the queenside.

12...♗e6

12...b4 is hardly an improvement and Black probably has to suffer more after 13 ♘xb3 ♕b6 14 ♘b5 0-0 (A beautiful variation showing the potential of White's position is 14...♘xb5 15 axb5 ♕xb5? 16 c7 ♗b7 17 ♖xa7!! and it's mate on d8 if Black accepts.) 15 ♗d4 ♕b8 16 0-0. The c6-pawn secures the win sooner or later.

13 axb5 ♕b6 14 ♘xb3 ♘xb5?

More resilient was 14...♖d8 15 ♕c2 a6 to exploit the hanging knight on b3. However, if White finds the super move 16 e3!!, with the idea of 16...axb5 17 ♘e2 ♗c4 18 ♗d4, he has very good winning chances.

15 ♘a4

Bareev converted his winning advantage after 49 moves.

146

Capablanca – Nimzowitsch
Bad Kissingen 1928

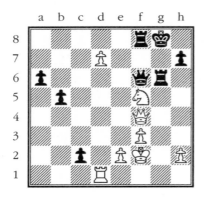

White to play

During the penultimate round in Bad Kissingen 1928 Spielmann and other players, who had finished their games, followed the dramatic encounter between Capablanca and Nimzowitsch. It seemed that Capablanca was in serious trouble and that only Nimzowitsch could win.

Black has an extra exchange and an annoying pin on the knight. Black's c-pawn seems more dangerous than White's d-pawn. Nimzowitsch had moved 34...c2 and the grandmasters went into a neighbouring room and analysed the position. They came up with 35 ♖c1? ♖g5 36 e4 ♛b6+ and White is forced to exchange queens with 37 ♛e3 when Black wins due to his material superiority. They expected Capablanca to lose.

Capablanca swiftly played **35 ♖d6!** and the game continued...

35...♛d8

(a) 35...♛xd6 36 ♘xd6 ♖xf4 37 d8♛+ ♖f8 38 ♛c7 ♖xd6! 39 ♛xc2! with a draw.

(b) 35...♛xf5 36 ♛xf5 ♖xd6 37 ♛xc2 ♖xd7 38 ♛a2+ ♖ff7 39 ♛xa6 ♖b7 when a draw is the most likely result.

(c) 35...c1♛? 36 ♛xc1 ♛xf5 37 d8♛ ♖xd8 38 ♖xd8+ ♔g7 39 ♛c7+ ♔h6 40 ♖d7 ♖f6 and White has the advantage due to Black's exposed king.

36 ♛e5!!

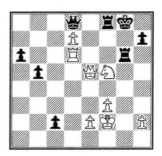

36...♖xf5

36...♖g2+?! 37 ♔xg2 ♛g5+ 38 ♔f2 c1♛ 39 ♘h6+! ♛xh6 40 d8♛ ♖xd8 41 ♖xd8+ ♛f8 (41...♔f7? 42 ♖d7+ ♔g8 43 ♛d5+! and Black is mated on the last rank.) 42 ♖xf8+ ♔xf8 43 ♛h8+ ♔f7 44 ♛xh7+ ♔f6 and Black has chances to draw thanks to his strong passed b-pawn.

Of course not 36...c1♛? 37 ♖xg6+ and mate next move.

37 ♖xg6+ hxg6 38 ♛e8+ ♖f8 39 ♛xg6+ Draw.

Spielmann writes that the miracle has happened. Capablanca had displayed his customary lightning-like perception of the board that other grandmasters were unable to see.

147

Petrosian – Veresov
USSR Championship 1947

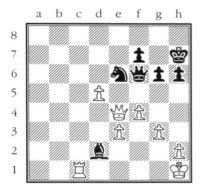

White to move

Don't forget that a pawn placed on the fifth rank is only three steps from queening and this fact alone is sometimes enough for a decisive combination.

37 ⬜d1!

There is a trap in the position since the seemingly good 37 dxe6? ♗xc1 38 e7 is met by the long arm of the queen, namely 38...♕a6! 39 ♔g1 ♕e2 40 e8♕ ♕e1+ and Black draws by perpetual check.

37...♘c5 38 ♕d4! Black resigns.

After 38...♕xd4 39 exd4 ♘e4 40 ⬜xd2! ♘xd2 41 d6 the d-pawn is unstoppable.

148

Chiburdanidze – Goldin
Palma de Mallorca 1989

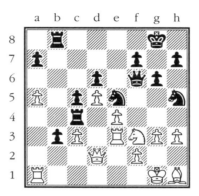

Black to move

In this position Black's rooks are the true heroes.

29...⬜a4!! 30 ⬜xa4

Forced as White cannot allow the black knight to c4.

30...b2 31 ⬜e1 b1♕

The most precise but another win was 31...♕xf3 32 ⬜b1 ♘xg3 33 fxg3 ♕xg3+ 34 ♔f1 ⬜f8!! 35 ⬜xb2 f5 with a winning attack.

32 ⬜xb1 ⬜xb1+ 33 ♘e1

33...♘d3!!

Very nice!

**34 ♕xd3 ♖xe1+ 35 ♔g2 ♖xh1!
36 e5**

If 36 ♔xh1 then 36...♕xf2 and
37...♘xg3+.

36...♖h2+!

Black finishes his beautiful
manoeuvre from b8-b1-e1-h1-h2 by
sacrificing the rook itself.

Both rooks were the true heroes
but in completely different ways!

The first rook was sacrificed on
the a-file to pave the way for
the passed pawn to promote, while
the other rook forced the king to
cede its protection of the important
f2-pawn.

This model game shows how
rooks should be sacrificed and not
only when they are placed on their
original squares.

There is even a book on this theme
of sacrificing two rooks when they
are placed on a1(a8) and h1(h8)
written by Seirawan and Minev.

149

Alekhine – Van Mindeno
Simultaneous exhibition,
Holland 1933

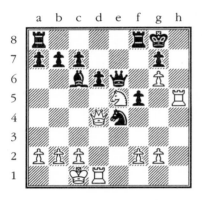

Black to move

16...dxe5??

After this fatal mistake Alekhine
announced checkmate in five
moves. Correct was 16...♕xa2!
threatening mate.

(a) 17 ♕c4+ ♕xc4 18 ♖dh1 is met
by 18...♕f1+!. It is necessary to see
this finesse otherwise Black would
be lost. 19 ♖xf1 ♘f6 (After this
move White cannot organise his
pieces for a mating attack along the
h-file.) 20 ♖h2 (20 ♖h4 ♗xg2)
20...♖fe8 21 ♖fh1 ♔f8 and Black
wins with his extra material.

(b) 17 b3 is met by 17...♘f6
and following 18 ♖h2 (18 ♖h4
♗xg2) 18...♗e4 19 ♕c3 ♗xc2!
is the most effective. 20 ♖dh1
(20 ♕xc2 ♕xc2+ 21 ♔xc2
♖fe8) 20...♕b1+ 21 ♔d2 ♘e4+
22 ♔e3 f4+ 23 ♔d4 c5+ 24 ♔c4 d5+

and White's queen is captured with check. Besides that White's king will fall within at most six moves.

17 ♖dh1

Black is clearly lost, because Black's queen must cover the classical diagonal.

17...♕xg6

There is nothing else to prevent mate on h8.

18 ♕c4+ ♗d5 19 ♕xd5+ ♕e6 20 ♕xe6+ ♖f7 21 ♖h8 mate.

150

Yusupov – Rebel 8
Match, Ischia 1997

White to move

22 ♕xd1!

Yusupov missed the winning continuation due to time pressure, since it was rapid chess with 30 minutes for the whole game. However, he did analyse this and a couple more moves besides, but

eventually settled for 22 ♗h7+ ♔h8 23 ♗g6+ ♔g8 with a draw.

22...♗g5

The only move.

23 ♘d5!

23 fxg5?? ♖f1+.

23...♕d8

Here Yusupov didn't see anything decisive and that's the reason he preferred to draw by perpetual check. He overlooked he could play an intermediate check...

24 ♗h7+! ♔h8

24...♔f7 25 ♕h5+.

25 fxg5! ♕xg5

25...♖f1+ doesn't work now: 26 ♕xf1 ♗xf1 27 ♗f5+ ♔g8 28 ♗xe6+ ♔f8 29 ♖h8 mate.

26 ♗g6+ ♔g8

Or 26...♕h6 27 ♖xh6+ gxh6 28 ♕a1+!.

27 ♘e7+! ♕xe7 28 ♖h8+ ♔xh8 29 ♕h5+ ♔g8 30 ♕h7 mate.

Part 3:

75 most important exercises in the Endgame

151

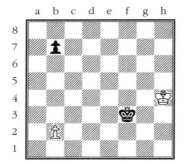

White to move

153

White to move

152

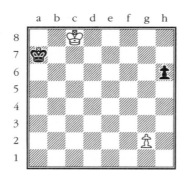

White to move

154

White to move

155

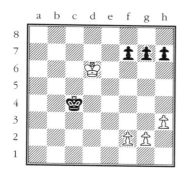

White to move

156

White to move

157

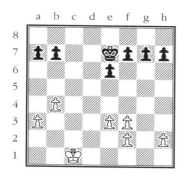

Black to move

158

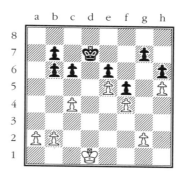

White to move

159

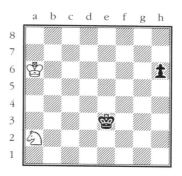

White to move

160

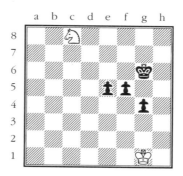

Black to move

161

White to move

162

Black to move

163

Black to move

164

White to move

165

White to move

166

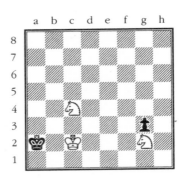

White to move

167

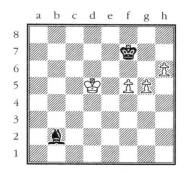

White to move

168

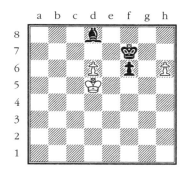

White to move

169

White to move

170

Black to move

171

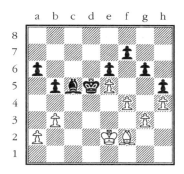

White to move

172

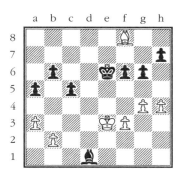

White to move

173

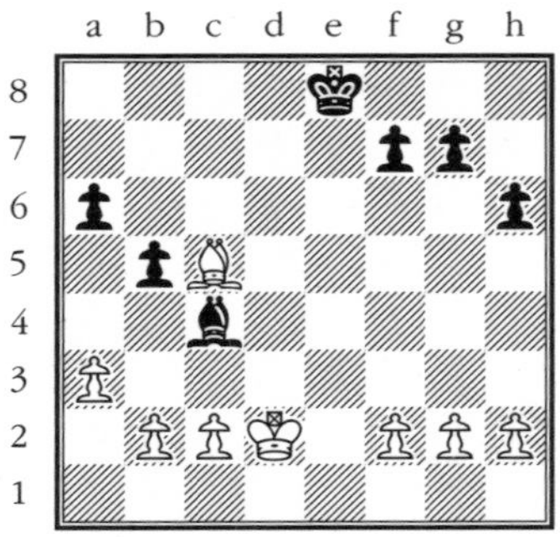

Black to move

176

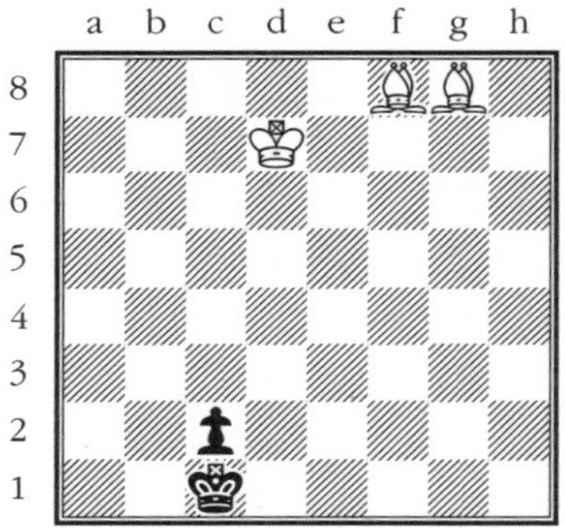

White to move

174

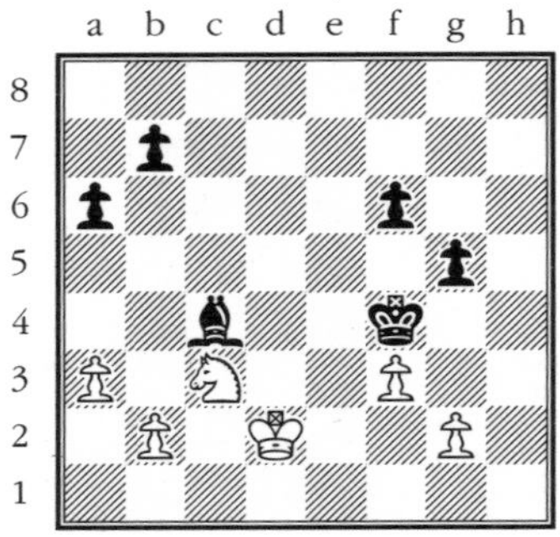

White to move

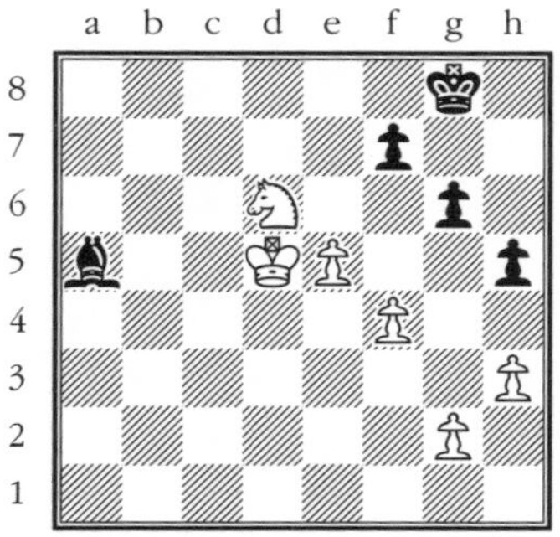

177

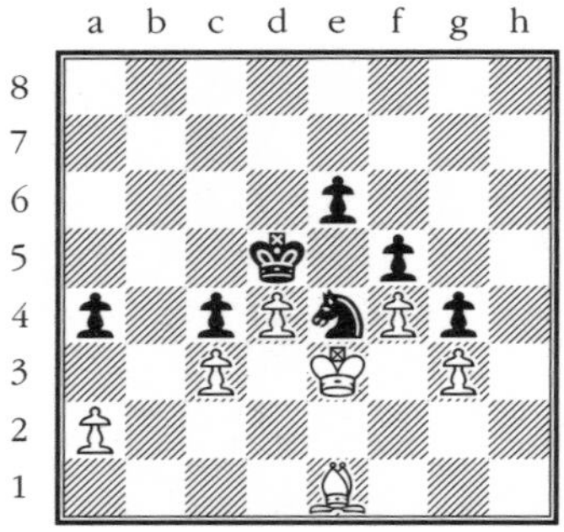

Black to move

175

White to move

178

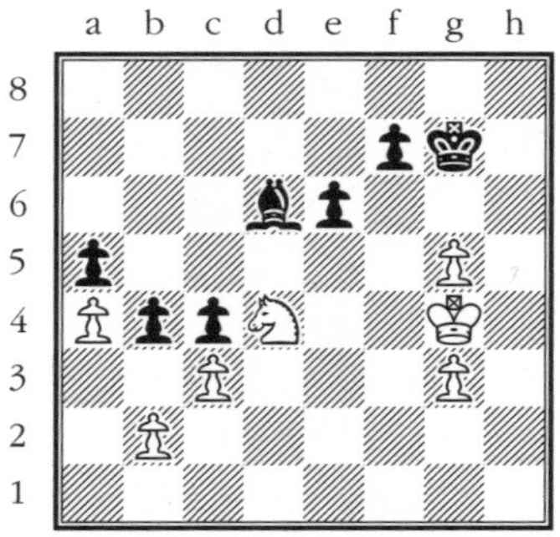

Black to move

210

179

Black to move

180

White to move

181

White to move

182

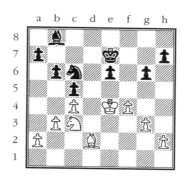

White to move

183

White to move

184

White to move

185

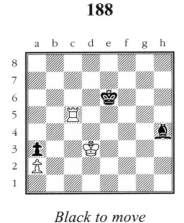

White to move

186

White to move

187

White to move

188

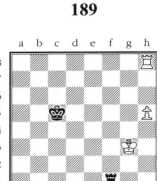

Black to move

189

White to move

190

White to move

191

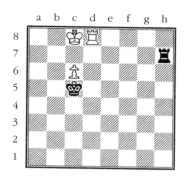

White to move

192

White to move

193

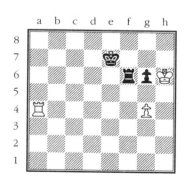

Black to move

194

Black to move

195

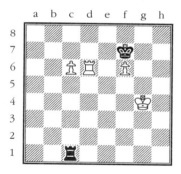

Black to move

196

Black to move

197

White to move

198

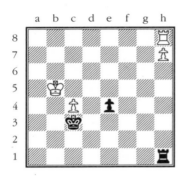

Black to move

199

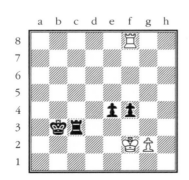

Black to move

200

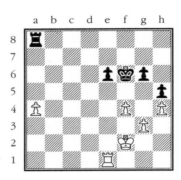

White to move

201

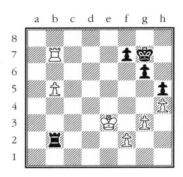

White to move

202

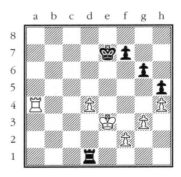

White to move

203

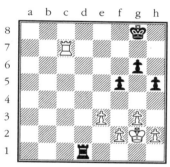

White to move

204

White to move

205

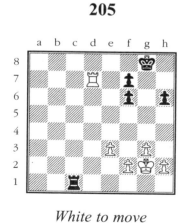

Black to move

206

White to move

White to move

207

White to move

208

White to move

209

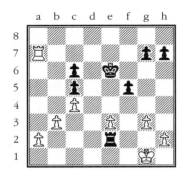

White to move

210

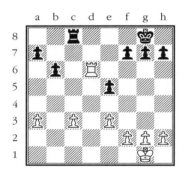

White to move

211

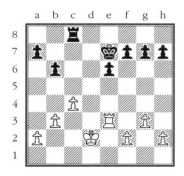

Black to move

212

White to move

213

White to move

214

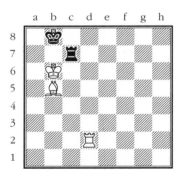

White to move

215

Black to move

216

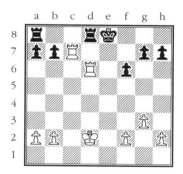

White to move

217

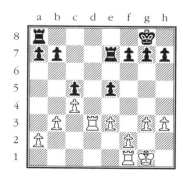

White to move

218

White to move

219

Black to move

220

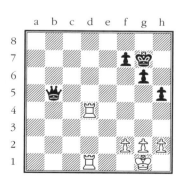

White to move

221

White to move

224

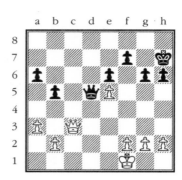

Black to move

222

White to move

225

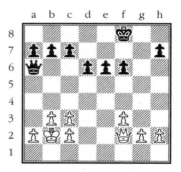

White to move

223

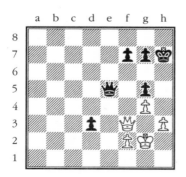

Black to move

Solutions to Exercises 151-225

151

Grigoriev
1938

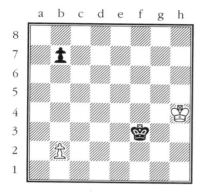

White to move

I have always been fascinated by pawn endings and solved more than a thousand of them. My favourite study composer is the Russian Nikolay Dmitrievich Grigoriev (1895-1938). Here is one of his magnificent studies:

1 ♔g5!

The only move. White must defend in such a flexible way that he sometimes goes for the enemy pawn and sometimes heads towards his own pawn, depending on Black's play.

1...♔e4

Black plays in a similarly flexible way having both pawns in mind.

This strategy applies the strongest pressure on White.

2 ♔f6! ♔d5 3 ♔e7!

3...♔c6

After 3...b5 White attacks the enemy pawn: 4 ♔d7! b4 5 ♔c7 ♔c5 6 ♔b7 b3 (6...♔b5 7 b3) 7 ♔a6 is a draw.

Black must be careful not to play for a win as he can even lose after 7...♔c4 8 ♔a5 ♔d3? 9 ♔b4 ♔c2 10 ♔a3 and White wins the pawn.

3...♔c5 is a draw as well if White immediately attacks the b-pawn by 4 ♔d7 b5 5 ♔c7 etc.

4 ♔e6!

The right direction. If 4 ♔d8? White loses contact with his b-pawn and to a certain extent the enemy b-pawn. He loses after 4...b5! 5 ♔e7 b4 6 ♔e6 ♔c5! 7 ♔e5 ♔c4 8 ♔d6 b3!.

4...b6 5 ♔e5 ♔c5 6 ♔e4 ♔c4 7 ♔e3 b5

7...♔b3 8 ♔d4 and White goes for the b5-pawn.

8 ♔d2 ♔b3 9 ♔c1 ♔a2

10 b4!

The only move to draw.

10...♔b3 11 ♔b1 ♔xb4 12 ♔b2

White maintains the opposition with an elementary draw. All 12 moves that have been played by White have been forced.

12...♔c4 13 ♔c2 b4 14 ♔b2 b3 15 ♔b1! ♔c3 16 ♔c1

Against a knight-pawn, 16 ♔a1 also holds the draw thanks to the stalemate trick after 16...♔c2.

16...b2+ 17 ♔b1 ♔b3 Draw.

A beautiful study which covers several important ideas to master in pawn endings. There is only one way to master such endings. First of all you must be familiar with the typical ideas and secondly you must calculate the variations without making any mistakes. For this reason I believe that pawn endings

are among the most instructive positions to study. In that way you practice ideas, calculation and learn the foundation for all endings.

152

Adamson
1915

White to move

The following study is composed by the British composer Henry Anthony Adamson (1871-1941). He was a skilled mathematician and in the area of chess he composed some very elegant and intricate pawn endings. This pawn ending is not as simple as it looks, so you've got to be careful before you think you have solved it!

1 ♔c7!

The idea is to gain a tempo before White goes after the h-pawn.

1...♔a6 2 ♔c6 ♔a5 3 ♔c5 ♔a4 4 ♔c4 ♔a3 5 ♔c3 ♔a2 6 ♔c2 ♔a3

Here comes the most difficult move in the whole study:

7 g3!!

The first time I tried to solve this intricate pawn ending, according to my notes, was on 7 February 1990 and I used the exclent book *Test your Endgame Ability* (Batsford 1988) by August Livshits and Jon Speelman. Then I missed the amazing move 7 g3!!. Three years later, on 15 February 1993, I got my revenge because this time I managed to see all the variations. Most probably I hadn't forgotten that the ability of the g2-pawn to move one or two steps can be decisive in pawn endings. The automatic 7 g4? is a draw after 7...♚b4 8 ♔d3 ♚c5 9 ♔e4 ♚d6 10 ♔f5 because of 10...h5!! 11 gxh5 ♚e7 12 ♔g6 ♚f8 13 h6 ♚g8 14 h7+ ♚h8 15 ♔h6 stalemate.

7...♚b4 8 ♔d3 ♚c5 9 ♔e4 ♚d6 10 ♔f5 ♚d5 11 g4!!

This is the moment to take another step forward.

11...♚d6

11...h5 doesn't work now for several reasons.

12 ♔g6 ♚e6 13 ♔xh6 ♚f7 14 g5 ♚g8 15 ♔g6

White wins. This beautiful study with only four pieces on the board should be regarded as one of the most aesthetic among this material.

This endgame can also be found in *Improve your Endgame* (Chess Enterprises 1990) by Eric Schiller. It's the only book which focuses solely on promotion in the endgame, with the help of 30 studies by well-known composers.

The following study I found in Tkachenko's book *The King Saves the Day* (Elk and Ruby 2018) which contains solely positions where the king is the hero.

153

J. Pospisil
The King Saves the Day 1996

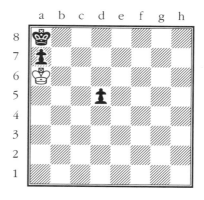

White to move

1 ♔a5!

1 ♔b5? ♚b7 2 ♔c5 ♚a6 3 ♔xd5 ♚b5 and Black's a-pawn promotes, for example 4 ♔d4 ♚b4 5 ♔d3 ♚b3 6 ♔d2 ♚b2. When Black controls the critical c1 square this endgame is

a win. 7 ♔d3 a5 8 ♔c4 a4 9 ♔b4 a3 etc.

1...♔b8!

If 1...♔b7 then 2 ♔b5.

2 ♔b4! ♔b7 3 ♔b5!

The opposition is more important than grabbing the pawn as quickly as possible. If 3 ♔c5? Then 3...♔a6 4 ♔xd5 ♔b5 and Black wins.

3...a5

Black's last attempt since 3...♔c7 4 ♔c5 is a clear draw.

4 ♔xa5 ♔c6 5 ♔b4 ♔d6 6 ♔c3 ♔e5 7 ♔d3

White has achieved an elementary draw despite the fact that he was two pawns down. The main reason was that he had more manoeuvring space than his opponent and that Black had an a-pawn which is useless in many pawn endings. It's obviously an easy win for Black if we move the position one file to the right.

Sergey Tkachenko is a member of the Ukrainian team which won the World Championship for Chess Composition 1997. He has written seven miniature books (15x10 cm) each of which contains 100 studies. This series of books is divided up according to which piece is the hero. They are very nicely presented and useful and there is no need for a chess board because most of the solutions are shorter than six moves. Solving them is more a matter of creativity and imagination rather than calculation. The advantage of working on such studies is not only that you learn the full capabilities of

the pieces but also that you develop your fantasy in the endgame while focusing on only one piece. These are the only endgame books I know which have a single piece as its principal theme. They contain creative and fantastic studies on World Championship level with many classic studies as well as a large number originating in Russia, some of them composed by Tkachenko himself.

154

Hašek
1928

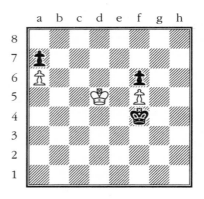

White to move

The following study is a beautiful example of both triangulation and corresponding squares.

1 ♔c6

1 ♔e6? ♔g5 is a draw. If you are unsure you can count White's and Black's pawn moves to their respective queening squares. It takes White seven moves to queen and Black seven as well so it's a draw. It's important to learn by heart that it

always takes five moves for a pawn to reach the ultimate square from its original position. This small piece of knowledge will facilitate the calculation of pawn races and is very important to master in order to speed up calculation.

1...♔e5!

The best defence is to follow White's king to the a-pawn. The pawn race after 1...♔xf5 2 ♔b7 is in White's favour. It will take Black six moves to queen but only five for White.

2 ♔c7!!

White is fooling Black like a skilled football player who dribbles with the ball. 2 ♔b7? ♔d6 3 ♔xa7 ♔c7 is an elementary draw.

2...♔d5 3 ♔d7!!

White has carried out a triangulation manoeuvre on the c6-c7-d7 squares and placed Black in zugzwang since he has to concede either the c6 or e6 square.

3...♔e5

Or 3...♔c5 4 ♔e6.

4 ♔c6!

The key to winning this pawn ending was to reach this position with Black to move.

4...♔xf5 5 ♔b7

White wins the pawn race. Viktor Korchnoi (1931-2016) used to say that triangulation is the ABC of chess and it certainly rings true in this study.

155

Kalinicev – Schulz
Cham 1992

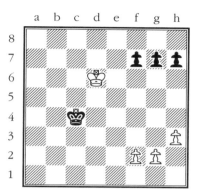

White to move

What's fascinating about this pawn ending is that it's an instructive example of how Nimzowitsch's theories work in practice.

1 ♔e7?

The first time I saw this endgame I wrote in my private annotations that it's "incredible that this move doesn't win!" From a visual point of view it certainly seems that White's king will wipe out the whole kingside of pawns like a vacuum cleaner, but that turns out to be an optical illusion. The key move to winning is to play according to Nimzowitsch's rule, which states that you should hem in the target before blockading it and only then destroy it!

1 g4! would have prevented Black from moving his f-pawn to f5. Then 1...♔d3 2 ♔e7 f6 3 ♔f7 ♔e2 4 f4 ♔f3 5 f5. The f-pawn is now

blockaded and a future attacking target. 5...♔g3 6 ♔xg7 ♔xh3 7 ♔xh7 (7 ♔xf6 ♔xg4 8 ♔e6 also wins but it's unnecessary to give Black some hope with his h-pawn even though that would be futile.) 7...♔xg4 8 ♔g6 and White's f-pawn decides.

1...f5

Another of Nimzowitsch's concepts – the pawn's lust to expand – is very visible in this position.

2 ♔f7 ♔d3 3 ♔xg7 f4!!

It's because of this move that Black surprisingly draws. Such moves are easy to overlook when calculating the variations, since it's easy to be carried away by 3...♔e2 4 f4 ♔e3 5 g3 (or simply 5 ♔xh7 ♔xf4 6 ♔g6) 5...h5 6 h4 ♔f3 7 ♔g6 ♔xg3 but then comes 8 ♔g5!

A famous zugzwang idea that I learned early in my chess career and never forgot. It still impresses me!

4 ♔xh7

If White persists in attacking the f-pawn it's still a draw after 4 ♔f6 ♔e2 5 f3 (It's too late to hem in the f-pawn in this position. 5 ♔f5 f3! is

another example of the pawn's lust to expand!) 5...♔f2 6 ♔f5 ♔xg2 7 ♔xf4 ♔xh3 8 ♔g5 ♔g3 9 f4 h6+ etc.

4...♔e2 5 g4 ♔xf2 6 g5 f3 7 g6 ♔g3! 8 g7 f2 9 g8♕+ ♔xh3

This endgame is an elementary draw thanks to the stalemate resource ...♔h1 when the queen checks on g3. One plausible variation is...

10 ♕c4 ♔g2 11 ♕g4+ ♔h2 12 ♕f3 ♔g1 13 ♕g3+ ♔h1! 14 ♕xf2 stalemate.

156

Bianchetti
1925

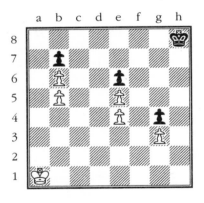

White to move

White wins by utilising the theory of "corresponding squares". An alternative terminology, but less popular, is "co-ordinate squares", which was used by Averbakh and Maizelis in *Pawn Endings* (Batsford 1974).

It isn't possible to win directly by penetrating to d6 or f4 because Black's king will stop the intruder. If White has his king on the c5-square Black will have his on the e7-square. This relationship between the critical squares means that the squares are corresponding to each other. If we go one step back we see that the d4-square corresponds to the f7-square because Black must be ready to meet ♔c5 with ...♚e7 and ♔e3 with ...♚g6. From the c3-square White's possible moves are ♔d4, ♔c4, ♔b4 and ♔d3. The only square from which Black's king can simultaneously reach f7, f8 and g7 is the g8-square. If we go backwards like this and check all the important squares and the corresponding ones we will have the following related couples:

c5 – e7, f4 – h5, d4 – f7, c4 – f8, d3 – g7, c3 – g8, b4 – f7, b3 – g7, b2 – h7, a3 – g8, a2 – h8, c2 – h8, e3 – g6, d2 – h7, e2 – h6, d1 – g7, e1 – g6, c1 – g8, b1 – g7

When we have solved the riddle as to which squares correspond to each other, with every move we will create subtle double-threats so that at all moments it will be impossible for Black to cover the critical square and he will be placed in a continual state of zugzwang. Bianchetti's solution to the study runs as follows:

1 ♔a2!!

The a2-square corresponds to the h8-square and is the only move to prepare a successful penetration. A direct winning attempt by taking the shortest route fails after 1 ♔b2? ♚h7!! 2 ♔c3 ♚g8! 3 ♔d4 ♚f7!

4 ♔c5 ♚e7 5 ♔d4 ♚f7 6 ♔e3 ♚g6 7 ♔f4 ♚h5 with a draw.

1...♚h7 2 ♔b2! ♚g7 3 ♔b3 ♚g8 4 ♔c3 ♚f8 5 ♔c4! ♚f7 6 ♔d4

This is the key position where Black is in zugzwang, because as we have seen in the table the d4-square relates to the f7-square. Black has to give way for the white king to penetrate either via d6 or f4.

Other cases of corresponding squares could have been possible if Cohn had come up with a better defence against Rubinstein in St Petersburg 1909, exercise 157, so check out this endgame as well! A simpler case is the study by Hašek 1928, exercise 154. If you are interested in learning more about corresponding squares in pawn endings I recommend *Pawn Endings* (Batsford 1974) by Averbakh/ Maizelis and *Endgame Preparation* (Batsford 1989) by Speelman who have written extensively on it.

157

Cohn – Rubinstein
St Petersburg 1909

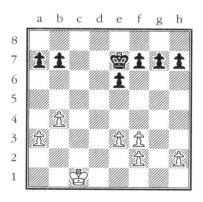

Black to move

This pawn ending is unique. If you only study one pawn ending with many pawns this is the one. It's probably the most famous that has ever been played in a game. I saw it for the first time many years ago in Bent Larsen's book *Du måste ha en plan* (Prisma 1977) and it was the first position in the book. It showed very clearly the use of a two-step-plan. Earlier in the game Rubinstein's opponent Cohn played the fatal 24 ♖c1?, allowing Rubinstein to exchange the rooks and obtain a winning pawn ending.

25...♔f6!

In the famous tournament book by the second world chess champion Emanuel Lasker (1868-1941) his sole comment with regard to Black's 25th move is: "An attack finely carried through with the smallest means."

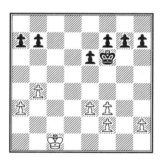

Black has a two-step-plan where everything is clear to the end, to use the words of Kotov. Larsen now writes that the plan is to attack the isolated h-pawn and thereby force the white king to g1. Black then activates his pawns on the kingside and exchanges them, thereby "clearing" the board so that the black king on h3 can go "west" and snatch a pawn, perhaps on e3 or e4, or

perhaps go all the way to the queenside.

26 ♔d2 ♔g5 27 ♔e2

It's easy to see that a counterattack by White loses after 27 ♔d3 ♔h4 28 ♔d4 ♔h3 29 ♔c5 ♔xh2 30 b5 ♔g2 31 ♔d6 h5 32 ♔c7 h4 33 ♔xb7 h3 34 ♔xa7 h2 35 b6 h1♕ 36 b7 ♕a1 37 b8♕ ♕xa3+ and Black exchanges queens and eliminates all the pawns.

27...♔h4 28 ♔f1 ♔h3 29 ♔g1 e5

The first part of the plan has been realised. Black's king is optimally activated so he can now win by activating all his pawns and decide the game with a breakthrough on the kingside.

30 ♔h1

Larsen gives 30 e4 g5 31 ♔h1 h5 32 ♔g1 h4 33 ♔h1 g4 34 fxg4 ♔xg4 35 ♔g2 h3+ 36 ♔f1 ♔f3 and Black wins. Speelman and Mestel analyse 30 a4 b6 31 b5 f5 32 ♔h1 g5 33 ♔g1 h5 34 ♔h1 h4 35 ♔g1 e4 36 fxe4 fxe4 37 ♔h1 ♔g4 38 ♔g2 h3+ 39 ♔g1 ♔f3 40 ♔f1 g4 with a win.

30...b5

A clever and principled move because Black secures an extra

tempo for himself on the queenside with the a-pawn.

31 ♔g1 f5 32 ♔h1 g5 33 ♔g1 h5 34 ♔h1 g4

All black pawns have been activated so now commences the first breakthrough.

35 e4

Cohn's last chance to stay in the game was 35 fxg4 hxg4 (Larsen gives only 35...fxg4 36 ♔g1 e4 37 ♔h1 h4 38 ♔g1 g3 39 hxg3 hxg3 40 ♔f1 g2+ 41 ♔g1 when Black exploits the reserve tempo he has saved by playing 41...a6 and thereby places White in zugzwang.) 36 ♔g1 f4 37 exf4 exf4 38 ♔h1.

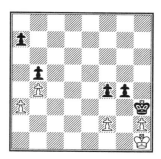

But now comes Mestel's suggestion 38...f3!! 39 ♔g1 ♔h4 40 ♔f1 (After 40 ♔h1 ♔g5 41 h3 gxh3 42 ♔h2 ♔g4 43 ♔g1 ♔f4 44 ♔h2 ♔e4 45 ♔xh3 ♔d3 46 ♔g4 ♔e2 47 ♔g3 a6 and Black's reserve tempo decides!) The trick is to reach this position (and the following ones at moves 41-42) with White to move since the h4-square corresponds to f1. 40...♔g5 41 ♔e1 ♔f4 42 ♔d2 ♔e4 43 ♔c3 ♔f5! White is now in zugzwang because Black threatens to capture the h2-pawn by ...♔g5-h4-h3xh2. If White tries to defend it

with 44 ♔d2 Black wins after 44...♔f4!, because the f4-square corresponds to d2 and it is White to move. For example, 45 ♔e1 (45.♔d3 ♔g5) 45...♔e4 46 ♔d2 ♔d4 47 ♔c2 ♔c4 places White in zugzwang and Black penetrates via either d3 or b3.

Note that the routine 38...g3?? looks like a win but is in fact an optical illusion. It's actually a forced draw after 39 hxg3 fxg3

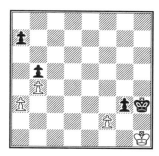

40 fxg3 (White can also draw by 40 ♔g1 g2 41 f4 ♔g4 42 ♔xg2 ♔xf4 43 ♔f2 ♔e4 44 ♔e2 ♔d4 45 ♔d2 ♔c4 46 ♔c2 a6 and now both 47 a4! and 47 ♔b2 lead to the desired result for White.) is the only move to win. One plausible variation is 40...♔xg3 41 ♔g1 ♔f3 42 ♔f1 ♔e3 43 ♔e1 ♔d3 44 ♔d1 ♔c3 because of the saviour in distress 45 a4!!. Black cannot play for a win with pawn(s) on the a-file so the last try is 45...a6 46 axb5 axb5 47 ♔c1 ♔xb4, but after 48 ♔b2 White has the opposition with an elementary draw.

35...fxe4 36 fxe4

Kmoch gives 36 fxg4 hxg4 37 ♔g1 e3 38 fxe3 e4 39 ♔h1 g3 with a win.

36...h4 37 ♔g1 g3 38 hxg3 hxg3 White resigns.

Don't forget this classic ending because knowledge of the position will be very beneficial for your overall understanding of chess, especially the type of pawn structure we have dealt with here and above all the value of an active king. You will find two more examples of this particular pawn ending hidden in other endgames, so remain alert!

158

A. Korolev – A. Shakarov
Correspondence, USSR 1976

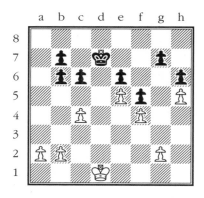

White to move

White has a very strong grip with his pawns on e5 and h5 and this, combined with the break c4-c5 and an invasion by his king, will prove decisive. It's fascinating to see that Black will resign in only three more moves, which at first glance might seem strange. However, it's White's superior pawn structure in all sectors of the board which secures White a decisive breakthrough, whereas Black's breaks are fruitless. White first manoeuvres his king to b4.

27 ♔c2! ♔c7

There is no time to create a passed pawn on the kingside with 27...♔e7 28 ♔c3 ♔f7 29 ♔b4 g6 30 hxg6+ ♔xg6 due to 31 c5! bxc5+ 32 ♔xc5 ♔h5 33 ♔d6 ♔g4 34 ♔xe6 and White decides.

28 ♔b3 ♔d7

28...b5 is pointless as after 29 cxb5 cxb5 30 ♔b4 ♔b6 31 b3 ♔c6 32 ♔a5 ♔d5 33 ♔xb5 ♔e4 34 ♔c5 ♔xf4 35 ♔d6 White queens the e-pawn in five moves.

Or 28...c5 29 ♔a4 ♔c6 30 g3 and Black is in zugzwang.

29 ♔b4

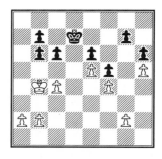

Black resigns.

White's next plan would have been to prepare the decisive break c4-c5. A possible continuation might have been 29...♔c8 30 a4 ♔c7 31 g3 ♔c8 32 c5! The right moment for the decisive break, since White gains control of the b6-square by force. 32...♔c7 33 cxb6+ ♔xb6 34 a5+ ♔a6 (34...♔c7 35 ♔c5 is a decisive penetration. Black has to yield the b6- or the d6-square, e.g. 35...♔d7 36 ♔b6 ♔c8 37 a6 bxa6 38 ♔xc6 etc.) 35 ♔c5 ♔xa5 36 ♔d6 ♔b4 37 ♔xe6 ♔b3 38 ♔d6 and White wins.

159

Grigoriev
1932

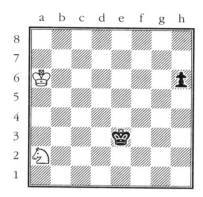

White to move

1 ♘b4

The first move is pretty obvious because the knight would not have much of a future on the other two available squares, because the king would easily neutralise it.

1...h5 2 ♘c6!

2 ♘d5+ ♚f3! neutralises the knight very effectively!

2...♚e4!

Black is using the maximum force of his king to restrict White's knight as much as possible. However, in this specific case the knight is too agile. After 2...h4 3 ♘e5 the draw is pretty clear as the knight will reach the key g4-square.

3 ♘a5!!

The prettiest move in the study. White must be careful. If the knight goes behind the pawn the black king will effectively restrict its activity.

After 3 ♘d8? h4 4 ♘e6 ♚f5 5 ♘d4+ ♚g4 the knight is unable to stop the h-pawn.

3...h4

3...♚d5 allows 4 ♘b3 h4 5 ♘d2 h3 6 ♘f1 with an elementary draw.

4 ♘c4

Not 4 ♘b3 ♚e3! and the knight is cut off from the h-pawn.

4...♚f3

As mentioned before, 4...h3 5 ♘d2+ followed by ♘f1 and ♘h2 is a draw, so Black must try to make White's task as difficult as possible.

5 ♘e5+! ♚g3

It looks like the knight is cut off but after...

6 ♘c4!

...it shows its enormous versatility by carrying out this nice manoeuvre back again, thereby mirroring 3 ♘a5!!. The knight is a very versatile piece indeed if one knows how to handle it and understand its capabilities.

6...h3 7 ♘e3 ♚f3

The knight controls the h-pawn after 7...♚f2 8 ♘g4+ or 7...h2 8 ♘f1+.

8 ♘f1

It's a fundamental draw. The king cannot drive away the knight from the key f1 or g4 squares. The beautiful knight manoeuvres 3 ♘a5!! and 6 ♘c4!, to contain the h-pawn, will be remembered as concrete evidence of how magical this piece can be. We can bring this knowledge to all phases of the game.

160

Skalkotas – T. Horvath
Athens 1983

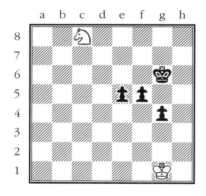

Black to move

In *300 Most Important Chess Positions* there were several examples of this material balance on the board. It's a really instructive type of endgame to learn the true value of the pieces in the simplest form. The knight is worth three pawns but only if the pawns are situated on the fifth rank from White's point of view, or fourth rank from Black's point of view. If the pawns have managed to cross the frontier line, as Nimzowitsch likes to call the borderline between the fifth

and fourth rank, the knight is powerless. The rule to learn in this ending is that if White has three connected pawns on the fifth rank they win against a knight if the pawns are supported by the king.

1...♔g5

1...e4! is the most precise continuation according to Tablebase. Black can follow up with ...♔g6-g5-f4 or ...♔g6-f6-e5 depending on White's reactions. 1...f4? would be a mistake due to 2 ♘d6 because it will be difficult to carry out the important move ...e5-e4.

2 ♔g2 e4 3 ♘e7

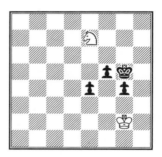

3...f4!

All black pawns are placed on the fifth rank and the king is supporting two of them. Since it's not possible to attack the e4-pawn Black is clearly winning according to the above mentioned rule.

4 ♔f2

In the next phase of this ending Black must be careful because there are pitfalls when one has to decide which pawn to advance. In this particular position Black can move any of the pawns that are supported by the king.

4...g3+!

The most effective move. 4...f3 also wins because White is in a kind of zugzwang so it's not possible to stop the further advance of the g- or e-pawn. For example 5 ♘d5 is answered by 5...♚h4. 4...e3+? 5 ♚e2 is a draw because it's not possible to advance the pawns without allowing a blockade or losing material. The most instructive variation is 5...♚h4 6 ♘d5! ♚g3 7 ♘f6! and Black cannot avoid the perpetual threats to the f4- and g4-pawns.

5 ♚g2 ♚h4?

After the simple and natural 5...♚g4 there is no knight check and the black pawns can advance to their queening squares.

6 ♘f5+

6 ♘g6+ is also good enough for a draw.

6...♚g4 7 ♘h6+ ♚g5 8 ♘f7+ ♚f6 9 ♘d8 ♚e5 10 ♘c6+?

The correct knight check was 10 ♘f7+! ♚d4 11 ♘g5! ♚d3

12 ♘e6 and White holds the draw by perpetual threats against the pawns on the fourth rank.

10...♚d5?

10...♚f5! wins after 11 ♚h3 e3! 12 ♘d4+ (12 ♚g2 ♚e4) 12...♚e4 13 ♘c2 e2 14 ♚g2 ♚d3 15 ♘e1+ ♚d2 16 ♘f3+ ♚d1 and Black promotes the e-pawn.

11 ♘e7+?

White can draw by the amazing move 11 ♘d8!!. After the further 11...♚d4 12 ♘e6+ ♚e3 White must find the only move 13 ♚h3!. It's important that the knight remains on e6 because that makes it impossible to win by 13...f3 14 ♚xg3 f2 15 ♚g2 ♚e2 due to 16 ♘d4+! ♚e1 17 ♘c2+.

11...♚d4 12 ♘g6 ♚e3 13 ♘e5 ♚d2 14 ♘g6 f3+! 15 ♚xg3 e3! 16 ♘e5

Or 16 ♚xf3 e2.

16...f2 17 ♘f3+ ♚e2!

The only move to win.

White resigns.

161

Prokeš
1946

White to move

This study is a typical but simpler case of corresponding squares. These are b2-d2, d3-b3 and a2 to e3. This means that the winning move is...

1 ♔a2!

1 ♔b2? would be answered by either 1...♔d2! or 1...♔d4!.

1...♔d3

1...♔d4 is met by 2 ♔b2!.

2 ♔b3! ♔d4 3 ♔b4 ♔d3

If 3...e5 then 4 ♔b5! ♔xc3 5 ♔c5 ♔d3 6 ♔d5.

4 ♔c5 ♔xc3 5 ♔d6

An immediate 5 e5 also wins.

5...♔d4 6 e5

And White wins.

162

Matlakov – Kramnik
World Blitz Championship 2019

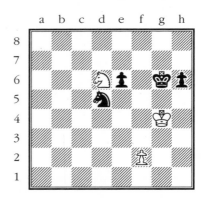

Black to move

I followed this endgame live and was convinced that it would end in a draw. Kramnik is well-known for his skill with the knight but I could never have imagined that he would win this ending. However, to my surprise, he did and how he did it was very impressive indeed.

55...e5 56 ♘c4 ♘f6+ 57 ♔g3 ♔f5

Black improves his position slowly but surely.

58 f3

Good move! There is no reason to give Black more terrain than necessary, neither technically nor psychologically.

58...♔e6 59 ♘e3 ♘d5

60 ♘g4

White wants to entice the h-pawn to move closer to the white king. White had a forced draw with 60 ♘xd5 ♔xd5 61 f4 e4 62 f5 ♔e5 63 f6 ♔xf6 64 ♔f4 with an easy draw but it was necessary to calculate five moves ahead and perhaps Matlakov trusted Kramnik's divine gift of intuition. This is perhaps too much to ask for, even at world elite level, since all players will be very tired by the last day of a demanding tournament.

60...h5 61 ♘f2 ♔f5 62 ♘e4 ♘f6 63 ♘d6+

This time the pawn ending after 63 ♘xf6? ♔xf6 is lost due to 64 f4 e4, since White cannot exchange the f-pawn for the e-pawn.

63...♔e6 64 ♘c4 ♔d5 65 ♘e3+ ♔d4 66 ♘f5+ ♔d3

Where is Black's king going? Don't the black pawns now risk becoming objects of attack?

67 ♔h4 ♔e2 68 ♔g5 ♘d5 69 ♘h4!

Impressive defensive play by Matlakov, although 69 ♔xh5 ♔xf3 was also a simple draw. There is no question that "everybody" (probably even Kramnik) thought that the game would end in a draw, since one of Black's pawns will inevitably fall.

69...♘f4

Kramnik defends the h5-pawn and leaves the e-pawn to its fate. It's a well-known fact that the rim-pawn is the knight's worst enemy.

70 ♔f5 ♔f2 71 ♔xe5 ♔g3 72 ♔f5!

Strongly played! Matlakov must have seen that the pawn ending (and the queen ending) is a draw since the simple continuation 72 ♘f5+ ♔xf3 73 ♔f6 is a draw as well.

72...♘h3!

As usual Kramnik impresses with his beautiful knight manoeuvres, which utilise all squares on the board, even squares you don't expect. Here it's possible that the players quickly calculated 72...♔xh4 73 ♔xf4 ♔h3 74 ♔g5 h4 75 f4 ♔g3 76 f5 h3 77 f6 h2 78 f7 h1♕ 79 f8♕ ♕h4+ 80 ♔g6 with a draw, but most probably they stopped their analysis already at move 74 since that is a well-known draw for experienced players at the highest level.

73 ♘g6

White is forced to move the knight and sacrifice the f3-pawn, but it doesn't matter because it's still an easy draw.

73...♔xf3 74 ♘e5+

The knight was excellently placed on g6 so one way to finish the game more quickly was 74 ♔f6 ♘f4 (74...♔g4 is a draw after 75 ♘e5+ and 76 ♘g6. Maybe someone might object that Black can play 74...♔e4 instead, but then the continuation would have been 75 ♘h4 ♘f4 76 ♔g5!) 75 ♔g5!.

74...♔g3

75 ♔e4??

The first mystery in this endgame is why Matlakov didn't go back with the knight by 75 ♘g6.

75...♘g5+??

If White's idea was 75...h4 76 ♘f3 that loses after 76...♘f2+ 77 ♔e3 h3 78 ♘d2 ♔g4+ 79 ♔e2 ♔g2 80 ♘f1 ♘e5 81 ♘e3+ ♔g1 82 ♘f1 ♘g6

83 ♘d2 ♔g2 84 ♘f1 (84 ♘f3 ♘e5!) 84...♔g1 85 ♘d2 ♘h4 86 ♘f1 ♘f5 87 ♘d2 ♘d4+.

Mystery number 2 is why Kramnik didn't play the normal move 75...♘f2+. It might seem surprising that Kramnik misses the natural knight move but he probably thought that the f3-square must be under control but unfortunately he forgot about White's king.

76 ♔e3??

Mystery number 3 is why Matlakov didn't play 76 ♔f5 followed by ♘g6 with a simple draw since 76...h4 77 ♔xg5 h3 78 ♘g4 doesn't lead to the desired success for Black.

76...h4 77 ♘d3 h3 78 ♘f2 h2 79 ♘h1+ ♔g2 80 ♔e2!

80...♘e4

The last trick is actually one of the big mysteries in chess: 80...♔xh1?? 81 ♔f2! is a well-known but still a very surprising draw. The player who has never seen this idea before should try to find out why this position is a draw, but the main reason is that the knight is not a perfect piece, it's human. An interesting parallel is that of an opposite coloured bishop to the queening square of a rim-pawn.

81 ♔e1 ♘g3 82 ♘f2 ♔f3 White resigns.

Beautiful play by Kramnik. This win secured him a fine third place in the blitz tournament.

163

Ilivitzky – Geller
Tbilisi 1949

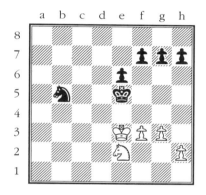

Black to move

The knight ending of three pawns against four on the same side of the board is difficult to hold if one sticks to a passive strategy. The best method is to centralise the king and knight and play actively with the f-pawn. The most resistant structure is one with pawns on the h2, g3 and f4-squares.

45...♘d6 46 ♘c1

Before it's too late White should have played 46 f4! which is the best defensive set-up for White. After 46...♔d5 47 ♘c3+ ♔c4 48 ♘e2 f6 49 ♘c1 ♘f5+ 50 ♔f3

♔d4 51 ♘b3+ ♔d5 52 ♘c1 e5 53 fxe5 fxe5 54 ♘a2 it's not clear how Black should proceed to make his pawn advantage decisive.

46...♘f5+ 47 ♔f2 ♔d5

To be considered was 47...g5 to prevent White from setting up his ideal position.

48 ♘d3

This was the last chance to play 48 f4! with drawing chances.

48...e5

From now on White's position gets harder and harder to defend.

49 ♘b4+

It's too late for 49 f4 because of 49...e4 allowing Black a passed pawn. After the further 50 ♘c1 h5 Black's space advantage and centralised pieces make White's position untenable. If playing actively with the f-pawn doesn't work one can try the second defensive idea which is to play actively with the g-pawn. In this endgame activity is highly important. White endeavours to reduce the number of pawns and sometimes he can even sacrifice his knight to draw.

49 g4 should therefore have been played. After 49...♘d4 White can manoeuvre his knight to e4 where it can disturb Black's position more efficiently.

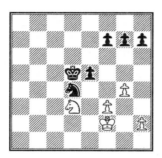

Then:

(a) 50 f4 looks like a good practical try if it weren't for 50...f6!. but not 50...e4? which is met by 51 ♘b4+ ♚c4 52 ♚e3! with definite counterplay. Then Black maintains great winning chances due to his strong centralised position. The small centre is conquered as can be seen if we go further into the variation: 51 fxe5 fxe5 52 ♚e3 ♘c2+ 53 ♚d2 ♘a3 54 ♚e2 ♘c4 55 ♘c1 e4 and Black is winning. The fundamental rule to hold the draw in this ending is not to lose control of the key e4 square if Black has created a passed pawn on e5.

(b) A likely variation is 50 ♘b2 50...♘e6 51 ♘d1 ♚d4 52 ♘e3 g6 53 ♘c2+. The idea is to play the king to e3 where it will control the vital e4-square, which is so important in this ending. This method, which we can call the second defensive method, is much better than the passive defence (third method) adopted in the game where White lost without much of a fight. 53...♚c3! Black prevents

White's intended king move to e3. 54 ♘e3 ♚d3 55 h4 ♘f4 56 ♘f1 ♘d5 57 ♘g3 ♘c3 Black has won the battle of the e4-square and on his next move plans to push the pawn to e4 with a theoretical win.

49...♚c5 50 ♘d3+ ♚d4 51 ♚e2

It's clear that White has chosen a passive strategy which is too risky in this type of endgame.

51...♘e7 52 ♘c1 f5 53 ♘b3+ ♚c4 54 ♘d2+ ♚c3 55 ♘b1+ ♚d4 56 ♘d2 ♘c6 57 ♘b3+ ♚c4 58 ♘d2+ ♚c3 59 ♘b1+ ♚d4

Step by step Black improves his position while retaining his domination of the centre. Black gains a tempo by triangulating on the c4-c3-d4 squares.

60 ♘a3 e4!

61 f4

The pawn wave and control of the e5-square offers little chance of survival, considering that Black already has decisive assets in his position. 61 ♘b5+ fails to 61...♚c5 with the double threat of ...♚xb5 and ...♘d4+. 61 fxe4 fxe4 allows Black to achieve his main goals in this ending, which are to get a passed pawn on the e-file while dominating the four squares in the middle of the board.

61...♚c5 62 ♚e3 ♘b4 63 h4 ♘d5+ 64 ♚d2 ♘f6 65 ♚e3 ♚b4 66 ♘c2+ ♚c3 67 ♘a3 ♘d5+ 68 ♚e2 ♚b3 White resigns.

The knight is trapped due to Black's possibility of ...♘c3+ if the knight moves to b5 or b1.

This endgame illustrates very well how to win against passive defence. It shows what happens if the defender waits too long with the important pawn-push to f4. Black's pieces were so active that it was impossible for White to set up a blockade and stop the pawn from reaching the critical e4-square. Activity is important in knight endings as well as rook endings.

164

Martirosyan – Tabatabaei
World Cup 2021

White to move

58 ♘xf3?

Nigel Short commented that the main reason for this "psychological error" was because of White's inability to sustain "prolonged tension."

If White had played any of the moves 58 ♘f1, 58 ♘b1, 58 ♘c4 or 58 ♚d1 the game might have continued for forty more moves and most probably ended in a draw. Note that 58 exd4? loses to 58...♘xd2! 59 ♚xd2 ♚xd4 60 ♚c2 e3.

58...gxf3+

58...d3+ followed by 59...gxf3+ leads to the same position by transposition.

59 ♚d2 d3

The only move, otherwise White wins!

60 ♚e1 ♚e5 61 ♚d1 ♚f5 62 ♚d2 ♚g4 63 ♚d1 ♚h3 64 ♚e1 ♚g2 65 g4 d2+ 66 ♚xd2

66 ♚d1 doesn't work on account of 66...♚xf2 67 g5 ♚xe3 68 g6 f2 and Black mates in two moves.

66...♚xf2 67 g5 ♚g1! White resigns.

The last move was overlooked by Martirosyan. After 68 g6 f2 69 g7 f1♕ 70 g8♕ ♕g2+ 71 ♕xg2+ ♚xg2 the pawn ending is clearly winning.

A cruel loss for Martirosyan but an important lesson not to stop analysing after seeing there is a check on g8, because perhaps the opponent has a counter-check!

165

Timman – Ree
Amsterdam 1984

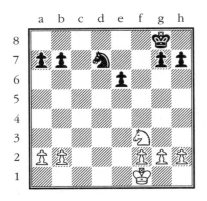

White to play

Pawn weaknesses are more serious in knight endings than in pawn endings because they can be attacked by two pieces. Here White has two pawn islands against Black's three.

24 ♘g5 ♘c5

24...e5 is playable but weakens the light squares in the central sector of Black's position.

25 b4 ♘a6

25...h6 leads to a lost pawn ending after 26 bxc5 hxg5 27 ♔e2 ♔f7 28 ♔f3 ♔f6 29 ♔e4 ♔e7 30 g4! followed by f2-f4. After the pawn exchange White decides the game by creating a distant passed h-pawn.

26 a3 ♘c7 27 ♔e2 h6?

Panchenko's recommendation 27...♘b5 is met by 28 a4 ♘c3+ 29 ♔d3 ♘xa4 30 ♘xe6 with good winning chances due to Black's disorganised position. Black's best

continuation is probably 27...b6 28 ♔d3 a6 29 ♔c4 h6 30 ♘e4 ♔f7 followed by ...♔e7.

28 ♘e4 ♔f8 29 ♘d6 b6 30 ♔d3 a6

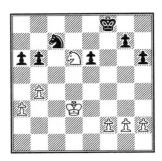

31 ♘c4?

Correct was 31 ♔d4! followed by ♔e5 when White is too active for Black to hold the game. The pawn ending which arises after 31...♘b5+ 32 ♘xb5 axb5 is lost: 33 ♔e5 ♔e7 34 h4 ♔d7 35 h5 ♔e7 36 g4 ♔d7 37 f4 ♔e7 38 g5 etc.

31...♘d5 32 ♔d4 ♔e7 33 g3?

33 ♔e5 was correct with good winning chances.

33...♔d7?

33...♔f6 was the correct defence.

34 f4 ♔c6 35 ♔e5

At last it's the white king's turn to attack Black's main weakness.

35...♘c7 36 ♘d6

A simpler continuation was 36 f5! exf5 37 ♔xf5 followed by ♔g6.

36...♔d7 37 f5

A nice transformation of positional advantages since White exchanges

238

Black's weak e6-pawn for activity. However it would have been better for White to play f4-f5 in conjunction with ♔xf5 as mentioned in the last comment.

37...exf5 38 ♘xf5 ♘e8

Too passive. More active continuations were either 38...a5 or 38...♘b5.

39 g4 ♘f6?

A blunder. 39...a5 was better.

40 h3?!

The tactical stroke 40 ♘xh6! wins a pawn for nothing. Presumably the players were in time pressure.

40...h5?

More resilient was 40...♘e8.

41 g5 ♘h7

Here the game was adjourned but it's too late to save Black's position.

42 h4 ♘f8 43 ♘xg7 ♘g6+ 44 ♔f6 ♘xh4 45 ♘xh5 ♔c6 46 ♘g3 ♔d5 47 a4! b5 48 a5 ♔c4

Both 48...♔d4 and 48...♔d6 would be met by 49 ♘f5+ so Black has to cede the e5-square.

49 ♘f5 ♘g2 50 ♔e5! Black resigns.

The g-pawn advances to g8.

166

Chéron
1955

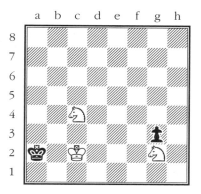

White to move

The pioneer of analysing the ending two knights versus one pawn was the Russian study composer Alexei Troitsky (1866-1942). He invented the so called **Troitzky-line** which is very important to know but not so difficult to learn by heart. as it's symmetrical and looks like an "M"! Don't forget it, as you will probably get it at least once in a lifetime as I have myself. Here follows a brief discussion of the Troitzky-line:

The key to winning this ending is to blockade the pawn with one knight and manoeuvre with the other knight and king and force Black to the edge of the board. When this is done White uses the knight, which blockaded the pawn, to checkmate the king. According to Troitzky and confirmed by Tablebase, in order to win, the pawn should not have passed any of the squares a4, b6, c5, d4, e4, f5, g6, h4 with the blockading knight on a3, b5, c4, d3, e3, f4, g5 or h3. Note again the shape of the structure which resembles the letter "M". If the knight blockades the pawn on any of these squares the position of the kings doesn't matter.

However an exception is the following position because the black king has already been driven to the edge of the board. White wins even though the pawn is far beyond the g6-square, according to the Troitsky line, and the reason is that Black's king is on the wrong edge of the board upon which the Troitzky-line loses its significance.

Here, in Chéron's study from 1955, White wants to have this position with Black to move because then Black will be forced to go into the corner.

1 ♔c3 ♔b1 2 ♔d2 ♔a1 3 ♔c1 ♔a2 4 ♔c2

The first mission is completed. It's Black to move.

4...♔a1

White now manoeuvres to get the same position but with a vertical opposition instead of a horizontal one.

5 ♔b3 ♔b1

In this position the plan is to manoeuvre the c4-knight and king in such a way that the c1-square is under control.

6 ♘b2 ♔c1 7 ♔c3 ♔b1 8 ♘d3 ♔a1 9 ♔c4 ♔a2 10 ♔b4 ♔a1 11 ♔a3 ♔b1

12 ♔b3

Now White has enough time to bring up the blockading knight to generate a timely mating net.

12...♔a1 13 ♘e3 g2 14 ♘c2+ ♔b1 15 ♘a3+ ♔a1 16 ♘b4 g1♕ 17 ♘bc2 mate.

166a

G. Svenn – Engqvist
Örebro 1995

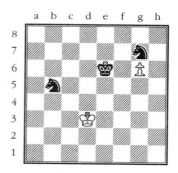

White to move

My first indirect experience of this rare but fascinating ending was as a junior in the late seventies when the highest rated player in my club SK-33 in Enköping, Anders Lundquist, reached the Troitzky ending when his game against Sven-Olof Andersson was adjourned. I recall how impressed I was that he managed to win what was to my eyes a rather intricate ending.

Approximately 25 years later I too got my once-in-a-lifetime experience of this rare but fascinating ending. As we have seen from the study by Chéron Black can only win against a g-pawn if that pawn is placed no further than g3 with a blockading knight on g4. In the above position I have only one small practical winning chance and that is to lure the king to a8 (according to the study by Chéron.) All other corners will be a safe haven for White's king. If the pawn promotes on g8 the queen will control important squares such as the b3-square as well as the g-file. The Swedish GM Ulf Andersson, who was present during this team competition in Örebro 1995, told me right after the game that the winning corner was a8. At the time this was all new to me but I was very impressed by Andersson's profound understanding of this rare but important ending.

58 ♔e3 ♔d5 59 ♔f4 ♔d4 60 ♔f3 ♘c3 61 ♔f4 ♘d5+ 62 ♔f3 ♔d3 63 ♔g4 ♔e4 64 ♔g3 ♔e3 65 ♔g4 Draw.

Here my opponent claimed a draw and surprisingly the arbiter accepted the claim despite the fact that I had some small practical winning chances. Moreover Svenn had only a few seconds left and I had 22 minutes for the rest of the game! My protest didn't help and later it turned out that the arbiter didn't know that with one pawn on the board Black has practical winning chances! He

thought it was an elementary draw since two knights cannot mate! Later I heard that he had bought all the endgame books he could get hold of in order to compensate for his wrong decision. From my point of view I don't mind so much about the split point as the fact that I never got the chance to play out this endgame in accordance with the 50 move rule!

167

B.Nikolić – Mozetić
Yugoslavia 1991

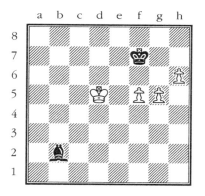

White to move

We know that a bishop is worth three pawns but everything depends on how far advanced these pawns are. Generally the further advanced, the stronger the pawns are, and the weaker the bishop. To my mind, this ending is the most instructive phase to learn and understand the real value of a piece.

1 ♔d6?

The only way to win is by 1 h7! with the threat of 2 f6 so Black has to reply 1...♔g7. Now White has to sacrifice the h-pawn by 2 ♔e6!!

(2 g6? is only a draw due to the stalemate trick 2...♔h8 3 ♔e6 ♗f6! and White cannot improve his position.) Then White wins after:

(a) 2...♗c1 3 g6 ♗b2 4 f6+ ♗xf6 5 h8♕+ ♔xh8 6 ♔xf6

(b) 2...♗c3 3 f6+ ♔xh7 4 ♔f7

(c) 2...♔h8 3 f6! (3 ♔f7? ♗c1 4 g6 ♗b2 5 f6 ♗xf6 6 ♔xf6 is stalemate.) 3...♗c3 (3...♗c1 4 g6 ♗h6 5 ♔f7) 4 ♔f7 ♗b2 5 ♔e8 ♗c3 (5...♔xh7 6 ♔f7! followed by g5-g6-g7 wins or 5...♗a3 6 g6 ♗f8 7 ♔f7!) 6 f7 ♗b4 7 f8♕+ ♗xf8 8 ♔xf8 ♔xh7 9 ♔f7 ♔h8 10 ♔g6 ♔g8 11 ♔h6! and White succeeds in promoting the g-pawn.

(d) 2...♔xh7 3 ♔f7!

This is the key position to remember in this ending. Now there is nothing Black can do to prevent White from advancing his pawns. After 3...♗c3 4 f6 ♔h8 5 g6 White wins because the pawn ending after 5...♗xf6 6 ♔xf6 ♔g8 7 g7 is conclusive.

White's unfortunate error gives the move to Black and now he has the chance to decide where White's pawns should be placed.

1...♗c1

1...♔g8!! was also playable. The waiting move 1...♗c3? would give White the move but with the king on d6 there are two wins: 2 g6+ (2 h7 also wins as mentioned before in the variation with the king on d5.) 2...♔f6 3 ♔d7! ♗d2 4 h7 ♔g7 5 f6+ ♔h8 6 ♔e6 ♗c3 7 g7+! ♔xh7 8 ♔f7.

2 g6+ ♔g8!!

2...♔f6? loses after 3 h7 ♔g7 4 f6+ ♔h8 5 ♔e6 ♗b2 (5...♗h6 6 ♔f7) 6 g7+ ♔xh7 7 ♔f7 and 2...♔f8? after 3 h7 ♗b2 4 ♔e6 ♔h8 (4...♔g7 5 f6+) 5 f6 ♗g7 6 fxg7+ ♔xg7 7 h8♕+ ♔xh8 8 ♔f6.

3 h7+ ♔h8! 4 f6 ♗b2 5 g7+ ♔xh7 6 ♔e6 ♗xf6 Draw.

After 7 ♔xf6 ♔g8 8 ♔g6 Black is stalemated.

168

Réti
1929

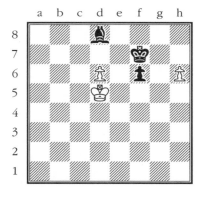

White to move

Judith Polgar has mentioned that Réti was one of her favourite composers. I wouldn't be surprised if she counted this as one of the most impressive studies by Réti.

1 ♔c6! ♗a5

White wins after 1...f5 2 ♔d5 ♗f6 3 d7 ♔e7 (3...♔g6 4 ♔e6) 4 d8♕+ ♔xd8 5 ♔e6 or 1...♔g6 2 ♔d7 ♗a5 3 ♔e6.

2 ♔d5! ♗c3 3 h7

Not 3 ♔c4? ♗b2 4 ♔d5 f5 5 ♔c6 f4.

3...f5 4 d7 ♔e7

It looks like White is completely lost but he's not. He can continue with the incredibly beautiful...

5 d8♕+!!

5 ♔c6? fails to the only move 5...♔d8! which prevents 6 ♔c7 when White would win.

5...♔xd8 6 ♔e6 f4 7 ♔d5!!

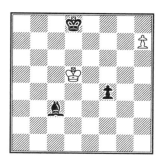

The core of the position. How is it possible that this position is a draw? The f-pawn seems unstoppable and the bishop controls the h8-square. One can understand that Réti was fascinated by the paradoxical idea that the white king can control the f-pawn by using the threat on the bishop on c3 as a springboard to gaining the necessary tempo.

7...f3 8 ♔c4! ♗f6 9 ♔d3

Black's king is now too far away to defend the f3-pawn so White can just pick it off. An amazing study in the spirit of Réti's immortal pawn ending.

169

Chéron
1956

White to move

1 ♗f7!

It's vital to prevent Black from occupying the h5-e8 diagonal. 1 h4? ♗g6 is a draw since the only way to put pressure on the bishop is by approaching it with the king, but then Black's king follows and puts pressure on the h-pawn. 2 ♔g4 ♔h2 3 ♔g5 ♔g3 is a clear draw.

1...♗e2 2 h4

This is the moment to advance the h-pawn.

2...♗d1 3 ♗g6!!

The bishop manoeuvre to f5 is the key to win. 3 ♔f4? is met by

3...♚h2 4 ♗g6 ♚h3 5 ♔g5 ♚g3. The ideal place for the king, if not in front of the pawn, is from the rear. 6 ♗h5 ♗a4 is a draw because White cannot control both the d1-h5 and h5-e8 diagonals. 7 ♗g4 ♗e8 8 ♗h5 ♗a4 9 ♗g6 ♗d1 etc. only repeats the position.

3...♗e2 4 ♗f5! ♗h5

5 ♔f4!

The right moment to approach with the king is when the bishop is on f5 because it's important to control both the g4- and g6-squares with the bishop as well as with the king. When this is accomplished White can react appropriately with the bishop according to Black's reply.

5...♚h2 6 ♔g5 ♗d1

If 6...♗e8 then 7 ♗g6!. Black's king is not on g3 so this vital move is playable. This is the reason the bishop must be placed on f5 otherwise Black gains the necessary tempo to play the king to its ideal square behind the pawn. After 7...♗a4 8 h5 ♗b3 9 h6 ♗g8 10 ♔f6 ♔g3 11 ♔g7 White wins.

7 ♗g4! ♗c2 8 h5 ♔g3 9 ♗f5 ♗b3 10 h6 ♗g8 11 ♔g6 ♔f4

12 ♔g7 ♔g5 13 ♗g6

This is an important zugzwang position to remember. The king wants to maintain the pressure on the h6-pawn but since the king move to h5 isn't legal Black has to move the bishop, but then the pawn is free to advance the desired steps.

170

Spassky – Karpov
Rapidplay, Porto Veccio 2006

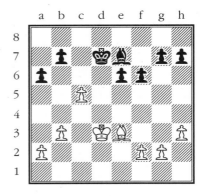

Black to move

White has the more active pawn majority and king so Black has to be very careful.

28...♗d8?!

Karpov missed an excellent opportunity to perhaps even turn the tables after 28...♔c6 29 ♔c4 (Note that 29 b4? ♔d5 would give Black the more active king and in conjunction with the activation of his majority [...e6-e5, ...f6-f5 etc.] it's only Black who can play for a win.) 29...a5 30 a3?

244

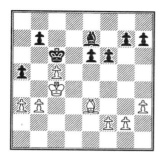

This natural move, preparing b3-b4, is a big mistake because of 30...♗xc5!!. Such a devilish move is very easy to miss, especially in the faster forms of chess or simply due to fatigue. It's like a shot out of the blue which is directed against the mobility of the pawns and the fact that the pieces are servants to the pawns, as Philidor realised long ago. 31 ♗xc5 b5+ 32 ♔d4 e5+ leads to a winning endgame for Black. In *300 Most Important Tactical Chess Positions* a similar idea was overlooked in position 206. If you are armed with such tactical ideas in minor piece endings you have an advantage because they are easily overlooked. After all, who expects explosions in such a quiet position?

29 b4 ♗c7 30 ♔c4 h5 31 a4 ♗e5 32 b5 axb5+ 33 axb5 ♔c7?!

More in harmony of the position was 33...♗c7.

34 g4!

White prepares f2-f4-f5. White wants to liquidate the e6-pawn to secure the d5-square for his king, so it will be able to penetrate further into the heart of Black's position.

34...hxg4 35 hxg4 ♔d7 36 f4 ♗b2 37 f5

37...e5?

37...♗e5 was the only move because control of the h2-b8 diagonal is crucial for both players. If Black waits with 37...♗a1? he loses by force after 38 ♗f4! because the black king is tied to the protection of the e6-pawn. White can now support the b-pawn to the promotion square by tactical means, because it is newly supported by the bishop placed on the ideal "London" diagonal. 38...♗b2 39 c6+! bxc6 40 fxe6+ ♔xe6 41 b6 and the pawn runs home.

38 ♔d5

Penetration of the fifth rank with king and pawns is often the key to winning many endings with few pieces. Here the g4-pawn plans to take further steps to clinch the game. Remember the Ulf Andersson game in the introduction!

38...♗a3 39 g5 fxg5

Black cannot allow the further advance g5-g6 because then ♗h6 would promote the g-pawn.

40 ♗xg5 ♗b2 41 ♗h4 Black resigns.

42 ♗g3 picks up both the e5- and g7-pawns.

245

171

Sveshnikov – Kasparov

USSR Championship, Minsk 1979

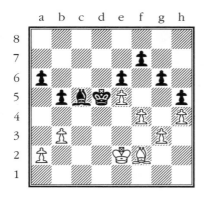

White to move

Kasparov moved the bishop from b4 to play the psychologically clever 34...♝c5!, instead of the objectively better centralisation into enemy territory with 34...♚e4 followed by 35...♝c3 and 36...♝d4. However, in such a situation it is easier for Sveshnikov to think that the exchange of bishops will be dead lost for White.

35 ♝xc5??

This is an incorrect "liquidation on the chessboard" to use the title of Joel Benjamin's interesting book which deals solely with transitions into pawn endings. As we can see here it's pretty common in practice to make mistakes in the transition phase. Skilled players sometimes wait for the right moment, for example when the opponent has less time on the clock, for such important decisions which might decide the game.

Correct was 35 ♝e3! and just maintain the tension between the bishops. After 35...♝xe3 (35...♝d4 is answered by 36 ♚d3 and 35...♝b4 by 36 ♚f3, controlling the important e4-square.) 36 ♚xe3 ♚c5 37 a3! the pawn ending is a draw, because Black cannot penetrate either on the queenside or in the centre.

35...♚xc5

Now White cannot prevent penetration on the queenside or in the centre.

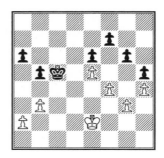

36 ♚d3

Black now wins with a two-step-plan. First the king moves to a3 and then the queenside pawns will decide by means of two breakthroughs. A zugzwang will arise after 36 a3 ♚d4 (or 36...b4 37 a4 ♚d4 38 ♚d2 a5) 37 ♚d2 a5 and Black's king penetrates on either side of the board.

36...♚b4 37 ♚c2 ♚a3 38 ♚b1

Do you recognize the theme from Rubinstein's most famous pawn endgame where the king was placed on h3?

38...a5 39 ♚a1 a4

The first breakthrough.

40 bxa4 ♔xa4 41 ♔b1

41 ♔b2 b4 42 ♔c2 ♔a3 43 ♔b1 b3 doesn't prevent the second breakthrough.

41...♔a3 42 ♔a1 b4 43 ♔b1 b3

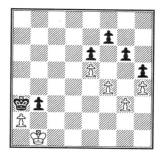

Now the second decisive breakthrough. After the exchange of pawns the black king walks east and slaughters all the white pawns.

White resigns.

172

Ljubojević – Karpov
Milan 1975

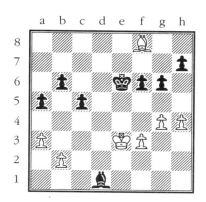

White to move

With correct defensive play by White, this position should result in a draw.

34 ♔e4

Ljubojević doesn't seem to have any plan and makes the first move in the wrong direction. According to Dvoretsky the simplest way to maintain the balance is to place the pawns on the opposite colour of the opponent's bishop. Plausible variations are 34 g5 (The principled move in this type of ending with bishops of opposite colours. It's surprising that Ljubojević doesn't play "according to the book".) 34...f5 (or 34...fxg5 then 35 hxg5 and 36 f4 followed by manoeuvring the king to the queenside.) 35 f4 ♔d5 36 ♗g7 ♔c4 37 ♔d2 and White has no problems holding the draw.

34...a4 35 h5

35 g5 f5+ 36 ♔e3 was still the simplest continuation and the principled way to hold the draw.

35...gxh5 36 gxh5 f5+ 37 ♔e3 ♔d5 38 h6 ♔c4 39 f4 ♔b3

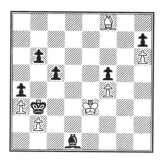

40 ♗g7?

40 ♔d2 still draws but it's necessary to analyse 40...♔xb2 in depth. 41 ♔xd1 ♔xa3 (41...c4 42 ♗g7+ c3 43 ♔e2! ♔c2! (43...♔xa3? 44 ♗xc3 b5 45 ♗e5 b4 46 ♗d6 ♔b3 47 ♔d3 and White

wins.) Black must prevent the king move to d3 while preparing ...b6-b5-b4 etc. White holds the draw by manoeuvring his king to the queenside: 44 ♔e3 b5 45 ♔d4 ♔d2 46 ♔c5 c2 47 ♗b2 c1♕+ 48 ♗xc1+ ♔xc1.

The pawn ending leads to a drawn queen ending after the forced sequence: 49 ♔xb5 ♔d2 50 ♔xa4 ♔e3 51 ♔b3 ♔xf4 52 a4 ♔g3 53 a5 f4 54 a6 f3 55 a7 f2 56 a8♕ f1♕ 57 ♕g8+ etc.) 42 ♔c2 ♔b4 43 ♔b2 b5 44 ♗d6 ♔c4 is also a draw but requires the specific knowledge that 45 ♔a3! is the only way to achieve this. Black's pawns mustn't reach the fifth rank (from Black's point of view).

40...♔c2

The game is decided because White's king can no longer defend the queenside and there are always possibilities of making breakthroughs with the pawns. Such a position is important to know and understand because White cannot prevent Black from creating a passed pawn.

41 ♗e5 ♗h5!

Black manoeuvres the bishop to b3 according to Nimzowitsch's famous principle that a weakness, in this case the b2-pawn, should be blockaded before attacking it.

42 ♗f6 ♗f7 43 ♗e5 ♗b3 44 ♗g7 b5

The queenside pawns advance to prepare the decisive breakthrough.

45 ♗f8 c4 46 ♗g7

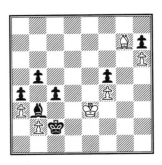

46...b4!

This breakthrough secures Black a passed pawn.

47 ♔d4

47 axb4 c3 48 ♗xc3 (48 bxc3 is met by the strong blockading-move 48...♗c4! and the a-pawn advances to a1 with decisive effect: 49 b5 a3 50 b6 a2 51 b7 a1♕ 52 b8♕ ♕g1+ 53 ♔f3 ♗d5+ 54 ♔e2 ♕g2+ 55 ♔e1 ♕g3+ 56 ♔e2 ♗c4 mate.) 48...a3 49 ♗e5 a2 This was the reason why the b2-pawn had to be blockaded. Now White cannot play the b2-pawn to b3 and control the promotion square a1.

47...c3! 48 bxc3 bxa3 49 c4 a2 50 ♔c5 ♔b1 51 ♔b4 a1♕ 52 ♗xa1 ♔xa1 53 c5 ♔b2 54 c6 a3 55 c7 ♗e6

Just in time to stop White's pawn.

56 ♔c5 a2 57 ♔d6 ♗c8 White resigns.

Don't forget this breakthrough with bishops of opposite colour. Apparently Ljubojević had overlooked these ideas, since he didn't go for the simpler option of placing the g-pawn on g5 as early as possible.

173

Carlsen – Caruana
Game 11, World Championship,
London 2018

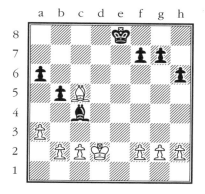

Black to move

30...h5!

Caruana plays according to the "book" and places his pawns on the same colour as his bishop. This makes it easier to protect the pawns and avoid an attack from the opponent's bishop. This is step 1 to hold the draw when one pawn down.

31 ♔e3 ♔d7!

Step 2 is to advance with the king to the flank where Black is one pawn down.

32 ♔d4 g6!

The pawn wave is completed on the kingside so now it's practically impossible for White to carry out a successful breakthrough on that side of the board.

33 g3 ♗e2 34 ♗f8 ♔c6!

When the defender has prevented the opponent's king penetrating on the queenside it's easy to hold the game and White can only play for a cheapo.

35 b3 ♗d1 36 ♔d3 ♗g4 37 c4 ♗e6 38 ♔d4 bxc4 39 bxc4 ♗g4 40 c5 ♗e6 41 ♗h6 ♗d5 42 ♗e3 ♗e6 43 ♔e5

White's last trick is to attack the kingside with his king and pawns and try to create a passed pawn with the help of a breakthrough.

43...♗d5 44 ♔f4 ♗e6 45 ♔g5 ♗d5

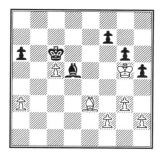

46 g4!

Step 1 for White to try to create a passed pawn on the kingside is to exchange the g-pawn for the h-pawn. It has easily been achieved.

46...hxg4

46...♗f3 also holds: 47 gxh5 (or 47 ♔f6 ♗xg4 48 ♔xf7 ♗f5) 47...gxh5 (But not 47...♗xh5?? 48 ♔f6.)

47 ♔xg4

Step 2 in White's plan to create a passed pawn on the kingside is to break with f4-f5 at the right moment and try to get a passed pawn on the h-file.

47...♗a2 48 ♔g5 ♗b3 49 ♔f6 ♗a2 50 h4 ♗b3 51 f4 ♗a2 52 ♔e7 ♗b3 53 ♔f6 ♗a2 54 ♔e7 ♗b3 55 ♔f6 ♗a2 56 f5! ♗b1!

The only defensive move is not that difficult to find.

57 ♗f2

57 ♔xf7 ♗xf5! 58 ♔f6 ♗e4 avoids the cheapo 59 h5.

57...♗c2! Draw agreed.

After Carlsen had assured himself that Caruana wouldn't play the suicidal 57...♗xf5?? 58 h5.

174

Chéron
1927

White to play

Chéron has shown in a few studies how to win with the bishop pair against a supported pawn one step from the queening square. After having seen his instructive studies one gets a really good feel for the

enormous working capacity of the two bishops when they are cooperating.

1 ♗g7!

White has to prevent 1...♔b2 which would draw.

1...♔d1

Black's best defence.

2 ♗b3 ♔d2

2...♔c1 with the threat 3...♔b1 is met by 3 ♗f7 ♔b1 (3...♔d1 4 ♗h5+!) 4 ♗g6 ♔c1 5 ♔c6 ♔d1 6 ♗h5+ ♔c1 7 ♔c5 and White wins by repeating the manoeuvre with the bishop and then approaching one step nearer the pawn with the king.

3 ♗a4!!

This beautiful move is the key to the win.

3...♔c1!

3...c1♕ is met by the skewer 4 ♗h6+.

4 ♗c6! ♔d1 5 ♗f3+ ♔d2 6 ♗h6+ ♔c3 7 ♗c1! ♔b3 8 ♗e4!

White wins. The c2-pawn is now firmly blockaded on c1 and under pressure from the other bishop. This perfect cooperation between the bishops makes it easy for White's king to pick it up.

175

Yurtaev – Serper
USSR 1988

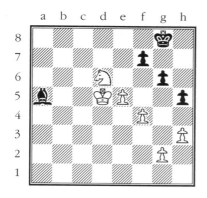

White to move

According to Fine the superior side with the knight should in general win, since he can convert the e- and f-pawns into a passed pawn by exchanging the enemy f-pawn. However if the superior side has the bishop there are drawing chances for the defender due to the bishop's inability to cover all the necessary squares.

1 ♘e4?

The knight was much better placed on d6. The simplest way to exploit White's superior activity is to manoeuvre the king to d7 followed by Fine's plan of converting the e- and f-pawns to a passed pawn on the e-file. Plausible variations are: 1 ♔c6! ♗b4 (1...♗d8 2 ♔d7 ♗h4 3 g3! ♗xg3 4 ♘xf7! and there are only three squares to queen the e-pawn.) 2 ♔d7 ♔f8 (2...h4 3 ♔e8 f6 4 ♔e7 fxe5 5 fxe5 and the e-pawn will win.) 3 g4 hxg4 4 hxg4 ♗a3 5 f5 gxf5 6 gxf5 ♗b4 7 e6 ♗xd6 8 ♔xd6 ♔e8 9 f6! ♔f8 10 e7+ ♔e8 11 ♔c5 ♔d7 12 e8♕+ ♔xe8 13 ♔c6 ♔d8 14 ♔d6 ♔e8 15 ♔c7 and White picks up the f7-pawn.

1...♗b6 2 f5?

This isn't the right procedure. White could still win by penetrating Black's position with 2 ♘f6+ ♔g7 3 ♔d6 ♗e3 4 g3 ♗c1 5 ♔e7 h4 6 ♘e8+ ♔g8 7 g4 ♗xf4 8 ♔f6 ♗h6 9 g5 ♗f8 10 e6 fxe6 11 ♔xg6 etc.

2...gxf5 3 ♘f6+ ♔g7 4 ♘xh5+ ♔g6 5 ♘f6 ♔g5 6 ♘e8 ♗f2 7 ♘d6 ♔g6 8 ♔c6 ♗d4 9 ♘c4 ♗c3 10 ♔d5 ♔g5 11 ♘d6 ♔g6 12 ♘b5 ♗b2

It was possible to draw by means of the following illustrative variation: 12...♗e1 13 ♘d4 ♗f2 14 ♘f3 ♗g3 15 ♔d6 f6! 16 ♔e6 fxe5 17 ♘xe5+ ♔g5 18 ♘f3+ ♔f4 19 ♘d4 ♗e1 20 ♘xf5 ♗c3 21 g3+ ♔f3! (21...♔g5? would be a mistake due to 22 ♘h4 and 23 ♘f3+.)

Despite the fact that Black is two pawns down, this position is a draw. White plays 22 ♔f7. This is White's best winning chance which requires

251

that Black finds the best moves with the bishop: 22...♗e5! 23 g4 ♔g2 24 h4 ♔f3 25 g5 ♔g4 26 ♔g6 ♗f4! 27 ♔f6 ♗c1 28 g6 ♗b2+ 29 ♔e6 ♗c3 and White is in zugzwang and cannot avoid loss of material.

13 ♘d4 ♔g5 14 g3! ♗c3 15 ♘f3+ ♔g6 16 ♔d6 ♗b4+ 17 ♔d7 ♗c3 18 ♔e7 ♔g7 19 ♔d7 ♔g6

20 e6?

20 ♔e7 forces Black to defend against the threat of 21 ♘h4+. After 20...♔g7 21 ♔e8!! Black is in zugzwang and has to move the bishop to a worse square. (An immediate 21 ♔d7 ♔g6 22 e6 would have led only to a draw after 22...fxe6 23 ♔xe6 ♗b4 24 ♘h4+ ♔g5 25 ♘xf5 ♗e1!) 21...♗b2 22 ♔d7 ♔g6 23 e6 fxe6 24 ♔xe6 ♗a3 25 ♘h4+ ♔g5 26 ♘xf5. This position is winning for White because Black cannot put any pressure on the g3-pawn.

20...fxe6 21 ♔xe6 ♗f6?

Black could draw by 21...♗a5 22 ♘e5+ (22 ♘h4+ ♔g5 23 ♘xf5 ♗e1! is a draw, for example 24 g4 ♗c3! 25 ♔d5 ♔f4. Black must stop White's king manoeuvre to e4 and f3. 26 ♔c4 ♗f6) 22...♔g5 23 h4+ ♔h5 24 ♔xf5 ♗c7! and the knight is

pinned on e5 due to the threat on the g3-pawn.

The game concluded:

22 ♘e5+ ♗xe5 23 ♔xe5 ♔g5 4 h4+ ♔g4 25 h5 Black resigns.

176

Hillarp-Persson – Ragger
Politiken Cup 2015

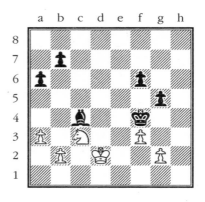

White to move

38 ♘e2+!!

This is a bold but correct decision to transfer to a pawn ending because on the surface it looks like a forced loss, according to the famous model example Cohn – Rubinstein, although it's actually a draw due to the pawn formation on the queenside.

38 ♘d1? would in the long run have led to zugzwang, for example 38...♔g3 39 ♘e3 ♗b5 40 ♔e1 a5 41 b3 ♗a6 42 ♔d2 ♔f2 43 b4 axb4 44 axb4 ♗b5 etc.

38...♗xe2

38...♔e5 39 ♔e3 keeps the endgame in balance.

**39 ♔xe2 ♔g3 40 ♔f1 b5 41 b4! f5
42 ♔g1 g4 43 fxg4 ♔xg4 44 ♔f2 f4**

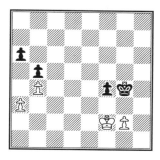

In this position the Swedish GM made the tragic-comic and premature decision to resign. Most probably he would have seen the forced draw if he had continued...

45 ♔g1 ♔g3 46 ♔f1 f3 47 gxf3

47 ♔g1?? fxg2 48 a4 bxa4 49 b5 a3 50 b6 a2 51 b7 a1♕ mate. White is only one tempo from a check on b8 but one tempo in chess is many times the whole life.

**47...♔xf3 48 ♔e1 ♔e3 49 ♔d1
♔d3 50 ♔c1 ♔c3**

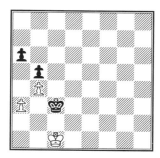

A most probable speculation is that he resigned due to the fact that he knew the example with Rubinstein so why suffer needlessly? It's human to think that Black always wins due to the extremely active king, but this position is an exception and this is why chess is so difficult and Hillarp-Persson can be fully excused. But now to the question: how is it possible that this position is a draw?

51 a4!

This is the key move.

51...♔xb4 52 axb5 axb5 53 ♔b2!

White's king has the opposition so it's an elementary draw. The difference compared with the Rubinstein game was that the e-pawns contributed to Cohn's fall. In Sveshnikov – Kasparov Black had four pawns on the queenside making it impossible to survive with a finesse like 51 a4! which was available for Hillarp-Persson if he had continued the game.

177

Henneberger – Nimzowitsch
Swiss Championship,
Winterthur 1931

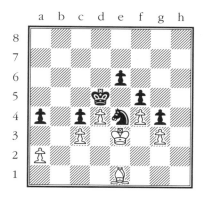

Black to move

To win this endgame Black must strive to place White in a zugzwang

253

position. Here it's necessary to carry out a triangulation manoeuvre twice to succeed.

48...♚d6 49 ♚e2 ♚c6 50 ♚e3 ♚d5

Now it's White's turn to move instead of Black's.

51 ♚e2 ♘d6 52 ♚e3

White must prevent the black king from penetrating the position via e4.

52...♘b5 53 ♗d2 ♘a3 54 ♗c1 ♘b1

A very uncomfortable knight for White!

55 ♗b2

55 ♗d2 loses after 55...♘xd2 56 ♚xd2 ♚e4 57 ♚e2 a3 and Black penetrates to f3 or d3.

55...a3 56 ♗a1

Black would like it to be his move so he has to make a second triangulation to achieve his dream!

56...♚d6 57 ♚e2 ♚c6

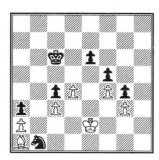

58 ♚d1

58 ♚e3 ♚d5 leads to a second complete triangulation. 59 ♚e2 (59 ♚f2 ♘d2 60 ♚e2 ♚e4! [Note the trap *60...♘b3?? 61 axb3 cxb3 62 ♚d3 and White wins. This was*

probably White's best practical chance to even win the game so always look for traps when a position is dead lost!] 61 ♚xd2 ♚f3 and the g-pawn queens after five more moves.) 59...♚e4 and Black penetrates further into the heart of White's position, for example 60 ♚e1 ♚e3!.

58...♚d5

Nimzowitsch has calculated the finish of the game exactly.

59 ♚c2 ♚e4 60 ♚xb1 ♚f3 61 ♗b2 axb2 62 a4 ♚xg3 63 a5 ♚h2 64 a6 g3 65 a7 g2 66 a8♕ g1♕+ 67 ♚xb2 ♕g2+

Everything goes like clockwork!

68 ♕xg2+ ♚xg2 69 ♚a3 ♚f3 70 ♚b4 ♚xf4 71 ♚xc4 ♚e3 72 d5 exd5+ 73 ♚xd5 f4 74 c4 f3 75 c5 f2 76 c6 f1♕ White resigns.

Black blocks the c-pawn on c8. Quite an exciting endgame!

178

Carlsen – Georgiadis
Biel 2018

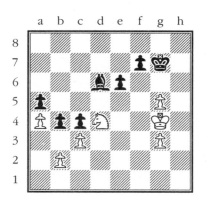

Black to move

Sometimes chess is a really cruel game. Black played the horrendous move...

46...b3??

Smyslov once expressed the view that one can play a perfect game for 39 moves and then make one mistake and the whole game is destroyed. This is a typical example of what the great chess coach Mark Dvoretsky would call "tragic-comics." Black could have played 46...♗e5 after which Carlsen would have been forced to find 47 ♘c2! to keep the balance, for example 47...bxc3 48 bxc3 ♗xc3 49 ♘e3 is a pretty certain draw.

47 ♘f3! Black resigns.

Georgiadis' resignation, after a long think, was perhaps slightly premature. He must have forgotten that there was a forced move which threatened to pick up both pawns by ♘f3-d2xc4-d2xb3. His last chance was to go for 47...♗a3 anyway and after 48 bxa3 b2 49 ♘d2 to play 49...♔g6. The best variation for White then would be 50 ♔f4 ♔h5 51 ♔e3 ♔xg5 52 ♔e2! ♔g4 53 ♔d1 ♔xg3 54 ♔c2. If White plays 52 ♔d4 instead then care is required so that after 52...♔g4 53 ♔xc4 e5! he doesn't play the natural-looking move 54 ♔d5??, which surprisingly is a forced draw by force after 54...♔xg3 55 ♔xe5 ♔f2. However White can still win by playing either 54 ♔b3 or 54 ♔d3.

It would have been interesting to see this endgame played out but one can also understand Georgiadis' disappointment as he had this game in the palm of his hand. It was also

ironic that it was the queenside knight which turned out to be the surviving hero, especially since Carlsen played the suspect and provocative 1 e4 c5 2 ♘a3?!. In the end Carlsen's opponent lost track of this queenside knight.

179

Saidy – Fischer
US Championship, New York 1964

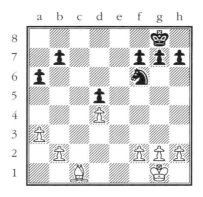

Black to move

It's very instructive to see how Fischer manages to outmanoeuvre Saidy in this seemingly drawish ending.

23...♘d7

The first step is to manoeuvre the knight to its best square e6 where it can exercise pressure on White's only weakness.

24 ♔f1 ♘f8 25 ♔e2 ♘e6 26 ♔d3 h5!

Next step is to activate the king on the white kingside squares while grabbing space with the pawns. In the long run Black's only chance to win is if he manages to create a second weakness on the kingside.

27 ♗e3 ♔h7 28 f3

White adopts a waiting strategy and places his pawns on white squares according to Capablanca's rule which states that you should place your pawns on the opposite colour of your own bishop.

28...♔g6 29 a4 ♔f5 30 ♔e2 g5 31 ♔f2 ♘d8 32 ♗d2 ♔g6 33 ♔e3 ♘e6 34 ♔d3 ♔f5 35 ♗e3 f6

Black plays according to the no-hurry principle because the f-pawn wants to go to f4.

36 ♔e2 ♔g6 37 ♔d3 f5 38 ♔e2

38 g3 (activity!) was also good here with excellent drawing chances. For example 38...f4 39 gxf4 g4 40 fxg4 hxg4 41 ♗f2 ♘xf4+ 42 ♔e3 ♔f5 43 ♗g3 etc.

38...f4 39.♗f2 ♘g7

39...g4 was also playable and part of Black's plan but Fischer prefers first to manoeuvre his knight to f5 which is the best position for this piece.

40 h3

A more active defence was 40 g4 fxg3 41 ♗xg3 ♘f5 42 ♗e5.

40...♘f5 41 ♔d3 g4! 42 hxg4 hxg4 43 fxg4 ♘h6

It's clear now that White's second pawn weakness is g2.

44 ♗e1?

White should have stuck to passive defence with 44 ♔e2 ♘xg4 45 ♗g1 with the threat of getting rid of his g2-weakness by 46 ♔f3 and g3 at an appropriate moment. A plausible variation is 45...♔f5 46 ♔f3 ♘f6 47 ♗h2 ♘h5 48 a5 ♔g5 49 g4 fxg3 50 ♗xg3 with a draw.

44...♘xg4

44...♔g5, followed by 45...♔xg4 and 46...♘f5, leads to the same position as in the game.

45 ♗d2 ♔f5 46 ♗e1 ♘f6 47 ♗h4 ♘e4 48 ♗e1 ♔g4 49 ♔e2 ♘g3+

Black prepares the decisive manoeuvre ...♘f5-h4.

50 ♔d3

50 ♔f2 ♘f5 51 ♗c3 ♘e3 52 ♔g1 ♘d1! and Black wins a pawn or the pawn ending.

50...♘f5 51 ♗f2 ♘h4 52 a5

The pawn ending after 52 ♗xh4 ♔xh4 53 ♔e2 ♔g3 54 ♔f1 f3 55 gxf3 ♔xf3 is the key to winning the game.

52...♘xg2 53 ♔c3 ♔f3 54 ♗g1 ♔e2 55 ♗h2 f3 56 ♗g3 ♘e3 White resigns.

As 57...♘f5 follows next move.

180

Reshevsky – Woliston

US Championship, New York 1940

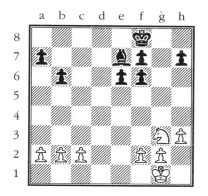

White to move

The computer evaluates this position as completely equal but in practice it's harder to play with the black pieces. Black not only has three pawn islands but must also face a pawn majority on the queenside. The first step for both players is to activate their kings.

24 ♔f1 ♔e8 25 ♔e2 ♔d7 26 ♔d3 ♔c6

It's slightly harder for Black to find a good place for his king since the knight can control both coloured squares.

27 ♘e2

Next step is to improve the pieces and pawns on the kingside.

27...♗c5

According to Capablanca's famous rule in such endings Black should place the pawns on opposite coloured squares to his bishop so as to compensate for lack of white square control. Thus 27...f5! was the correct move. After the further 28 ♘d4+ ♔d7 29 g4 fxg4 30 hxg4 a6 the position is balanced.

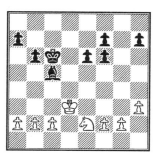

28 f4

Here White could have played 28 ♘d4+! followed by g2-g4, preventing Black from improving his pawn position on the kingside. Then 28...♗xd4? 29 ♔xd4 with the idea g2-g4 leads to a lost pawn ending. Instead 28...♔d6!? might be best when 29 g4 ♔e5 30 ♘c6+ ♔f4 31 ♔e2 b5 would give Black an active position with counterplay as 32 ♘d8 is answered by 32...♗e7. However 29 ♘b5+ ♔e5 30 ♘xa7 ♗xf2 31 c4 leads to a situation where White can play for two results.

28...b5?

Now it will be easier for White to create a passed pawn on the queenside. It's better for Black to follow Steinitz's famous rule and not move the queenside pawns at all. 28...f5! 29 g4 fxg4 30 hxg4 ♗f8!, followed by ...♗g7 or ...♗h6, would have made White's task much more difficult if not impossible.

29 g4

29 ♘d4+! ♚b6 30 g4 was even stronger since the defending king is more decentralised compared with the game.

29...a6 30 ♚e4

Here we can see why it was so important to place the f6-pawn on f5. White's king is centralised on e4 and in the future f4-f5 will be a decisive break.

30...♝f8

According to Reshevsky "The only good piece is a working piece. A piece that is undeveloped, out of play, passive, or hampered by pawns is not a good piece." Here the knight is clearly superior to the bishop due to its higher level of manoeuvrability.

31 ♘d4+ ♚d6 32 ♘b3

White plans the knight manoeuvre to d2 followed by c2-c4 while Black is marking time.

32...♝e7 33 ♘d2 ♝f8 34 c4 ♚c5 35 cxb5

35...axb5?

35...♚xb5 was more resistant since it's harder to create a passed pawn with the enemy pawn on a6 than on b5.

According to Fine "White has achieved the ideal end-game position – Black's pawn majority is immobilised, White's king is well centralised, and he has a good knight against a poor bishop. The rest merely involves setting up an outside passed pawn on the queenside and forcing a decisive gain of material on the other wing."

36 ♘b3+ ♚d6 37 ♘d4 ♚c5 38 f5!

The right moment for this decisive pawn break.

38...e5 39 ♘f3

White now plans the break g4-g5 which is on a black square.

39...h6 40 h4 ♝e7 41 h5! ♝d6

42 a3

As so often with a strategy on a specific colour square the decisive breakthrough often takes place on the opposite colour. The most convincing win was therefore 42 g5!! Surprisingly this attack on a strongpoint was overlooked by Reshevsky as well as the annotators.

42...fxg5 (42...hxg5 43 h6 ♗f8 44 h7 ♗g7 45 ♘h2 and Black is helpless against the manoeuvre ♘g4-h6-f7 followed by h8♕. If the black king manoeuvres to cover the f7-pawn White decides with his queenside pawn majority by patiently playing a2-a3, b2-b3 and a3-a4.) 43 ♘h2 ♗f8 44 ♘g4 ♔d6 45 ♘xe5 ♔e7 46 ♘g4 ♗g7 47 ♔d5 and White is technically winning.

42...b4

42...♔c4 43 ♘d2+ ♔c5 44 b4+ ♔c6 45 ♘f3 ♗f8 46 g5! hxg5 (46...fxg5 47 ♘xe5+ ♔c7 48 f6! ♔d6 49 ♔f5! ♔d5 50 ♘xf7 g4 51 ♔xg4 ♔e6 52 ♘d8+ ♔xf6 53 ♘c6 and the b-pawn falls in two moves.) 47 ♘h2 ♗g7 48 ♘g4 ♔d6 49 h6 ♗h8 50 h7 ♗g7 51 ♘h6 ♔e7 52 ♔d5 and White picks up the b-pawn.

43 a4

43 g5!! was still the most convincing win.

43...b3 44 ♘d2 ♔b4 45 a5 ♔xa5 46 ♘c4+ Black resigns.

This endgame teaches among other things that it's a good policy to exchange major pieces when one has the better pawn structure.

181

Gledura – Anand
Gibraltar Masters 2016

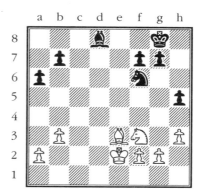

White to move

Black has just made the positional error 28...h6-h5? instead of either one of the normal centralising moves 28...♔f8 or 28...♘d5. White exploited Anand's last move with...

29 ♗g5!

White exploits the possibility to both reduce the knight to passivity by a pin and exchange it at an appropriate moment.

29...♔f8 30 ♔d3 ♔e8 31 ♗xf6! ♗xf6 32 ♔e4

It's difficult for Black to cover the white squares since Black's knight isn't left to cover them.

32...♗d8 33 ♘e5 ♔e7 34 ♔d5

White starts to get a strong positional bind on Black's position due to his space advantage.

34...♗b6?

34...♗c7 35 ♘d3 ♔d7 36 ♘c5+ ♔c8 was a better defensive

possibility. If now 37 ♘e4 then 37...♔d7.

35 ♘d3 ♔d7 36 ♘c5+ ♗xc5

36...♔c8 doesn't work on account of the weak d6-square. 37 ♘e4 (37 ♔d6 is also strong.) 37...♔d7 38 ♘d6 ♗xf2 39 ♘xb7 and Black cannot simultaneously hold the critical d6 and c5 squares.

37 ♔xc5

This pawn ending is an easy win for White, because his king is too active. White wins either on the queenside or on the kingside depending on Black's method of defence.

37...♔c7

Nor does 37...h4 help after 38 ♔b6 ♔c8 39 g3 g5 40 gxh4 White must be careful. Black's threat was the decisive 40...g4!. A typical variation now is the following: 40...gxh4 41 f4 f6 42 f5 ♔b8 43 b4 ♔c8 44 a3 ♔b8 45 a4 ♔c8 46 ♔a7 ♔c7 47 b5 axb5 48 axb5 b6 49 ♔a6 and White wins the b6-pawn.

38 h4 ♔d7 39 ♔b6 ♔c8 40 b4 ♔b8 41 f3 ♔c8 42 g4 hxg4 43 fxg4

♔b8 44 h5 f6 45 a4 ♔c8 46 ♔a7 ♔c7 47 b5 a5 48 ♔a8 Black resigns.

182

Smyslov – Golombek
London 1947

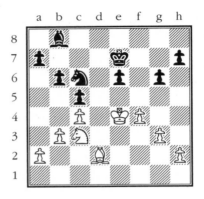

White to move

White has a minimal advantage due to his more active king and bishop, which will soon be placed on c3. Note also that Black has three pawn islands against White's two. A similar position arose between Gheorghiu and Fischer at the Siegen Olympiad 1970 but in that game Black had his bishop more actively placed on g7. That game ended in a draw.

33 ♘d1!

White plans to place his bishop on c3 and manoeuvre the knight to g4 so he can attack the h7-pawn and weaken Black's pawn chain.

33...♗d6

33...e5 weakens the d5-square and after 34 f5 the black bishop becomes worse. White has a clear advantage because apart from these two positional advantages there is a third one: it will be easier to create a passed pawn on the kingside. A plausible variation is 34...gxf5+ 35 ♔xf5 ♘d4+ 36 ♔e4 h5 37 h3 ♔e6 38 g4 hxg4 39 hxg4.

34 ♘f2 ♘d8

Black plans to manoeuvre the knight to f7 but this is a rather passive defence. Levenfish wrote that he was surprised by the manoeuvre of the black knight, since he thought the knight was well placed on c6. He recommends a different but stronger defensive set-up after the moves 34...♔f7 35 ♗c3 ♗e7. Black tries to manoeuvre his bishop to the long diagonal in the spirit of Gheorghiu – Fischer but this is promptly prevented with 36 ♘g4 although Black still has reasonable drawing chances after 36...♗d6.

35 ♗c3 ♘f7 36 ♘g4 h5

Levenfish recommends 36...♔d8 and only after 37 ♘f6 to play 37...h5.

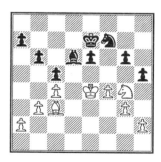

37 ♗f6+!

This strong bishop check helps to fix all Black's pawns on the kingside and in the centre.

37...♔d7 38 ♘f2 ♗c7

38...♗e7 39 ♗c3 g5? only helps White to create a passed pawn on the kingside after 40 fxg5 ♘xg5+ 41 ♔f4.

39 ♘d3 ♔c6 40 ♘e1!

White plans to bring the knight to h4.

40...♘d6+

The game was adjourned at this point.

41 ♔d3 ♘f5 42 ♘f3

All Black's pawns are fixed except the pawns on the queenside.

42...♔d7 43 ♔e4 ♘d6+ 44 ♔e3 ♘f5+ 45 ♔f2 ♗d6

45...a6 is answered by 46 a4.

46 h3! ♗c7 47 g4 hxg4 48 hxg4 ♘h6 49 ♔g3

49...♘f7?

A better defence was 49...♔e8 50 ♗e5 (50 ♘g5 ♔d7) 50...♗d8 51 ♗b8 ♘f7 (51...a6 52 ♘e5 g5 53 ♘c6 ♗f6 54 ♔e5 ♗xe5 55 ♘xe5 gxf4+ 56 ♔xf4 with a win according to Smyslov.) 52 g5 (52 ♗xa7 ♗c7 53 a4 g5 and Black wins the pawn back.) 52...♚d7 53 ♗e5 a6 54 ♗c3 b5 55 ♚h3 (55 ♘h4 is met by 55...e5! 56 f5 gxf5 57 g6 ♘h6 58 ♗xe5 bxc4 59 bxc4 ♚e6 60 ♘f3 and 55 ♚g4 by 55...bxc4 56 bxc4 ♚e8 57 ♗e5 ♗a5) 55...♚e8 56 ♚g4 bxc4 57 bxc4 ♗b6.

50 g5 ♗d8 51 ♚g4 ♗xf6 52 gxf6 ♚d6 53 ♘e5! Black resigns.

183

Gutmans – Tseitlin
USSR 1976

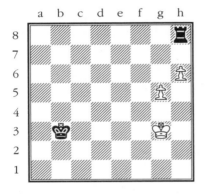

White to move

According to the American endgame expert, GM Edmar Mednis (1937-2002), "Of the various rook vs. multiple pawn endgames, the one of greatest practical importance is rook vs. two connected passed pawns. It usually results from a queening race where one side has given up its rook for the enemy pawn".

52 ♚f4?

It's easy to think that White should support the pawns while at the same time shielding against the black king, but this road only leads to a draw. The quickest, simplest and only way to win is by preparing the pawn-push of the g-pawn, but first the h6-pawn must be defended by the king: 52 ♚h4! (or 52 ♚g4!) 52...♚c4 53 ♚h5 ♚d5 54 g6 ♚e6 55 g7 ♖a8 56 h7 ♚f7 57 h8♕ and White wins.

52...♚c4

53 ♚e5

53 ♚f5 is trickier. Then:

(a) The natural 53...♚d5? loses to 54 g6 ♖xh6 55 g7 ♖h1 56 g8♕+.

(b) 53...♚d4! holds since there is no check on g8 after 54 g6 ♖xh6 55 g7 ♖h5+ 56 ♚f4 ♖h1!. After 57 g8♕?? (Correct is 57 ♚f5) 57...♖f1+ Black even wins.

(c) 53...♖f8+! holds as well after 54 ♚e6 (or 54 ♚g4 ♚d5! 55 g6 ♚e6 56 g7 ♖g8) 54...♖h8!.

53...♚d3!

Black attacks the g-pawn from behind but this was not the only defence. 53...♚c5 is also a draw after 54 ♚f6 ♚d6 55 ♚g7 ♖a8 56 h7 ♚e6 57 h8♕ (57 g6 ♚f5) 57...♖xh8 58 ♚xh8 ♚f5.

54 ♚f6

54 ♔f5 ♔e3 55 g6 ♖xh6 56 g7
leads nowhere after 56...♖h5+!.

**54...♔e4 55 ♔g7 ♖a8 56 h7 ♔f5
57 g6 ♔g5 58 h8♕ ♖xh8 59 ♔xh8
♔xg6 Draw.**

184

Kovalevskaya – Zhu Chen
Women's Olympiad, Moscow 1994

White to move

There are many names for
endgames that can be analysed with
100 percent accuracy, since there are
so few pieces on the board. We can
call these exceptionally important
endgames "Tablebase" "theoretical",
"precise", "technical" or "concrete"
endgames. Every concrete endgame
leads either to a forced win or a
forced draw. None of these
endgames has an evaluation but only
a result. Because of this you must
master them 100 percent. These
specific endgames go against
intuitive play and will from to time
arise in your own games. It's
possible to check such endgames
with the help of seven-piece-
endgame Tablebases or by
specialised endgame books by

Karsten Müller and John Nunn
where Tablebase has been used.

On this occasion White has a
concrete endgame which should
have been learned by heart. It's not
enough to know the result, one must
also know the method to achieve the
desired result. Here the White player
unfortunately destroyed her nice
pawn chain by playing the
aggressive...

66 f5+?

After the game Vladimir Kramnik
showed that it's a draw by doing
nothing and keeping the pawn chain
intact. 66 ♔g3! ♖g1+ 67 ♔h3 ♔f5
68 ♔h2 ♖a1 69 ♔g2! If Black plays
69...♔xf4 the pawns are free to
advance. For example 70 h7
(70 g6 is also a draw.) 70...♖a2+
(70...♖a8? 71 g6) 71 ♔h3 (71 ♔f1
♖a8 72 g6 ♔f3 73 ♔g1 ♔g3
74 ♔f1 etc.) 71...♖a3+ 72 ♔h4 ♖a1
73 ♔h5! Note that if the pawn chain
is placed one step further back
on the board, according to the
configuration f3-g4-h5, it's a loss as
has been shown by Chéron in 1927.
It's very important that the pawn
chain, with the spearhead on h6, is
close to the queening square.

66...♔h7 Black resigns.

Black realises that White will pick
up all the pawns after 67 ♔h5
(67 ♔g3 ♖f1 68 ♔g4 ♖f2! loses in
the same fashion.) 67...♖h1+
68 ♔g4 ♖f1!.

Black has forced a zugzwang
situation and the f-pawn is forced to
move giving Black the opportunity
to block all the pawns from g6 and
then pick them off one by one. This

concrete endgame has been known since 1843.

There are several dozen of these concrete endgames to master. A professional like Kramnik knows them. One can compete with the great majority of opponents by learning around two dozen of the most important concrete endgames so don't forget them!

185

Neumann – Steinitz
Baden-Baden 1870

White to move

This is a theoretical draw, regardless of who is to move. It's not possible for the attacker to gain the opposition. This type of position normally arises with the defender to move because White has promoted his g-pawn to a knight, rather than to a queen, so as to give check to the king on f6, otherwise it would have been mate on c8.

115 ♘h6

Obviously the only move but it's just enough to hold the draw.

115...♖h7

If Black tries to improve his king with 115...♔f6 White responds with disturbing checks after 116 ♘g8+ ♔g6 117 ♘e7+ etc. It's impossible for the attacker to break this cooperation between the defender's pieces.

116 ♘g4?

When the knight becomes separated from its king it's often possible to catch the knight. So the main rule is to keep the knight as close to the king as possible. 116 ♘g8 is a simple draw, because it's not possible to create a zugzwang situation. For example 116...♖f7+ 117 ♔e8 ♖f1 White's king is cut off but it doesn't mean anything. The most important thing is to keep the knight close to the king. 118 ♘h6 (118 ♘e7 also works because White can move the main defensive position to the queenside after 118...♖a1 119 ♘c8 ♖a8 120 ♔d8 etc. This is the main set-up to remember.) 118...♖a1 119 ♔f8 etc.

116...♖h4

116...♖h3! was immediately winning. The king cannot move due to mate or pin of the knight, while the knight has no squares where it will not be captured.

117 ♘e3 ♖e4 118 ♘d1

Remember the rook's position after 118 ♘g2 because it amounts to a total domination of the knight.

118...♖f4+

Black manoeuvres to f3 with tempo in order to limit the knight's radius of action even further.

**119 ♔g7 ♖f3 120 ♔g6 ♔e5
121 ♔g5 ♔d4 122 ♔g4 ♖f1
123 ♘b2 ♖b1 124 ♘a4 ♖b4 White
resigns.**

The knight is finally trapped.

Gustav Neumann was an exceptionally strong player and according to Chessmetrics.com he was ranked number one in the world for eighteen months during the period 1868-1870. If he can lose this endgame anyone can and as a matter of a fact even modern players at a high level have succumbed in this ending. In *300 Most Important Chess Positions*, position 212, I have shown how the strong GM Bacrot lost a drawn position against Kamsky in Sofia 2006. So don't forget to study and practice the key positions where the knight is close to the king and where it is cut off!

186

Vancura
1925

White to move

1 ♔h5!!

The trap in this beautiful study is that 1 ♔f5? leads to a draw after

1...♖e8! 2 ♘g6 ♔d6 (2...♔d7 also works.) 3 ♘f8 ♔e7! 4 g8♕ ♖xf8+. Also 1 ♔f7? ♖f3+ followed by 2...♖g3 draws.

1...♖e8

1...♖h3+ 2 ♔g4 ♖h1 3 ♘g6 ♖g1+ 4 ♔f5 ♖f1+ 5 ♔e6! ♖e1+ 6 ♘e5+ and White queens the pawn.

1...♖e1 2 ♘g6 ♖e8 3 ♔h6!! (3 ♘f8 ♖e1 4 ♘e6 also wins but the main variation is two moves faster.) 3...♔d6 4 ♘f8 ♖e1 5 g8♕ ♖h1+ 6 ♔g7 This was the point in playing 3 ♔h6!!, because after 6...♖g1+ White has 7 ♘g6.

2 ♘g6 ♖a8

2...♔d6 3 ♘f8 ♖e1 4 ♘e6! ♖e5+ 5 ♔g4 ♖e1 6 ♔f5 ♖f1+ 7 ♔g6 ♖g1+ 8 ♘g5 and the pawn promotes.

3 ♔h6!!

3 ♘f8 is two moves slower due to 3...♖a1! because White must repeat the position.

3...♔b5!

The trickiest defence which demands precise play by White.

4 ♘f8 ♖a6+ 5 ♔h5!

The only move to win.

5...♖a1 6 ♘e6!

The most effective move with the knight.

6...♖a8

6...♖h1+ 7 ♔g6 ♖g1+ 8 ♘g5.

7 ♘c7+

And White wins.

187

Chéron
1926

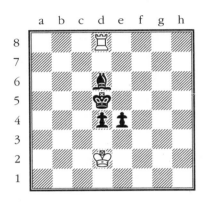

White to move

There are several positions which are not related to the notorious endgame of rook and bishop versus rook where it's useful to understand Szén's method of defence. Here White uses the same method of pinning the bishop. It's important to learn by heart that such a position should always be drawn.

1 ♔e2 ♔c6 2 ♔d2 ♗b4+ 3 ♔e2 ♗c5

If 3...♔c5 then 4 ♖e8. By alternating the attack on the e-pawn and back again to the d-file White can force the draw: 4...♔d5 5 ♖d8+ ♔c4 6 ♖e8 d3+ 7 ♔e3 ♗c5+ 8 ♔xe4 d2 9 ♖d8.

4 ♔d2

The method of alternating between the d-file and the e-file doesn't work here.

After 4 ♖e8 ♔d5

(a) Not 5 ♖d8+? ♔c4 6 ♖e8 d3+ 7 ♔d2 e3+ 8 ♔d1

...because a position such as this with the two pawns placed just two squares from the promotion squares is lost and it doesn't matter if the bishop is black-squared or white-squared. Black wins after 8...♔d5 9 ♔e1 (After 9 ♖d8+ ♔e4 10 ♖e8+ ♔f3 11 ♖e6 ♗b4 12 ♖f6+ ♔e4 13 ♖e6+ ♔f4 White is in zugzwang because 14 ♖e8 [14 ♖f6+ ♔e5] is answered by 14...♔f3) 9...♗d4 10 ♔d1 ♗e5 Note how Black is using the bishop to protect the king from checks. 11 ♖e7 ♔e4 12 ♖e8 ♔f5 13 ♖f8+ ♔g4 14 ♖e8 ♗f4 15 ♔e1 ♔f3 White cannot check the king so Black wins after 16 ♖e6 ♗g3+ 17 ♔d1 e2+.

(b) But 5 ♔d2 ♗b4+ (5...d3 6 ♔c3) 6 ♔d1 d3 7 ♖d8+ ♔c4 (7...♗d6 8 ♔d2!) 8 ♖e8! and the position is drawn.

4...♔b5 5 ♖e8!

The simplest way to draw.

5...♗b4+ 6 ♔e2 d3+ 7 ♔e3 d2 8 ♖d8

It's a clear draw.

187a

von der Lasa
1843

White to move

If we move all the black pieces one rank up the board, it's still a win. The fact that the black pawns are only two steps away from queening is the decisive factor when Black has a bishop.

1 ♖d7

White's plan is to play a waiting game but it doesn't help despite the fact that the important d-file is controlled all the time. 1 ♔e1 ♔c5 followed by ...♗c4 and ...♔b4 would have led to the same play as in the main variation. For example 2 ♖c8+ ♔b4 3 ♖d8 ♗c4 4 ♔d1 ♔c3 5 ♖d6 ♗b3+ 6 ♔e1 ♗f7 etc.

1...♔c5

Black wants to manoeuvre his king to c3 without losing his bishop of course.

2 ♖d8 ♗c4

An impossible position has arisen for White because there is no way to

prevent both ...♔b4 and ...♔d4 followed by ...♔c3.

3 ♖d7 ♔b4 4 ♖d8 ♔c3 5 ♖d6 ♗b3+ 6 ♔e1

6...♗f7

A clever waiting move. White's king cannot move so White is forced to place his rook on a worse square. White could only hope for 6...d2+? 7 ♔e2 d1♕+ 8 ♖xd1 ♗xd1+ 9 ♔xe3 with a draw.

7 ♖d7

7 ♖c6+ ♗c4 8 ♖d6 d2+ wins. The difference, compared with the sixth move, is that now the e2-square is under Black's control. 7 ♖d8 ♗c4 8 ♔d1 ♗e6! 9 ♔e1 ♗g4 would not have made any difference.

7...♗c4 8 ♔d1 ♗e6! 9 ♖c7+ ♔d4

White cannot prevent the bishop check on b3 or g4.

The critical position to remember is the one with the bishop on d5 but as mentioned before a dark-squared bishop would have won as well.

267

187b

von der Lasa
1843

White to move

If a knight is placed on d5 it's only a draw so in this particular ending the knight is clearly weaker than the bishop. Naturally more accuracy is required when the black pawns are only two squares from queening.

1 ♔e1!

The only move to draw. According to *Encyclopaedia of Chess Endings* (Belgrade 1986) 1 ♖d7 is a draw but it's not because the king and knight can set up ideal positions. White's checks are limited when the rook is situated on d7 rather than on the perfect square d8. A plausible winning line is 1...♔c5! 2 ♖d8 ♘c3+ 3 ♔e1 ♔c4 4 ♖d7. White maintains the pressure on the d-pawn to stop Black's king from manoeuvring to c2 when the d-pawn would be unstoppable. 4...♘e4 5 ♔d1 (5 ♖d8 ♔c3 6 ♖c8+ ♔b2) 5...e2+ 6 ♔e1 ♘g5 7 ♖c7+ ♔b4 8 ♖b7+ ♔c5 9 ♖e7 ♘f3+ 10 ♔f2 ♘d4 11 ♔e1 ♔c4 12 ♖c7+ ♔b3 13 ♖b7+ ♔c3 14 ♖c7+ ♔b2 15 ♖b7+ ♔c1 and Black wins.

1...d2+

If Black manoeuvres his pieces to the kingside by 1...♔e4 2 ♖e8+ ♔f3 3 ♖f8+ ♘f4 it's still a draw after 4 ♔d1!.

2 ♔e2 ♔c4 3 ♖c8+ ♔b3 4 ♖d8!

The d-file is the key to holding the draw.

4...♘c3+ 5 ♔xe3

The key procedure to remember is Szén's method which is based on pinning. Easy stuff to remember if you are familiar with Szén's defensive pattern!

188

Timman – Velimirović
Rio de Janeiro 1979

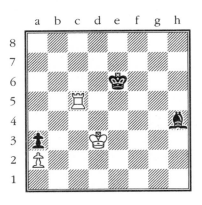

Black to move

This fascinating endgame with rook and a pawn on a2 against bishop and a black pawn on a3 has been heavily analysed by the great Swiss endgame analyst André Chéron (1895-1980). He's mostly famous for his four-volume

Lehr- und Handbuch der Endspiele (copyright 1952) where this specific endgame with the pawn structure a2 versus a3 can be found on as many as 14 pages!

Subsequently this endgame occurred in the twice-adjourned game Timman – Velimirovic, Rio de Janeiro 1979. The Dutch GM Jan Hein Donner (1927-1988) wanted to help Timman and equipped with Chéron's extensive analysis wrote about it in the Dutch newspaper *De Volkskrant* (1979). He wrote: "There might just be some readers to whom these endless sequences of moves appear rather crazy. I can only find it very interesting. Sheer genius always manifests itself on a square inch."

Jan Timman tells the whole story on 24 pages in two different chapters in his book *Studies and Games* (Cadogan 1996). His second, the Swedish endgame genius Ulf Andersson, helped him for a whole week, mostly at night and they managed to improve on Chéron's painstaking work.

Today Tablebase is available on the Internet and it's easy to check when the ending is a draw and when it's a win. The following moves have exclamation marks attached to the moves when they are regarded as best according to Tablebase.

The actual position is a draw. White's main plan to play for a win is to get a position where it's decisive to capture the a3-pawn so as then to be able to win the pawn ending with the remaining rook pawn. The only way to succeed with

this plan is if Black is too passive with his king.

64...♗f6!

The only move to draw. Obviously Black strives to anchor the bishop on b2 where both the pawn and the bishop are conveniently protected. However the problem for the defender is that he must be careful, otherwise White can create zugzwang positions where the bishop is forced to move to a less secure square.

65 ♖c6+ ♔e7

It's still a draw but principally the more active 65...♔f5 should have been played to control the centre.

66 ♔e4 ♗b2! 67 ♔d5 ♔f7! 68 ♖e6

68...♔f8?

This is a decisive mistake because the king is far worse placed here. Timman writes that it took him two years to understand that this move was the decisive mistake. According to Tablebase it's now a forced mate in 56 moves. All legal moves on the long diagonal were actually a draw except 68...♗e5?.

Timman gives the waiting move 68...♗a1. The black king keeps the pressure on the e6-rook, which is ideally situated on e6, where it cuts off the king horizontally as well as vertically. A plausible drawing line is 69 ♖e3 ♗b2 70 ♔d6 ♔f6! 71 ♖f3+ ♔g5! (71...♔g6! is a draw as well.) 72 ♔d5 ♔g4! (72...♔g6! or 72...♗c1! also holds.) 73 ♔e4 ♔g5! The only move. It's useful to remember that Black always draws with the king on f7 or g6 (as well as g5 and g4.) Black has to adapt to White's piece placement and avoid the last rank or file.

Timman also gives the variation: 68...♗f6 69 ♔d6 ♗b2 70 ♔d7 ♗c3 71 ♖e3 ♗b2 72 ♖f3+ ♔g6 73 ♔e6 ♔g5! 74 ♖f5+ ♔g4! 75 ♖f1 ♔g5 76 ♔d5 ♔g4 77 ♔e4 ♔g5! 78 ♖f5+ ♔g6! 79 ♔f4 ♗a1 80 ♖a5 ♗b2 81 ♖a6+ ♔f7 82 ♔f5 ♔e7! 83 ♖e6+ ♔d7. White cannot make progress, because he doesn't have access to the e5-square. However, even if the king were placed on d5 it would be a draw if Black to move plays ...♗c1. Note that the key to holding the draw is to place the king in diagonal opposition as we saw after moves 74, 78 and 83.

69 ♔e4! ♔f7 70 ♔f5!

This is the point. White's king has manoeuvred to the strong f5 square whereas Black's king is completely cut off from most sectors of the board. Black cannot hold his position on f7 and that is why his position is lost.

70...♔f8

70...♗c1 71 ♖c6 ♗b2 72 ♖c7+ and Black's king is forced to the last rank anyway.

71 ♔g6! ♗c3 72 ♖a6! ♗b2 73 ♖a7! ♔e8 74 ♔f5! ♔f8

74...♔d8 loses much more quickly after 75 ♔e6! ♗c8 76 ♔d6! ♔b8 77 ♖d7! with the idea 77...♔c8 78 ♔c6! ♗c1 79 ♖d3! ♗b2 80 ♔b6 wins.

This position isn't difficult but important to know since one of the goals, if Black manoeuvres to the queenside along the last rank, is to reach this zugzwang. Precisely this position can be found among Chéron's own compositions and was created in 1948. He composed hundreds of endgame studies which were published in his monumental endgame books. It's hard to ignore him, because there is a lot of knowledge and wisdom which can be extracted from his painstaking work.

75 ♔e6! ♔g8 76 ♖f7!

Black's king is suffocating more and more due to lack of space.

76...♗c3 77 ♖f3

77 ♔e7!.

77...♗b2

Here the game was adjourned and Timman sealed...

78 ♔e7!

Immediately after the game Velimirović argued that the position was a draw and mentioned that Botvinnik had failed to win a similar endgame against Flohr but apparently the game did not even exist! Timman had brought the book with rook endings by Chéron to Rio and found the exact position which stipulated a win for White, whoever is to move, on page 323 in the updated version. In this position Andersson and Timman managed to improve on Chéron's analyses so that White could win even quicker to avoid the fifty-move draw rule, which states that a player can claim a draw if no capture has been made and no pawn has been moved in the last fifty moves.

78...♔h7 79 ♖g3! ♔h6

80 ♔d6!

Andersson improves on Chéron's suggestion 80 ♔e6! ♔h5 81 ♔f5 (81 ♔d5! would be two moves quicker.) 81...♔h6 82 ♔e4 ♔h5 83 ♔f4 (83 ♔d5! or 83 ♔d3 was two moves quicker.) 83...♔h6 84 ♔f5 (84 ♔e4! was one move quicker.) 84...♔h7 85 ♔e4 ♔h6 86 ♔d5 ♔h5 87 ♔c4 ♔h4 88 ♖g8 which is four moves slower compared with the game.

80...♔h5 81 ♔c5! ♔h4

Black has to upset White's cooperation otherwise White decides with 82 ♔b4 and 83 ♖xa3.

82 ♖g8! ♗e5!

The best move. White mates in 42 moves.

83 ♔d5

According to Timman this is an important move to force 83...♗b2, but one move faster to mate was by 83 ♔b4! or 83 ♔c4!.

83...♗b2 84 ♔c4!

This is the same position Chéron analysed in the comments to the eightieth move.

84...♗f6

The most precise move was 84...♗e5! which was expected by Timman since this was the main variation of the analysis. Chéron didn't strive like Tablebase to find the quickest way to win, and his analyses which run on several pages have been neatly arranged by Donner and Max Leo Pam: 85 ♔b3! ♗d6 86 ♖g6! ♗f8 87 ♔c4! ♔h5 88 ♖g8! ♗e7 89 ♖g2 ♗d6 90 ♔d5! ♗b4 91 ♖g3! ♔h4 92 ♖b3! ♗f8 93 ♖f3! ♗e7 94 ♔e6! ♗c5 95 ♖c3!

271

Timman/Andersson had, contrary to Chéron, realised that it wasn't necessary to chase the bishop on the a3-f8 diagonal so they preferred 95 ♖d3!, complemented by the following variations:

(a) 95...♔g4 When the bishop isn't anchored on b2 this square is mined as has been demonstrated by Chéron/Timman/Andersson: 96 ♖c3! ♗f8 97 ♖c8! ♗h6 (97...♗g7 fails to 98 ♖g8 and is the main reason g4 is a bad square for the king. It's not possible to anchor the bishop on b2.) 98 ♖c4+! ♔g5 99 ♔f7! It's zugzwang. Black cannot prevent 100 ♖c3 next move and winning the pawn. For example 99...♔f5 is a good square for the king but with the badly placed bishop 100 ♖c3 decides.

(b) 95...♗f8 96 ♔f6 ♔h5 This move loses in 16 moves so a better defence was 96...♗c5 which loses in 30 moves. 97 ♖d8 (97 ♖d4! was discovered by Hans Böhm to be the most precise move which was later confirmed by Tablebase. It wins in 16 moves compared with 97 ♖d8 which wins in 21 moves.) 97...♗b4 The only move to avoid the loss of the bishop. 98 ♖d5+ (98 ♖d3!) 98...♔h6 99 ♖d3! ♔h5 100 ♔f5 (100 ♖e3!) 100...♔h6 101 ♖g3

(101 ♔f6!) 101...♗c5 102 ♖g4! It's necessary to prevent the bishop manoeuvre ...♗c5-d4-b2. (However according to Tablebase White earns two moves by giving check first 102 ♖g6+! ♔h5 103 ♖g4!) 102...♔h5 (102...♗e7!)

According to Timman this position has been overlooked by Chéron despite the fact that it's important and can arise in several variations.

103 ♖c4 (103 ♖a4!) 103...♗d6 104 ♔e6! ♗f8 105 ♔f7 (105 ♔f6!) 105...♗d6 106 ♖d4 (106 ♔e6!) The bishop must abandon the a3-f8 diagonal so White wins the pawn after 107 ♖d3.

Chéron's analysis beginning with 95 ♖c3 continues 95...♗f8 96 ♖c8 ♗g7 97 ♔f5! ♗b2 98 ♖d8 ♔h5 99 ♖d6! ♔h4 100 ♖d3! ♗c1 101 ♖c3 ♗b2 102 ♖e3! ♗c1 103 ♖e1! ♗b2 104 ♖g1! ♔h3 105 ♔f4! ♔h2 106 ♖g4! ♔h3 107 ♔f3! ♔h2 108 ♖h4+ ♔g1 109 ♖h3 ♗d4 110 ♔e2! ♗c5 111 ♔d1 ♔g2 112 ♖d3! ♔f2 113 ♔c2! ♔e2 114 ♖c3 ♗b4 115 ♖h3 ♗d6 116 ♔b3! ♔d2 117 ♖h6 ♗c5 118 ♖c6 ♗e7 119 ♖c7! ♗f8 120 ♖c8! ♗e7 121 ♖e8! ♗c5 122 ♔c4! ♗f2 123 ♖a8! and White wins.

It's not bad to find the 28 strongest white moves out of 39 according to Tablebase which shows what a great analyst Chéron was. It's easy to forget that he was the pioneer of this ending before the team Timman/Andersson and Tablebase improved the variations. However most of the ideas and critical positions had already been discovered by Chéron and later it was mainly a matter of making the variations more precise.

85 ♖g6! ♗g5 86 ♔d5! ♗c1

Chéron gives the amazing variation 86...♔h5 87 ♖c6!! ♗d2! 88 ♔e6! ♔g5! 89 ♖c4! ♔h6 90 ♖c2! ♗e1! 91 ♖h2+ ♔g5 92 ♖h3! ♗b4 and now 93 ♖f3! resembles the earlier mentioned 95 ♖d3!!.

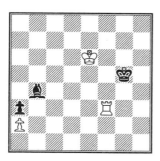

Black's best is the "forbidden" move 93...♔g4 when White wins with the familiar method 94 ♖b3! ♗f8 (94...♗c5 95 ♖c3 ♗f8 96 ♖c8 ♗h6 97 ♖c4+ ♔g5 98 ♔f7) 95 ♖b8! ♗h6 96 ♖c8! ♗d2 97 ♖c2! ♗h6 98 ♖c4+! ♔g5 99 ♔f7! etc.

87 ♔e4

87 ♔e5!.

87...♗b2 88 ♔f5

88 ♔f4!.

88...♔h5 89 ♖d6! ♔h4 90 ♖d3! ♗c1 91 ♖c3

91 ♖d1!.

91...♗b2 92 ♖e3! ♗c1 93 ♖e1!

93...♗d2

Timman and Andersson analysed 93...♗b2 94 ♖g1! ♔h3 95 ♔f4! ♔h2 96 ♖g4! ♔h3 97 ♔f3! ♔h2 98 ♔f2! (Faster than Chéron's variation as given by Donner/Pam: 98 ♖h4+ ♔g1 99 ♖h3 ♗d4 100 ♔e2! ♗c5 101 ♔d1 ♔g2 102 ♖d3! ♔f2 103 ♔c2! ♔e2 104 ♖c3 ♗b4 105 ♖h3 ♗d6 106 ♔b3! ♔d2 107 ♖h6 ♗c5 108 ♖c6 ♗e7 109 ♖c7! ♗f8 110 ♖c8! ♗e7 111 ♖e8! ♗c5 112 ♔c4! ♗f2 113 ♖a8!) 98...♗f6 (98...♔h3 99 ♖a4 Black is in zugzwang and has to move the bishop which gives White a decisive tempo. 99...♗c1 100 ♔e2 ♔g3 101 ♔d1 ♗b2 102 ♔c2 ♔f3 103 ♔b3 ♔e3 104 ♖xa3 ♗xa3 105 ♔xa3 The a-pawn promotes after the forced sequence 105...♔d4 106 ♔b4 ♔d5 107 ♔b5 ♔d6 108 ♔b6 ♔d7 109 ♔b7 ♔d6 110 a4 ♔c5 111 a5 ♔b5 112 a6) 99 ♖g2+! ♔h1 100 ♔f1! ♗b2 101 ♖g3 (101 ♖e2!) 101...♔h2 102 ♖b3!

♗c1 103 ♔e2 ♔g2 104 ♔d1 ♗b2 105 ♔c2 and 106 ♖xb2.

94 ♖h1+! ♔g3 95 ♖d1! ♗b4

The typical idea to win this ending is to cut off the king as much as possible. Now it's forced to move to the second rank.

96 ♖d3+! ♔f2 97 ♔e4! ♔e2 98 ♔d4! ♗c5+ 99 ♔c4! ♗e7 100 ♖h3! ♗d6 101 ♔b3

101 ♖h4!.

101...♗f8! 102 ♖h8! ♗d6

102...♗c5! 103 ♖c8! ♗d6! 104 ♖a8!.

103 ♖a8! Black resigns.

103...♔d3 loses the bishop due to the pin on the d-file so White decides the game by capturing on a3 next move.

I can only wholeheartedly agree with Donner, who said that this ending was interesting and obviously Chéron, Timman and Andersson must have felt so too. It's very instructive regarding the importance of an anchored bishop. When the bishop is somewhere on the a3-f8 diagonal White can profit from it by excellent cooperation between the king and the rook. The forbidden square g4 is also typical for this endgame and something to remember. Another piece of information is that it's not possible to win only by playing on white squares. In some positions White's king and rook are on two black squares at the same time! The overall strategy is to play on the white squares but often the decisive move is on a black square.

In my opinion a thought-provoking idea is that one should embrace classical endgame books by Averbakh, Berger, Chéron, Euwe, Fine, Keres and Rabinovich because they were, with the exceptions of the great endgame composers, pioneers in how to learn and play endgames. Today we have Tablebase but it's not a good teacher, unless you complement it with books by Dvoretsky, Nunn and Müller. To get a true feeling for the endgame we all need to work hard, like for example Chéron did with the example we have just examined. It's even more important today due to lack of adjournments. We don't get this feeling when we work with Tablebase. A big problem working solely with Tablebase is finding out which is the best move in practice when several options are available and all lead to a draw. I hope I have instilled a passion for combining work with Tablebase together with reading books by the great pioneers of the endgame, especially the ones written by really hard-working authors. By the way, I also recommend Timman's book *Studies and Games* for his painstaking analyses and how he pays homage to Chéron where, among other things, writes that "in spite of his enormous contribution to endgame theory, little attention had been paid to his demise in the international chess press."

189

Ju Wenjun – Goryachkina
Women's Grand Prix,
Skolkovo 2019

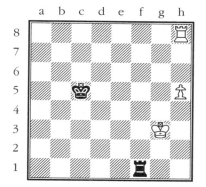

White to move

The worst pawn for the attacker is to be left with a rook-pawn, but here White is winning, because the black king is outside the square of the pawn. It would have been a draw with the pawn on h4 because then Black could pick any move with his king to go the d-file.

56...♖h1

Tablebase gives 56...♖g1+ 57 ♔f3 ♖h1 58 h6 ♔c6 59 ♔g4 (59 h7? at once is met by 59...♔b7. White can no longer win because of checks if White tries to support the h-pawn with his king.) 59...♔c7 60 ♔f5 ♔c6 61 ♔g6 ♖g1+ Black must disturb White with a check otherwise he would liberate his rook. 62 ♔h7 ♔d7 63 ♖g8 ♖e1 64 ♖g6! ♖e8

65 ♖f6! ♖e1 66 ♔g7 ♖g1+ 67 ♖g6 ♖e1 68 h7 and the pawn queens.

57 ♔g4??

When I followed the game live I saw in a second that White should play 57 h6, with the threat of h7 followed by a check and promotion. A plausible variation is 57...♔c6 (57...♔d6 58 h7 ♔e7 59 ♖a8! ♖xh7 60 ♖a7+ is a notorious tactic in this kind of endgame which everyone must know.) 58 ♔g4 ♖h2 59 ♔f5 ♖h1 60 ♔g6 ♖g1+ 61 ♔h7 ♔d7 62 ♖g8 and White wins.

57...♔d6

The black king is too close and it's a draw.

58 h6

58 ♖e8 was a better winning attempt but it's still a theoretical draw after 58...♖h2 59 ♔g5 ♖g2+ 60 ♔f6 ♖f2+ 61 ♔g7 ♖g2+ 62 ♔h7 ♖h2 63 h6 ♔d7! 64 ♖e1 ♖g2. Black needs to prevent White from controlling the g-file otherwise White can play his rook to the g-file followed by ♔h7-g7. 65 ♔h8 ♖g3 66 h7 ♖g2 This is a well-known drawn position, since White doesn't have time to manoeuvre the rook to

g8 without allowing the black king to reach f7 when the white king would be trapped forever in the corner.

58...♚e7 59 h7 ♚f7 60 ♖a8 ♖xh7 Draw.

Why does a world champion make such a mistake as 57 ♚g4?? ? Such an endgame is important to know even for a much lower rated player. Maybe she expected a check and was mentally prepared to move the king. When the check didn't happen she may have thought that it didn't matter that she moved the king and suppressed the ability to be flexible in her mind.

I'm pretty sure that if Ju Wenjun had been on a training camp, and her coach had given her this position as an exercise, she would probably have seen the solution in a few seconds, since we are dealing with fundamental endgame knowledge.

This ending with a rook-pawn that we have just looked at is not the only important one. I would strongly urge the reader to study the other famous positions by Karstedt (1909), Vancura (1924) and Troitzky (1896).

They can be found in most books dealing with fundamental rook endings. They can also be found as positions 224-226 in *300 Most Important Chess Positions*. Embrace them and you will increase your winning chances as well as drawing chances because these endgames will appear again and again in your games. They are the foundation of all rook endings.

190

Robertie
Basic Endgame Strategy 1998

White to move

Due to the rook's dynamic mobility in endgames, White sometimes has to consider whether to cut off the king on the file or the rank. An exclamation mark is attached to the attacker's move when it's regarded as the best move by Tablebase.

1 ♖h4!

It's correct to cut off the black king along the rank rather than on the file, since the rook has the double function of building a bridge to defend against the black rook's checks. If it's White's turn to move, with the rook on h4, he would play 2 b4 followed by ♚b2-b3 etc. with an easy win. 1 ♖d7? is incorrect, since White doesn't have the possibility of building a bridge to avoid Black's checks. Without the help of the rook White must manoeuvre the king to c3 or a3 to support the pawn on b4, but as soon as the king is played to the c- or a-file Black checks. After 1...♚e4 it's no longer possible for White to improve his position.

1...♚d3 2 ♖a4!

2 b4? is too early since White's king isn't supporting the pawn. After 2...♚c3 the pawn falls.

2...♖h8 3 ♚a2! ♖h2

4 ♖g4

White prepares ♚a3 and b2-b4. 4 ♚a3! ♖h1 5 ♖a5 ♖a1+ 6 ♚b4 ♖h1 7 ♖c5 is Tablebase's suggestion.

4...♖f2 5 ♚a3! ♖f1 6 b4! ♚c3 7 ♚a4! ♖a1+

If 7...♖f8 then 8 ♖g5!.

8 ♚b5 ♖a8 9 ♖g3+! ♚d4 10 ♚c6! ♖c8+ 11 ♚b7! ♖c1 12 b5! ♚c5 13 b6! ♖b1 14 ♚c7!

White wins. Black cannot stop the pawn from promotion.

One reason rook endings are complicated is that one must always think what is the most effective file or rank for the rook. Notice how White had to alter the position of his rook several times due to the changing circumstances.

191

Chéron
1947

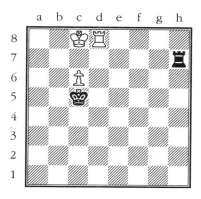

White to move

1 ♖d7!

White must show patience before moving the pawn to c7 and getting a pure Lucena position. If an immediate 1 c7? then 1...♚c6 is a draw since White's rook is unfortunately placed.

1...♖h1 2 ♚b7!!

2 c7? still doesn't work due to 2...♚c6. 2 ♚c7? is also wrong because of 2...♖h6.

2...♖b1+ 3 ♚c7

Now this move works since the black rook cannot threaten the c6-pawn in a convenient way.

3...♖a1 4 ♖d2 ♖a7+ 5 ♚b8! ♖a1 6 c7

At last White has reached a Lucena position. The conclusion could be...

6...♖b1+ 7 ♚c8

...with the idea 8 ♔d8 and after...

7...♖h1

White simply plays...

8 ♖b2

...followed by a king move to the b-file with an easy win.

192

Rohde – D. Cramling
Innsbruck 1977

White to move

This instructive position, which must be regarded as the most important Philidor position, is actually similar to a study by Kopaev from 1955 which can be found in *Comprehensive Chess Endings – Rook Endings* by Averbakh and Kopayev (Pergamon Press 1987). However, in his study the pieces were placed on the queenside, with the exception of the black rook, which was placed on e1. The position from the game arose 22 years later in the World Junior Championship and all pieces, except

the black rook, were placed on the kingside.

70 ♔e6!

White exploits the unfortunate position of the rook which is unable to check the white king on the sixth rank according to Philidor's scheme. 70 ♔f6? ♖e1! is the famous position by Philidor, published in 1777, where he showed that it is a draw. 71 ♔e6 (71 e6 ♖f1+ or 71 ♖h8+ ♔d7 and the pawn cannot advance. This is the main point of placing the rook on the e-file.) 71...♔f8! The principled move is to move the king to the "short side" to provide leeway for the rook on the queenside. 72 ♖h8+ ♔g7 73 ♖e8 (If instead 73 ♖a8, which actually contains no threat, the simplest reply is 73...♖e2!) 73...♖a1! The principled continuation is to defend with rook checks by using the "long side". 74 ♖d8 (74 ♔d7 ♖a7+ 75 ♔c6 ♖a6+ 76 ♔b7 ♔f7!) 74...♖e1! 75 ♔d6 ♔f7. White is unable improve his position and can only repeat what has happened before: 76 ♖d7+ ♔e8 77 ♖a7 ♖e2 78 ♔e6 ♔f8! with a draw.

70...♔f8!

As we have seen before the king moves to the short side so that the rook can use the long side for checks. It would principally be wrong to move the king to the long side because after 70...♔d8 71 ♖h8+ ♔c7 72 ♔e7 ♖g1 73 e6 ♖g7+ 74 ♔f6 followed by e7 it turns out that the short side is too short for the rook.

71 ♖f7+!

An important intermediate check because if immediately 71 ♖a7? Black draws after either 71...♖e1 or 71...♖b1.

71...♔g8

71...♔e8 72 ♖a7 and now the move to the short side with 72...♔f8 doesn't help because White's rook has made the long side shorter by placing his rook on the a-file. (72...♔d8 leads to the same situation after 73 ♖a8+ ♔c7 74 ♔e7 ♖h1 75 e6 ♖h7+ 76 ♔f6 ♖h6+ 77 ♔f7 ♖h7+ 78 ♔g6 etc.) 73 ♖a8+ ♔g7 74 ♔e7 ♖b1 75 e6 ♖b7+ 76 ♔d6 ♖b6+ 77 ♔d7 ♖b7+ 78 ♔c6 and the pawn advances to e7.

72 ♖d7!

White gains time and manages to exploit the abysmal position of the black king which stands too far away from the e-pawn's promotion square. 72 ♖a7? ♖e1! The only move to draw. White cannot win since 73 ♔f6 ♖f1+ 74 ♔e7?? fails to 74...♖f7+ and Black wins. But not 72...♔f8? 73 ♖a8+ ♔g7 74 ♔e7 ♖b1 75 e6 and the long side has actually become the short side because the white rook has "stolen" the important a-file from Black and made the chessboard one-eighth

shorter for Black. This is a very important concept that can be used in the middlegame as well. The idea of reducing the board to seven ranks instead of eight has been shown in another form in the games Petrosian – Gufeld, USSR Championship 1960 and Carlsen – Ivanchuk, Forus 2008 which is position 98 in *300 Most Important Chess Positions*.

72...♖e1

Against other rook moves White would have played 73 ♔e7 exploiting the fact that Black's king isn't placed on f8 where it belongs in this type of ending.

73 ♔f6! ♖f1+ 74 ♔e7

Now it's clear why it was important to place the rook on d7 because the check on f7 is harmless.

74...♖a1!

74...♖f7+ 75 ♔d6 ♖f8 (75...♖f1 76 e6 ♖d1+ 77 ♔e7 ♖a1 78 ♖d2) 76 e6 ♖a8 77 ♔e5! (77 ♔e7? ♔g7! is an elementary draw.) 77...♔f8 78 ♔f6 ♖b8 79 ♖f7+ ♔g8 80 ♖g7+ ♔h8 81 ♖g5 and White wins.

75 e6?

An error that was made after the time control. Kopaev has proved in his study that White wins after 75 ♖d2!, exploiting the abysmal position of the king. 75...♖a7+ Black obviously doesn't want to be forced to place his king on the edge of the board so this check is practically forced. 76 ♔f6 ♖f7+ 77 ♔e6 ♖f1 (77...♖a7 doesn't work on account of 78 ♖d8+) 78 ♖a2! White's rook manoeuvre from d7-d2-a2 is quite amazing and shows the inherent dynamism in the rook by exploiting the files and ranks in this manner. It's necessary to reduce the number of squares available for the black rook otherwise Black would draw by using the a-file himself. 78...♔g7 (78...♖e1 79 ♔f6 ♖f1+ 80 ♔e7 ♖f7+ 81 ♔d6) 79 ♖a7+ ♔g6 (79...♔f8 80 ♖a8+ ♔g7 81 ♔e7 is the same position as the main variation.) 80 ♖a8 ♔g7 81 ♔e7 ♖f7+ (81...♖b1 82 e6) 82 ♔d6 ♖b7 83 e6.

75...♔g7!

Black improves the position of his king.

76 ♖d6

76 ♔e8+ ♔f6 77 e7 ♔e6 is a draw.

76...♖a8!

The only move to prevent White from winning with 77 ♔e8 followed by e6-e7.

77 ♖d1

Black draws easily after 77...♖a7+ 78 ♔e8 ♔f6 etc. Jon Speelman wrote in *Analysing the Endgame* (Batsford 1988) that when he became acquainted with the endgame Rohde – Cramling in a magazine it took him a considerable time to understand what was going on. So it's not an easy endgame but if you really study it you will understand so many other important positions which can arise from Philidor's position. One must have a very detailed feeling for when the rooks or the kings are misplaced and how to deal with precise moves and manoeuvres.

193

Taimanov – Estevez Morales
Brno 1975

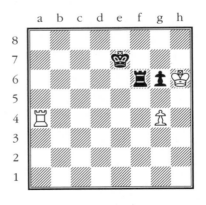

Black to move

46...g5+?

46...♔f7 is the principled move. Black's plan to draw is simply to place the king on the queening square g8 and the rook on f8. A plausible continuation is 47 ♖a7+ ♔g8 48 g5 ♖f8 (Note that 48...♖b6? leads to the Lucena position after 49 ♖a8+ ♔f7 50 ♔h7! Now White plans ♖g8 followed by ♖g7+ and ♖xg6 with a winning rook endgame, since White controls the important g8-square. 50...♖b1 51 ♖a7+ ♔f8 52 ♔xg6 ♖g1 53 ♖a8+ ♔e7 54 ♖g8 ♖g2 55 ♔h7 and White wins.) 49 ♔xg6 ♖b8. This is one of the few rook endings where the right defensive policy is to play passively. The idea of playing the rook to f8 doesn't work against the central or bishops'pawns.

47 ♔xg5 ♖f1 48 ♖a7+ ♔f8 49 ♔g6 ♖f2 50 g5

Black cannot prevent White from setting up a Lucena position.

50...♖b2 51 ♖a8+ ♔e7 52 ♔g7 ♖f2 53 g6 ♖f1 54 ♔g8 ♖g1 55 g7

The celebrated Lucena position has been reached. This is the most famous rook ending after Philidor's position.

55...♖g2 56 ♖f8 Black resigns.

A possible line is 56...♖h2 57 ♖f4! ♖h1 58 ♖e4+ ♔d6! 59 ♔f7 ♖f1+ 60 ♔g6 ♖g1+ 61 ♔f6 ♖g2 62 ♖e6+! ♔d7 63 ♖e5 followed by 64 ♖g5.

194

Suetin – F. Portisch
Budapest 1977

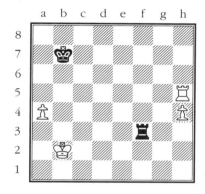

Black to move

If Black has an active rook there are chances of holding the draw even when two pawns down.

1...♖f4! 2 ♔b3 ♔a6! 3 a5

From now on White's rook cannot move without giving up one of the pawns and this is the main reason Black holds the draw, since the remaining pawn is a rook pawn.

3...♖e4 4 ♔c3 ♖f4 5 ♔d3 ♖g4 6 ♔e3 ♖c4 7 ♔f3 ♖c3+

It's not necessary to cut off the king on the fourth rank because it's on its way to g3 to liberate the rook. Black holds the draw by just ignoring the a-pawn and playing according to Vancura's idea and checking the king from the side.

8 ♔e4 ♖c4+ 9 ♔d5 ♖g4

Maintaining the pressure on the h4-pawn obliges White to keep his rook in a passive position.

10 ♔e6 ♖c4 11 ♖h8 ♔b7!
12 ♖h7+

12 h5 is answered by 12...♖c6+ (12...♖c5 is also good enough for a draw.) 13 ♔d5 ♖a6! 14 ♔e5 ♖xa5+ Black even has time to take the unimportant a-pawn and reach a pure Vancura position after 15 ♔f6 ♖c5!.

Black holds the draw by using the long side for the rook according to the method of Vancura. This particular rook ending is the third most important to know after Philidor and Lucena. A plausible variation to play out this position is 16 h6 ♖c6+ 17 ♔g7 ♖c7+ 18 ♔g8 ♖c8+ 19 ♔g7 ♖c7+ 20 ♔f6 ♖c6+ 21 ♔e5 ♖g6 The simplest. 22 h7 (22 ♔f5 ♖c6 23 ♔g5 ♖c5+!) 22...♖h6 23 ♔f5 ♖h1 24 ♔g6 ♖g1+! 25 ♔f7 ♖h1. White's king cannot escape the checks from the rook when defending the pawn, so the position is a dead draw.

12...♔a6 Draw.

What's interesting with this ending is how closely related it is to the Vancura position from 1924.

195

Larsen – Torre
Interzonal, Leningrad 1973

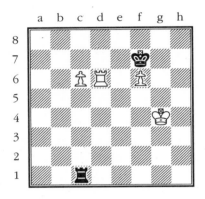

Black to move

The only chance to hold the draw when two pawns down is by full activation of king and rook.

82...♔g6!

Black prevents the white king from reaching one of the crucial squares g5 or f5.

83 ♔f3

83 ♔f4, planning to cross the e-file, is stopped by 83...♖e1!. There is no way for White to improve his position. After 84 ♔f3 ♖e5 85 c7 ♖c5 one of the pawns falls.

83...♖e1! 84 ♔f4 ♖e2!

The only move.

85 ♖d5

85...罝c2!

85...含xf6? allows White's rook to be placed behind the c-pawn and this is decisive as the following variation shows: 86 罝c5 罝e8 87 罝f5+!

This is the point: Black's king is not able to cross the e-file. 87...含g6 (87...含e7 leads to a lost pawn ending after 88 罝e5+ 含f7 89 罝xe8 含xe8 90 含e5 含e7 91 含d5 含e8 92 含e6!) 88 罝e5 罝c8 89 罝e6+ 含f7 90 含e5 罝c7 91 含d5 (91 含d6? 罝xc6+) 91...罝c8 92 罝e1 followed by 含d5-d6-d7 with an easy win.

86 罝d6 罝e2! 87 f7+

White tries a last shot.

87...含xf7 88 含f5

Or 88 c7 罝c2 89 罝h6 含e7.

88...含e7

Note that 88...罝f2+? 89 含e5 含e7 90 罝d7+ 含e8 91 含d6 helps White to construct a Lucena position.

89 罝d7+ 含e8 90 含f6 罝e1 91 罝d5 罝c1 92 罝d6 罝f1+ 93 含e6 罝e1+ 94 含d5 罝d1+ 95 含c5 罝xd6 96 含xd6 含d8 Draw.

196

Radjabov – Grischuk
Candidates, London 2013

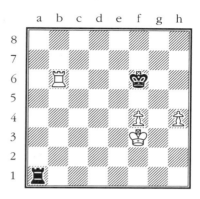

Black to move

63...含f5

Grischuk chooses the most active set-up according to the general rule in this ending, which stipulates that the king meets a rook check on the rank by moving forward. The main thing in this ending is to avoid the back rank with the king because this abysmal position normally leads to a lost endgame as has been shown in the famous endings Capablanca – Kostić, Havana 1919 and Leko – Carlsen, Moscow 2009. The classical defence according to the most famous model endgame Gligoric – Smyslov, Moscow 1947, is to play 63...含g7 until forcibly driven away. The king answers a check from a pawn by blockading it and can usually respond to a rook check on the g-file by moving to either side, but f7 represents the easiest defence. The ideal square for the defending rook is a1 where its fundamental assignment is to prevent the enemy king from penetrating Black's position. There it has possibilities of checking or cutting off the enemy king on the fifth, sixth, seventh or eighth rank as well as on the three files behind the white pieces. The dynamism of the rook is the key to holding this ending.

64 ♖b5+

White must dislodge the king from its active position. 64 h5? ♖a3+ and 65...♔xf4 is an easy draw.

64...♔f6 65 ♔g4 ♖g1+

Black plays according to the same principle as White and dislodges the king.

66 ♔h5 ♖h1 67 ♖a5 ♖h2 68 ♖a8 ♖h1

Black maintains the pressure on the h4-pawn so White cannot improve his position with ♔h5-h6 and h4-h5.

69 ♖g8 ♔f7 70 ♖g4 ♔f6 71 ♖g8

71 ♔h6 doesn't lead to the desired result if Black continues maximum activity with his king and rook. After the principled moves 71...♔f5 72 ♖g5+ ♔xf4 73 h5 ♖a1 74 ♖g7 ♔f5 75 ♖f7+ ♔e6 76 ♖f2 ♖g1 it's an elementary draw.

71...♔f7 72 ♖c8 ♔f6 73 ♖c5 ♖h2 74 ♖g5 ♖h1 75 ♔g4

75...♖g1+ 76 ♔f3 ♖f1+

Note how Black uses the h-, g- and f-files to disturb White with checks as well as putting pressure on the h-pawn and the f-pawn.

77 ♔g3 ♖g1+ 78 ♔f2 ♖h1 79 h5 ♖h4

Even the fourth rank is used to put pressure on both pawns!

80 ♔g3 ♖h1 81 ♖a5

Of course 81 ♖g6+ is answered by 81...♔f5!.

81...♖g1+ 82 ♔f2 ♖h1 83 ♔g2 ♖h4 84 ♔f3 ♖h1 85 h6 ♖xh6!

A very nice trick, which is the simplest way to draw, but by no means the only move.

86 ♖a6+ ♔f5 87 ♖xh6 stalemate.

If you have the possibility of defending according to this model game, then you should do so because the classic model ending Gligorić – Smyslov, Moscow 1947, demands more knowledge of the subtleties in the position.

196a

Carlsen – Aronian
Tripoli 2004

White to move

Carlsen is famous for having lost this ending despite the fact that it's a draw. Carlsen's mistake was that he let the opponent's king penetrate his position and support one of his pawns.

74 ♔f3?

The definite turning-point in this ending. 74 ♔f4 or 74 ♔g4 would have prevented the penetration of Black's king. It would have been pointless to try the manoeuvre ...♔f7-e7-d6 because of 74...♔f7 75 ♔f5 ♖f2+ 76 ♔g4 ♔e6 77 ♔g3 ♖c2 78 ♖h5 and Black is cut off on the fifth rank since 78...f5 is met by 79 ♔f4 with an immediate draw due to 80 ♖h6+ next move.

74...♔f5

Surprisingly there is no way to stop the black king from penetrating all the way to White's first rank.

75.♖h5+ ♔e6?

Correct was 75...♔g6 76 ♖h8 ♔g5!! and White is in zugzwang.

77 ♖h7 is met by the finesse 77...♖c1! 78 ♖xh2 ♖c3+ 79 ♔e4 f5+ and Black wins easily due to White's king being cut off on the third rank.

76 ♖h8?

The rook was perfectly placed on h5 where it prevented the enemy king from entering the fifth rank. Better was 76 ♔g3 ♔f7 77 ♖h8 ♔g6 78 ♔f4! or 78 ♔g4! to prevent penetration.

76...♔e5

From now on Black's king is unstoppable. The main target square is g1 to escort the pawn to h1.

77 ♖e8+ ♔d4 78 ♖d8+ ♔c3

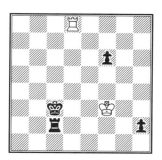

79 ♖h8

79 ♖d1 leads to a more complicated line after 79...f5 80 ♔g3 ♔c4 81 ♖a1 ♖a2 82 ♖b1 ♖d2 83 ♔f3 ♔c5 84 ♔f4 ♔d4 85 ♖a1 (85 ♔xf5 ♖g2 86 ♖h1 ♔e3) 85...♖f2+ 86 ♔g3 ♖a2 87 ♖e1 ♖e2 88 ♖f1 ♔e3 89 ♖f3+ ♔d2 90 ♖f1 ♖e1 91 ♖f2+ ♔e3 92 ♖xh2 f4+ 93 ♔g4 ♖g1+ 94 ♔f5 f3 and Black wins.

79...♖d2! 80 ♔g3 ♔d3 81 ♔f3 ♔c2 82 ♔g3 ♔d1! White resigns.

The king-march to g1 is unstoppable. 83 ♖xh2 loses the pawn ending after 83...♖xh2 84 ♔xh2 ♔e2 85 ♔g3 ♔e3 86 ♔g4 ♔e4 87 ♔g3 f5 88 ♔f2 ♔f4 and Black has the opposition.

197

Makarov
The Endgame 2007

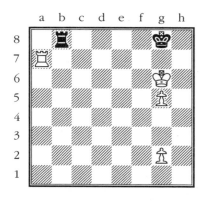

White to move

Normally doubled pawns lead to a draw but there is one exception that everybody should know. White wins by forcing the exchange of rooks.

1 ♔h6 ♖c8

If 1...♖b6+ then 2 g6 ♖b8 3 g4 ♖c8 4 g5 ♖b8 5 ♖a6 ♖c8 6 g7! ♖b8 7 ♖f6 and 8 ♖f8+.

Here 6 ♖f6 also wins but complicates matters after 6...♖c1 7 g7 ♖h1+ 8 ♔g6 ♖h6+! 9 ♔f5 ♖h1 because here White must find 10 ♖e6!!. White wins after 10...♔xg7 (10...♖a1 11 ♔g6 ♖a6!

12 ♖f6! ♖b6! 13 ♔h6! and Black's rook is hanging because there is no longer any stalemate.) 11 ♖e7+ ♔f8 12 ♖a7 ♖b1 13 ♔g6! since he cannot prevent White from setting up a Lucena position. 13...♖g1 14 ♖a8+ ♔e7 15 ♖g8! followed by 16 ♔h7.

2 g6 ♖b8

3 ♖a6!

This is the key manoeuvre which Black cannot prevent. The rook is on its way to f6 and f8 after g6-g7 has been played.

3...♖c8

3...♖f8 4 g4! (4 g7? ♖f6+! is what Black is hoping for.) 4...♖b8 5 g7 ♖c8 6 ♖f6 and White wins as in the main variation.

4 g7

4 ♖f6? at once is a draw after 4...♖c1 or 4...♖c4.

4...♖b8 5 ♖f6 ♖a8 6 g4 ♖b8 7 g5 ♖a8 8 ♖f8+ ♖xf8 9 gxf8♕+ ♔xf8 10 g6 ♔g8 11 g7 ♔f7 12 ♔h7

White queens.

198

Akhsharumova – J. Bellin
Women's Olympiad, Novi Sad 1990

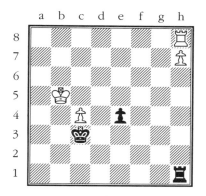

Black to move

64...e3?

Black could have drawn by playing as actively as possible with the rook. Correct was 64...♖b1+! 65 ♔c6 (or 65 ♔c5 ♖h1) 65...♖h1 66 c5 (After 66 ♖e8 the simplest draw is 66...♔d4 67 h8♕+ ♖xh8 68 ♖xh8 ♔xc4) 66...♔c4!! 67 ♔b6 (67 ♖e8 is answered by the intermediate check 67...♖h6+! before capturing on h7 next move with check again.) 67...♖b1+ 68 ♔c7 ♔xc5 69 ♖e8 ♖h1 70 h8♕ ♖xh8 71 ♖xh8 e3 72 ♖e8 (72 ♖h4 ♔d5) 72...♔d4 73 ♔d6 ♔d3 74 ♔e5 e2 75 ♔f4 ♔d2.

65 ♖e8 ♖xh7 66 ♖xe3+ ♔d4 67 ♖e1!

The strongest move but not the only way to win. 67 ♖g3 ♖h5+ 68 ♔b4 ♖h1 69 ♖g4+ ♔e5 70 ♔c5 was an alternative continuation. The idea is to reach the Lucena position with the king on c8 and the pawn on

c7. Note that 67 ♖f3? would not win due to 67...♖h5+ 68 ♔b4 ♖h1 69 ♖f4+ ♔e5 70 ♖g4 ♔d6 and Black has gained a crucial tempo to place the king so it can control the pawn.

67...♖b7+

If 67...♖h5+ then 68 ♔b4.

68 ♔c6 ♖b2 69 ♖c1 ♖h2 70 c5 ♖g2 71 ♔b6 Black resigns.

199

Fransson – Cirić
Marseille 1981

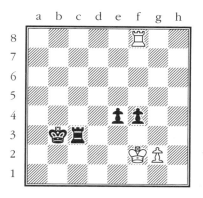

Black to move

Here Black has two connected pawns placed on the fifth rank and on top of that one of the pawns is passed. White has no defence after...

1...♖c2+ 2 ♔f1

(a) 2 ♔g1 ♔c3! 3 ♖xf4 e3 and White cannot stop the black pawn from promoting: 4 ♖f8 ♖c1+ 5 ♔h2 e2 6 ♖c8+ ♔b2!

(b) 2 ♔e1 ♔c3! 3 ♖xf4 ♔d3 4 ♖f8 (4 g3 e3) 4...♖c1+ 5 ♔f2 e3+ and Black wins.

2...♔c3! 3 ♖xf4

More resilient was to cut off the king. After 3 ♖d8! ♖a2! Black has to prepare the pawn-push to e3. (An immediate 3...e3?? fails to 4 ♖c8+ ♔d2 5 ♖xc2+ ♔xc2 6 ♔e2 ♔c3 7 g3 with a draw.) 4 ♖d7 e3 5 ♖d8 ♖f2+ 6 ♔g1 ♖d2! 7 ♖c8+ ♔d3 8 ♖d8+ ♔e2 9 ♖f8 ♔d1 10 ♖a8 ♔e1 and White cannot prevent ...e3-e2, ♖d2-d1 and ♔e1-d2.

3...♔d3 4 g4 e3 5 ♖f8 ♖c1+ White resigns.

White saw that 6 ♔g2 e2 7 ♖d8+ ♔c2 8 ♖e8 e1♕ 9 ♖xe1 ♖xe1 10 ♔f3 ♔d3 11 ♔f4 ♔d4 12 ♔f5 ♔d5 13 g5 ♖f1+ 14 ♔g6 ♔e6 would have won easily for Black.

199a

Bayer – Polasek
Luxembourg 1986

White to move

Two connected pawns but without any passer make the defence more difficult if the pawns are located on the fifth rank.

1 g6+ ♔f6

1...♔e7 2 ♖g8 ♔f6 3 ♖f8+ is a transposition to the main variation.

2 ♖f8+ ♔e5 3 f6!!

Note the devilish trap 3 ♖f7? ♖a1 4 ♖xg7?? ♔f4 5 ♔h6 ♖h1 mate. 3 ♔g5? ♖a1 4 ♖e8+ ♔d6 5 ♖e4 (5 f6 ♖g1+ 6 ♔h5 ♖h1+!) 5...♖g1+ 6 ♖g4 ♖f1 7 ♖f4 ♖g1+.

3...♖xf6 4 ♖f7 ♔e6 5 ♖xg7 ♖f1 6 ♖a7 Black resigns.

It's impossible for Black to avoid Lucena's position. The pawn will advance to g7 and the king to g8 with an elementary win.

200

Yusupov – Timman
Candidates, Linares 1992

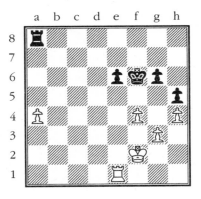

White to move

We have been taught by Tarrasch that a rook should be deployed behind a passed pawn, but there are several exceptions to this rule that the advanced player should know. For example if the enemy king blockades the pawn it makes more sense to protect the pawn from the side, since it then also takes part in

288

the play on the opposite wing. Here we see another exception to the rule.

35 ♖a1?

35 ♖e4! was correct. From this location the white rook protects the pawn as well as the centre and the kingside. This would not have been possible by following the universal rule by Tarrasch. Then:

(a) 35...♔e7 36 ♔e3 ♔d6 37 ♔d3 and White's king reaches the queenside with an easy win.

(b) 35...♔f5 36 ♖e5+ followed by 37 a5 leads to a similar ending which arose in the game Averbakh – Euwe, Zürich 1953 which was easily won by White. Everything is protected after ♖g5 and White can support the a-pawn with the king: 35...♖a5 36 ♔e3 ♔f5 37 ♖e5+ ♖xe5+ 38 fxe5 ♔xe5 39 a5 ♔d5 40 a6 ♔c6 41 ♔f4 etc.

35...♖a5!

Black blockades the pawn and prepares some pawn exchanges.

36 ♔e3 e5!

Of course not 36...♔f5? 37 ♔d4 ♔g4 38 ♖a3 and everything is protected.

37 ♔e4

37 fxe5+ ♔xe5 38 ♔d3 ♔d5 39 ♔c3 ♔c5 (39...♔c6 40 ♔b4 ♖e5, followed by ...♔b6 and rook checks, also works.) 40 ♔b3 g5! and White cannot make any progress.

37...exf4 38 ♔xf4 ♔e6 39 ♔e4

White can try 39 ♖e1+ ♔f6 40 ♖e4 but after one more pawn

exchange with 40...g5+ 41 ♔e3 gxh4 42 gxh4 the position is drawn. For example, 42...♔f5 43 ♔d3 ♖a8 44 ♖b4 ♔e6! 45 ♔c4 ♔d6 46 ♔b3 ♖a5 47 ♖c4 ♖a8 and it's hard for White to make any progress.

39...g5! 40 hxg5 ♖xg5 41 ♔f3 ♖a5 42 ♖e1+ ♔f5 43 ♖e4 ♖c5 44 ♖e3 ♖a5 45 ♖a3 ♔e5 46 ♔e3 ♔e6 47 ♔e2 ♔d6 48 ♔f2 ♔e6 49 ♖e3+ ♔d5 50 ♖a3 ♔e6 51 ♔e3 h4! 52 g4

52 gxh4 ♖h5 53 ♔d4 ♖xh4+ 54 ♔c5 ♔d7 is an elementary draw.

52...♔f6 53 ♔f4 ♔g6 54 ♔f3 ♔g5 55 ♖a2 h3 Draw.

201

Spassky – Antoshin
Sochi 1965

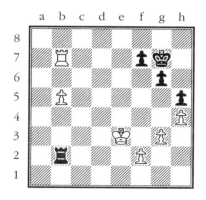

White to move

It's well-known that an a-pawn is a draw when the attacker has a passive rook against an active rook behind the passer as was shown ten years ago by Kantorovich and Poghosyan. I recommend *Dvoretsky's Endgame Manual* if you want to study this endgame in depth. With a b-pawn

White's winning chances increase. The reason is that the attacker's king can support the b-pawn one move quicker compared with an a-pawn. In situations where the defender has given up his rook for the b-pawn the king has gained a tempo when it returns to base. So in total White can gain two tempi and that is crucial when pawn races are involved because the result of the game often depends on just one or two tempi. Here the rook is excellently placed on b7 because it prevents the enemy king from manoeuvring to g4 via f6 and f5. White has created a pawn wave on the kingside which is the best pawn formation because White has only one weakness on f2. Black has also placed the rook on the best square where it pressurises two pawns simultaneously. Black's pawn formation is the best since the h-pawn has already made a move and this can be important in a future pawn race.

46 ♔d4!

The right moment to abandon the f2-pawn. 46 b6 ♔f6 transposes to Feletar - Z. Zelić, Hrvatska 1995. That game continued: 47 ♔d4! ♖xf2 (47...g5) 48 ♖c7 ♖b2 49 b7 ♔f5 50 ♖xf7+ ♔g4 51 ♔c3 ♖b6 52 ♖g7 (A simpler win was 52 ♖f4+ ♔xg3 53 ♖b4 ♖xb7 54 ♖xb7 ♔xh4 55 ♔d3 etc.) 52...♔h3 53 ♔d4 g5 54 hxg5 ♔xg3 55 g6 Black resigns.

46...♖xf2

46...♔f6 47 b6 transposes to the aforementioned game.

47 ♖e7 ♖b2

47...g5 48 hxg5 ♖f5 49 ♖e5 ♖f3 50 ♖e3 ♖f5 51 ♖b3.

48 ♔c4 ♔f6 49 ♖e3! ♔f5 50 ♖b3 ♖c2+

The pawn ending after 50...♖xb3 51 ♔xb3 is lost. Then a plausible variation is 51...♔e5 52 ♔b4 ♔d6 53 ♔a5 ♔c7 54 ♔a6 ♔b8 55 ♔b6 f6 56 ♔c5 g5 57 ♔d5 ♔c7 58 ♔e6 ♔b6 59 ♔xf6 gxh4 60 gxh4 ♔xb5 61 ♔g5 ♔c6 62 ♔xh5 ♔d7 63 ♔g6 ♔e8 64 ♔g7.

51 ♔d5 ♔g4 52 b6 ♖c8 53 b7 ♖b8

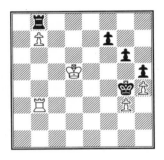

54 ♔e5

54 ♔c6 also wins after 54...f6 55 ♔c7 ♖g8 56 b8♕ ♖xb8 57 ♖xb8 (57 ♔xb8? g5! is a draw.) 57...♔xg3 58 ♖g8 and White's king is close enough.

54...f5

54...g5 55 hxg5 ♔xg5 56 ♖b4 f5 57 ♔d6 f4 58 gxf4+ ♔f5 59 ♔c7 ♖xb7+ 60 ♔xb7 h4 61 ♔c6 h3 62 ♖b3 ♔g4 63 ♖xh3 wins.

55 ♔f6 f4 56 gxf4 ♔xh4 57 ♔xg6 ♔g4 58 f5 h4 59 f6 h3 60 f7 h2 61 ♖b1 ♖xb7

If 61...♔g3 then 62 ♔g7.

62 ♖xb7 h1♕ 63 ♖b4+ ♔h3 64 f8♕ ♕g2+ 65 ♔h7 ♕c2+ 66 ♔h8 ♕c3+ 67 ♔g8 ♕g3+ 68 ♕g7 Black resigns.

202

Ghitescu – Rajković
Skopje 1984

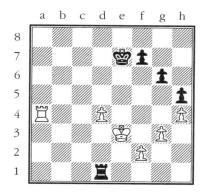

White to move

1 ♖a2!

White plays according to Tarrasch's procedure of placing the rook behind the passed pawn and that is the correct strategy here.

1...♔e6 2 ♖d2 ♖a1 3 ♔f4 ♖a5?

3...f6 was necessary.

4 ♖e2+?

White misses the beautiful win 4 d5+!! ♖xd5 (4...♔f6 5 ♖d4! followed by 6 d6.) 5 ♖xd5 ♔xd5 6 ♔g5.

This pawn ending is very useful to know because it's a very common pawn structure. White is winning due to the fact that the pawn break f4-f5 cannot be prevented. This position clearly shows the benefit of a more active king. 6...♔e5 7 f3! ♔e6 8 f4 ♔e7 9 f5 gxf5 10 ♔xf5 and White not only wins the h-pawn but also the pawn ending.

4...♔d6 5 ♖b2 ♔e6 6 ♔e4 ♖a1?

6...♔d6 is better.

7 d5+! ♔f6 8 ♖d2

8 ♔d4 was also good.

8...♔e7

He should try 8...♖a7.

9 ♔e5?

Correct was 9 d6+! ♔d7 10 ♔e5 ♖a5+ 11 ♔f6 ♖f5+ 12 ♔g7 ♖f3 13 ♔h6 ♖f6 (13...♖f5 14 f4 ♖f6 15 ♔g7 ♖f5 16 ♖d3) 14 f4 ♖xd6 15 ♖xd6+ ♔xd6 16 f5! gxf5 17 ♔xh5 ♔e5 18 ♔g5 and White wins.

9...♖e1+

After 9...f6+ 10 ♔f4 ♔d6 Black has an ideal defensive position so White cannot win.

10 ♔f4 f6 11 ♖a2

A better try was 11 ♖d4 ♖a1 (11...♔d6? 12 ♖e4!) 12 ♖e4+ ♔f7 13 ♖b4 ♔e7 14 ♖b7+ ♔d6 15 ♖b6+ ♔e7 16 ♖e6+ ♔f7 17 ♖e2 with the plan ♔e4, however if Black plays 17...♖a4+ 18 ♔e3 g5! the game will end in a draw anyway.

11...♖e5! 12 ♖a7+ ♔d6! 13 ♖a6+ ♔e7 14 ♖a7+ ♔d6 15 ♖a6+ ♔e7 16 d6+ ♔d7 Draw.

56 ♔b4!

The idea of sacrificing a pawn in exchange for penetration into the enemy territory is a clear parallel to Capablanca's famous endgame against Tartakower.

56...♖d3?

56...♖xd4+? 57 ♔a5 followed by ♔b6 and ♔xc6 wins in the same fashion as Capablanca defeated Tartakower. Correct was 56...♖a1! and White's king is unable to penetrate Black's position. A draw is the most likely outcome despite the fact that White has an extra pawn.

57 ♔a5 ♖xd4

Cutting off the king with 57...♖b3 fails to 58 ♔a6 followed by 59 ♖b7. If 58...♔c8 then 59 ♖e7 decides.

58 ♔b6 ♖d7 59 ♖xd7+ ♔xd7 60 ♔b7 Black resigns.

203

Capablanca – Stearns
Simultaneous exhibition,
Cleveland 1922

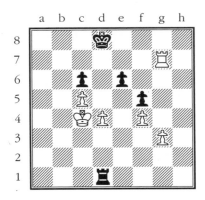

White to move

204

Engqvist – B. Kristensen
Hafnarfjördur 1996

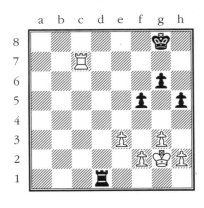

Black to move

During the game I thought I had some winning chances due to Black's passive king and my extra pawn. However, as I played on I realised that it was practically impossible to win. At home I asked GM Mikhail Gurevich online if White had any winning chances but he thought it was a draw. So here we can establish another rule that if Black can play both ...h5 and ...f5 it doesn't matter if Black's king is passive as long as the black rook can stop White's king from marching to g5, and that isn't particularly difficult.

34...♖a1

Black plans 35...♖a2 to make it difficult for White to activate his king but first he reduces the activity of White's rook which now has only seven files to play on.

35 ♖d7

The rook is slightly better placed here because in some positions ♖d4, where it's protected, is a useful move.

35...♖a2!

The best square for Black's rook.

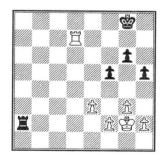

36 h3

The idea is to get a passed pawn on e4 with the break g3-g4 at the right

moment to exploit Black's pawn position on f5. The other winning attempt is to try to penetrate to g5, but if Black just maintains the pressure on f2 it's still a draw after 36 h4 ♖b2 37 ♔f3 ♖a2 (Another way to draw is 37...♖b4 38 ♖d4 ♖b2 but the other line liquidates all pawns except the h-pawn.) 38 ♔f4 ♖xf2+ 39 ♔g5 ♖f3 40 ♔xg6 ♖xg3+ 41 ♔xf5 ♖xe3 42 ♔g6 ♖e6+.

36...♔f8 37 ♔f3 ♖b2 38 ♖a7 ♖b4

Black plans the profitable exchange of his h-pawn for White's g-pawn or f-pawn. White's dream in this ending is to get rid of his h-pawn so Black's plan has to be stopped.

39 ♖d7 ♖b2

39...h4? 40 ♖d4 would lose the pawn since Black cannot exchange on d4.

40 g4! hxg4+ 41 hxg4 fxg4+ 42 ♔g3

One of the reasons that Black's pawn structure h5-g6-f5 is so resilient is that Black secures the exchange of two pawns instead of one. Now White has to recapture the pawn with the rook and then Black's king is liberated from the last rank.

42...♖a2 43 ♖d4 ♔f7 44 ♖xg4

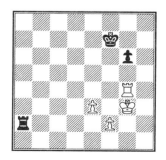

During the game I still thought I had some winning chances but it's actually a very simple draw. This is an important position to keep in mind, since it's a natural outcome of endings with four pawns versus three pawns if the defender knows the perfect set-up.

44...♖a1 45 ♖b4 ♔f6 46 ♖b6+ ♔f5 47 f3 ♖a3 48 e4+ ♔g5 49 ♖b5+ ♔f6 50 ♔g4 ♖a1 51 ♖b6+ ♔f7 52 ♖d6 ♖g1+ 53 ♔f4 ♔e7 54 ♖a6 ♖g2 55 ♔e3

55 ♔e5 ♖g5+ prevents the white king from any further penetration.

55...♔f7

The principled 55...g5! would have fixed the f3-pawn.

56 f4 ♖g4!

Kristensen's method is to prevent the king from penetrating to the central square e5 via d4.

57 ♖a1 ♖h4 58 ♔f3 ♖h3+ 59 ♔g4 ♖h2 60 ♖a7+ ♔e6!

60...♔f6? 61 e5+ ♔e6 62 ♔g5 ♖g2+ 63 ♔h6 followed by 64 ♖a6+ wins the g6-pawn, because White can use the important outpost on f6 for his rook if necessary.

61 e5

With the pawn on e4 61 ♔g5 ♖g2+ 62 ♔h6 ♖g4 is a simple draw.

61...♖g2+ 62 ♔f3 ♖g1 63 ♖a6+ ♔e7 64 ♖f6 ♔e8 65 ♔e4 ♔e7 66 ♖d6 ♖e1+ 67 ♔d5 ♖d1+ 68 ♔c6 ♖c1+ 69 ♔d5 ♖d1+ 70 ♔c5 ♖c1+ 71 ♔b4 ♖e1!

Black strives for the Philidor position.

72 ♖xg6 ♖e4+ 73 ♔c5 ♖xf4 74 ♔d5 ♖a4 75 ♖g7+ ♔e8 76 ♔e6

76...♖a6+!

This defence was published by Philidor 1777 and is the number one position to know when studying rook endings. By controlling the sixth rank White cannot penetrate Black's position.

77 ♔f5 ♔f8 78 ♖d7 ♔e8 79 ♖b7 ♔f8 80 e6

Here I offered a draw because after 80...♖a1 White's king is prevented from reaching the sixth rank due to the rook check with an elementary draw. After this game I learned that it's pretty easy to hold three pawns versus four if you know this indestructible position with pawns on h5 and f5.

Four years later I learned that in a similar position, in the 14th game of their World Championship match, London 2000, Kramnik had the possibility of playing 46 f3-f4 with an immediate draw against Kasparov. The authors of the book *Kasparov – Kramnik London 2000*, Nigel Davies and Andrew Martin, at that time wrote: "It seems that almost everyone knew about this apart from Kramnik!"

However, you might just as well reverse it and say that if Kramnik didn't know it, who did? It wasn't clearly formulated in the endgame books during those days. However, after the World Championship match you could find this important bit of knowledge in *Fundamental Chess Endings* by Müller/Lamprecht (Gambit 2001) and Jeremy Silman's *Complete Endgame Course* (Siles Press 2007).

204a

Piket – Kasparov

KasparovChess Grand Prix 2000

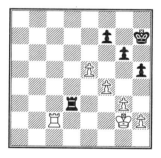

White to move

If the defender is unable to stop the e-pawn from advancing to the fourth or fifth rank, as we saw in the previous example, more care is required. Kasparov didn't manage to hold this position, where White has a nice pawn chain with the e5-pawn as a spearhead. White's dream is to have his king on g5 and then set up a pawn duo with f4-f5.

41 ♔h3! ♖e3?

41...g5! would have spoiled White's plan completely. After

42 fxg5 ♔g6 43 ♖f2 ♔xg5! 44 ♖xf7 ♖e3 45 ♖e7 ♖e2 46 ♖e8 ♔f5 47 e6 ♔f6 48 e7 ♔g7! it's an easy draw. Interestingly the active defence starting with 43...♔xg5 has been overlooked by annotators of this endgame.

42 ♔h4?

42 ♖c7 ♔g7 43 ♔h4 and 44 ♔g5 is the winning continuation as we'll see in the game.

42...♔g7?

42...♔h6 43 ♖c7 ♖e2 was the only defence. After the further 44 g4 ♔g7 45 h3 hxg4 46 hxg4 ♖e4 47 ♔g5 ♖e1 White cannot win.

43 ♔g5?

43 ♖c7 ♖e2 44 ♔g5 should have been played.

43...♖e1?

A comedy of errors but don't forget that this is actually a rapid game played on the Internet. Averbakh's suggestion 43...♖a3 44 ♖c7 ♖a5 was correct. One forced line is 45 ♖e7 ♖b5 46 f5 gxf5 47 e6 f4+! 48 ♔xf4 ♔f6 49 ♖xf7+ ♔xe6.

44 ♖c7 ♖e2

The clever defence 44...♖e4, which prevents f4-f5 due to mate on g4, is met by the nice waiting move 45 ♖a7. White wins after 45...♖b4 by 46 g4! hxg4 47 f5 gxf5 48 e6.

45 ♖e7! ♖a2

There is also 45...♖e4.

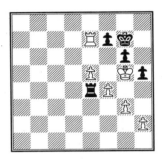

This position has occurred in three games. (Stean – Hartston, Brighton 1972, Ionov – Karasev, Leningrad 1983 and Matveeva – Rappoport, Baku 1983) White wins as follows: 46 e6! (46 h3? ♖e3 47 g4 hxg4 48 hxg4 ♖e1 49 f5 ♖xe5 50 ♖xe5 f6+ 51 ♔f4 fxe5+ 52 ♔xe5 gxf5 is a draw.) 46...♖xe6 47 ♖xe6 fxe6 48 h3 ♔f7 49 ♔h6 ♔f6 50 g4 h4 51 g5+ ♔f5 52 ♔g7 ♔xf4 53 ♔xg6 e5 54 ♔h5 e4 55 g6 e3 56 g7 e2 57 g8♕ e1♕ 58 ♕g5+ ♔f3 59 ♕g4+.

46 f5!

White's dream has been achieved. Note that 46 e6? didn't work on account of 46...♖a5+ 47 ♔h4 ♔f6.

46...gxf5 47 e6

Here we see the point of White's 46th move; there is no check along the fifth rank since the f5-pawn shields the rook.

47...h4 48 ♖xf7+ ♔g8 49 ♔f6 **Black resigns.**

205

P. Karlsson – Engqvist
Uppsala 1979

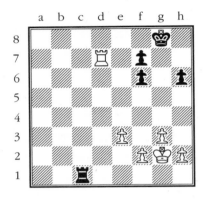

White to move

37 ♔f3

Znosko-Borovsky suggests the clever idea, and probably the only realistic winning plan, of placing the rook on g4 to force Black to declare his intentions with his king. If Black places it on f8 White can strive for the following set-up: pawns on f3 and e4 and then to advance his king to h5 targeting the weak h6-pawn. If Black tries to stop the king when it is on h4 by placing his rook on the fifth rank White can advance the f-pawn to f5 blocking the rook. If Black meets the check on g4 with ...♔h7 White can try to reach the other side with his king and focus his attention on the f-pawns or a rook exchange.

37 ♖d4!?, with the idea 38 ♖g4+, cannot be stopped by 37...h5? due to 38 ♖d5 h4 39 g4 followed by

40 ♖h5 or 40 ♔h3. However note that if the black king was already placed on g7 then the h5-pawn could be defended by ...♔g6. The best defence is 37...♖c5! 38 ♖g4+ ♔f8 or 38...♔h7 and if White plays 39 e4 with the plan f4-f5 Black can simply exchange the e4-pawn by playing 39...f5 making it easier to draw. It's all about activity.

37...♖c5

A good square for the rook where it covers the fifth rank and prevents any penetration by the white king as well as any space-gaining pawn moves.

38 ♔f4 ♔g7 39 h4 ♔g6

Black exploits the damaged pawn structure and plays as actively as possible with the king by placing it on g6.

40 e4 h5

Black has positioned all his pieces as actively as possible according to the golden rule in rook endings.

41 f3 ♖c3 42 ♖d6 ♖c4

Black must prevent e4-e5.

43 g4

There are no profitable pawn exchanges for White and he has to content himself with a passed h-pawn which is the worst extra pawn to have.

43...hxg4 44 fxg4 ♔g7

Black must defend against g4-g5 and withdraws his king one step.

45 ♔f5 ♖c1

Black is threatening mate.

46 g5 fxg5 47 ♔xg5 ♖g1+ 48 ♔h5 ♖e1 49 ♖d4 ♖g1 50 e5 ♖e1 51 ♖g4+ ♔h7 52 ♖g5 ♖f1 53 ♔g4 ♖g1+ 54 ♔f5 ♖f1+ 55 ♔e4 ♖d1 56 h5 ♖h1 57 ♔d5 ♖d1+ 58 ♔c6 ♖f1 59 ♔d6 ♔h6 60 ♖g8 ♔xh5 Draw.

A well played ending by both players. I was helped by the fact that I already knew the famous endgame Eliskases – Bogoljubow, match, 1939 from one of Euwe's endgame books, which taught me that the position is easier to defend with the g-pawn on f6 rather than on g7.

206

Ribli – Korchnoi
Baden-Baden 1981

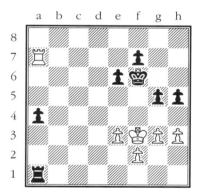

White to move

Rook endings with an outside passed pawn on the queenside and four against four on the kingside increase the winning chances for the superior side compared with three against three on the kingside. The crucial factor is the placement of the rooks. Here the attacker has the passive rook and the defender the

297

active rook, so normally this position should end in a draw. However, as Korchnoi writes in his book *Practical Rook Endings* (Editions Olms 1999), "the weaker side must, as usual, play precisely." White has already made a slight mistake by avoiding 34 h4, setting up a pawn wave with the pawns on f2-g3-h4. This omission has permitted Black to grab space with 34...g5 which has restricted White's possibilities on the kingside. Korchnoi is also critical of 37 e3 which has weakened the second rank. We are coming into the game at move 38.

38 ♖a5!

The most logical place for the rook where it puts pressure on the g5-pawn and indirectly the h5-pawn. It also prevents the king manoeuvre to the queenside via the central squares.

38...a3

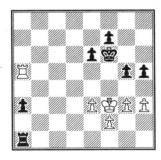

39 g4

Korchnoi comments: "After all the inaccuracies committed by White, he is already experiencing some difficulties. Naturally, he tries to gain some space on the kingside. If White had abstained from any activity and just made waiting moves with his rook, while Black had played straightforwardly, e.g. 39 ♖a8 ♖a2 40 ♖a5 ♔e7 41 ♖xg5 ♖d2 42 ♖a5 (42 ♖xh5? ♖d5 43 ♖h8 ♖a5) 42...a2, then White would have had a wide choice of plans involving e3-e4, g3-g4 and h3-h4, and, in view of the possibility of creating a passed h-pawn, his position would certainly be less threatened than in the game."

39...h4

Now White not only has the problem of the a-pawn to deal with, but also an additional fixed weakness on h3.

40 ♔g2 ♔g6

41 ♖a6?

Ribli wants to prevent activity with ...f7-f5 but the real threat is the king manoeuvre to the queenside. Here the game was adjourned and according to Korchnoi the position at this particular moment is won. However, he didn't find any win during the break of one and a half hours. In *Practical Rook Endings* he recommends the following line leading to a draw: 41 ♔h2! f6 Black plans to bring out his king to f7 and then manoeuvre to the queenside along the 7th and 8th ranks. 42 ♖a7 f5

43 f4! a2 (43...fxg4 44 hxg4 a2 45 ♖a6 ♖e1 46 f5+ ♔f6 47 ♖xa2 ♖xe3 48 ♖a6) 44 gxf5+ ♔xf5 45 ♖a5+ ♔f6 46 fxg5+ ♔g6 47 e4 e5 48 ♔g2 ♔h5 49 ♔h2 ♖e1 50 ♖xa2 ♖xe4 51 ♖g2 ♔g6 52 ♔g1.

41...♔g7 42 ♖a7

42...♔f6?

Korchnoi gives the winning variation 42...♖a2! 43 ♔f3 ♔f8 44 e4 (44 ♖a8+?! ♔e7 45 ♖a7+ ♔d6 46 ♖xf7 ♖c2 47 ♖a7 a2 48 e4 (48 ♔e4 ♖xf2) 48...e5 49 ♔e3 ♔c5) 44...e5 45 ♔e3 ♔e8 46 ♖a5 f6 47 ♖a7 ♔d8. The king manoeuvres to b8 and then to b3 with a win.

43 ♖a8?

43 ♖a5! should have been played. Now Black has the chance to win again.

43...♔e7?

Korchnoi gives 43...♔e5! 44 ♖a5+ ♔e4 45 ♖xg5 ♖c1 46 ♖a5 ♖c3 47 ♖a7 ♔d3 48 ♖xf7 ♔c2 49 ♖a7 ♔b2 and Black wins in all variations. For example:

(a) 50 ♔f3 a2 51 ♖xa2+ ♔xa2.

(a1) 52 g5 ♔b3 53 ♔g4 ♖c2 54 f4 ♔c4 55 ♔h5 ♔d3.

(a2) 52 ♔f4 ♖c2 53 f3 (53 ♔g5 ♖xf2 54 ♔xh4 ♖e2 55 g5 ♖xe3 56 ♔g4 ♖e1 57 h4 ♔b3) 53...♖h2.

(b) 50 g5 a2 51 g6 a1♕ 52 ♖xa1 ♔xa1 53 ♔f3 ♖c1 54 ♔g4 ♖g1+ 55 ♔h5 ♔b2 56 ♔h6 ♔c3 57 g7 ♔d3 58 ♔h7 ♔e2.

44 ♖a7+ ♔e8? 45 ♖a8+ ♔d7 46 ♖a7+ ♔c6 47 ♖xf7 ♖b1

47...♔b6 is met by 48 ♖f8. 47...♔d5 is trickier to meet but if one finds 48 ♖c7! it's a clear draw after 48...e5 49 ♖c3 e4 50 ♔h2 ♖f1 51 ♖xa3 ♖xf2+ 52 ♔g1.

48 ♖a7 ♖b3 49 f4! gxf4 50 exf4

White's passed pawn secures the draw.

50...♔b6 51 ♖a8 ♖g3+ 52 ♔h2 ♔c5 53 f5 exf5 54 gxf5 ♔b4 55 f6 ♖f3 56 ♖b8+ ♔c3 57 ♖a8 Draw.

206a

Bisguier – Udovčić
Zagreb 1955

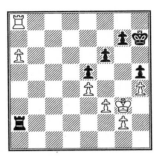

White to move

When each player has four pawns on the kingside, the attacker has better winning chances than with fewer pawns. The reasons are threefold:

(1) He can put more pressure on the black pawns with g2-g4.

(2) He can prepare g2-g3 followed by f2-f4.

(3) His king can more easily find safety amongst the black pawns, because it's less likely that all pawns on the kingside will disappear from the board.

44 ♔h2 ♖a1 45 g4

The other plan was 45 g3 followed by f2-f4.

45...hxg4 46 fxg4 ♖a4 47 a7!

This pawn-push indirectly defends the e4-pawn while preparing a king manoeuvre to a safe square on the black kingside.

47...♖a2+ 48 ♔g3 ♖a3+ 49 ♔f2 ♖a2+ 50 ♔e3 ♖a3+ 51 ♔d2 ♔g6 52 h5+ ♔g5

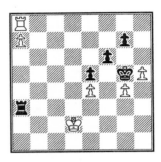

53 h6!

A typical finesse where this tactical pawn break is combined with a passed pawn on the seventh rank.

53...♔g6

53...♔xh6 54 ♖h8+ or 53...gxh6 54 ♖g8+ are not playable.

54 hxg7 ♔xg7 55 ♔c2 ♖a2+ 56 ♔b3 ♖a1 57 ♔b4 ♖a2 58 ♔b5

White's king is on its way to e6 or f5 followed by the decisive break g4-g5.

58...♖b2+ 59 ♔c6 ♖a2 60 ♔d6 ♖a6+ 61 ♔e7 ♖a5 62 ♔e6 ♖a3

If 62...♖a6+ then 63 ♔f5.

63 g5 fxg5 64 ♔f5 ♖f3+ 65 ♔xg5 Black resigns.

Black is in zugzwang after 65...♖a3 66 ♔f5 ♖a5 67 ♔e6 ♔h7 68 ♔f6. He then loses the e5-pawn and White soon promotes the passed e4-pawn.

207

Capablanca – Beaumont
Simultaneous exhibition,
Leeds 1919

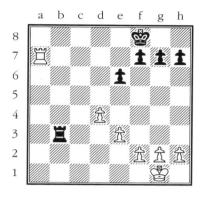

White to move

Rook endings with connected pawns, five versus four on the same side, are surprisingly difficult to find in endgame literature. The key to creating winning chances is to establish a passed pawn on the d-file.

32 g4!

A good move which seizes space and prepares the activation of the king.

32...g5?!

A better defence was 32...罝b5!. Now it will be easier for Capablanca to exchange the h-pawn for Black's g-pawn (or create a weakness on h6). It was this profitable exchanging strategy which laid the foundations for his classical wins against Duras, New York 1913 (Position 247 in *300 Most Important Chess Positions*) and Yates, Hastings 1930. In both these classic rook endings he had

four connected pawns versus three connected pawns on the kingside. It's useful to know these endings as it's sometimes possible to transpose to an advantageous four vs. three ending.

33 當g2

White could have exploited the passive position of the king by immediately attacking the g5-pawn with 33 罝a5! because after 33...h6 34 h4 Black is practically forced to accept the pawn exchange 34...gxh4, which is in White's favour after 35 罝h5.

33...當g7 34 當g3 當g6

It was more important to activate the rook with 34...罝b2! and put pressure on the f2-pawn.

35 h4! h6!

36 h5+!

Plan B, if White doesn't manage to force Black to exchange the g-pawn for the h-pawn, is to create a second weakness on h6. The main problem for Black is that he has to defend against d4-d5, after preparatory moves like f2-f3, and e3-e4 at an appropriate moment. The disappearance of the h-pawns after 36 hxg5 hxg5 makes the position more compact, which should make Black's defensive task easier.

36...♔g7 37 ♔f3 ♔f8 38 ♔e4 ♖b2 39 f3 ♖b3 40 ♖a8+ ♔g7

Black might try 40...♔e7?, hoping for 41 ♖h8 ♔f6 42 ♖xh6+? ♔g7 when White's rook is trapped. But instead 42 ♖h7! dispels the illusion that 42...♖b8 traps White's rook because after 43 f4 White already threatens to grab the h6-pawn followed by fxg5.

41 f4 gxf4

This is an advantageous exchange for Black since the f-pawn is more valuable than the g-pawn. Anyway Black would otherwise have to reckon with both 42 fxg5, giving White an outside passer, or 42 f5 followed by 43 fxe6 which is a profitable exchange for White.

42 ♔xf4

It's important to keep alive the pawn push e3-e4 with the idea of d4-d5.

42...♔f6

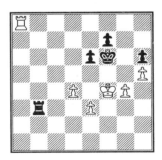

43 ♖g8

The plan to place the rook behind the d-pawn and play e3-e4 and d4-d5 doesn't work due to the weak g5-square. One plausible variation is 43 ♖a1 ♖b2 44 ♖d1 ♖f2+ 45 ♔g3 ♖e2 46 ♔f3 ♖a2 47 e4 ♔g5! 48 ♖d3 ♖a1 49 d5 exd5 50 exd5 f5! 51 gxf5 ♔xf5 52 d6 ♖a8 and the d-pawn is doomed.

43...♖c3 44 e4

Maybe Capablanca realised that the intended 44 g5+ hxg5+ 45.♖xg5 would give Black too good drawing chances after 45...♖c1! (Note that 45...♖xe3? fails to the pretty intermediate move 46 ♖f5+! exf5 47 ♔xe3 ♔g5 48 d5 and one of the pawns will promote.) 46 ♖g3 ♖h1 47 ♔g4 ♔g7 48 e4 ♔h6 and the h-pawn falls with a draw.

44...♔e7?

Black could draw with 44...♖d3! 45 e5+ (Or 45 ♖h8 ♔g7 46 ♖d8 ♔f6) 45...♔e7 46 ♔e4 ♖g3. This drawing opportunity proves that the ending was not so easy for Capablanca nor was it as simple as it looks.

45 e5?

45 ♖h8 wins after 45...♔f6 (or 45...♖d3 46 ♖xh6 ♖xd4 47 g5 ♖d1 48 ♖h8 and Black is lost) 46 ♖xh6+ ♔g7 47 g5 ♖d3 48 d5 exd5 49 ♖d6!!.

45...♖c4 46 ♔e4 f5+?

Black draws after 46...♖c1 followed by ...♖e1+ and ...♖d1.

47 exf6+ Black resigns.

207a

Liu – Bu
Qinhuangdao Open 2011

White to move

Compare the following position with Capablanca – Beaumont. Here it's easier to create a passed pawn on the d-file, due to the fact that White's e-pawn is situated on the fourth rank.

31...♔e6!

This preparation for ...f7-f5 is the most sophisticated way to exploit the vulnerability of the e4-pawn. The immediate 31...e6, with the idea of 32...d5, makes White's defence easier after 32 ♖c6! which forces a four versus three ending after 32...d5 (32...♔e7 33 ♖c7+ ♔e8 34 ♔f4! and Black is too passive to create a passer on the d-file.) 33 exd5 ♖xd5.

32 ♔f4 f5! 33 exf5+

If White allows the f-pawns to be exchanged on e4 his pawns will no longer be connected and Black can still establish a passed pawn on the d-file after due preparation.

33...♖xf5+ 34 ♔e3 h5

There is no reason to allow White more space than necessary. Now the h4-pawn is fixed and a future target for the black rook.

35 ♖c8?

The rook belongs on the fourth rank.

35...♖c5 36 ♖g8 ♔f7 37 ♖d8 ♖c2

A further pawn is lost.

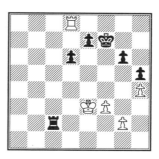

38 g4

The nice variation 38 g3 ♖g2 39 ♔f4 e5+ 40 ♔e3 ♔e7! 41 ♖g8 ♖xg3 42 ♔f2 ♔f7! would secure the extra pawns.

38...♖h2 39 ♔f4 ♖xh4 40 ♖h8 ♖h3! 41 ♖h7+ ♔f8 42 g5 ♖h1 43 ♔g3 ♖g1+ 44 ♔h4 ♖e1 45 ♖h8+

White must avoid 45...♔g8 46 ♖h6 ♔g7 when the rook is imprisoned.

45...♔g7 46 ♖d8 ♖a1 47 ♔g3 ♖a5 48 f4 ♔f7 49 ♖b8 ♖a3+ 50 ♔g2 ♔e6 51 ♖f8 h4 52 ♔h2 ♖g3 53 ♖h8 ♔f5 54 ♖xh4 ♖e3 55 ♔g2 ♖e4 White resigns.

56 ♔g3 would have been answered by 56...e5! after which White's position collapses.

207b

Marangunić – Simić
Yugoslavia 1972

White to move

1 ♖b5 f6 2 ♖b7

2 ♖b8+! ♔g7 3 ♖b7+ ♔g8 (The king would be abysmally placed after 3...♔h6 4 h4) 4 h4 would have gained a tempo to get rid of the weakness on h2.

2...♖e1 3 ♖b2

White probably didn't like 3 ♔f3 due to 3...g5, creating a weakness on h2, or 3 e3 because of 3...♖d1.

3...♔f7

3...g5 was more to the point.

4 f4?

4 h4 should have been played.

4...h5?

4...exf4 5 gxf4 h5 was the correct way to play for a draw which would indeed have been pretty certain as White has too many pawn weaknesses. At the moment he has to cover the e2- and h2-pawns and if he advances the e-pawn two steps there are three weaknesses on d3, f4

and h2. So there is no way for White to successfully activate his position. Black's rook is too active and White has two pawn islands to take care of.

5 fxe5 fxe5 6 ♔f3 ♖a1 7 ♔e4 ♖a5 8 e3 ♔f6 9 ♖b6+ ♔f7 10 h3 ♖c5 11 ♖d6 Black resigns.

207c

Ståhlberg – Danielsson
Sweden

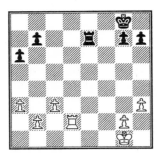

White to move

One of Rudolf Spielmann's important rules in rook endings is to manoeuvre the king to the pawn majority, where it belongs, before moving any pawns so they can be supported by the king. An exception of course is when the pawns win automatically without any assistance of the king. In this position White should not rush the advance of the pawns but strive to post his king on c2 before pushing them. White can do this by simply playing...

1 ♔f2

...followed by 2 ♖e2 and 3 ♔e1 etc. Note that this plan is all the more effective since the black king cannot defend against the pawn majority since it is cut off from the main scene of action. Black cannot agree to a rook exchange as eventually White will create a passed pawn on the queenside, supported by his king, and that will secure him an easy win. The king is better than a rook to support a pawn, even when the rook is placed behind the pawn! Here White's rook stands perfectly on the second rank where it not only supports the pawn majority from behind but also protects the g2-pawn to avoid any serious counterplay on the kingside.

208

Turov – Mikhalevski
Rilton Cup, Stockholm 2015

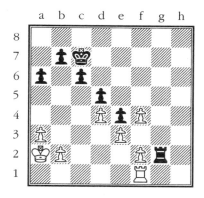

White to move

39 ♔b3 b6 40 ♔c3 a5

Or 40...c5 41 dxc5 bxc5 42 b4!.

41 b4!

White starts a minority attack! The normal move 41 ♔d2, planning to liberate the rook on f1, is strongly answered by 41...c5! 42 ♔e2 (If 42 dxc5 bxc5 43 ♔e2 a4 and White's

b2-pawn is a future target for Black's rook after 44 ♖h1 ♖g8 followed by ...♖b8.) 42...cxd4 43 exd4 ♖h2 44 ♖g1 ♖h4! 45 ♔e3 ♖h3+. (White shouldn't allow Black to play his rook to b3.) 46 ♖g3 ♖xg3+ 47 fxg3 and the pawn ending is an easy draw due to Black's far advanced protected passed pawn.

41...axb4+

41...a4 seems more logical due to the fact that it opens a possible way to penetrate White's position via b7-a6-c4. Then:

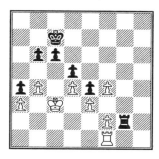

(a) After 42 ♔d2 ♔b7 43 ♔e2 ♔a6 44 ♖h1 ♔b5 45 ♖h6 ♖g7 Black has counterplay with ...♔c4 and ...♔b3 so the position is balanced.

(b) Upon 42 b5 the drawback to 42...c5 is that the b5-pawn can be troublesome for Black after 43 f5 ♖g5 44 f4! ♖xf5 45 ♖h1 but with 42...cxb5 43 ♔b4 ♔c6 44 ♖c1+ ♔b7 45 ♔xb5 (45 ♖c2 ♔a6) 45...♖xf2 46 ♔xa4 ♖b2 Black can play for mate with ...♔a6 and ...b5 so White has to place the rook on the sixth rank and when Black attacks e3, White attacks d5. White's king is offside in this variation so Black's drawing chances should be good.

42 axb4

42 ♔xb4 followed by a4 was another option.

42...♖g8?

42...b5 43 ♔d2 ♖g8 was a simpler way to achieve a draw. White's weakness on b4 makes it difficult to play for a win.

43 b5!

Allowing this strong move makes it questionable whether Black can hold the rook ending.

43...cxb5 44 ♔b4 ♖a8 45 f3 exf3 46 ♖xf3

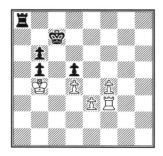

46...♔d6

Black cannot stop the pawn from advancing to f6. After 46...♖a1 47 f5 ♖b1+ 48 ♔c3 ♔d7 49 f6 ♔e8 50 ♖f5 ♔f7 51 ♖xd5 ♔xf6 52 ♖d6+ ♔f5 53 ♖xb6 ♔e4 54 ♖e6+ ♔d5 55 ♖e5+ White has two connected pawns in the centre.

47 f5 ♔e7 48 f6+ ♔f7 49 ♔xb5 ♖b8 50 ♖f5 ♔e6 51 ♖f1 ♔f7 52 ♖f3 ♖d8 53 ♔xb6 ♖c8 54 ♖f5 ♔e6 55 ♔b7 ♖h8 56 ♖f3 ♔f7 57 ♔c6 ♖h5 58 ♖f4 ♖g5 59 e4

White liquidates to the ending rook and pawn against rook.

59...dxe4 60 ♖xe4 ♔xf6

When Black's king is cut off White wins if the passed pawn has advanced a few steps. This is a classic rook ending which must be mastered at all levels.

61 d5 ♖g1 62 d6 ♖c1+ 63 ♔b6 ♖b1+ 64 ♔c7 ♖c1+ 65 ♔d8 ♖a1 66 d7 ♔f7

The famous Lucena position has arisen.

67 ♖f4+

White is so focused on playing the Lucena position that he forgets that Black's rook isn't placed on c1. He could have simply played 67 ♖c4 followed by moving the king to the c-file.

67...♔g7 68 ♔e7 ♖e1+ 69 ♔d6 ♖d1+ 70 ♔e6 ♖d2

The spite checks 70...♖e1+ 71 ♔d5 ♖d1+ 72 ♖d4 lead to nothing. White is already prepared to build a bridge with his rook on the fourth rank.

71 ♖f5! Black resigns.

Now after the further 72 ♖d5 White will promote to a major piece.

209

Lilienthal – Smyslov
USSR Absolute Championship
1941

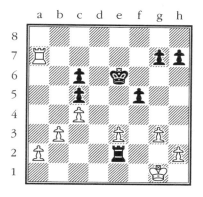

White to move

Black is a pawn down with bad pawns on the queenside. However Black's king and rook are more active and these factors secure the draw.

29...g5! 30 ≜xh7 ≜xa2

30...g4 was also possible, for example 31 ≜h6+ ♔e5 32 ≜xc6 ≜xa2 33 ≜xc5+ ♔e4 34 ≜d5 ≜a1+ 35 ♔f2 ≜a2+ 36 ♔e1 (36...≜a1+? 37 ♔e2 wins.) 36...≜b2! and despite the fact that Black is three pawns down it's a draw.

31 ≜h6+

A more interesting line would arise after 31 g4 fxg4 32 ≜h6+ ♔e5 33 ≜xc6 ♔e4 34 ≜xc5 ≜b2 35 b4 ♔xe3 (35...≜xb4? 36 ♔f2) 36 b5 g3! 37 hxg3 g4 38 ≜f5 ≜b1+ 39 ≜f1 ≜b2 40 ≜a1 ♔f3 41 ≜a3+ ♔e2 with a positional draw.

31...♔e5 32 ≜xc6 ♔e4 33 ≜xc5 f4! 34 exf4 ♔f3

Black is four pawns down but is threatening mate thanks to his enormous activity and White's badly placed king.

35 h3 ≜a1+ Draw.

It's a draw by perpetual check. A good example showing that king + rook activity can be worth a pawn apiece!

210

Turova – Goganov
Rilton Cup, Stockholm 2015

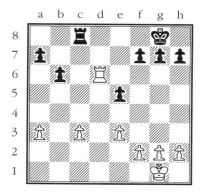

White to move

24 ≜d1?

White breaks a well-known classical principle that you should always be active in rook endings. Here the simplest way to reach a draw was 24 ≜d7 a5 25 ≜b7 h5 26 ≜xb6 ≜xc3 27 h4 ≜xa3 because after 28 ≜a6 it's a theoretical draw. White has the more active rook which is necessary if you want to hold the draw with a pawn deficit. The most famous model game of this ending is Ribli – Korchnoi, Baden Baden 1981, exercise 206.

24...♔f8 25 ♖c1 ♖c4

Note how Black manoeuvres on the key squares in the spirit of Staunton.

26 ♔f1 ♔e7 27 ♔e2 ♖a4 28 ♖a1 ♔d6 29 ♔d2 ♔d5 30 ♔c2 ♔c4

Black's king uses the white squares as well when it manoeuvres.

31 ♔b2

White has managed to defend the queenside pawn weaknesses with his king but the price is a decentralised king, which Black exploits.

31...♖a5 32 ♖d1 ♖d5

If 32...♖b5+ 33 ♔c2 ♖b3 White has the chance to activate his rook with good drawing chances after the sequence 34 ♖d7 ♖xc3+ 35 ♔b2 ♖b3+ 36 ♔a2 ♖d3 37 ♖c7+ ♔d5 38 ♖xf7 with merciless pressure on the exposed pawns on the seventh rank.

33 ♖xd5 ♔xd5

34 ♔b3

34 ♔c2 ♔c4 and White will eventually lose control of either the b3- or the d3-square.

34...♔e4!

This king centralisation decides the game.

35 ♔c4

35 ♔c2 b5 36 ♔d2 ♔d5 37 ♔c2 ♔c4 would not have helped.

35...a6 36 a4 f5 37 f4 exf4 38 exf4

38...h5!

After this strong move White is in a kind of zugzwang because all moves make his position worse. Note that the seemingly obvious 38...♔xf4? gives White good drawing chances in the queen ending after 39 ♔d4! a5 40 ♔c4 ♔e3 41 ♔b5 f4 42 ♔xb6 ♔f2 43 c4 ♔xg2 44 c5 f3 45 c6 f2 46 c7 f1♕ 47 c8♕ ♔xh2 48 ♕c2+.

39 g3 h4 40 gxh4 g6

A immediate 40...♔xf4 was also fine.

41 ♔b4 ♔xf4 42 c4 ♔e3 43 a5 bxa5+ 44 ♔xa5 f4 45 c5 f3 46 c6 f2 47 ♔xa6

It's mate after 47 c7 f1♕ 48 c8♕ ♕b5.

47...f1♕+ 48 ♔a7 ♕c4 49 ♔b7 ♕b5+ 50 ♔c7 ♔d4 White resigns.

211

U. Andersson – Brynell
Malmö 1994

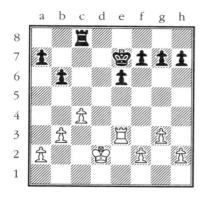

Black to move

It's very instructive to study how Ulf Andersson managed to win this equal rook ending against the strong Swedish player Stellan Brynell who seven years later became a GM.

28...♖c5

28...f6 29 f4 ♖d8+ 30 ♖d3 ♖xd3+ 31 ♔xd3 was perhaps not to Black's liking even though it should be a draw.

29 ♔c3 ♖f5

Black plays well with his rook and puts pressure on one of White's tactical weaknesses.

30 f3

It's instructive that Andersson plays this modest move with the f-pawn, ceding space, instead of 30 f4 setting up a pawn wave.

30...h5

Black plans ...g7-g5-g4 to fix the h2-pawn.

31 b4

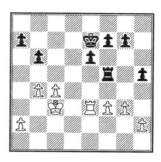

31...a5

This looks like a step in the wrong direction. It loses at least a tempo which could have been used on the kingside to improve Black's pawn position. Black breaks the classical rule that one shouldn't weaken oneself (the b6-pawn) where one is under attack so it's more logical to activate the pawns on the kingside with 31...g5.

Perhaps Black didn't like the fact that the a7-pawn could come under fire after 32 ♔d4 ♔d6 33 ♖a3, but as a matter of fact the a7-pawn is just as weak as the f3-pawn and the position is mutually balanced.

32 a3 ♔d6 33 ♔d4 g5 34 ♖d3 ♖e5 35 ♔c3+ ♔c7

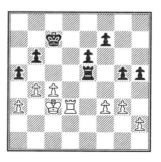

Black's king is best placed on the same side as the white pawn majority.

36 ♔d2

White must prevent the incursion of the black rook to e2.

36...g4 37 ♖e3

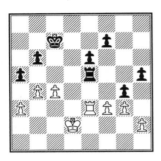

37...♖f5

Black cannot exchange to a pawn ending because after 37...♖xe3? 38 ♔xe3 ♔d6 (38...gxf3 39 ♔xf3 axb4 40 axb4 e5 41 g4 h4 [*41...hxg4+ 42 ♔xg4*] 42 g5 ♔d6 43 ♔e4 ♔e6 44 h3 f6 45 gxf6 ♔xf6 46 ♔d5) 39 fxg4 hxg4 40 ♔f4 f5 41 ♔g5 ♔e5 42 bxa5 bxa5 43 c5 ♔d5 44 ♔f6 White wins.

38 ♔e2 axb4

38...gxf3+ 39 ♖xf3 ♖e5+ 40 ♔d2 f5 41 ♖f4 ♔c6 42 ♖h4 b5 was a more active continuation to achieve a draw.

39 axb4 ♔d6

39...e5 would put more pressure on the white pawn minority.

40 ♖d3+ ♔c6 41 f4 h4

Black's plan is to activate the rook via h5 and down the h-file.

42 ♔e3 hxg3 43 hxg3 ♖h5 44 ♔d4

44...♖h1

The most active continuation but passive defence with 44...f6 also holds the game. 45 ♖e3 ♔d6 46 c5+ bxc5+ 47 bxc5+ ♖xc5! (47...♔d7 48 ♖a3 ♖h1 49 ♖a7+ ♔c6 50 ♖a6+ ♔d7 51 ♖d6+ ♔e7 52 ♔c4 ♖c1+! 53 ♔b5 ♖c3 and Black has counterplay against the pawn on g3.) 48 ♖xe6+ ♔xe6 49 ♔xc5 ♔d7!! The pawn ending is drawn despite the fact that Black loses the g-pawn after 50 f5 (50 ♔d5 ♔e7) 50...♔c7 51 ♔d5 ♔d7 52 ♔e4 ♔d6 53 ♔f4 ♔d5 54 ♔xg4 ♔e5.

45 ♔e5 ♖c1

The simplest way to draw was to play Krasenkov's suggested 45...♖f1 with the idea of 46...♖f3 so as to win the g3-pawn. If White replies 46 ♖d6+ ♔c7 47 ♖d2 Black draws either by 47...♖g1 48 ♖d3 ♖f1 which repeats the position or 47...♖f3 48 ♖g2 ♔d7 49 ♔f6 ♔e8 50 c5 bxc5 51 bxc5 ♔d7 52 ♔xf7 e5.

46 ♔f6 ♖xc4 47 ♔xf7 ♖e4
48 ♔e7 ♔b5 49 ♖d6

49...♖e3

Black could draw more easily by
49...♖xb4 50 ♖xe6 ♖b3 51 f5 ♖xg3
52 f6 ♖f3 53 f7 g3 54 f8♕ ♖xf8
55 ♔xf8 g2 56 ♖g6 ♔c4! Black
supports the b-pawn while stopping
the white king from drawing closer
as much as possible. 57 ♔e7 b5
58 ♔d6 b4 59 ♖g4+ ♔c3 60 ♔c5 b3
61 ♖g3+ ♔c2 62 ♖xg2+ ♔c3
63 ♖g3+ ♔c2 64 ♔c4 b2
65 ♖g2+ ♔b1! 66 ♔b3 ♔a1
67 ♖xb2 stalemate.

50 ♖xe6 ♖xg3 51 f5

51...♖f3?

51...♖a3! was the only move to
draw. 52 f6 ♖a7+ 53 ♔f8 g3 54 f7 g2
55 ♖g6 g1♕ 56 ♖xg1 ♔xb4.

52 f6 g3 53 f7 g2 54 ♖g6 ♖e3+
55 ♔f8 g1♕ 56 ♖xg1 ♔xb4 57 ♖f1
♖a3 58 ♔e7 ♖a8 59 f8♕ ♖xf8
60 ♖xf8 **Black resigns.**

212

Johansson – Lind
Uppsala 2016

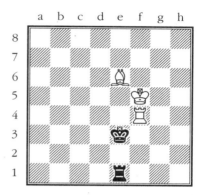

White to move

A very instructive rook and bishop
versus rook ending arose in the sub-
group of the Swedish Championship
in Uppsala 2016 between the former
Swedish champion IM Jan Johansson
and the strong player Jan-Olov Lind.
This ending will demonstrate
different kinds of defensive as well
as attacking methods which you
should master – and these ways of
playing will be served to you on a
silver platter.

75 ♖a4 ♔f2

75...♔d3 looks more natural, since
it follows Cochrane's principle to
play the king in the opposite
direction of the opponent's king.
Besides it's logical to keep the
defending king on the central

311

squares as long as possible and set up a defence with the rook on the third rank. However, it's a matter of taste whether you want to go for the third-rank-defence, as advocated by the Czechoslovak-German GM and theoretician Ludek Pachman (1924-2003), or the more popular second-rank-defence recommended by the Polish GM Wlodzimierz Schmidt (1943-).

76 ♗d5 ♖e2

Lind's defensive technique is to follow the advice which was introduced by Schmidt. Today this is the most common method of defending this ending. It's relatively easy to handle if you understand the justification for it and know the available tricks. The alternative is to follow in the spirit of Pachman and continue the third-rank-defence by 76...♔e3 77 ♔e5 ♔d3+ 78 ♗e4+ ♔c3 followed by ...♖e3.

77 ♔f4 ♖d2

This is an ideal position for the second-rank-defence. It's supposed to be one square between the defending king and rook and the rook should be placed in diagonal opposition to the enemy king. This is the key position to remember!

78 ♗e4 ♖e2 79 ♖a7 ♖d2 80 ♖h7 ♔e2

80...♖e2 was also good.

81 ♖h1 ♔f2 82 ♖a1 ♖b2 83 ♖d1 ♔e2 84 ♖h1 ♖d2!

84...♔f2?? 85 ♖h2+ shows why it's so important to have the black rook close to its own king. However; 84...♔d2 was playable since it moves the second-rank-defence two squares to the left and combines it with Cochrane's famous escape method.

85 ♖h3 ♔f2! 86 ♖g3 ♔e2 87 ♖h3 ♔f2 88 ♗d3!

White tries to loosen up Black's second-rank-defence.

88...♔g2

One important point with the second-rank-defence which doesn't work with the third-rank-defence is the stalemate finesse 88...♔e1 89 ♔e3 ♖e2+! 90 ♗xe2 stalemate.

89 ♖g3+ ♔f2!

89...♔h2!?, according to Cochrane's recipe, was playable but why go to the edge of the board when it's not necessary? More precise defence is required the fewer squares the defending king has available.

90 ♖f3+ ♔g2

90...♔e1? 91 ♖f1 mate.

91 ♗f1+

91 ♔g4 ♖f2 92 ♖g3+ ♔h2 93 ♗e4 (93 ♖h3+ ♔g1 94 ♗e4 ♔f1 and the king escapes to the seventh rank.) 93...♖f4+! 94 ♔xf4 stalemate.

91...♔g1 92 ♔e3! ♖a2 93 ♗d3 ♔g2 94 ♖f7

With skilful play White has managed to destroy Black's second-rank-defence.

94...♖a3!

Black switches to another defensive system which is Szen's method and rests on the idea of pinning the enemy bishop from the rear with the rook. This defence is more difficult, because in the long run the defender must have the long side available for the king.

95 ♖g7+ ♔h3

The simplest is to place the king in front of the king since White cannot move forward with the king due to the hanging bishop. This is the main idea with Szen's defence. However 95...♔h2, in the spirit of Cochrane, was playable since there is no mate after 96 ♔f2? ♖xd3.

96 ♔e4 ♖b3 97 ♗f1+ ♔h4

97...♔h2 98 ♖g2+ ♔h1 was also possible because Black's king is only in the corner for a moment due to White's lack of harmony.

98 ♔f4 ♖b4+ 99 ♔f5 ♖a4 100 ♗b5 ♖b4 101 ♗f1 ♖a4 102 ♗g2 ♖a5+ 103 ♔f4

103...♔h5?!

Here Black could have played the clever 103...♖g5! and return to the second-rank-defence. 104 ♖h7+ ♖h5 105 ♖a7 ♖a5! 106 ♖d7 ♖g5 (But not 106...♖a4+? 107 ♗e4 which is Philidor's famous position from 1749.) 107 ♗f3 ♖g4+! etc.

The reason the second-rank-defence is regarded as the best is because of all the stalemate possibilities it contains and which was clearly visible in this variation.

104 ♗e4

104...♔h4??

After Black's 103rd move more precise defence was required. 104...♖a6 was the only move. Now White wins according to the analyses of Philidor. However, it's not at all simple even if you have seen it before. It requires a lot of practice and understanding regarding the optimal cooperation between White's three pieces. Particularly, how to play with the rook and bishop is the key to winning this position.

105 ♖g1 ♖a3 106 ♖g4+ ♔h5

107 ♖g7??

The intricate win, which everybody should know and master, runs: 107 ♖g5+! ♔h4 (107...♔h6 108 ♔h4 ♖g6+ ♔h5 109 ♖d6 Black's rook must not be allowed to reach the important third rank! 109...♖a4 110 ♖d1 ♔h6 111 ♖d7 and

it's impossible to parry the mate without losing the rook.) 108 ♖g6!. The key to winning is control of the third rank and finding the delicate bishop manoeuvre. 108...♖a5 109 ♗c6!

This bishop move is the key to the solution of how to win Philidor's famous position. Black is in zugzwang because the important rook check on a4 isn't possible and that was the only way to disrupt the harmony in White's position. This beautiful and hard to find manoeuvre was discovered by Philidor, the unofficial world champion, already during the 18th century! Today only the very best endgame players understand this intricate position! The best defence is 109...♖c5 (109...♔h5 110 ♖d6 ♔h4 111 ♖d1 ♖a3 (111...♔h5 112 ♗e4!) 112 ♗d7!

Note the effectiveness of the bishop, especially its control of the vital a4 and h3 squares. 112...♔h5 113 ♖d6 and White wins. Elegant!) 110 ♗f3 ♖c4+ 111 ♗e4 ♖c5 112 ♖g4+ ♔h5 113 ♖g2 ♔h6 114 ♖g6+ ♔h5 115 ♖d6 ♖c4 116 ♖d7. The bishop controls the important c6-square and Black's fate is sealed.

107...♖a6

Now it's a draw.

108 ♖b7 ♖d6 109 ♖a7 ♖b6 110 ♖c7 ♖d6 111 ♖c1 ♔h6 112 ♗f5 ♔g7 113 ♔e5 ♖a6 114 ♖c7+ ♔f8 115 ♗e6 ♖a1 116 ♔f6 ♖f1+ 117 ♗f5

Black again applies Szen's defensive method and here it's easy to see that it's a draw due to the fact that Black's king has the long side available.

117...♖e1

The only move is easy to find.

118 ♖h7 ♖g1 119 ♖f7+ ♔e8

The simplest is to go to the long side but 119...♔g8 is also a draw.

120 ♖e7+ ♔f8

Cochrane would have preferred 120...♔d8.

121 ♖c7 ♖e1! 122 ♖c3 ♖e2 123 ♖f3 ♖e7

The second-rank-defence or Schmidt's defence if you so prefer.

124 ♖a3

124 ♗e6 ♖f7+! is the typical stalemate motif when playing this defence.

124...♖f7+ 125 ♔g6 ♖g7+ 126 ♔h6 ♖e7 127 ♗d3 ♖e1 128 ♗f5 Draw.

212a

Pachman
Endspielpraxis im Schach 1977

Black to move

Pachman recommends the third-rank-defence, which is the most logical.

1...♖g3! 2 ♖a4

The idea is that White cannot hold the third rank after 2 ♖a3+ ♔f2. 2 ♖d8 ♖f3! 3 ♗e4 ♖g3 4 ♔f5. Otherwise Black plays 4...♖g5+ and goes back to g3. 4...♖g7 (4...♖h3? fails to 5 ♖d3+) Black must abandon the third rank, because 5 ♖d3+ ♚e2 6 ♖a3 (White would like to harmonise his position by means of 6 ♚f4 ♖f7+ 7 ♗f5? but 7...♖xf5+ destroys White's intentions.) 6...♖f7+. Black prevents White from setting up an ideal position with a king on f4 and a bishop on f5 followed by ♖a2+. 7 ♚e5 ♚f2 8 ♚d4 ♖d7+ 9 ♗d5 ♖e7 10 ♖h3 ♖e8 etc.

2...♖f3 3 ♗g4 ♖g3 4 ♖b4

Forcing Black to move his king to the second rank, but only temporarily.

4...♚d2!

If 4...♚f2 then 5 ♚f4.

5 ♚f4

Otherwise Black goes back with his king to e3.

5...♚c3 6 ♖e4 ♖d3 7 ♚e5 ♖g3 Draw.

Black just continues his third-rank-defence.

212b

Centurini
1867

White to move

1 ♖f2

White can place the rook anywhere between f1-f5.

1...♖g6 2 ♖f1!

This is the point. Black must abandon the important g-file.

2...♖h6

Precisely this position arose in the Swedish Championship in Sunne 2015 between IM Axel Smith and GM Tiger Hillarp-Persson.

3 ♖a1!

In the game followed 3 ♖g1?? ♖f6! Now it's a theoretical draw after Black has taken over the important f-file. The game continued 4 ♖g2 ♖f1 5 ♖g6 ♖f2 6 ♗d5 ♖f1 7 ♖g8+ ♚f8 8 ♖g4 ♖f6+ 9 ♚e6 ♖f1 10 ♖c4 ♚f8 11 ♖c8+ ♚g7 12 ♖g8+ ♚h7 13 ♖g3 ♚h6 14 ♚e5 ♖f8 15 ♗f5 ♖a8 16 ♚f4 ♖a6 17 ♖e3 ♖a4+ 18 ♖e4 ♖xe4+ 19 ♗xe4 with a draw.

3...♚f8 4 ♖g1 ♖h8 5 ♚d7!

White prevents Black from playing ...♚e8 and places Black in zugzwang.

5...♖h7+ 6 ♚d8 ♖h8

316

6...♖d7+ is no stalemate after 7 ♗xd7.

7 ♖g2 ♖h7 8 ♖g8 mate.

213

Lolli
1763

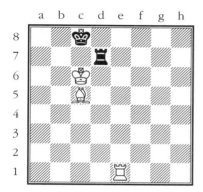

White to move

Of all the pawnless endings rook and bishop versus rook is the most important since it often arises in actual play and is fairly difficult. This is the same position as Philidor's famous position from 1749 but moved one file to the left. The winning technique is a little different from Philidor's due to lack of space on the queenside. First the enemy rook must be forced to the eighth rank.

1 ♖e8+

1 ♗b6? is met by the stalemate idea 1...♖c7+! and this is the reason White has to force the rook away from this so useful rank for the defender.

1...♖d8 2 ♖e7

2...♖d2!

This is the best place for the rook. The last-rank-defence 2...♖g8 is more interesting with Lolli's position than with Philidor's due to the fact that White's rook has less space on the left side of the board. The most effective win is 3 ♖a7 (John Nunn in *Secrets of Pawnless Endings* (Gambit 1994/2002) suggests the following more practical variation: 3 ♗d6 ♔d8 4 ♖e6! ♖h8 5 ♗e5 ♖f8 6 ♗g7 ♖g8 7 ♗f6+ ♔c8 8 ♖e1 ♖f8 9 ♗g7 ♖g8 10 ♖a1 wins.) 3...♔b8 4 ♖b7+ ♔a8 (4...♔c8 5 ♗d6). With the king in the corner White has accomplished a great deal. He just has to manoeuvre correctly with the rook and avoid stalemate. 5 ♗d6

5...♖c8+ (5...♖g1 6 ♖h7 ♖c1+ 7 ♗c5 ♖b1 8 ♖h4! and White mates on the a- or h-file depending on

Black's reply. Note the stalemate idea after 8 ♖h2 ♖b2! which is always on the agenda with the king in the corner. This is the reason 9 ♖h4! should be played.) 6 ♗c7 ♖g8 (6...♖xc7+ 7 ♔xc7!) 7 ♖b1 ♖g6+ 8 ♗d6 ♖g7 9 ♖e1 ♖h7 10 ♖e8+ ♔a7 11 ♗c5+ and mate in two moves.

3 ♖h7!

An important tempo is gained by forcing the black rook away from the second rank.

3...♖d1

The strongest defence because now White must force the rook to the fatal third rank. If Black switches to the last-rank-defence with 3...♖d8...

...it's clever because when the rook is on d8 the standard manoeuvre 4 ♖a7 ♔b8 5 ♖b7+ ♔c8 6 ♗d6? fails to 6...♖xd6+ with a draw. However correct is 4 ♗e7! ♖g8! 5 ♖h1!. (The trap set by Black's last move was that 5 ♗d6? is met by 5...♔d8! with the idea 6 ♖a7 ♔e8.) Now there is nothing Black can do to prevent ♖h1-a1-a8 mate since White has the key move ♗d6 if the king moves to b8 or the rook checks. Note that 4 ♗d6? at once

doesn't work due to 4...♖d7! 5 ♖xd7 stalemate.

4 ♖a7 ♖b1

5 ♗a3!

This is the key move just as ♗b3 was played in Philidor's position. The defender's rook is forced to enter the fatal third rank.

5...♖b3

If 5...♔b8 then 6 ♖h7!. Due to lack of space on the queenside White cannot win as in the method given in Philidor's position. This win is specific for Lolli's position. 6...♔a8 7 ♖h4 ♖b7 8 ♖d4 and Black finds himself in an amusing zugzwang. 8...♔a7 9 ♖a4+ ♔b8 10 ♗d6+.

6 ♗d6 ♖c3+ 7 ♗c5 ♖b3

Or 7...♔b8 8 ♖h7 and mate on the eighth rank.

8 ♖c7+!

When the opponent's rook is placed on the third rank it's important to check in order to force the king to decide which side to go to.

8...♔b8

8...♔d8 9 ♖f7! and Black cannot move the rook to e3. This is the main reason that Black's rook is worse placed on the third rank compared with the second or first.

9 ♖h7 ♚a8 10 ♖h4!

White mates since Black is unable to control the rank as well as the file.

214

Lolli

1763

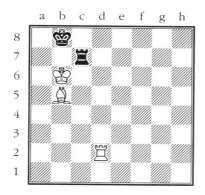

White to move

The Italian theoretician Giambattista Lolli (1698-1769) published another, much more complicated, study with this material where he moved all the pieces one file to the left. The difference with the former study by Lolli (compared with Philidor 1749 and the present one by Lolli) is that now the position is drawn. The main reason is that Black's king is closer to the edge of the board. The attacker's only chance to win is to obtain Philidor's position but this isn't possible with best play. Note that it's impossible to strive for Lolli's method with a bishop on c5 due to the opposite colour of the bishop! With a white-

squared bishop you have to place it on f5 which is rather distant in this position.

1 ♖d8+ ♖c8 2 ♖d7 ♖c2

In this position 2...♖c1 or 2...♖c3 are equally good. The most important thing to know is that the last-rank-defence is a theoretical loss. The best move on the last rank is 2...♖f8?, but White wins by placing his bishop on c6 followed by a rook manoeuvre to the a-file. However, with the rook on f8 Black will be able to flee with his king to e7 without losing the rook and so the winning procedure is to set up a position where Black's rook is forced to g8 or h8 because then White wins the rook. Here follows one principal variation which looks quite complicated, but the main thing is to understand when to play according to the pattern ♗c6 and ♖a8. Of course the only way to conduct this endgame perfectly is by practising it with the computer. 3 ♗c6 ♚c8! 4 ♖d6!. (4 ♖a7? is useless with the rook on f8 due to 4...♚d8 5 ♖a8+ ♚e7 and the rook is defended.) Black is in zugzwang. It's important not to allow Black's rook to control the sixth rank. 4...♖g8 5 ♗d5 ♖f8 6 ♗e6+ ♚b8 7 ♗f5 ♚a8 8 ♗d7 ♚b8 9 ♖h6 ♚a8 10 ♖h7 ♚b8 11 ♖h4 ♖g8 This is the signal to regroup according to the mating pattern. 12 ♗c6! ♚c8 13 ♖a4 ♚d8 14 ♖a8+ and White wins the rook.

3 ♖f7 ♖c3 4 ♗a4 ♖c1

The only move to draw!

5 ♗c6 ♖b1+

6 ♔c5!

White's only practical chance to win is by trying to transpose to a Philidor position.

6...♖b2

6...♖c1+? 7 ♔d6 ♖d1+ 8 ♗d5 ♖c1 9 ♖b7+ ♔c8 10 ♖a7 ♔d8 would be a Philidor position.

11 ♖f7 ♖e1 12 ♗f3! Compare this important bishop manoeuvre with 5 ♗a3! in the study by Lolli (1763) exercise 213. Black is in zugzwang. 12...♖e3 places the rook on the fatal third rank. 13 ♗c6 ♖d3+ 14 ♗d5 ♖e3 (The variations 14...♔e8 15 ♖g7! and 14...♔c8 15 ♖a7! show how fatal the third rank is in Philidor's position.) 15 ♖d7+! This check is always important when the enemy rook is placed on the third rank.

Now the king has to decide which way to go. 15...♔e8 (15...♔c8 16 ♖a7 wins immediately since 16...♖b3 isn't playable.) 16 ♖a7 ♔f8 17 ♖f7+ ♔e8 18 ♖f4! ♔d8 (18...♖d3 19 ♖g4!) 19 ♗e4! This is the reason the rook must be placed on f4. 19...♔e8 20 ♗c6+ ♔d8 21 ♖f8+ and mate.

7 ♗d5 ♖h2!

The only move to draw.

8 ♖b7+

After 8 ♔d6 Black must reply with the only move 8...♖h6+!. The main point of checking from the side is to upset Philidor's position. 9 ♗e6 ♖h1 The position is a theoretical draw. It's important not to place the rook behind in the spirit of Cochrane and give White a position which resembles Philidor's position.

8...♔c8 9 ♖e7 ♔b8!

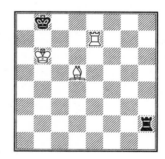

10 ♔b6

10 ♔c6 ♖h6+! 11 ♗e6 ♖h1 12 ♖b7+ ♔a8 13 ♗d5 ♖h6+ 14 ♔b5 (14 ♔c5 ♖c6+! is an instant draw.) 14...♖h5! 15 ♖d7+ ♔b8 16 ♔b6 ♖h6+! 17 ♗c6 ♔c8! 18 ♖e7 ♖d6. There is no way White can break down Black's defence.

10...♖c2!

It's a draw because White lacks space on the queenside for decisive manoeuvres and it's also hard to get a Philidor position by manoeuvring the king to d6.

10...♖b2+? 11 ♔c6 is a win because Black has no check on the sixth rank. Black lags one tempo behind after 11...♖h2 and White exploits that by 12 ♖b7+ ♔a8 (12...♔c8 13 ♗e6+ ♔d8 14 ♔d6 ♖d2+ 15 ♗d5 is a Philidor position.) 13 ♖b1! ♖c2+ 14 ♔b6+ ♔b8 15 ♗e6! ♖e2 16 ♔c6+ ♔a8 17 ♖a1+ ♔b8 18 ♗d5 ♖h2 19 ♖b1+ ♔a7 20 ♗e4 ♖h6+ 21 ♔c5 ♖b6! 22 ♖g1! (22 ♖xb6? is stalemate.) 22...♖a6 23 ♖g8 ♖a5+ 24 ♔c6 ♖h5 25 ♖g7+ ♔a6 26 ♗d5 ♖h6+ 27 ♔c5 ♔a5 28 ♖b7 ♖g6 29 ♖b1 ♖g4 30 ♖b2 ♖h4 31 ♖b7 ♖h6 32 ♗f7! ♖f6 33 ♗c4 ♖f5+ 34 ♗d5 ♖f6 35 ♖b5+! ♔a6 36 ♖b1 ♔a7 37 ♖b7+ ♔a6 38 ♖e7! ♖f5 39 ♖e8 wins.

11 ♗b3

11 ♗e4 ♖c7! draws.

11...♖c1!

11...♖c3? 12 ♗e6 and White has no saving check on b3.

12 ♖d7 ♔c8! 13 ♖d2 ♖b1! 14 ♖d3 ♖b2!

Black has played four 'only moves' in a row which shows that there are significant winning chances for the attacker even in theoretically drawn positions.

15 ♔c6 ♖b1

16 ♗d5

16 ♗e6+ ♔b8 17 ♖d8+ ♔a7 18 ♖d7+ ♔b8! (18...♔a8? 19 ♗d5 ♖c1+ 20 ♔d6+ is the Philidor.) 19 ♗d5 ♖c1+ 20 ♔d6 ♖c7! and White cannot avoid stalemate or the exchange of rooks.

16...♖c1+ 17 ♔d6 ♖c7! 18 ♖a3 ♖d7+! 19 ♔e6 ♖d8!

What an incredibly strong rook manoeuvre!

20 ♖a7 ♔b8! 21 ♖b7+ ♔c8

It's a draw.

214a

von der Lasa
1843

White to move

If Philidor's or Lolli's position is shifted to the edge of the board White wins.

1 ♖f1

1 ♖c8+ ♖b8 2 ♖c7 is useless due to the stalemate resource 2...♖b7.

1...♖b1!

Back rank defence with 1...♖b8 loses after 2 ♗c7 ♖e8 3 ♗d6. Black is tied down to the back rank and must defend against ♖f7 and ♖a7 mate. 3...♖d8 4 ♖f6 ♖c8 5 ♔b6 ♖d8 6 ♖h6 ♖g8 7 ♖h7 ♖g7 8 ♖h8+ and mate. 1...♖a7+ 2 ♔b6 ♖b7+ 3 ♔c6 ♖b2 4 ♗b6 ♖c2+ 5 ♗c5 ♖b2 6 ♖a1+ ♔b8 7 ♗d6+ and mate in two moves.

2 ♖f6!

White plans to reach a Lolli position which is a win with a black-squared bishop and then the best defence is to place the rook on the second rank.

2...♖b2

If 2...♖b7 then 3 ♗b6 ♖a7+ 4 ♔b5 ♖h7 5 ♔c6. The regrouping of the king avoids stalemates and prepares for the final mate. 5...♖h8 6 ♗c7 ♖g8 7 ♗d6 ♖g5 8 ♖f1 ♖a5 9 ♖f8+ ♔a7 10 ♗b8+ ♔a6 11 ♖f7 and mate in two.

3 ♗b6 ♖a2+ 4 ♔b5 ♔b7 5 ♖f7+ ♔c8 6 ♔c6 ♖c2+ 7 ♗c5

A winning Lolli-position has been reached. The main variation is...

7...♖d2 8 ♖h7 ♖d1 9 ♖a7 ♖b1 10 ♗a3! ♖b3 11 ♗d6 ♖c3+ 12 ♗c5 ♖b3 13 ♖c7+! ♔b8 14 ♖h7 ♔a8 15 ♖h4! and White wins.

215

Kotov – Pachman
Venice 1950

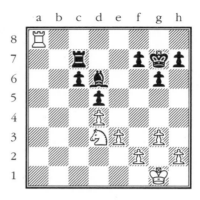

Black to move

A typical endgame which can arise after a successful minority attack on the queenside is the following. Pachman played...

42...♔f6

...which is not so bad even though it has been criticised due to White's response. Kotov suggests 42...h5 and Pachman wants to improve with 42...f5. Kotov's suggestion is less weakening and is to be preferred to prevent White's next move.

43 g4!

This move creates a potential weakness on h7.

43...♔e6

A more active continuation was 43...♔g5 44 h3 f5 45 gxf5 (45 f4+ ♔h4! 46 gxf5 ♔g3! with serious counterplay: for example 47 f6 is answered by 47...♖f7) 45... ♔xf5.

44 ♔g2 ♖b7 45 ♖e8+ ♖e7 46 ♖h8

f6 47 h4 ♖b7 48 ♔f3 ♖f7 49 ♖e8+ ♖e7 50 ♖d8 ♖a7 51 ♘c5+ ♔e7

If 51...♗xc5 then 52 dxc5 ♖a6 (52...♖d7 53 ♖c8) 53 ♖d6+ ♔e7 54 g5!.

52 ♖c8

52 ♖h8 ♗xc5 53 ♖xh7+? ♔f8! and Black wins a piece.

52...♗xc5

Or 52...♖c7 53 ♖h8.

53 dxc5

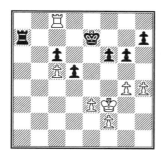

Now we have a pure rook ending where Black has two pawn weaknesses distant from each other.

53...♔d7 54 ♖h8 ♔e6 55 ♖d8 ♔e7

If 55...♖c7 56 ♖d6+ ♔e5 57 ♔e2 g5 Black must prevent mate in two. 58 ♔f3! Black is in zugzwang and has to make a move which worsens his position. 58...♖c8 59 ♖d7 and White wins the h-pawn as well as the rook ending.

56 ♖d6 ♖a6 57 g5

White secures the e5-square for his king.

57...fxg5 58 hxg5 ♔f7 59 ♔g3

59 ♔f4 ♖a4+ 60 ♔g3 was the alternative but certainly not 60 ♔e5?? ♖e4 mate.

59...♔e7 60 f3 ♖a3 61 ♔f4 ♖a4+ 62 ♔e5 ♖a3

Or 62...♖a6 63 ♖e6+ ♔d7 64 ♔f6.

63 ♖xc6

Here 63 ♖e6+ ♔d7 64 ♔f6 d4 65 ♖d6+ (65 exd4? ♖xf3+) 65...♔c7 66 ♖xd4 ♖xe3 67 ♖f4 followed by ♔g7 wins.

63...♖xe3+ 64 ♔xd5 ♖d3+

If 64...♖xf3 65 ♖c7+ ♔e8 66 ♖xh7 ♖f5+ 67 ♔e6 ♔d8 68 ♔d6 ♔e8 69 c6 and the pawn promotes.

65 ♔e4 ♖c3 66 f4 ♖c1 67 ♖c7+

67...♔d8

67...♔e6 contains a trap and should be tried as the last hope to save a clearly lost position. 68 ♔d4 (The trap is that 68 ♖xh7? ♖xc5 69 ♖g7 ♖c4+ 70 ♔f3 ♖c6!! is a draw due to stalemate after 71 ♖xg6+ ♔f5 72 ♖xc6.) 68...♖d1+ 69 ♔c4 ♖f1 70 ♖c6+ ♔e7 71 ♖f6 and Black cannot save the game.

68 ♖xh7 ♖xc5 69 ♖f7 Black resigns.

216

Hammer – Keymer
Xtracon Chess Open, 2018

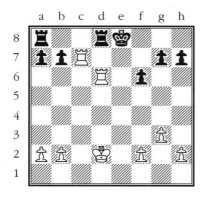

White to move

22 ♖d3!!

Hammer displays fine positional sense and manages to gain a tempo for his king. Compare the move played with 22 ♖xd8+? ♖xd8+ 23 ♔e3 ♖d7 24 ♖xd7 ♔xd7 25 ♔d4 and the centralisation on the fourth rank is not enough to win the pawn ending.

22...♖xd3+ 23 ♔xd3 ♖d8+ 24 ♔c4 ♖d2

Or 24...♖d7 25 ♖xd7 ♔xd7 26 ♔d5.

With the king on the fifth White wins after 26...h5 27 b4 g5 28 f4 g4 29 b5 ♔e7 30.a4 ♔d7 31 a5 because Black is in zugzwang, due to the extra move with the f-pawn. 31...♔e7 (31...a6 32 bxa6 bxa6 33 f5) 32 a6 bxa6 33 bxa6 ♔d7 34 f5 When the pawns are placed as they are on the queenside White's target is the f-pawn rather than the a7-pawn. 34...♔e7 35 ♔c6 ♔e8 36 ♔d6 (36 ♔b7? ♔d7 37 ♔xa7 ♔c7 and the white king will be trapped in the corner due to stalemate.) 36...♔f7 37 ♔d7 ♔f8 38 ♔e6 ♔g7 39 ♔e7 etc.

25 ♖xb7 ♖xf2 26 a4

The rook ending is winning because of White's more active king, while his pawn majority on the queenside will soon be transformed into a passed pawn.

26...a5 27 b3?

White should have played 27 b4 axb4 28 ♔b3!.

27...♖xh2 28 ♖xg7 ♖c2+?

This loses a tempo so better was 28...h5 29 ♔b5 ♖b2.

29 ♔b5 ♖b2 30 ♔xa5 ♖xb3 31 g4! ♖e3 32 ♖xh7

32...♖e5+?

Better was 32...♖e4. For example 33 ♔b5 ♔d8 34 a5 ♔c8 35 a6 ♔b8 36 ♖g7 ♖f4 and White cannot win the pawn on f6 without losing the one on g4. There is no zugzwang as Black can go back and forth between a8 and b8 with his king.

33 ♔b6 ♖e6+ 34 ♔b7 ♖e5 35 ♖h5! ♖e7+ 36 ♔c6 ♖e6+ 37 ♔c7 ♖e7+ 38 ♔d6 ♖e4 39 a5 ♖xg4 40 a6 ♖a4 41 ♖h8+ ♔f7 42 a7! Black resigns.

42...♖xa7 is met by 43 ♖h7+.

217

Bu Xiangzhi – Moiseenko
Politiken Cup, 1914

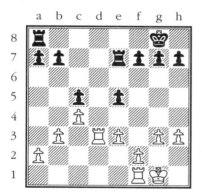

White to move

I was impressed when I followed how the Chinese grandmaster Xiangzhi Bu managed to win this symmetrical double rook ending when his sole advantage was control of the only open file.

23 ♖fd1 ♔f8 24 ♔g2 f6

24...e4 would only lead to an artificial pawn weakness on e4 after 25 ♖d6! ♖ae8 26 ♖1d5 b6 27 g4 followed by ♔g3 and eventually ♔f4.

25 ♖d6! ♖ae8 26 ♖1d5

White plays as actively as he can with his rooks placed on the d-file controlling the sixth and fifth ranks.

26...b6 27 ♔f3 ♔f7 28 ♔e4

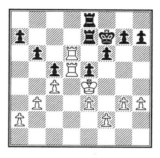

The difference in activity between the rooks and the kings is striking. All three pieces are dominating the centre. Most chess players know the importance of the principle of activity, but it's also important to understand that control of the centre is the same thing as having more activity than the opponent. This is the main reason control of the centre is important in all phases of the game.

28...h5 29 ♖d7! g6 30 ♖5d6!

White has in effect "castled" the rooks and changed the placement of the d5-rook which now stands on d7. The d5-square has been evacuated for the king so it will be possible to penetrate further into Black's position on the queenside.

30...♜xd7

Desperation, but what else?

31 ♜xd7+

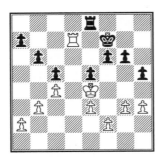

31...♚e6

The pawn ending arising after 31...♜e7 32 ♜xe7+ ♚xe7 33 ♚d5 is winning for White due to his more active king placed in the centre on the fifth rank. Black will eventually run out of pawn moves and as a consequence of that will land in zugzwang. Plausible variations are 33...♚d7 34 a4 a5 (34...g5 35 a5 bxa5 36 ♚xc5 and White wins the a5-pawn) 35 e4 g5 36 g4 h4 37 f3 and Black's king must make room for its white counterpart to penetrate further.

32 ♜xa7 ♜d8 33 ♜b7 f5+ 34 ♚f3 ♜d6 35 g4

I followed the game live and noticed that Xiangzhi Bu played pretty quickly in this stage of the endgame, which is technically winning, since White has an active rook and an extra pawn. These types of advantages are usually enough to win rook endings.

35...hxg4+ 36 hxg4 ♚f6 37 ♚g3 e4 38 gxf5 ♚xf5 39 a4 ♚e5 40 ♜b8

♚f5 41 ♚h4 ♜f6 42 ♜c8

The pawn break a4-a5 will definitely decide the fight on the queenside.

42...♚e5 43 a5! bxa5 44 ♜xc5+ ♚d6 45 ♜d5+ ♚c6

46 ♚g3!

Tempting was 46 ♜xa5 with two connected passed pawns but Black gets a passed pawn on the e-file after 46...♜xf2 so Xiangzhi Bu's more pragmatic move feels safer.

46...♜f3+ 47 ♚g2 ♜f5 48 ♜xf5 gxf5

This leads to a winning queen ending by force and then to a winning pawn ending again!

49 ♚g3 ♚c5 50 ♚f4 ♚b4 51 ♚xf5 ♚xb3 52 c5 a4 53 c6 a3 54 c7 a2 55 c8♛ a1♛ 56 ♛b7+!

Black has to accept the exchange of queens or give up the e4-pawn with check.

56...♚c2 57 ♛xe4+ ♚b3 58 ♛d3+ Black resigns.

White secures the exchange of queens on the d4-square next move.

218

Nunn
Secrets of Pawnless Endings 2002

White to move

According to John Nunn in *Secrets of Pawnless Endings* (Gambit 1994, 2002), if you look at only one position in the notorious queen versus rook endgame, this is the one to study. Black applies a third-rank-defence which is tricky to break down unless one knows the method beforehand.

1 ♕f4!!

Nunn writes that "this is the paradoxical move which provides the key to success. Moving the queen away from its dominating position is so unexpected that you just have to know it."

1...♔d7

Any move along the third rank loses the rook and that is why it's so strong to place the queen on f4 in this particular position. 1...♔c8 2 ♔c5 ♖a6 (The only rook move to hold on to the third-rank-defence. If 2...♔b7 3 ♕e4+ ♔a7 4 ♕d4! ♖b7

5 ♔c6+ ♔b8 6 ♕h8+ ♔a7 7 ♕d8 etc.) 3 ♕e4 ♔c7 (The rook cannot move along the sixth rank because after 3...♖h6 4 ♕g4+! it will fall in a couple of moves.) 4 ♕e7+ ♔b8 5 ♔b5 and Black's third-rank-defence is broken.

5...♖a7 6 ♕d8+ ♔b7 7 ♕d4! After this strong move Black is compelled to move his king. 7...♔b8 8 ♔b6 ♖b7+ 9 ♔a6 White has destroyed Black's second-rank-defence as well, since 9...♖c7 is met by 10 ♕d8+ ♖c8 11 ♕b6+ ♔a8 12 ♕b7 mate. This is a very instructive variation which demonstrates how to break down the defence on the third, second and first ranks.

2 ♕a4+

White plays a kind of four-rank-attack.

2...♔c7 3 ♕a7+ ♖b7

4 ♕c5+

White has already broken Black's third-rank-defence so now White has to break Black's second-rank-defence.

4...♔b8 5 ♔d6 ♖h7 6 ♕e5

The simplest is to strive for Philidor's position.

6...♔a7

If 6...♖c7 then the simplest is to manoeuvre with the queen so it's Black's turn to move. 7 ♕f4! ♔c8 8 ♕f5+ ♔b8 9 ♕e5! After the further 9...♖b7 10 ♔c6+ ♔a7 11 ♕a1+ ♔b8 12 ♕a5 we have reached the familiar Philidor position.

7 ♔c6 ♖b7 8 ♕a1+ ♔b8 9 ♕a5

Black is forced to move his rook away from the king and White will win it with the help of forced checks.

9...♖b1 10 ♕e5+ ♔a7 11 ♕d4+ ♔a8 12 ♕h8+ ♔a7

12...♖b8 gives White the opportunity to show off with the queen's long arm. A move such as 13 ♕a1 mate is always a pleasure to administer.

13 ♕h7+

The formula to win with queen versus rook can be broken down into three steps:

(1) Break down the third-rank-defence with a four-rank attack.

(2) Break down the second-rank-defence by penetrating with queen and king.

(3) Win the rook by checking the black king.

If you know this technique you know the most important method to win against another human being. In practice the third-rank-defence is a good defence because you just shuffle the rook back and forth along the third-rank and if your opponent doesn't know the fourth-rank-attack it will be difficult to win.

The pragmatic way now is to take advice from the silicon monster Tablebase, rather than learning the best moves by heart. It's pretty useless when it comes to practical chess as there is little risk that any human will defend with the same precision as Tablebase.

219

Pachman – Guimard
Buenos Aires 1955

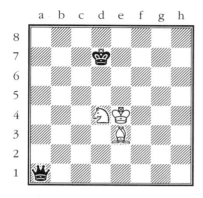

Black to move

According to Tablebase it takes 74 moves to mate White. The moves have an exclamation mark attached to them when Tablebase agrees it's the fastest way to mate.

68...♕a8+! 69 ♔d3!

White's dream position is to have the king on b1 and the bishop on b2 which is an impregnable fortress. 69 ♔e5 Centralisation means nothing in this type of ending due to the monochromy of the white squares. 69...♕e8+ 70 ♔f4 ♔d6 71 ♘f3 (71 ♘f5+ ♔d5 72 ♘g3 ♕f7+ 73 ♔g4 ♔e5) 71...♔d5 and White's pieces are slowly but surely driven to the edge of the board.

70 ♔c3

It's not possible to set up a fortress. After 70 ♔c2 ♔d6 71 ♗d2 ♔d5 72 ♗c3 ♔c4 73 ♗b2 White is threatening 74 ♔b1 but Black prevents it with either 73...♕g6+! or 73...♕a2. After the further

74 ♔c1 ♕g1+ 75 ♔c2 ♕e1 White is in zugzwang and loses a piece.

70...♔d6! 71 ♘c2!

White can forget about any fortress and that means White isn't able to combat Black on the light squares. Zugzwang and loss of a piece is unavoidable in the long run.

71...♔e5! 72 ♗c1 ♔e4! 73 ♗a3! ♕d3+! 74 ♔b2! ♕c4

Black penetrates further and further into White's position by utilising the light squares. 74...♕h3 and 74...♕g3 followed by ...♔e4-d5 are Tablebase's suggestions.

75 ♗b4! ♕b5

Better is 75...♔d3! 76 ♘e1+ ♔e3 77 ♘c2+ ♔e2.

76 ♔b3 ♕d5+ 77 ♔c3! ♕e5+ 78 ♔b3! ♕e6+ 79 ♔a4!

If 79 ♔c3 then 79...♔d5! 80 ♔b3! ♕f7!!.

79...♔d3! 80 ♘a3 ♕d7+ 81 ♔b3! ♕a7!

82 ♗d6!

82 ♗c3 ♕f7+ 83 ♔b4 ♕b7+ 84 ♘b5 ♕e7+ 85 ♔a4 (85 ♔b3 ♕c5

86 ♔a4 ♔c4) 85...♔c4 and Black wins material.

82...♕f7+! 83 ♔b4! ♔d4

83...♔e4!.

84 ♗c5+ ♔d5! 85 ♘b5 ♕f4+

85...♕b7!.

86 ♘d4

86 ♗d4! ♕f8+! 87 ♔a5! ♔c4! 88 ♘c7! ♕b4+! and Black can take the bishop without having to worry about a knight fork!

86...♕d2+

86...♕b8+! and White loses the bishop or the knight

White resigns.

White will lose the bishop because after 87 ♔a4! follows ♕a2+! (and not 87...♔c5?? 88 ♘b3+) and 88...♕c4+.

220

Gurgenidze – Averbakh
Baku 1961

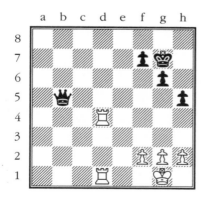

White to move

39 h4 ♕e2 40 ♖1d2 ♕e1+ 41 ♔h2 ♕e5+ 42 g3 ♕e1 43 ♔g2 ♔h6 44 ♖d1 ♕e2 45 ♖d7

White has a typical three-step-plan to win this position:

(1) Put pressure on f7 and force the pawn forward.

(2) Double rooks on the seventh rank and force the black queen into a passive position.

(3) Advance the king and at an appropriate moment exchange into a winning pawn ending.

45...♕c2 46 ♔g1 f5

Black should wait as long as possible before moving the f-pawn so more stubborn was 46...♕e2

47 ♖e1 ♕c8 48 ♖ee7 ♕h8 49 f4! ♕a1+ 50 ♔h2 ♕b2+ 51 ♔h3 ♕h8 52 ♖b7 ♕g8 53 ♖f7

White prepares to transfer his king to a more active position on the queenside.

53...♕h8 54 ♔g2 ♕g8 55 ♔f2 ♕h8 56 ♔e2 ♕e8+ 57 ♔d2 ♕d8+ 58 ♔c2 ♕c8+ 59 ♖bc7 ♕h8 60 ♔d3 ♕d8+ 61 ♔c4 ♕g8 62 ♔c5 ♕h8 63 ♖h7+! ♕xh7 64 ♖xh7+ ♔xh7 65 ♔d5 ♔g7 66 ♔e6 Black resigns.

White wins by penetrating to g8 after the forced 66...♔h6 67 ♔f6 ♔h7 68 ♔f7 ♔h6 69 ♔g8.

221

Botvinnik – Minev
Olympiad, Amsterdam 1954

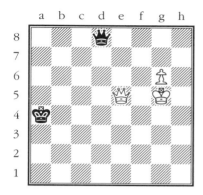

White to move

During an analysis Botvinnik found the correct way to win when the enemy king is placed far away from the pawn.

74 ♕f6

Botvinnik obtained a similar position ten years earlier against Ravinsky (Moscow 1944) and from that experience (the game lasted 126 moves!) he learned one of the rules for this endgame and that is that one should avoid placing the king in front of the pawn. This rule is still valid today and confirmed by Tablebase, so for this reason 74 ♔h6 ♕h4+ 75 ♔g7 was avoided. According to Tablebase, it's a draw after 75...♔a3!. Botvinnik understood that queen endings should not be played like rook endings way before Tablebase could give us the correct answer. However, according to Tablebase 74 ♔f5! is best. This is logical, because why should the queen abandon the

centralised post on e5? According to computer analysis the following continuation is possible: 74...♕c8+ 75 ♔f4 ♕c1+ 76 ♕e3 ♕c7+ 77 ♔g4 ♕d7+ 78 ♔h4 Black can blockade the pawn with 78...♕g7 (78...♕d8+ 79 ♔g3 and Black has run out of checks.) while taking control of the important long dark diagonal. The ideal defensive system for Black is to have the king on a1, while the black queen controls the long dark diagonal, so White has a theoretical win after 79 ♔g5.

74...♕d5+ 75 ♕f5 ♕d8+ 76 ♔h5

Another useful rule is to place the king on the same file or rank where the defender's king is standing, or if this isn't possible, to place it on an adjacent file or rank. This rule is also valid when there are more pawns present on the board.

76...♕e8

If 76...♕d1+ then 77 ♕g4+. White counter-checks by interposition. 76...♕h8+ is answered by 77 ♔g4 ♕g7 (77...♕d4+ 78 ♕f4 and White's queen is pinned on the fourth rank.) 78 ♕f7! ♕c3 79 g7 and White wins, since the checks end after 79...♕c8+ 80 ♔h4 ♕d8+ 81 ♔g3 ♕g5+ (81...♕d3+ 82 ♕f3!) 82 ♔f3!.

77.♕f4+?

In *Decision making in Major Piece Endings* (Quality Chess 2020) Gelfand gives a variation according to Botvinnik's concept of "king to king", which elaborates on the idea that the white king should approach the black king: 77 ♔g4! ♕e2+ 78 ♔f4 ♕d2+ 79 ♔e5 ♕a5+ 80 ♔e6 ♕c7 81 ♕d5! ♕b6+ 82 ♕d6 ♕e3+ 83 ♔d5! ♕d3+ 84 ♔c5

84...♕b5+ (or 84...♕c3+ 85 ♔b6 ♕g7 86 ♕e6. Tablebase gives the un-human continuation 86 ♔a6!! ♔b3 87 ♕d5+ ♔c2 88 ♕c6+ ♔d2 89 ♔b6! ♔d3 90 ♕d6+ ♔e4 91 ♕e6+! ♔d3 92 ♔c5 ♕a7+ 93 ♔c6 ♔c2 94 ♕c8!! The so-called distant "queen to king" is a typical device as well to utilise in such endings. 94...♔c1 95 ♕c7! ♕a6+ 96 ♕b6! ♕c8+ 97 ♔d6 ♕f8+ 98 ♔c7 ♕g7+ 99 ♔c8 ♕h8+ 100 ♔b7

♔c2 101 ♕c7+ ♔b2 102 g7 ♕g8 103 ♕b6+ ♔a2 104 ♕a7+ ♔b3 105 ♕d4! This strong centralisation of the queen secures mate in 53 moves.) 85 ♔d4 ♕b2+ 86 ♔d5 ♕b5+ 87 ♕c5 ♕d7+ 88 ♔e5 ♕g7+ 89 ♔f5 ♕d7+ 90 ♔f6 ♕d8+ 91 ♕e7 ♕b6+ 92 ♔f7 ♕b3+ 93 ♔f8 ♕f3+ 94 ♕f7 ♕a3+ (94...♕a8+ shows why a4 is a bad square for the king after 95 ♕e8+.) 95 ♔e8 ♕e3+ 96 ♕e7 followed by 97 g7.

77...♔a5??

In those bygone days the recommendation was to keep the defending king on a5 or a4 but today we know that this is a losing strategy due to the method discovered by Botvinnik. Black should have played 77...♔a3!, which is a theoretical draw, and strive to reach the drawing zone, i.e. any of the squares a2, b2, b1 or a1. When Black's king is inside the rectangle it's easier for Black to annoy White with checks due to the fact that he is unable to interpose with cross-checks. According to theory such a position with the king in the drawing zone is a draw. However, in practical chess the optimal square is a1 due to stalemate ideas. For example a promoted queen on g8 and the other queen placed on the b-file stalemates Black's king. The second-best square is a2. In *Shakhmatny Bulletin* (1971 No. 2) Faibisovich suggests that the b-file is less favourable for Black than the a-file and calls the b1- and b2-squares the "dangerous zone". The safer squares a1 and a2 he calls the "non-dangerous zone".

78 ♕d2+ ♔a4 79 ♕d4+ ♔a5 80 ♔g5 ♕e7+ 81 ♔f5!

Botvinnik approaches the enemy king on the same file to increase the chances for a counter-check by interposition. This "king-to-king-method" is the key when playing this ending where the opponent's king is completely misplaced.

81...♕f8+ 82 ♔e4!

Black has run out of checks because the king is abysmally placed on a5. Every check by Black is countered by an interposition check.

82...♕h6

83 ♕e5+

More precise was an immediate 83 g7. According to Averbakh it's always a win when the pawn is on g7 and the queen is centralised on d4, even if the defending king is placed on one of the four squares in the lower left corner. Don't forget this simple but important fact.

83...♔a4 84 g7 ♕h1+ 85 ♔d4

White approaches the black king again. This method of using the same rank (or adjacent rank) as the opponent's king is typical for queen and pawn endings. 85 ♔f5! is two moves faster and is following the same principle.

85...♕d1+ 86 ♔c5 ♕c1+

Or 86...♕c2+ 87 ♔d6.

87 ♔d6

The continuation 87 ♔d5 ♕c8 88 ♕e4+ ♔b5 89 ♔e5 ♕c3+ 90 ♕d4 ♕g3+ 91 ♔f5 ♕f3+ 92 ♕f4 ♕d3+ 93 ♕e4 ♕d7+ 94 ♔f6 ♕d8+ 95 ♕e7 is just as effective and also wins.

87...♕d2+

If 87...♕h6+ 88 ♔d5! or 87...♕a3+ 88 ♔c7!.

88 ♔e6 ♕a2+ 89 ♔d5 ♕e2+ 90 ♔d6 ♕h2+ 91 ♔c5!!

Black resigns.

A very nice conclusion to the game. All checks are answered by a counter-check. The Swedish GM Gideon Ståhlberg (1908-1967) gives the following plausible continuation in the Swedish book *Damslutspel* (Rabén & Sjögren, 1963): 91...♕c2+ 92 ♕c4+ ♔a3! 93 g8♕ (93 ♕xc2? is stalemate!) 93...♕f2+ (93...♕f5+ 94 ♕gd5 ♕f8+ 95 ♕d6) 94 ♔b5 ♕b2+ 95 ♔a6 ♕f6+ 96 ♕ge6. Ståhlberg's analysis fittingly stops here. Black has run out of checks and stalemate traps and has to succumb to a slow mate or he can be generous and continue with the amusing and painless 96...♕e5 97 ♕b3 mate.

Surprisingly this endgame cannot be found in *Queen and Pawn Endings* (Batsford, 1975) by Averbakh or in *Understanding the Queen Endgames* (Russell Enterprises, 2021) by Müller and Konoval. In my opinion this is the most important queen ending to know when trying to understand the secrets of how to play queen and pawn against queen. Gelfand writes that "Botvinnik's play in this game is a big part of the development towards this insight in the pre-computer era." The technique "king to king" should be understood 100 percent since it's fundamental for all queen endings, even with several pawns. If you learn only one queen ending with one pawn, this is definitely the one to embrace.

222

Velimirović – Marjanović
Yugoslav Championship,
Vrbas 1982

White to move

It's easiest to win with central- or bishop-pawns because these pawns provide better shelter compared with knight- and rook-pawns. The only chance for Black to draw is if the king is placed in front of the pawn or at least very near it. Here White's pawn is supported by the king and eventually the queen will support it as well. Another problem is that Black's king is badly placed, making it more difficult for Black to check the king or pin the pawn. A better place for the black king would have been on h2 but White would still win with best play.

63 ♕b8+ ♔c4 64 ♕b5+ ♔c3 65 ♔b7 ♕h1+ 66 c6 ♕e4 67 ♕c5+ ♔d2 68 ♔a7 ♕a4+ 69 ♔b6! ♕b3+ 70 ♔a5!

This technique – king to queen – is important to remember. White limits the black queen's mobility by approaching it while exploiting the placement of Black's king.

70...♕a2+ 71 ♔b5! ♕a8

Black has run out of checks since 71...♕b3+ is answered by 72 ♕b4+. This is the main idea with the "king to queen" method.

72 c7 ♕c8

72...♛b7+ is met by 73 ♚a5! ♛a8+ 74 ♚b6!. White uses the king to queen method and forces the black queen in front of the passed pawn.

73 ♚b4

It was simpler to approach the enemy queen by 73 ♛d6+ ♚e3 74 ♚b6! ♚e2 75 ♚a7!!. (An immediate 75 ♛d8? ♛e6+ is a draw according to Tablebase.) followed by 76 ♛d8.

73...♚e1 74 ♛c1+ ♚f2 75 ♚a3

75...♚g3

It doesn't help to check because after 75...♛a6+ 76 ♚b2 ♛b5+ 77 ♚a1 ♛a6+ 78 ♚b1 Black must blockade the pawn anyway.

76 ♛c4 ♚h2

Black has reached the ideal square, but too late!

77 ♛c2+ ♚g3 78 ♚b2 ♚f4 79 ♚c1

With the queen blockading the pawn on a light square White should place the king on a dark square. Now it's only a matter of manoeuvring the queen to d8 or b8.

79...♚e5 80 ♛c6 Black resigns.

After 80...♚f4, 81 ♛d6+ followed by 82 ♛d8 is decisive.

This game explains the technique of "king to queen" whereas the previous game with Botvinnik demonstrated the technique of "king to king". Embrace both of them and you will have learned the most important techniques when dealing with queen endings.

223

Romanishin – Karpov
USSR Championship 1983

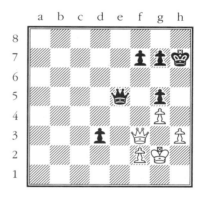

Black to move

I remember in the 80s how impressed I was by Karpov's queen manoeuvres in this ending. At first sight it seems that the draw is close since the pawns on d3 and f7 are both threatened. The d3-pawn is Black's only chance to win and the f7-pawn protects the king from queen checks along the h5-e8 diagonal. Karpov manages to find an excellent move which guarantees the win for Black.

45...♛b5!

Black protects the pawn while simultaneously protecting the important e8-square. Of course not 45...d2? 46 ♕d3+.

46 ♕e4+

46 ♕xf7 is not possible due to 46...d2 47 ♕f3 ♕b1 48 ♕f7 ♕e4+! 49 f3 ♕e2+ and Black wins. Note the decisive manoeuvre to e2 via e4 and how Black took advantage of White's exposed king.

46...♔h6

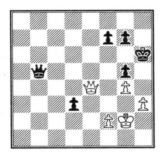

47 ♕d4

More resilient was 47 f4 gxf4 48 ♕xf4+ (48 h4 g5!) 48...♔h7 49 ♕e4+ g6 50 ♕d4 ♕c6+ 51 ♔g3 ♕c7+ 52 ♔g2 ♕c2+ 53 ♔g3 d2 54 ♕d5, although Black nevertheless wins by approaching his queen with his king.

One plausible variation is 54...♔g7 55 ♕e5+ ♔f8 56 ♕h8+ ♔e7 57 ♕e5+ ♔d7 58 ♕d5+ ♔c7 59 ♕xf7+ ♔d6 60 ♕f6+ ♔d5 61 ♕f7+ ♔d4 62 ♕f6+ ♔c5 63 ♕f8+ ♔c4 64 ♕f7+ ♔c3 65 ♕f6+ ♔b3 66 ♕f7+ ♔b2 and White's next queen check is answered by a counter-check.

47...♕c6+ 48 ♔g3 ♕c7+

More precise was immediately 48...♕c2. For example 49 ♕e4 ♕c7+ 50 ♔g2 ♕d6.

49 ♔g2 ♕c2 50 ♕e4

50 ♕d5 loses to 50...d2 51 ♕xf7 ♕e4+! 52 f3 ♕e2+ 53 ♔g3 ♕e5+ 54 ♔f2 ♔h7.

50...♕c3 51 ♕d5 d2 52 ♕xf7 ♕c6+ 53 f3 ♔h7 54 ♕b3 ♕d6

With the queen behind the passed pawn the game is decided.

55 ♕c2+ ♔h6 56 ♕d1 ♕d3 57 ♔f2 ♔g6 58 ♔g2 ♔f7 59 ♔f2 ♔f8 60 ♔g2 ♔e7 61 ♔f2 ♔d6 62 ♔g2 ♔c5 White resigns.

224

Marshall – Maróczy
Ostende 1905

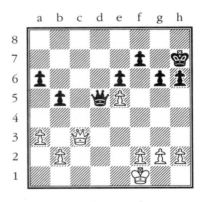

Black to move

The decisive factor is that Black's queen is far more active than White's.

31...♕d1+ 32 ♕e1 ♕d3+ 33 ♔g1

If 33 ♕e2 then 33...♕b1+.

33...♕c2! 34 ♕a1

A better defence was 34 b4 ♕b2 35 g3 ♕xa3 36 ♔g2 and Black has to prove how to exploit his extra pawn on a6.

34...a5!

Black wants to fix the b2-pawn.

35 g3

It's too late for 35 b4? axb4 (35...♕a4 also works, as 36 bxa5 is met by 36...b4) 36 axb4 ♕e4! and White cannot cover his two tactical pawn weaknesses as well as his back-rank.

35...a4

36 f4

36 ♕a2 ♕d1+ 37 ♔g2 g5 incarcerates the white queen on the a2-square. The only way to liberate it is by sacrificing the b-pawn. A pragmatic move was 36 ♔g2 when Black has to decide whether to take the pawn immediately by 36...♕e4+ 37 ♔g1 ♕xe5 which liberates White's queen a little or to improve his position on the kingside. A plausible variation is 36...g5 37 h3 ♔g7 38 ♔g1 ♔g6 39 g4 h5 40 ♕f1! ♕xb2 41 ♕d3+ ♔h6 42 ♕d6 ♕c1+ 43 ♔g2 ♕f4 44 gxh5 g4 45 hxg4 ♕xg4+ 46 ♔h2 ♕f3! (46...♕xh5+? 47 ♔g3 activates White's king too much.) 47 ♕f8+ ♔h7! 48 ♕c5

(48 h6 is not as dangerous as it looks due to 48...♕xf2+ 49 ♔h1 ♕h4+ 50 ♔g1 ♕xh6 51 ♕xf7+ ♕g7+) 48...♔g7! 49 ♕xb5 ♕xf2+ 50 ♔h3 ♕f3+ 51 ♔h4 ♕xa3 and Black wins.

36...♔g8!

White is in zugzwang.

37 h3

This weakens the g3-square but White couldn't avoid the loss of a pawn anyway after 37 ♔h1 h5 38 ♔g1 ♔g7 39 ♔h1 h4 40 gxh4 ♕e4+ 41 ♔g1 ♕xf4 42 ♕e1 ♕d4+ 43 ♕f2 ♕xe5 and Black wins.

37...h5 38 h4 ♔g7 39 ♔h1 ♕f2 40 ♕g1 ♕xb2 41 ♕c5 b4 42 f5!?

42 ♕e7 b3 43 ♕f6+ ♔g8 44 ♕d8+ ♔h7 45 ♕d7 ♕b1+ 46 ♔g2 ♕f5 47 ♕b7 ♔g7 and the b-pawn soon promotes.

42...exf5 43 e6 bxa3 44 exf7

44 ♕e7 is harmless, because Black controls the important long dark diagonal so he can play the calm 44...a2 45 ♕xf7+ ♔h6 46 ♕f8+ ♔h7 47 ♕f7+ ♕g7.

44...♔xf7 45 ♕c7+ ♔e6 White resigns.

225

Maróczy – Marshall
Karlsbad 1907

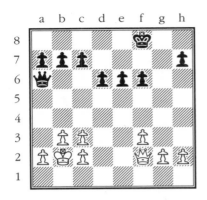

White to move

If you study only one player conducting queen endings then Géza Maróczy (1870-1951) has several model examples of how to play artistically. Here he shows how to exploit the advantage of having a safe king while the opponent's king doesn't have a reliable shelter.

23 ♕h4!

Apart from the fact that Black's king is exposed and his queen is decentralised, Black has four tactical pawn weaknesses. White actually wins a pawn by force.

23...♔g7 24 ♕g4+ ♔f7 25 ♕h5+

Interestingly Maróczy missed 25 ♕h3! with an immediate win of either the h7-pawn or the e6-pawn which cannot be covered with a single move. Sometimes it's more difficult to see backward queen manoeuvres, especially when one is focused on penetrating moves.

25...♔g7 26 ♕e8

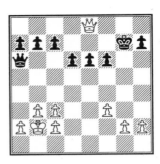

White has managed to penetrate Black's position and this was possible due to his safe king on the queenside. Note the important defensive function of the b-pawn and the double c-pawns which protect the king from disturbing queen checks.

26...♕e2

26...d5 (or 26...e5 27 ♕d7+ ♔h6 28 ♕xc7) 27 ♕e7+ ♔g6 28 h4! (White plays for mate or to win pawns on the kingside, because this is more important than 28 ♕xc7, which loses the momentum.) 28...♕d6 29 h5+ ♔xh5 30 ♕xh7+ ♔g5 31 ♕g7+ ♔f4 32 ♕g4+ ♔e3 (32...♔e5? 33 g3) 33 ♕d4+ ♔e2 34 ♕xf6 and White wins with the g-pawn.

27 ♕e7+ ♔g6

28 ♕f8

This indirect protection of the g2-pawn shows the great patience and technique Maróczy had when playing queen endings, which by the way was his favourite ending. However, due to Black's exposed king it was possible to create a passed pawn and not care if Black gets one as well, as long as White is one tempo faster. Pachman analyses 28 ♕xc7 ♕xg2 29 ♕xb7 ♕xh2 30 ♕xa7 h5 31 a4 h4 32 a5 h3 33 ♕b8! ♕h1 34 a6 h2 35 a7 ♕xf3 36 ♕g8+ ♔f5 37 ♕h7+ followed by 38 ♕xh2 with a win. According to the tournament book the reason for Maróczy's choice was the following: "There were good winning chances also in the trivial variation 28 ♕xc7 ♕xh2 29 ♕xb7 ♕xh2 30 ♕xa7. But Maróczy wanted to proceed in a way that made the win certain. For this purpose he had first to render harmless Black's kingside pawns (especially those on f6 and h7), after which a decisive advantage on the queenside could no longer elude him."

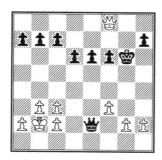

28...e5

Marshall mobilises his pawn majority in the centre and hopes either to disturb White's king by ...d6-d5-d4 or to obtain a passed pawn by ...f6-f5-e4. However this is difficult when having an exposed

king, as Maróczy clearly shows. It's fruitless to attack the c3-pawn with ...d5-d4 or ...b5-b4. For example 28...♕e5 29 ♕b8 d5 30 ♕xa7 b6, with the idea of ...d5-d4, is met by 31 ♕a8! d4 (31...♕xh2 32 ♕g8+ or 31...♔g7 32 ♕c6 d4 33 ♕d7+) 32 ♕e4+. These variations clearly show that the key idea in queen endings, with many pawns and an exposed king, is to simultaneously play against the pawns and the king. It's in accordance with the principle of the two weaknesses.

29 ♕g8+ ♔h6 30 h4! ♕f2

Counterplay attempts like 30...d5 followed by ...d4 don't work either, despite the fact that the queen seems to have lost contact with his queenside. A. Panchenko gives 31 g4 ♕xf3 32 g5+ ♔h5 33 ♕xh7+ ♔g4 34 g6 d4 35 cxd4 exd4 36 ♕xc7 and White controls c3.

31 ♕f8+ ♔g6 32 h5+! ♔xh5

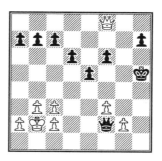

33 ♕g7!!

Beginning with 28 ♕f8, Maróczy has displayed a very fine touch how to handle queen endings in a less violent manner compared with the computer's brute force suggestions. For Maróczy, queen endings were an art form but for the computer just raw calculation. We will never be able to play complicated queen endings like the computer but we can learn to apply Maróczy's delightful technique how to handle them. If the pawns were the soul of chess for Philidor, it was the queen that was the soul of chess for Maróczy, because he preferred to play with queens on the board. Obviously we can learn a lot from him about how to handle the queen in other phases as well, but it's most clearly seen in the ending, due to the enormous scope available for the queen. Here on g7 it's like a tank ready to shoot in several directions.

The move played by Maróczy is all the more impressive due to the fact that it competed with the tempting continuation 33 ♕f7+ ♔h4 34 ♕xf6+ ♔g3 35 ♕g7+ (35 ♕g5+? ♔h2) but it turns out that it's only in Black's interest to reach this position after 35...♔f4, due to the importance of the g2-pawn. Black simply plans 36...h5 followed by 37...h4 and 38...♕g3 and the g2-pawn will be lost. If White eliminates pawns on the seventh rank by 36 ♕xh7 ♕xg2 37 ♕xc7 ♔xf3 38 ♕xb7+ e4 Black will possess a dangerous passed e-pawn. The golden rule in queen endings is not the material in itself, it's all about getting such a threatening passed pawn.

33...♕d2

Some of the tournament participants regarded 33...f5 as a lifeline but it turns out to be insufficient after 34 ♕xc7!! (Stockfish) when it's difficult for Black to achieve counterplay in the centre or on the kingside. 34 ♕xh7+

♔g5 35 ♕xc7 ♔f4 36 ♕g7! also wins but gives Black a more compact and active position and is unnecessary when there are more reliable continuations.

34 ♕xh7+ ♕h6 35 g4+ ♔g5 36 ♕xc7

The tournament book has the following interesting words to describe Maróczy's ingenious play: "The fact that Maróczy only now consumes this pawn – which he could have done on the 28th move – is an admirable example of self-mastery and asceticism. The virtue of abstinence now finds its well-earned reward."

36...♔f4 37 ♕xb7 ♕h1

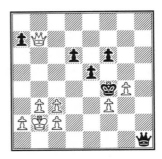

38 ♕b4+!

"The most precise" according to Panchenko. Pachman gives two exclamation marks for this artistic move. This is the kind of technical chess we want to assimilate. Brute force suggests the winning and unimaginative continuation 38 ♕xa7 ♕xf3 39 b4 e4 40 b5 e3 41 b6 e2 42 b7 e1♕ 43 ♕d4+ ♕ee4 (43...♔g5 44 b8♕) 44 ♕xf6+ ♔e3 45 ♕xf3+ ♔xf3 46 b8♕ d5 47 ♕b4 ♔xg4 48 a4.

38...♔xf3 39 ♕xd6

White's c3-pawn has become a very dangerous passer and Black's e-pawn is less dangerous for the exposed king.

39...♔xg4

39...♕h6 is met by the reply 40 ♕d3+! followed by 41 c4 and 39...♕h8 by 40 ♕d7!. In both variations White controls the enemy e-pawn, due to Black's exposed king, while preparing the advance of the c-pawn.

40 c4!

It's more important to advance the c-pawn than to join the Pawn Grabber's Society by 40 ♕xf6 and allow the strong queen centralisation 40...♕d5!. According to Panchenko Black would even have drawing chances. 41 c4 would be harder to carry out due to 41...♕d4+ 42 ♔a3 ♕c5+, but if White plays 43 b4! (43 ♔a4? e4 is a clear draw.) 43...♕xc4 44 ♕xe5 ♕xc2 45 ♕d4+ ♔g3 46 b5! White would keep his winning chances alive. Note that the greedy and decentralising 46 ♕xa7? allows a draw by perpetual check after 46...♕c3+ 47 ♔a4 ♕c2+ 48 ♔b5 ♕e2+ etc.

40...e4 41 c5!

41 ♕xf6 is also clever since 41...e3? is met by 42 ♕d4+ ♔f3? 43 ♕d5+ and 41...♕h5 42 ♕d4! pins the pawn while preparing 43 c5.

41...f5 42 c6

42...♕h8+

The control of this important diagonal doesn't mean anything anymore and is just a temporary defence of the critical c8-square where all the pieces are drawn like magnets. 42...e3 loses after 43 ♕d4+ ♕e4 44 ♕xe4+ fxe4 45 c7 e2 46 c8♕+ ♔g3 47 ♕c3+ ♔f2 48 ♕f6+ ♔g2 49 ♕h4 ♔f1 50 ♕f4+. Note how difficult it was for Black to advance his pawn(s) due to his exposed king. The queen has so much scope that the white king can just sit and watch without any need or obligation to cooperate with her majesty.

43 c3!

This is a good pawn shelter along the long dark diagonal but note that it weakens the second rank which sometimes is important. However now the queen controls the h2-square. The problem with 43 ♔a3? is that it allows 43...♕c3 because this is the ideal square for the queen as it controls the c-pawn(s) and supports the e-pawn.

43...e3 44 ♕g6+!

A good move which exploits the fact that Black has no pawn shelter behind his back. 44 c7 e2 45 ♕e6? e1♕! 46 ♕xe1 ♕h2+ with a draw shows what can happen if White is careless and forgets about stalemates!

44...♔f4 45 c7 e2 46 ♕e6!

Now this works since the black king obstructs the h2-b8 diagonal.

46...♔f3

What else? The e-pawn needs protection. 46...♕h2? 47 ♕d6+ gives White two queens. Of course not 47 c8♕? e1♕+ 48 ♔a3 ♕xe6! (48...♕c1+? 49 ♔b4) 49 ♕xe6 ♕h8!).

47 ♕xf5+

Maróczy's continuation is crueller than 47 c8♕ ♕xc8 48 ♕xc8 e1♕ 49 ♕xf5+ which is just a matter of effortless technique.

47...♔g2

Now Maróczy could have been even crueller! 47...♔g3 would have

avoided the staircase manoeuvre made by White.

48 ♕g4+ ♔f2 49 ♕f4+ ♔g2 50 ♕e3!

Of course we are all dream of performing a staircase manoeuvre with the queen but what is really happening is that Maróczy is playing with Marshall like a cat with a mouse.

50...♔f1 51 ♕f3+ ♔e1

52 ♕f4!?

My guess is that Maróczy was waiting for Marshall to resign so he's not in any hurry to finish him off as in the variations after 52 ♕f5! ♔d2 53 ♕g5+ (or 53 c8♕ ♕xc8 54 ♕xc8 e1♕ 55 ♕d7+ followed by a check on the e-file, the pragmatic solution) 53...♔e1 54 ♕d8 – the cruel continuation.

52...♕c8 53 ♕d6 ♔f2 54 ♕d8 e1♕

Understandably 54...♕xc7 55 ♕xc7 e1♕ 56 ♕xa7+ wasn't to Marshall's liking. Nor was the variation given by Pachman or the tournament book: 54...♕xd8 55 cxd8♕ e1♕ 56 ♕h4+.

55 ♕xc8 ♕d2+ 56 ♔a3 ♕c1+

342

56...♛d6+ 57 b4 and the king is secure.

57 ♔a4

Good, although elementary, technique! If the enemy queen checks on a black square the king moves to a white square to limit future checks. We all know that.

57...♛f4+ 58 c4 Black resigns.

Note how well White's c-pawns protected the white king throughout the whole game. And the b-pawn as well! Note also that the a-pawn was by no means useless. Its main defensive function was to be prepared for the pawn advance ...a5-a4 followed by an exchange on b3. I don't know any better model endgame showing the importance of a good pawn shelter and where this fact alone was so decisive. Never forget the main rules in queen endings, with many pawns distributed on both sides of the board, that a safe king and a far advanced passed pawn(s) are the two most important assets. I strongly urge the reader to assimilate this ending and even learn it by heart because I don't know any other queen ending that is more important than this, it's unique. The main thing is not only to embrace Maróczy's technique how to play with the queen in endings but above all how to play with the queen in all stages of the game.

Part 4:
75 most important tactical exercises in the Endgame

226

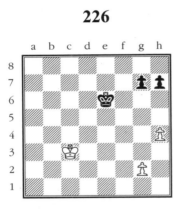

White to move

228

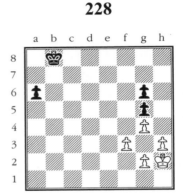

White to move

227

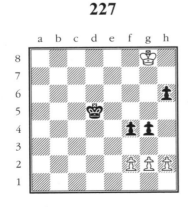

White to move

229

White to move

230

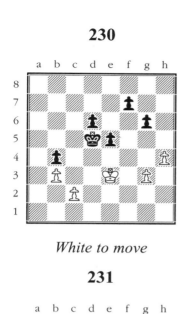

White to move

231

White to move

232

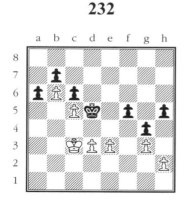

White to move

233

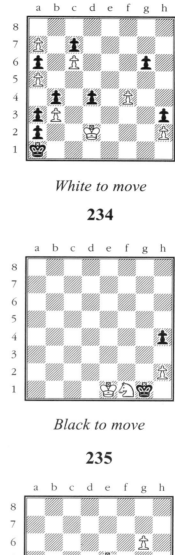

White to move

234

Black to move

235

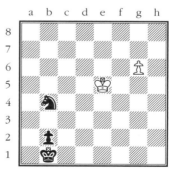

Black to move

236

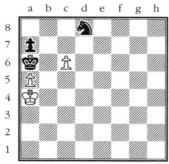

White to move

237

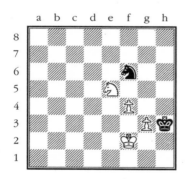

White to move

238

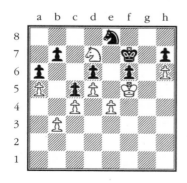

White to move

239

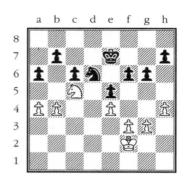

Black to move

240

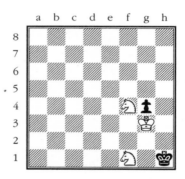

White to move

241

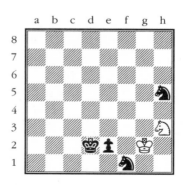

White to move

242

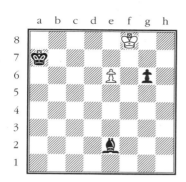

White to move

245

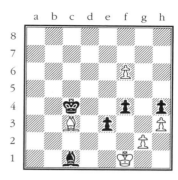

White to move

243

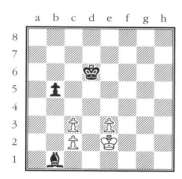

White to move

246

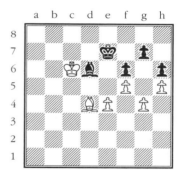

White to move

244

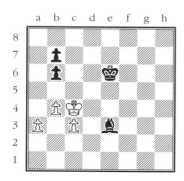

Black to move

247

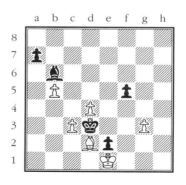

Black to move

248

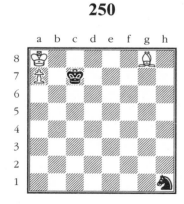

Black to move

251

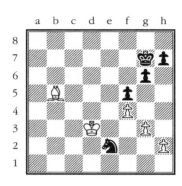

Black to move

249

Black to move

252

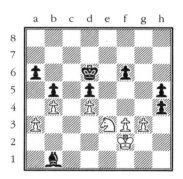

White to move

250

White to move

253

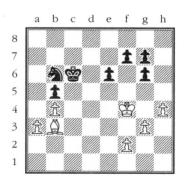

White to move

254

White to move

257

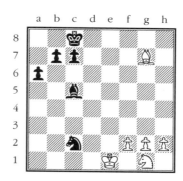

White to move

255

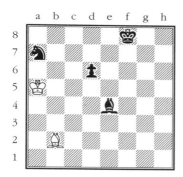

White to move

258

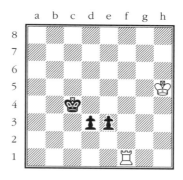

White to move

256

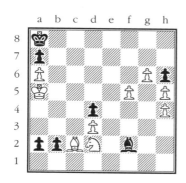

White to move

259

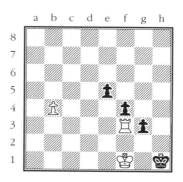

White to move

260

White to move

261

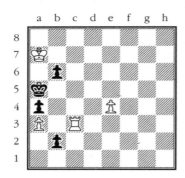

White to move

262

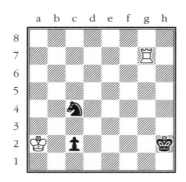

White to move

263

White to move

264

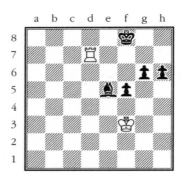

White to move

265

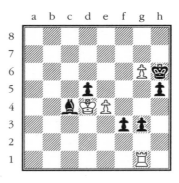

White to move

266

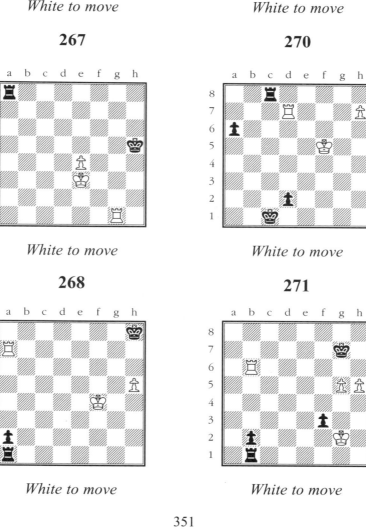

White to move

267

White to move

268

White to move

269

White to move

270

White to move

271

White to move

272

White to move

273

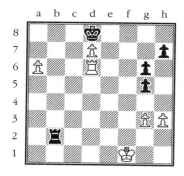

White to move

274

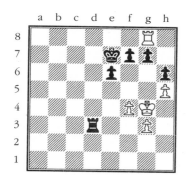

White to move

275

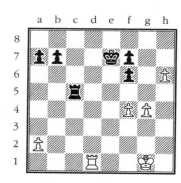

White to move

276

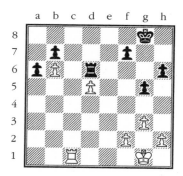

White to move

277

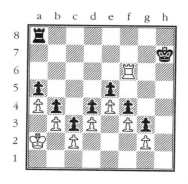

White to move

278

White to move

279

White to move

280

White to move

281

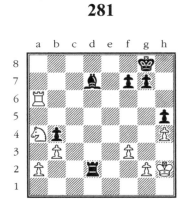

White to move

282

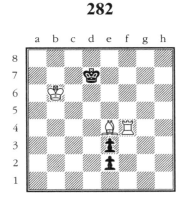

White to move

283

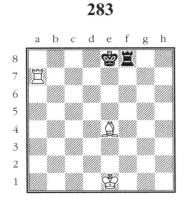

White to move

284

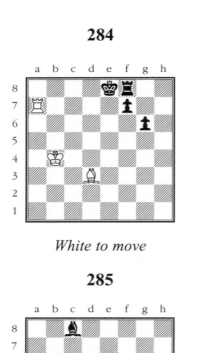

White to move

285

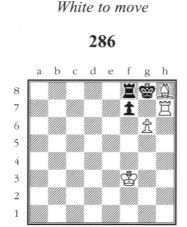

White to move

286

White to move

287

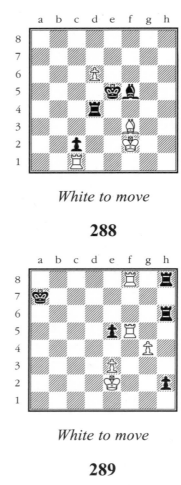

White to move

288

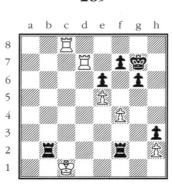

White to move

289

White to move

290

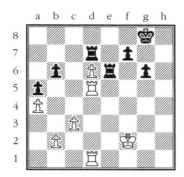

White to move

291

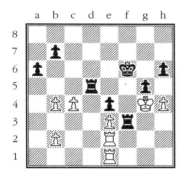

Black to move

292

White to move

293

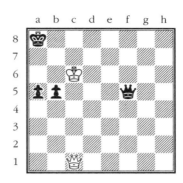

White to move

294

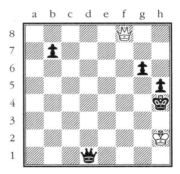

White to move

295

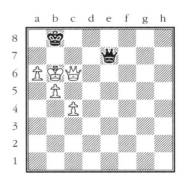

White to move

296

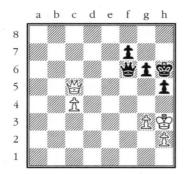

Black to move

299

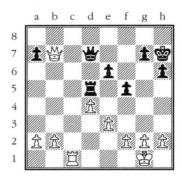

Black to move

297

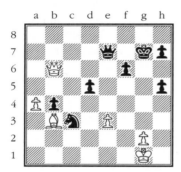

Black to move

300

White to move

298

Black to move

Solutions to Exercises 226-300

226

Korany
1956

White to move

1 h5!!

This is a typical tactical idea to remember. Instead of just letting Black take the pawn on h4 or h5 White sacrifices the pawn on h6 which at least secures him a better king position since Black must capture the h-pawn with the king. 1 ♔d4? ♔f5 loses the h-pawn and after 2 ♔e3 ♔g4 3 ♔f2 ♔xh4 Black's king is too active, which secures the win in this type of ending. 4 ♔f3 g5 5 ♔f2 g4 6 ♔f1 ♔g3 7 ♔g1 h5 8 ♔h1 h4 9 ♔g1 h3 10 gxh3 ♔xh3 is a likely continuation.

1...♔f5

If Black stops the pawn with 1...h6 White's king will be too active on the f5-square. 2 ♔d4 ♔f5 3 ♔d5 ♔g5 4 ♔e5 ♔xh5 5 ♔f5! is a draw. Had the black h-pawn been placed on its original square h7 Black could play his king to h4 since the g6-square would be under control. Now it's a draw after 5...g5 6 g3.

2 h6!

This is an important tactical idea to remember and one which can be used in other types of endings as well. The idea is either to destroy Black's pawn formation or to secure space for the king.

2...g5

2...gxh6 3 ♔d2 ♔g4 4 ♔e2 ♔g3 5 ♔f1 is obviously a draw when Black has only h-pawns on the board.

3 ♔d4 ♔g6 4 ♔e5 ♔xh6

5 ♔f6!

White penetrates deep into Black's position and secures the draw. 5 g4? ♔g6 6 ♔e4 h5 7 ♔f3 fails to 7...h4.

357

5...♚h5 6 ♚g7!

White must continue the penetration of Black's position. d6 ♚f5? loses to 6...♚h4 7 g3+ ♚h5 8 ♚f6 ♚g4!.

6...h6

6...♚h4 7 ♚xh7 g4 8 ♚g6.

7 g3!

7 ♚h7 g4 8 g3 ♚g5 followed by ...h5-h4 doesn't work.

7...g4 8 ♚f6

This is the point. Black is stalemated.

227

Chéron
1955

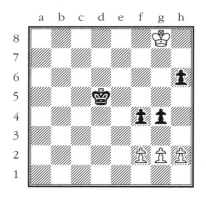

White to move

1 ♚g7!

White must derive benefit from the fact that his king is closer to the enemy pawns than the black king. However, it's also important to prevent the enemy king from reaching the e6-square in the crucial position after 1 ♚h7? h5 2 ♚g6 h4

4 g3 hxg3 5 hxg3 fxg3 6 fxg3 ♚e6! 7 ♚g5 ♚f7 8 ♚xg4 ♚g6! when Black has the opposition.

1...h5 2 ♚f6!

This is the point. White indirectly attacks the pawns while preventing the opponent's king from reaching one of the key squares.

2...h4 3 g3!

White must be careful as 3 ♚g5? g3! gives Black a passed pawn by force after either 4 fxg3 h3! or 4 hxg3 f3!.

3...hxg3 4 hxg3 fxg3 5 fxg3 ♚e4 6 ♚g5 ♚f3 7 ♚h4 ♚e4 8 ♚xg4

White wins by promoting the g-pawn.

A nice study by Chéron showing that it's possible to win with a seemingly decentralised king as well as passive pawns. It's only a matter of activating them in the most precise manner to create a win "out of nothing".

228

Berger
1889

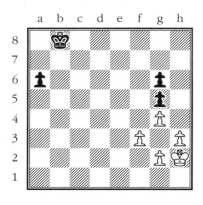

White to move

White's position looks pretty hopeless due to the fact that White's king is too far away from the enemy a-pawn, so what's the miracle?

1 f4!

White cannot play for promotion with 1 h4? since the king covers the square of the g-pawn after 1...gxh4 2 f4 ♚c7! 3 f5 gxf5 4 g5 ♚d7.

1...♚c7

Black must be careful as 1...gxf4? loses to 2 h4 and White queens first on h8 with check.

1...a5? also loses the pawn race after 2 h4 (2 f5 wins as well after 2...gxf5 3 h4! gxh4 4 g5) 2...a4 (2...gxh4 3 f5 gxf5 4 g5) 3 h5 gxh5 4 fxg5 a3 5 g6 a2 6 g7 a1♛ 7 g8♛+ ♚c7 8 gxh5 and the queen endgame is winning.

2 fxg5 a5 3 ♚g3! a4 4 ♚h4! a3 5 g3 a2 stalemate.

Black could never have avoided the beautiful stalemate constructed by White as the miracle was predestined.

229

Speelman
Endgame Preparation 1989

White to move

When at least three pawns are placed opposite each other it's always possible to create a passed pawn by means of a breakthrough. However, more space is required, as well as a defending king which is outside the critical promotion square.

1 h5!

The only move to win. The other three breaks lose:

(a) 1 g5 hxg5 2 f5 gxh4.

(b) 1 f5 gxf5 2 e5 fxe5 3 g5 f4.

(c) 1 e5 fxe5 (1...f5? 2 h5 gxh5 3 gxf5 exf5 4 e6) 2 h5 exf4.

1...gxh5

1...g5 is met by another breakthrough 2 e5! fxe5 and then a third 3 f5! followed by f5-f6-f7-f8♛+.

2 e5! fxe5 3 f5!

White wins the pawn race due to the check on f8 so this study would not have worked if it were not for the check on f8. For example, with the black king on a4 the position is a draw.

The study by Chéron, exercise 227, contains this important tactical idea concealed in the variations.

230

Kaiszauri – Velikov
1972

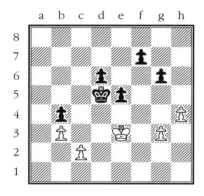

White to move

Black is a pawn up but a more important factor is the distribution of the pawns. White can create two distant passed pawns.

52 g4 f5?

The only move to draw was 52...♔e6. After the forced 53 h5 gxh5 54 gxh5 d5 White could have chosen one of two variations leading to queen endings:

(a) 55 c3 bxc3 56 ♔d3 d4 57 h6 ♔f6 58 b4 e4+ 59 ♔c2 e3 60 ♔d3 ♔g6 61 b5 f5 62 b6 f4 63 b7 e2 64 ♔xe2 f3+ 65 ♔xf3 c2 66 b8♕

c1♕ with a draw, or

(b) 55 h6 ♔f6 56 ♔d3 e4+! (56...♔g6? loses after 57 c3 e4+ 58 ♔c2!) 57 ♔d4 ♔g6 58 c3 e3! 59 ♔xe3 bxc3 60 b4 f5 61 ♔d3 (61 b5? f4+) 61...d4 62 b5 f4 63 b6 f3 64 b7 f2 65 b8♕ f1♕+ 66 ♔xd4 with a draw as well.

53 gxf5 gxf5 54 h5 f4+ 55 ♔d2 ♔e6 56 c3 bxc3+ 57 ♔xc3

White's two passed pawns are decisive factors as White manages to blockade Black's pawns.

57...f3 58 ♔d2 d5 59 h6 ♔f6 60 ♔e3 e4 61 b4 d4+ 62 ♔f2 d3 63 ♔e3 Black resigns.

The white king has no problems keeping the three connected pawns at bay, whereas Black's king is powerless against the two distant passed pawns placed on different sides of the board.

231

Kazantsev

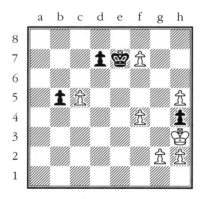

White to move

1 ♔g4! b4

1...♔xf7 gives White the necessary time to catch the b-pawn after 2 ♔f5 b4 3 ♔e4.

2 ♔f5 b3

2...h3 3 g3! b3 4 ♔g6 ♔f8 5 h6 b2 6 h7 b1♕+ 7 f5 ♕b2 8 h8♕+ ♕xh8 9 f6 d6 10 c6!. Of course not 10 cxd6? ♕xf6+ 11 ♔xf6 and Black is stalemated.

3 ♔g6 ♔f8

3...b2 4 ♔g7 b1♕ 5 f8♕+ ♔e6 6 ♕f7 mate.

4 h6 b2 5 h7 b1♕+ 6 f5 ♕b2

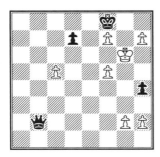

7 h8♕+!!

This is the beautiful point of the study.

7...♕xh8 8 f6!

Black is in zugzwang.

8...h3 9 g3

White takes away the last h4-square from the trapped queen.

9...d6 10 c6

White wins. But not 10 cxd6? which leads to stalemate after either 10...♕xf6+ 11 ♔xf6 or 10...♕h4 11 gxh4.

232

A. Lundin – Barkhagen
Swedish Championship,
Helsingborg 1991

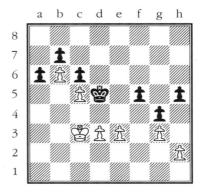

White to move

At this exciting stage in the game Black offered a draw which was accepted. The reason for the draw offer was that Barkhagen saw the possibility...

46 d4 ♔e4

However, Barkhagen missed that he could have won by playing 46...a5 47 ♔b3 and now the beautiful "impossible" break 47...f4!!

Then:

(a) 48 exf4 ♔xd4 49 ♔a4 ♔c4 50 ♔xa5 ♔xc5 51 f5 (51 ♔a4

♔xb6! It's fascinating how easy it is to be fooled by the eye. Black can actually capture all the pawns on d4, c5 and b6 and still be able to control the promotion square of the f-pawn!) 51...♔d5 52 ♔b4 ♔e5 53 ♔c5 ♔xf5 54 ♔d6 c5! The only move to win. 55 ♔xc5 (55 ♔c7 c4 56 ♔xb7 c3 57 ♔a6 c2 58 b7 c1♕ 59 b8♕ ♕a3+ and after the exchange of queens Black picks up both white pawns.) 55...♔e5 and Black wins the b6-pawn.

(b) 48 gxf4 h4 (Black must be careful as 48...♔e4? is a draw after 49 f5 h4 [49...♔xf5?? 50 d5 even wins for White.] 50 f6 g3 51 hxg3 hxg3 52 f7 g2 53 f8♕ g1♕ and White cannot win due to his exposed king.) 49 f5 g3 50 f6 g2 51 f7 g1♕ 52 f8♕ ♕xe3+ and Black wins the queen ending.

47 ♔c4

...followed by 48 d5 with a win, for example:

47...♔xe3 48 d5 cxd5+ 49 ♔xd5 f4 50 gxf4 h4 51 c6 bxc6+ 52 ♔e6! g3 53 hxg3 h3 54 b7 h2 55 b8♕ h1♕ 56 ♕e5+ and f4-f5 next move with a winning queen ending. Quite an amazing game because all three results were possible as well as different kinds of endgames. This is exciting chess we really like to see!

233

Amirov
Prace 1966

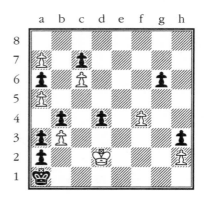

White to move

1 ♔c1!

1 a8♕? is a draw after 1...♔b2! 2 ♕h8 a1♕ 3 ♕xd4+ ♔a2 4 ♕xa1+ ♔xa1 5 ♔c1! ♔a2 6 ♔c2.

1...d3 2 a8♕ d2+ 3 ♔xd2 ♔b1

3...♔b2 4 ♕h8+ ♔b1 5 ♕a1+! ♔xa1 6 ♔c2! g5 7 f5 and White wins the pawn race by mating on the long black diagonal.

4 ♕xa6 a1♕ 5 ♕f1+ ♔a2 6 ♕xa1+ ♔xa1 7 ♔c1!

7 ♔c2? leads to a draw because of stalemate after 7...g5 8 a6 g4 9 a7 g3 10 a8♕ gxh2 11 ♕h8+ ♔a2 12 ♕xh3 h1♕ 13 ♕xh1. This is the reason White must play the king to c1.

7...g5 8 a6 g4 9 a7 g3 10 a8♕ gxh2 11 ♕h8+ ♔a2 12 ♕xh3 and White wins easily.

An instructive study to practice the queen's long arms.

234

Chéron
1926

Black to move

1...♔g2 2 ♔e2 h3

2...♔g1 3 ♔f3 ♔xf1 4 h3 and White picks up the h-pawn.

3 ♘e3+!

The key to the win is to mate!

3...♔xh2

3...♔g1 4 ♔f3 ♔xh2 5 ♔f2 makes no difference.

4 ♔f2 ♔h1 5 ♘f1 h2 6 ♘g3 mate.

235

S. Mohr – Conquest
Gausdal 1988

In the following position 98...♔c1? 99 g7 b1♕ was played but now, sadly for White, he lost on time before promoting to a queen on g8. That position would have been a theoretical draw. But Black can win by forcing the white king to a most unfortunate diagonal.

Black to move

98...♘d5! 99 ♔xd5

This square is mined but 99 g7 ♘e7 100 ♔f6 ♘g8+ 101 ♔f7 ♔a2 102 ♔xg8 b1♕ also loses as White is saddled with a g-pawn. Black wins by approaching the g-pawn with the queen and king.

99...♔c2 100 g7 b1♕ 101 g8♕ ♕b3+

The diagonal skewer on b3 (or a2), along the classical diagonal to g8 is decisive.

236

Weenink
Op de Hoogte 1918

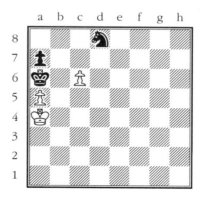

White to move

1 c7 ♘b7! 2 c8♖!

2 c8♕? is stalemate and 2 ♔b4 ♘d6 3 ♔c5 ♘c8 4 ♔c6 ♔xa5 5 ♔b7 ♘e7 6 ♔xa7 is also a draw.

2...♘xa5 3 ♖c5!

Not 3 ♖c7? ♔b6 with a draw.

3...♘b7 4 ♖c6 mate.

A nice study with few pieces!

237

Grischuk – J. Polgar
Biel 2007

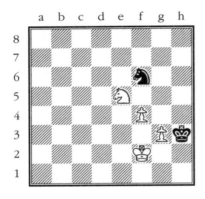

White to move

61 ♔f3?

This natural move, which is easy to make with the hands, leads to a forced draw. But White missed a pretty easy win with 61 f5 followed by 62 ♔f3. One forced line would have been 61...♘e4+ 62 ♔f3 ♘xg3 63 f6 ♘f5 64 f7 ♘d4+ 65 ♔e4 ♘e6 66 ♔f5 ♘f8 67 ♔f6 ♘h7+ 68 ♔e7 (68 ♔g7? ♘g5 is an instant draw because two knights cannot defeat one knight.) followed by manoeuvring the knight to f6.

61...♘g4!

The best female player of all time, Judit Polgar, has the following to say about this episode: "After making this spectacular move, I still thought my position was lost. But Alexander's long think made me look deeper into what was happening on the board. My calculations showed that we had constructed a drawing study!"

62 ♘d3

62 ♘xg4 leads to an unusual stalemate picture.

62...♘h2+! 63 ♔e4 ♘g4! 64 ♘e5 ♘f6+ 65 ♔f3 ♘g4!

Interestingly it's a positional draw. It doesn't even help that White changes the position to avoid the blockade and the stalemate.

66 ♘c4 ♘h2+ 67 ♔e4 ♘f1!

Black wisely adapts to the new circumstances. 67...♘g4? would have been an error due to 68 ♘e3 and White has managed to lift the blockade.

68 ♘e3 ♘xg3+ 69 ♔e5 ♔h2 70 ♔d6 ♘h5 71 f5 ♘g7 72 f6 Draw.

The fork on e8 is coming next move.

238

Hernandez Onna – Sula
Olympiad, Thessaloniki 1984

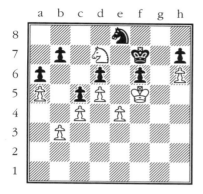

White to move

It's rare to see such a penetrated position and what is worse for Black is that White will penetrate even further!

47 ♘f8!!

One of the most incredible penetrations of a position ever witnessed!

47...♚xf8

47...♚g8 48 ♘xh7! ♚xh7 49 ♚e6 ♚xh6 50 ♚e7 ♘g7 51 ♚xf6 followed by ♚e7 and ♚xd6. Black is utterly slaughtered.

48 ♚e6

Note that the king in the heart of Black's position is supported by the whole pawn chain.

48...♘g7+

Even worse would have been 48...♚g8 49 ♚e7 ♘g7 50 hxg7 h5

51 ♚xf6 h4 52 e5 and White queens last but with check and mate on h8.

49 hxg7+ ♚xg7 50 ♚xd6 h5 51 ♚e7 h4 52 d6 h3 53 d7 h2 54 d8♕ h1♕

A transposition to a queen ending is small consolation when White has a forced win.

55 ♕f8+ ♚h7 56 ♕f7+ ♚h8 57 ♕xf6+ ♚h7 Black resigns.

Black had only to look forward to a clearly lost pawn ending after 58 ♚f7 ♕h5+ 59 ♚f8 ♕g4 60 ♕f5+ ♕g6 61 ♕h3+ ♕h6+ 62 ♕xh6+ ♚xh6 63 e5 and so wisely resigned.

239

Bajer – Tringov
Ljubljana 1969

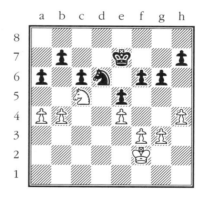

Black to move

41...b6!!

This move is forced if he is to keep his winning chances alive. Otherwise White plays 42 a5 next move and freezes the queenside.

42 ♘xa6

White has to accept the gift but the knight will be out of play for some time to come. 42 ♘d3? would have been answered by 42...♘c4 followed by ...♚e7-d6 and ...a6-a5 with a win thanks to the extra pawn.

42...♚d8

43 h5?

White feels obliged to do something radical but the idea of sacrificing the h-pawn and picking it up with the king isn't realistic. The only chance to play for a draw was 43 g4 ♚c8 44 ♚e3 g5 (44...♚b7 45 b5 cxb5 46 axb5 ♘xb5 47 ♘b4 ♘c7 48 f4! exf4+ 49 ♚xf4 ♘e6+ 50 ♚e3 ♘f8 51 ♚d4 with serious drawing chances for White, due to his more active pieces.) 45 h5 ♚b7 46 b5 cxb5 47 axb5 ♘xb5 48 ♘b4 ♘c7 49 ♚d3 b5 50 ♚c3 ♚b6 51 ♚b3 ♚c5 52 ♚c3 and White has constructed a fortress.

43...gxh5 44 ♚g2 ♚c8 45 ♚h3 f5

Or 45...♚b7 46 b5 c5.

46 exf5 ♘xf5 47 b5 c5! 48 ♚g2

If 48 a5 then 48...c4 49 axb6 c3 50 ♘b4 ♘d4.

48...h4! 49 f4 exf4 50 gxf4 c4! 51 ♘b4 c3 52 ♚f3 ♘d4+ 53 ♚g4 c2

54 ♘d3

54 ♘xc2 ♘xc2 55 ♚xh4 ♘d4 56 ♚g5 ♘e6+ 57 ♚f5 ♘xf4 would have been a hopeless variation to play.

54...♘f5!! White resigns.

This strong move could have been played already on move 53. White can only watch while the black king approaches the queenside.

240

Loyd
Chess Monthly 1858

White to move

One of the greatest problem composers, if not the greatest, Samuel Loyd (1841-1911) constructed this nice "miniature chess study". According to another great – if not the greatest – study composer Genrikh Kasparian (1910-1995) it means that the position should not involve more than seven pieces (or less) on the board.

1 ♘h3!

A very nice way to win the notorious ending two knights versus a pawn.

1...gxh3 2 ♔f2 h2 3 ♘g3 mate.

241

Herbstman/Kubbel
1937

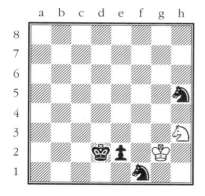

White to move

1 ♘g1 ♘e3+ 2 ♔h3 ♘f4+

Even the famous last trick to win with three knights against one doesn't work due to 2...e1♘ 3 ♘f3+!! ♘xf3 and White is stalemate. It's important to memorise

the pattern because it might appear in a real game!

3 ♔h2 ♘g4+

And here the "clever" 3...e1♘ also fails – not to stalemate but to a decisive double threat after 4 ♘f3+! ♘xf3+ 5 ♔g3!.

4 ♔h1

It's still not possible to win by any kind of promotion due to stalemate.

4...♘f2+

4...e1♘ 5 ♘f3+! ♘xf3 is a more obvious stalemate because of the cornered king.

5 ♔h2 e1♘

6 ♘f3+!! ♘xf3+ 7 ♔g3

A decisive double threat?

7...♔e3

No, but an incredible stalemate!

In fact the position is so incredible that I guess it could never happen in real life.

This is one of the most amazing studies I have ever seen. Embrace it for its sheer beauty rather than practicality.

242

Réti
Narodni Listy 1928

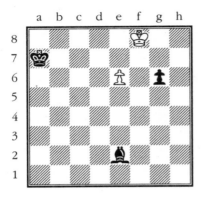

White to move

1 ♔e7!! g5

Forced, as 1...♗b5 2 ♔f6 ♗e8
3 ♔e7 leads to eternal threats on the
bishop and the pawn.

2 ♔d6 g4 3 e7

3 ♔c5 is the right move but in the
wrong position. Black wins after
3...g3 4 e7 ♗h5!.

3...♗b5 4 ♔c5!

This is the key position of the
study and the whole point. White's

king utilises the black bishop as a
springboard to gain the necessary
tempo and reach the square of the
enemy pawn. This idea mirrors
Réti's famous pawn ending (1921)
where the king manoeuvre ♔h8-g7-
f6-e5 contained a similar double
threat as the three first moves in this
study. One important difference
though is that it's more difficult to
find the first move in this study
compared with the immortal study
from 1921.

Réti continued the development,
and produced different angles, of
this incredible geometrical idea that
he started in 1921 and showed that
this illusionary concept is not valid
exclusively for pawn endings but
bishop endings as well. Several of
Réti's studies had this amazing idea
as its core, because of its illusory
nature, beauty and importance. This
is Réti's eternal painting just as
Monet's water lily paintings!

**4...♗e8 5 ♔d4 ♔b7 6 ♔e4 ♔c7
7 ♔f4 ♗h5**

8 e8♕

Black's bishop is overloaded so
it's a draw after...

8...♗xe8 9 ♔xg4

243

Dvoretsky
2000

White to move

Superficially this position looks to be clearly lost because how can White prevent the capture on c2 or the escape of the bishop via a2? Well, the solution is to play...

1 c4! b4!

Not 1...bxc4 2 ♔d2 ♔c5 3 ♔c3 and ♔b2 next move traps the bishop.

2 ♔d1!

2 ♔d2? ♔c5 3 ♔c1 ♗a2 4 c3 bxc3 (4...b3 5 ♔b2 is an elementary draw.) 5 ♔c2 ♔xc4 and Black wins.

2...♔c5 3 ♔d2 ♔xc4 4 ♔c1 ♗a2

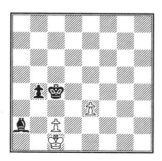

5 ♔d2!!

An amazing zugzwang has arisen. 5 ♔b2 seems to draw but it's an illusion after the devastating 5...♗b3!! 6 cxb3+ ♔d3 and Black wins by picking up all the pawns after 7 ♔c1 ♔xe3 8 ♔c2 ♔e2 9 ♔b1 ♔d3 10 ♔b2 ♔d2 11 ♔b1 ♔c3 12 ♔a2 ♔c2 13 ♔a1 ♔xb3 14 ♔b1 ♔a3!.

5...♔c5

5...♗b1 6 ♔c1 ♗a2 7 ♔d2!! and we are back where we were before.

6 c3 b3 7 ♔c1

Now it's an elementary draw.

7...♔c4 8 ♔b2 ♔d3 9 e4 ♔xe4 10 c4 ♔d4 11 c5 ♔xc5 12 ♔c3 ♔d5 13 ♔b2 ♔d4 14 ♔a1 ♗b1

14...♔c3 is stalemate.

15 ♔xb1 ♔c3 16 ♔a1

Black cannot avoid stalemate despite the fact that the bishop on a2 is no more.

244

Schmittdiel – Aseev
Mehlingen 1990

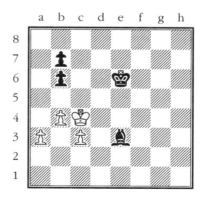

Black to move

White's plan is simply to exchange off all the white pawns.

1...♔d6

The ideal square for the king is to control the c5-square.

2 ♔b5 ♗f2

Black waits with the bishop while controlling the c5-square.

3 a4 ♗e3 4 c4 ♗f2 5 a5 bxa5?

5...♗e3! should have been played. After 6 axb6 (6 c5+ ♗xc5! is the key idea to win and the main reason why control of the critical c5 square was so important. The bishop ending will be a pawn ending after 7 bxc5+ bxc5 and then following the further 8 ♔b6 c4 9 ♔xb7 c3 10 a6 c2 11 a7 c1♕ 12 a8♕...

...a queen ending arises which is reminiscent of Lolli's famous study from 1763. Black wins by force after 12...♕b1+ 13 ♔c8 ♕c2+. The queen approaches closer and closer in a staircase-like manoeuvre after 14 ♔b7 ♕b3+ 15 ♔c8 (15 ♔a6 ♕a4+ 16 ♔b7 ♕b5+ 17 ♔a7 ♔c7 18 ♕c6+ ♔xc6! 19 ♔a8 ♕b7 mate.) 15...♕c4+ 16 ♔b7 ♕b5+ 17 ♔c8 ♕d7+ 18 ♔b8 ♕c7 mate.

Black wins either by controlling the important b8-square with:

(a) 6...♗f4! 7 c5+ ♔d5 8 c6 (8 ♔a5 ♔c4 9 ♔a4 ♗e5 10 ♔a5 ♗c3 11 ♔a4 ♗xb4 12 c6 bxc6 13 b7 ♗d6) 8...bxc6+ 9 ♔a6 ♔c4 10 ♔a5 (10 ♔b7 ♔b5) 10...♔b3 11.b5 c5.

Or by putting pressure on the b4-pawn with...

(b) 6...♗d2 7 c5+ ♔d5 8 c6 bxc6+ 9 ♔a4 ♔d4 10 b7 ♗f4 11 ♔b3 ♗c7 12 ♔a3 ♔c3 13 ♔a4 ♔c4 14 ♔a3 ♔b5 15 ♔b3 ♗d6! and Black is in zugzwang.

(c) Worse is 6...♗f2? as there is no longer any purpose in controlling the c5-square. White draws after 7 c5+ ♔d5 8 c6! bxc6+ 9 ♔a6 ♗g3 10 b7 ♗b8 (10...♗c7 11 b5 c5 12 ♔a7 c4 13 b6! ♗d6 14 b8♕ ♗xb8+ 15 ♔xb8 c3 16 b7 c2 17 ♔a8 c1♕ 18 b8♕) 11 ♔b6! ♗d6 12 ♔a5! ♔c7 13 ♔a6 and White holds the draw by triangulating on the squares b6-a5-a6.

6 bxa5 ♗a7

7 c5+!

Black must have overlooked this tactical possibility. If at first 7 a6? then 7...b6 would have won.

7...♗xc5 8 a6 Draw.

245

Smyslov
1976

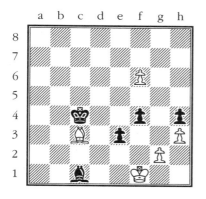

White to move

1 f7 ♗a3 2 ♗g7 f3!

The trickiest defence.

3 gxf3

3 f8♕? ♗xf8 4 ♗xf8 e2+ 5 ♔f2 fxg2 and one of the pawns promotes.

3...♔d3

4 f8♗!!

A very beautiful and unusual underpromotion.

If 4 f8♕? e2+ 5 ♔f2 (5 ♔e1 ♗xf8 6 ♗xf8 ♔e3 and Black picks

up White's remaining pawns.) 5...♗c5+!! 6 ♕xc5 e1♕+! 7 ♔xe1 stalemate. Note that the bishop on g7 is superfluous in creating the stalemate and that it would have been a more beautiful stalemate without it, controlling the d4- and c3-squares, which now are doubly controlled. A superfluous piece is never attractive.

4...e2+ 5 ♔f2 e1♕+ 6 ♔xe1 ♔e3

Black tries to pick up the rest of the pawns but it fails due to...

7 f4!

If 7 ♗xa3? ♔xf3 and White loses the h3-pawn with an obvious draw.

7...♔xf4 8 ♔f2 ♗c1 9 ♗h6+

White wins with a skewer.

246

Belyavsky/Mikhalchisin
1992

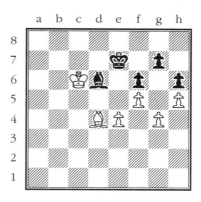

White to move

1 g5!!

This "impossible move" is the key to the win. The transition to a pawn ending by 1 ♗c5? looks like it's winning but is actually a draw after 1...♗xc5 2 ♔xc5 ♔d7 3 ♔d5 ♔e8!! (3...♔e7? loses to 4 e5 fxe5 5 ♔xe5 ♔f7 6 f6! gxf6+ 7 ♔f5.) 4 ♔e6 ♔f8 5 e5 is met by 5...fxe5 6 ♔xe5 ♔e7 and Black has the opposition.

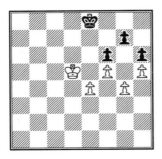

White has an extra pawn, a more active king as well as more active pawns, but amazingly it's still a draw. There is no way to break Black's resistant position.

1...hxg5

1...fxg5 2 ♗xg7 g4 3 e5 is a massacre, to put it mildly.

1...♗f4 2 gxf6+ gxf6 3 ♔d5 ♔f7 4 ♔c4! ♗d6 (4...♗c1 5 ♔d3 ♗g7 6 ♗c5 ♗f4 7 ♗e3! ♗e5 8 ♔c4 and White wins by penetrating to e6 with his king.) 5 ♗e3 ♗f8 6 ♔d5 ♗g7 7 ♗c5 ♗h8 8 ♗a3 ♗g7 9 ♗d6 ♗h8 10 e5 ♗g7 (10...fxe5 11 ♗xe5 ♗xe5 12 ♔xe5 ♔e7 13 f6+ ♔f8. Now White wins by triangulation after 14 ♔e4 ♔g8 15 ♔f4 ♔f8 16 ♔e5) 11 e6+ ♔e8 12 ♔c6 ♗h8 13 ♗f8! ♔xf8 14 ♔d7 and the e-pawn promotes.

An alternative win after 1...♗f4 is 2 g6 ♔e8 3 ♗c5 ♗g5 4 ♔d5 ♗d2 5 ♔e6 ♗a5 6 ♔e7 ♗c3 7 ♗d6 ♗d4 8 e5 ♗c3 9 exf6 ♗xf6 10 ♗e5 ♗xe5

11 ♔xe5 ♔e7 12 ♔e4 (12 f6+? gxf6+ 13 ♔f5 leads to a draw after both 13...♔e8 and 13...♔f8) 12...♔f6 13 ♔f4 ♔e7 14 ♔e5.

2 ♗xf6+! ♔xf6

If 2...gxf6 then 3 h6 ♔f7 4 ♔xd6 g4 5 e5 g3 6 e6+.

3 ♔xd6 g4 4 e5+ ♔xf5

Or 4...♔f7 5 e6+ ♔e8 6 f6 gxf6 7 h6.

5 e6 g3 6 e7 g2 7 e8♕ g1♕ 8 ♕e5+ ♔g4 9 ♕xg7+ and White wins.

A very instructive position. Not only because of the bishop ending in itself but also because of the two important pawn endings which formed part of this ending. Pawn endings are the foundation of all endings, and should be properly understood, even though these endings are less common than for example rook endings.

247

Ettlinger – Capablanca
New York 1907

Black to move

Emanuel Lasker was impressed with Capablanca's play in this bishop ending and wrote: "At this moment one would suppose that White could secure at least a draw. The actual termination is therefore a great surprise."

1...♗c7

Black could also win by 1...♗a5 but the move played by Capablanca is more forcing as well as prettier.

2 ♗f4 ♗a5 3 ♗d2 f4!

The key move which opens the floodgates to mate.

4 gxf4

If White obstructs Black's cunning idea with 4 b6 Black continues the march of the f-pawn: 4...f3! 5 bxa7 ♗c7! (5...f2+? 6 ♔xf2 ♔xd2 7 a8♕ e1♕+ 8 ♔g2) 6 ♔f2 ♔xd2 7 a8♕ e1♕+ 8 ♔xf3 ♕e2 mate.

4...♗d8 White resigns.

247a

G. Abrahams – Booth
1923

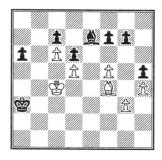

White to move

Before we end this section on tactical bishop endings, where the bishops are of the same colour, I want to show an elementary case of several decisive breaks. Here White sacrifices three pawns and a bishop to achieve his goal to queen the c-pawn.

1 f6!

Sacrifice number one!

1...gxf6

1...♗xf6 is answered by 2 ♗xd6+!.

2 g4!

Sacrifice number two!

2...hxg4 3 h5 ♗f8

4 h6!

Sacrifice number three is the nicest one and in accordance with the tactical idea of overloading.

4...♗xh6 5 ♗xd6+!

Sacrifice number four!!

This was really a sacrifice as 5 ♗xh6?? g3 would have won for Black.

5...cxd6 6 c7 Black resigns.

White is one tempo ahead in the short pawn race.

248

Shirov – Andersson
Biel 1991

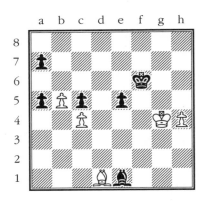

Black to move

Shirov has said that it was this ending, initiated by Andersson, that inspired him to make the immortal bishop sacrifice 47...♗h3!! against Topalov in Linares 1998.

44...♗xh4!!

It's important to take control of the g5-square and get rid of the passed h-pawn to be able to win this particular ending. 44...♗d2?, with the threat 45...e4, would have led to a draw after 45 ♔f3 since White doesn't control the important g5-square. After the further 45...♗e1 46 h5 ♔g5 47 ♔e4 ♗c3 48 ♔d5 ♗d4 Black has the g5-square but as the king must control the protected h5-pawn it's not possible for Black to penetrate.

45.♔xh4

Accepting the sacrifice gives Black the f5-square and works as a decoy to make possible a penetration via the centre to the white queenside. If White ignores the sacrifice Black will penetrate anyway due to the numerous weaknesses. White must cover the a-pawn, the e-pawn and the penetration squares via the kingside as well as via the queenside and that is way too much. For example after 45 ♗c2 ♗e1 46 ♗a4 ♗d2 Black threatens 47...e4. After the further 47 ♔f3 (47 ♗c2 doesn't help due to the principle of the two weaknesses. Black replies 47...e4! 48 ♗xe4 a4 followed by ...a3, ...♔e5-d4.) 47...♔f5 48 ♗c2+ e4+ 49 ♗xe4+ (49 ♔e2 is met by ♗f4 followed by ♔e5-d4.) 49...♔e5 and Black wins.

If White covers the central squares, Black penetrates via the kingside. One plausible variation is 45 ♔f3 ♗e1 46 ♗c2 ♗c3 47 ♔e4 ♔g5 48 ♔f3 ♔h4 49 ♗d1 ♔h3 50 ♗c2 ♔h2 51 ♗d1 ♔g1 52 ♔e2 ♔g2 53 ♗c2 ♔g3 54 ♔e3 ♗d4+ 55 ♔e2 ♔f4 followed by ...e5-e4 and ...♔f4-e5.

45...♔f5!

Black must keep the pawn on e5 for the time being and penetrate via e4 and d3. 45...e4? 46 ♔g3 ♔e5 47 ♔f2 ♔d4 48 ♔e2 ♔xc4 49 ♔e3 ♔xb5 50 ♔xe4 leads to a drawn position.

46 ♔g3 ♔e4 47 ♔f2 ♔d3 48 ♔e1

48...♚xc4

It wasn't necessary to take the c4-pawn but it works when Black's e-pawn is on e5. Compare this with the following variation: 48...e4 49 ♗a4 (49 ♗g4 a4 50 ♚d1 a3 51 ♚c1 e3 52 ♚b1 e2 53 ♗xe2+ ♚xe2 54 ♚a2 ♚d3 and Black wins the pawn ending.) 49...♚c3! (It's very important not to clear the c4-square with 49...♚xc4? because later on White can draw by using the c4-square for the king in a pawn ending.

An illustrative variation is 50 ♚d2 ♚b4 51 ♗c2 a4 52 ♗xe4 a3 53 ♗b1 ♚b3 54 ♚c1! a2 55 ♗xa2+ ♚xa2 56 ♚c2 ♚a3 57 ♚c3 ♚a4 58 ♚c4. If White's pawn had been on c4 this square wouldn't have been available and Black would have won.) 50 ♚e2 ♚b4 51 ♗c2 a4 52 ♗xe4 a3 53 ♗b1 ♚b3! (Note the instructive mistake 53...♚c3? 54 ♗a2 ♚b2 55 ♚d2 ♚xa2 56 ♚c2 with a draw.) followed by 54...♚b2 and the a-pawn promotes.

49 ♚d2 ♚b4

49...♚d4 also won but not 49...♚xb5? 50 ♚c3 which is a draw.

50 ♚c2 e4 51 ♗g4 a4 52 ♗f5 e3 53 ♗e6 c4 White resigns.

249

Kotov – Botvinnik
Moscow 1955

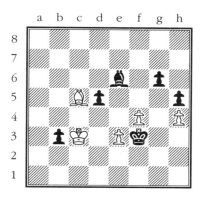

Black to move

A common winning method in bishops of opposite colours is to create two passed pawns. Here Botvinnik sacrificed two pawns but in return obtained two passed pawns with decisive effect.

59...g5! 60 fxg5

Or 60 hxg5 h4 61 ♗d6 ♗f5 62 g6 ♗xg6 63 f5 ♗xf5 64 ♚xb3 ♚g2.

60...d4+!

Now the b3-pawn is defended. Note also the important fact that Black's bishop single-handedly controls White's passed pawns, whether they are on the e- or the d-file.

61 exd4

61 ♗xd4 ♚g3 62 g6 ♚xh4 63 ♚d2 ♚h3! 64 ♗f6 h4 65 ♚e2 ♚g2! and the h-pawn will be supported on the critical h2-square.

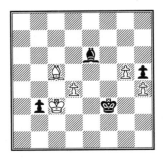

61...♔g3!

An instructive variation is 61...♔g4? 62 d5 ♗xd5 63 ♗f2 which only goes to prove that sometimes one has to manoeuvre over minefields (the black squares) to achieve the goal.

62 ♗a3

62 ♗e7 ♔xh4 63 g6+ ♔g4 is also an instructive variation, which clearly shows the difference between the locations of the passed pawns. All White's pawns can be controlled along the g8-a2 diagonal by the defending bishop, which also defends the passer on b3! This means the h-pawn is just free to advance without any obstacles whatsoever.

62...♔xh4 63 ♔d3 ♔xg5 64 ♔e4 h4

64...♔g4 was also good to support the h-pawn.

65 ♔f3

65 d5 ♗xd5+ 66 ♔xd5 h3.

65...♗d5+ White resigns.

After the further 66 ♔f2 ♔f4 Black manoeuvres to c2 and

captures White's bishop after the inevitable ...b3-b2. Then the h-pawn decides.

250

K. Richter
1910

White to move

Black's plan is to mate on b6 so White has to prevent the knight from reaching any of the five white squares a4, c4, d5, d7 and c8. The main line is...

1 ♗a2

The classical diagonal is the best waiting-diagonal because the four squares c4, d5, d7 and c8 can be controlled by the bishop provided it is placed on the right square. For example the knight on d6 cannot reach c8 (or c4) if the bishop stands on e6.

1...♘f2 2 ♗g8

The bishop waits on the classical diagonal until the knight reaches a critical square.

2...♘d3

3 ♗c4

(a) 3 ♗f7 ♘c5 4 ♗e8 or the more spectacular...

(b) 3 ♗d5 ♘c5 4 ♗c6! ♚xc6 5 ♔b8 would be a draw as well.

(c) However note that 3 ♗a2? would be an error due to 3...♘c5! and White cannot prevent the knight from reaching either of the d7 or a4 squares. For this it is necessary that the bishop controls the a4-e8-diagonal.

(d) 3 ♗e6? is also bad due to 3...♘e5 leading to zugzwang as White loses control of either d7 or c4 with his next move. The same goes for...

(e) 3 ♗b3? ♘b2! and Black wins.

This is a pretty good endgame to practice with a faster time control so if you have the possibility to play it out with a friend or a computer you should do so. You will not only develop a deeper appeciation of the pieces concerned but also increase your understanding of the important concept of corresponding squares.

3...♘c5 4 ♗b5 ♘e4 5 ♗c4 ♘d6 6 ♗e6

6 ♗a6 was also good.

6...♘b5 7 ♗g8 ♘c3

7...♚c8 followed by mate on c7 will never work because of 8 ♗e6+.

8 ♗b3! Draw.

251

Reshevsky – Tatai
Netanya 1973

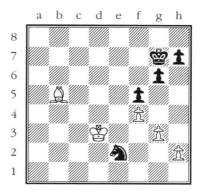

Black to move

Black's knight is trapped but it's nevertheless a forced draw after...

50...♘xf4+!

A slower draw is 50...♘g1 51 ♔e3 g5! 52 fxg5 ♘h3 53 ♗d3 ♚g6 54 ♚f3 ♘xg5+ 55 ♚f4 ♘e4!! 56 ♗xe4 fxe4 57 ♚xe4 ♚g5

...and Black holds the draw thanks to his active king. Lolli understood this many years ago in 1763. A plausible line is 58 ♔f3 h5!. The principled move. After 59 h3 Black continues with the only move 59...♔f5! to be followed by 60 ♔e3 ♔e5 and White cannot win. White can only win if it's Black to move, but it's impossible to gain the necessary tempo. The golden rule for Black is not to allow the king to reach the fourth rank.

51 gxf4 g5! 52 fxg5 h6

White cannot avoid the notorious endgame bishop + rook pawn, which is a draw when the queening square is of a different colour to that of the bishop.

252

Karpov – Kasparov
Game 9, World Championship,
Moscow 1984

White to move

47 ♘g2!!

An extraordinarily deep move and easy to miss as the h-pawn normally

is the knight's worst enemy. The Dutch GM Jan Timman writes in *The longest game* (2019) that this is "one of the most brilliant moves in the entire chess history." The key is that White is increasing his manoeuvring space since now not only is the f4 square available, but h4 as well. This continuation is absolutely the best practical chance because by avoiding the automatic 47 gxh4 ♗g6 48 ♔g3 ♔e6 49 ♘g2 ♔d6 50 ♘f4 ♗f7 51 ♘d3 ♗e6 52 ♘c5 ♗c8, where Black covers the a6-pawn and the f5-square, White would most probably not have won.

47...hxg3+

47...h3? 48 ♘f4 ♗f5 49 ♘xh5 ♔e7 50 ♘f4 followed by g3-g4 and ♔f2-g3 wins the h-pawn.

48 ♔xg3

White now wins the h5-pawn by force.

48...♔e6

Another, more passive defence was 48...♗g6 49 ♘f4 ♗f7 50 ♔h4 ♔e7 51 ♘xh5 ♔e6! 52 ♘g7+ ♔e7 etc.

49 ♘f4+ ♔f5 50 ♘xh5

Black must now defend against the knight manoeuvre ♘g7-e8-c7xa6.

50...♔e6 51 ♘f4+ ♔d6 52 ♔g4 ♗c2 53 ♔h5 ♗d1 54 ♔g6 ♔e7

54...♗xf3? 55 ♔xf6 leads to a technically winning endgame. White conquers the e5-square after a knight manoeuvre to f5 and then the d5-pawn is lost.

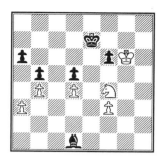

55 ♘xd5+?

Karpov makes an instructive mistake as the d5-square becomes vacant. This is surprising since he clearly understood this concept with his revolutionary 47th move. Twelve years after this game was played Timman prepared a lecture in Tilburg on the theme of "knight versus bad bishop". On that occasion he discovered that 55 ♘h5! was the right move. After 55...♗xf3 56 ♘xf6 ♗e4+ 57 ♔g5 White would have excellent winning chances due to the fact that the d5-pawn hasn't been captured yet and Black's king will play a passive role.

55...♔e6

55...♔d6 56 ♘xf6 ♗xf3 is a draw because White's king is not placed on e5 which would have secured the win in line with the comment on move 54.

56 ♘c7+ ♔d7

The other continuation 56...♔d6 57 ♘xa6 ♗xf3 58 ♔xf6 ♔d5 59 ♘c7+ ♔xd4 60 ♘xb5+ ♔c4 followed by 61...♔b3 was a simpler draw. Now Black loses a tempo with the king to reach the available dream square d5.

57 ♘xa6 ♗xf3 58 ♔xf6 ♔d6 59 ♔f5 ♔d5 60 ♔f4 ♗h1 61 ♔e3

Black is two pawns down but amazingly the game is now a positional draw if White is not allowed access to d3 and c3 with his king.

61...♔c4 62 ♘c5 ♗c6 63 ♘d3 ♗g2 64 ♘e5+ ♔c3 65 ♘g6 ♔c4 66 ♘e7

66...♗b7?

The definite turning-point in the game. 66...♗h1! should have been played according to GMs Aivars Gipslis (1937-2000) and Adrian Mikhalchishin (1954-).

It's an important principle to keep the bishop away from forks. The main variation is like a study: 67 ♘c8 ♔d5! 68 ♔d3 ♗e4+ 69 ♔c3 ♔c6 70 ♘e7+ ♔d6 71 ♘g8 ♔e6 72 ♘h6 ♗f3 The enemy knight is kept at bay. 73 ♔d3 ♗h1! 74 ♘g4 ♗f3 75 ♘e3 ♔d6

Quite amazingly it doesn't matter that the knight has come home because the key c3 square cannot be reached by the knight. There is no way to get round this as 76 ♔d2 ♗h5 77 ♘d1 ♔d5! 78 ♘c3+ ♔xd4 79 ♘xb5+ ♔c4 is an elementary draw thanks to the weakness on a3.

67 ♘f5 ♗g2 68 ♘d6+ ♔b3 69 ♘xb5 ♔a4 70 ♘d6 Black resigns.

There is no question that Karpov improved his winning chances because of his clever idea to increase the manoeuvring space for his pieces. It is beneficial to compare this game with Morozevich – Lputian, exercise 48, where Morozevich found a similar idea but in a totally different situation.

253

Zlatanović – Yordanov
Skopje 2017

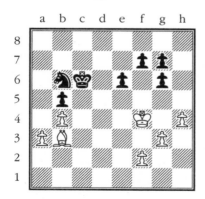

White to move

42 ♗xe6!!

Very nice. However note that this sacrifice would have been less

effective with the g6-pawn placed on h7.

42...fxe6

42...f6 43 ♗f7 only prolongs Black's fate.

43 ♔g5 Black resigns.

It takes White only six moves to queen the h-pawn compared to nine moves for Black to queen his b-pawn.

254

G. Shkrl
Concluding part of a study 1978

White to move

Always look for mate when the defending king is in the corner!

1 ♘e8!! ♘f5+

1...♘xe8 2 ♔f8 and it's mate next move thanks to zugzwang.

2 ♔f8 ♘xh6 3 ♘d6

Zugzwang!

3...♘g4 4 ♘f7 mate.

255

Hildebrand
1983

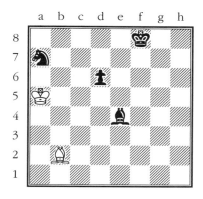

White to move

1 ♔b6!

This is all about penetrating Black's position as much as possible. 1 ♗a3? ♘c8 would prevent the king from penetrating by controlling all the vital squares on the queenside.

1...♘c8+

1...♘c6 2 ♔c7 ♘a5 3 ♗a3 and Black's sole pawn is doomed.

2 ♔c7 ♗f5 3 ♗a3 ♔e7 4 ♗b4 ♗d7 5 ♗a3 ♔e6

6 ♔d8!

White prevents the knight from activating thanks to a stalemate trick. The waiting move 6 ♗b4? would have given Black the chance to improve his position by using the fork as his principal weapon. 6...♘a7 (6...♘e7? would be a mistake because of the stalemate after 7 ♗xd6 ♘d5+ 8 ♔d8 ♔xd6. However 6...d5 followed by 7...♘e7 would have worked.) 7 ♗xd6 ♘b5+ 8 ♔d8 ♘xd6 and Black wins.

6...d5

6...♘a7 7 ♗xd6 ♔xd6 stalemate or 7...♘c6+ 8 ♔c7 with a draw.

7 ♗c5!

"The bishop dominates the knight" is a common theme to look out for in this type of ending. Here it is seen in its ideal and purest form. It is vital to prevent the pawn from reaching the d3-square so the bishop cannot be better placed than on c5 where it completely paralyses Black's position and places him in a neat zugzwang.

7...♘d6

There are no other reasonable moves.

381

8 ♗xd6 ♔xd6 stalemate.

A very nice and instructive study by Alexander Hildebrand (1921-2005) who was one of the most famous Swedish study composers. The superb bishop on c5 is unforgettable!

256

Smyslov
1936

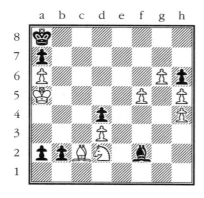

White to move

1 ♗b1!

1 ♘b1? a1♕+ 2 ♔b5 ♕a2 and 1 g7? a1♕+ 2 ♔b5 ♕g1 are both losing for White as Black has the passed g-pawn under control.

1...a1♕+ 2 ♔b5 ♗g3

Black cannot stop the g-pawn from queening so he plays for stalemate. 2...♕a3 3 g7 and Black cannot prevent the pawn from being promoted on g8.

3 g7 ♗b8!

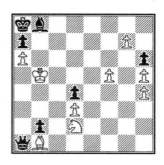

4 g8♗!!

The underpromotion to a bishop is necessary to avoid 4 g8♕? ♕a4+ 5 ♔xa4 stalemate.

4...♗f4

Mate was threatened on d5. After 4...♗e5 White can just play on as if it were a knight versus bishop ending. An illustrative variation is 5 ♗ga2! ♔b8 6 ♔c6 ♔c8 7 ♘e4 ♔d8 8 f6 ♔e8 9 f7+ ♔e7 10 ♔b7 and White wins with his a-pawn.

5 ♗ga2!

Black's queen is jailed for life.

5...♗xd2 6 f6! ♗f4 7 f7 ♗d6 8 ♔c6 ♗f8 9 ♔c7

Mate on d5 follows.

Don't forget to solve more studies by the creative and imaginative Vasily Smyslov (1921-2010).

He was the best study composer of all the world champions.

257

B. Svensson – Ornstein
Swedish Championship,
Helsingborg 1991

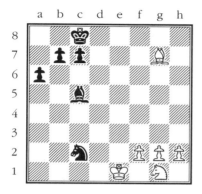

White to move

A unique position!

36 ♔e2

36 ♔d2 was more flexible.

36...♘d4+ 37 ♔e1?

Activity is more important than a pawn so correct was 37 ♔d3! ♘e6 38 ♗e5 ♗xf2 39 ♘f3 followed by h2-h4 and g2-g4 etc. with balanced play.

37...♘e6

The knight is well-placed in the centre so more logical was to improve his position with either 37...♔d7 or 37...b5.

38 ♗c3?

38 ♗e5 would have prevented Black's next move. This would have been in the spirit of the bishop move to c5 in Hildebrand's study, exercise 255.

38...♘f4! 39 g3

39 ♔f1 b5 and 40...b4 underlines another drawback to the bishop's placement on c3. Black gains important tempi.

39...♘d3+ 40 ♔e2 ♘xf2 41 ♘f3

41...♘e4?

More important than centralising the knight was either activation of the king with 41...♔d7 or constructing a blockade on the kingside with 41...♘h3.

42 ♗d4?

This is a serious mistake which activates Black's pawns in the knight ending for free. 42 ♗e5 followed by 43 g4 should have been played.

42...♗xd4 43 ♘xd4 c5 44 ♘c2 ♔d7 45 ♔f3 ♘d6 46 h4 b5 47 h5 b4 48 g4 ♔e6 49 ♔f4 a5 50 h6 ♔f7 51 ♔e5 ♘c4+ 52 ♔d5 b3 White resigns.

Black gained a bunch of tempi, not only against the bishop, but also against the knight (43...c5 and 52...b3) so the result was never in doubt.

258

Prokeš
1939

White to move

It looks tough to hold the draw when Black's pawns are so close to the queening squares and in addition can gain a tempo on the white rook. The reason White can hold this position is because the white king, believe it or not, is close enough.

1 ♔g4 e2

A less spectacular variation is 1...d2 2 ♔f3 ♔d3 3 ♖a1 e2 4 ♖a3+ ♔c2 5 ♖a2+ ♔c1 6 ♖a1+ ♔b2 7 ♔xe2 with a draw.

2 ♖c1+ ♔d4

After 2...♔b3 3 ♔f3 d2 4 ♖b1+ ♔c2 5 ♔xe2! ♔xb1 6 ♔xd2 all pieces have disappeared from the board.

3 ♔f3 d2 4 ♖c4+!!

This beautiful sacrifice is the main point of the study. White transposes to a drawn pawn ending.

4...♔d3

4...♔xc4 5 ♔xe2 ♔c3 6 ♔d1 ♔d3 stalemate.

5 ♖d4+!! Draw.

Again this beautiful trick!

259

Hildebrand
1963

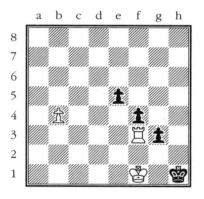

White to move

1 ♖f2!

This is the correct way to proceed. 1 b5? g2+ 2 ♔e2 g1♕ 3 ♖f1 fails to 3...f3+ 4 ♔e1 f2+ 5 ♔e2 ♔g2 and Black wins.

1...gxf2

1...f3 doesn't work due to the decisive pin after 2 ♖xf3 g2+ 3 ♔e2 g1♕ 4 ♖f1. 1...e4 2 ♖xf4 is the pragmatic win but then 2 ♖g2 e3 3 b5 e2+ 4 ♖xe2 f3 5 ♖e1! also wins.

2 b5 e4 3 b6 e3 4 b7 f3 5 b8♖!

5 b8♕? gives Black the rare opportunity to sacrifice all his pawns with check and be rewarded with a stalemate. 5...e2+ 6 ♔xf2 e1♕+ 7 ♔xe1 f2+ 8 ♔xf2 stalemate.

5...♔h2 6 ♖e8

White wins as all the pawns are picked up.

260

Helmertz – Wernbro
Lund 1973

White to play

Here White made some indifferent moves and soon resigned. However he could have salvaged a draw with the ingenious continuation...

1 b4!! ♖xb4

1...♖xd6 2 bxc5 ♖d1 is a draw.

2 d7 ♖d4

2...♖b8 3 ♔c4 ♖d8 4 ♔xc5 ♖xd7 5 b4 and Black's king is too far away.

3 b4!! ♖xd7 4 bxc5

And White draws easily after 5 ♔c4 and c5-c6.

261

A. dall'Ava
L'Italia Schacchistica 1938

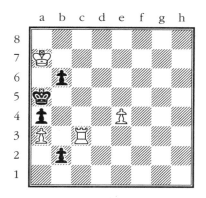

White to move

1 ♖g3!! b1♕ 2 ♖g5+ b5

2...♕b5 is met by 3 ♖f5! ♕c5 4 ♖xc5+ bxc5 5 e5 c4 (5...♔b5 6 ♔b7) 6 e6 c3 7 e7 c2 8 e8♕ c1♕ 9 ♕e5+ ♕c5+ 10 ♕xc5 mate.

3 ♖g6!

The reason White placed the rook on the g-file was to avoid a saving check on g1.

3...♕g1+ 4 ♖xg1 b4 5 ♖g5 mate.

A really fine study.

262

Myllyniemi
1965

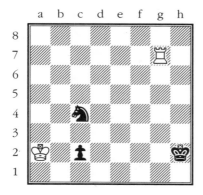

White to move

1 ♖h7+ ♔g2 2 ♖g7+ ♔f2 3 ♖f7+ ♔e2 4 ♖e7+ ♔d2 5 ♖d7+ ♔c3

6 ♖c7!

6 ♖d1? cxd1♗! The underpromotion to a bishop is sometimes, if rarely, the only way to win. This we have learned from Smyslov's studies.

6...c1♕

6...c1♖ is a theoretical draw.

7 ♖xc4+ ♔xc4 stalemate.

263

Gusev – Zhukhovitsky
1958

White to move

1 ♗d5+!

The stalemate idea 1 ♗g2?? fails to 1...♔a3 because now it's White's turn to move instead of Black's. For example after 2 ♗f1 ♖c2, mate cannot be prevented.

1...♔a3 2 ♗g2!

Black is in zugzwang.

2...♖h5 3 ♗d5!

White threatens to capture the a2-pawn with an immediate draw.

3...♖h2

4 ♗g2!

The same position, but with opposite colours, arose in the game Hedge – Palatnik, Calicut 1988, but Black resigned as he wasn't familiar with the stalemate idea. Without the a2-pawn White would draw easily by placing the bishop on e4 as ♗b1 would be possible after a check on the first rank. It's useful to know this stalemate idea with the pawn on a2 controlling the important b1-square.

264

Parr – Farrand
England 1971

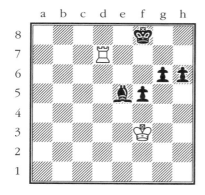

White to move

White secures a half point pretty easily after...

1 ♖d5! ♗f6

1...♗c7 2 ♖d7 ♗a5 3 ♖d5 doesn't prevent White's draw mechanism and it's the same problem after 1...♗h2 2 ♖d2 since 2...♗g1 is answered by the double threat 3 ♖g2.

2 ♖xf5! gxf5 3 ♔f4 Draw.

265

Kotov
1964

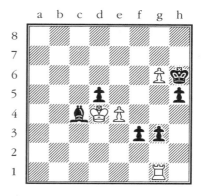

White to move

1 g7!

1 ♖xg3? f2 2 g7 dxe4! and Black wins.

1...f2

Or 1...♔xg7 2 ♖xg3+.

2 g8♘+! ♔h7 3 ♘f6+ ♔h8

Another interesting variation is 3...♔h6 4 ♘g8+ ♔g5! 5 ♖xg3+ ♔f4 6 ♖g6! (But not 6 ♖g7? dxe4 and Black wins.) 6...f1♕ 7 ♖f6+ ♔g3 8 ♖xf1 ♗xf1 (8 exf4 loses after 8...h4 9 d6 ♗b5.) 9 ♘e7! and the position is drawn.

4 ♖xg3 dxe4 5 ♖g7!!

The key-move to the study, exploiting the ability of the newborn knight to check with tempo.

5...♔xg7 6 ♘xh5+ ♔g6 7 ♘g3 ♗d3 8 ♔e3 Draw.

266

Smyslov
1938

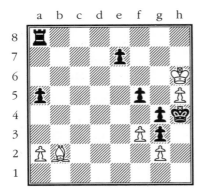

White to move

1 ♗f6+!!

A clever way to prevent the effectiveness of a check on a6.

1...exf6 2 f4

This is the first point. Black's king is confined.

2...♖h8+

2...a4 3 a3 and Black is forced to move the rook.

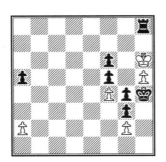

3 ♔g7!

3 ♔g6? ♖xh5 4 ♔g7 ♖g5+ 5 ♔h8 ♔h5 6 ♔h7 ♖g6 7 a3 (7 a4 ♖g5

8 ♔h8 ♔h6 and White is forced to capture the rook.) 7...♖h6+ 8 ♔g7 a4 and White is in zugzwang.

3...♖xh5

3...♖b8 4 ♔g6! keeps the black king in the box while preparing h5-h6-h7 followed by ♔g6-g7.

4 a4!

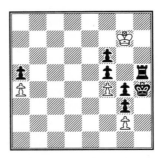

Black is in an incredible zugzwang.

4...♖g5+ 5 ♔h8!

5 ♔h7? ♔h5 and Black wins.

5...♖g6 6 ♔h7 ♔h5 7 ♔h8 ♖h6+

7...♔h6 is stalemate with the rook on g6 rather than g5.

8 ♔g7! ♖g6+ 9 ♔h8!

9 ♔h7? ♖g5 10 ♔h8 ♔h6 and White must capture on g5.

9...♔h6

Smyslov has managed to construct an imaginative study where the rook is eternally trapped without looking trapped. The white king's claws are just enormous in this specific position as the rook as well as the king just couldn't get out!

267

Chéron
1926

White to move

Black's king is cut off but White's king has problems escorting his pawn to the promotion square if it weren't for the fact that White can do this by simultaneously exploiting the abysmally placed black king.

1 e5!

It's useless to centralise the king at this stage. 1 ♔f4 with the threat 2 e5 is met by 1...♖f8+, for example 2 ♔e5 ♖e8+ 3 ♔f5 ♖f8+ 4 ♔e6 ♖e8+ 5 ♔d5 ♖d8+ 6 ♔c4 ♖e8 etc.

1...♖a4!

White's king is cut off from its own pawn but paradoxically White can push his pawn nearer the promotion square.

2 e6!! ♔h6

2...♖a6 3 ♔f4! restores the tactical cooperation between White's forces. 3...♖xe6 is answered by 4 ♔f5.

3 e7!!

Again, the same incredible idea but the pawn and the black king are one step further up the board.

3...♖a8 4 ♔f4!

The most precise move but 4 ♔e4 and 4 ♔d4 win as well. It's all about controlling the key squares e5 or f5.

4...♖e8 5 ♔f5! ♖xe7 6 ♔f6

Black must sacrifice his rook and succumb to mate after 8 moves.

268

Ponziani
1769

White to move

1 ♔g5!

The king is too far away from the enemy pawn so the only way to save half a point is to shield itself in front of the h-pawn.

1...♖g1+ 2 ♔h6 a1♕ 3 ♖a8+! ♕xa8 stalemate.

This tactical idea only works with a rook pawn.

269

Bernstein – Smyslov
Groningen 1946

White to move

Even one of the greatest endgame players, Vasily Smyslov, could make elementary mistakes. Here he had mistakenly played the pawn to b2 instead of 59...♔e4 with an easy win and became a victim of a stalemate trap.

60 ♖xb2! ♔g4

60...♖h2+ 61 ♔f3 ♖xb2 stalemate.

61 ♔f1 Draw.

Be careful not to fall into this trap as an attacker and look out for it as a defender, because there is pretty good chance your opponent will fall for it.

If Smyslov could forget or overlook it anyone can.

What's interesting about the next position is that Black can also draw a rook down.

270

Wahlund – Lundbäck
Stockholm 1990

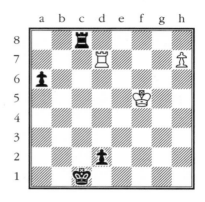

White to move

1 ♖c7+! ♖xc7

After 1...♔b1!? 2 ♖xc8 d1♕ 3 h8♕ Black draws by starting to check on one of the squares f3, d7 or d3. For example 3...♕f3+ (Of course not 3...♕d5+? 4 ♕e5) 4 ♔g6 ♕g4+ 5 ♔h7 ♕h5+ 6 ♔g8 ♕g6+ 7 ♔f8 (Covering the check with the queen is no good because of the unprotected rook after 7 ♕g7? ♕e6+) 7...♕f5+ 8 ♔e7 ♕e4+ 9 ♔d6 ♕d3+ 10 ♔c5 ♕c2+ 11 ♔b4 a5+! The only move to keep the perpetual check going. 12 ♔xa5 ♕a2+! 13 ♔b4 and now the stalemate trick 13...♕b3+!! (13...♕a3+!! also works.) is an extra opportunity since the a-pawn has been captured. 14 ♔xb3 stalemate. There was no way to escape the checks and the main reason was White's decentralised pieces.

2 h8♕ d1♕ 3 ♕a1+ ♔d2 4 ♕d4+

Of course not 4 ♕a5+? ♖c3.

Draw.

There is no way for Black to escape the perpetual check. Black's king cannot abandon the queen and has to defend it after every check on g4, g1, d4, a4 and a1.

271

Hillarp Persson – Livner
Lund 2015

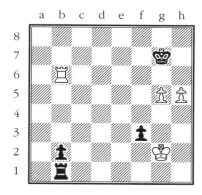

White to move

79 ♔h2??

White holds the draw with the study-like 79 ♔f2! ♖h1 80 h6+ ♔h7 81 ♖b7+ ♔g6 82 ♖b6+ ♔xg5 83 h7! This is the tactical shot which can easily be missed. After 83...♖xh7 84 ♔xf3! (84 ♖xb2?? ♖h2+) 84...♖h2 85 ♔e3 the b2-pawn falls into White's hands.

79...f2 80 h6+

80 ♖g6+ ♔f7 81 ♖f6+ ♔e7 82 ♖xf2 ♖h1+ 83 ♔xh1 b1♕+ 84 ♔g2 ♕b5 and Black wins.

80...♔h7 81 ♖b7+ ♔g6 82 ♖g7+ ♔f5

A quicker win was 82...♔h5! 83 h7 ♔g4! 84 h8♕ ♖h1+! 85 ♔xh1 b1♕+ 86 ♔h2 ♕g1 mate.

83 ♖f7+ ♔xg5 84 ♖xf2 ♖h1+ 85 ♔xh1 b1♕+ 86 ♔g2 ♔g4

Simpler was 86...♔xh6.

87 ♖d2 ♕b6 88 h7 ♕b7+ 89 ♔f2 ♕xh7

90 ♖d4+ ♔f5 91 ♔e3 ♔e5 92 ♖c4 ♕h3+ 93 ♔d2 ♔d5 94 ♖b4 ♕f3 95 ♖b7 ♕f2+ 96 ♔d3 ♕g3+ 97 ♔c2 ♔c4 98 ♖b2 ♕g7 99 ♔c1 ♕g6 100 ♔d2 ♕d3+ 101 ♔c1 ♕e3+ 102 ♔d1 ♕g1+ 103 ♔d2 ♕g5+ 104 ♔c2 ♕e5 105 ♔b1 ♔c3 106 ♔a1 ♕a5+ 107 ♔b1 ♕a4

The famous zugzwang position which was discovered by Philidor in 1777 has been reached. White loses the rook by force.

108 ♖b8 ♕d1+ 109 ♔a2 ♕a4+

Faster was 109...♕d5+ 110 ♔a1 ♕h1+ 111 ♔a2 ♕h2+ etc.

110 ♔b1 ♕e4+ 111 ♔a1 ♕h1+ 112 ♖b1

112 ♔a2 ♕h2+ and the rook is lost.

112...♕a8 mate.

A more detailed discussion on the queen vs. rook ending can be found in exercise 218.

272

Kotov
1976

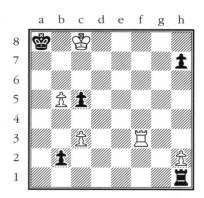

White to move

The Russian GM Alexander Kotov (1913-1981) is mostly known for several great books he wrote, for example about Alexander Alekhine. He was also a skilled study composer as the following position shows.

1 c4!

Another, more prosaic win is 1 b6 b1♕ 2 ♔c7 ♕xb6+ (2...♖f1 3 ♖xf1 ♕xf1 4 b7+ ♔a7 5 b8♕+ ♔a6 6 ♕b6 mate.) 3 ♔xb6 ♖b1+ 4 ♔xc5 and White wins the rook ending.

1...♖a1

1...♔a7 2 ♖a3+ ♔b6 3 ♖a6 mate and 1...b1♘ 2 ♖f6 lose more quickly than the main variation.

2 b6 b1♕ 3 ♖f1! h6 4 h3! h5 5 h4

A beautiful zugzwang has arisen. The queen is overloaded because it has to control b7 as well as a1, but now it must give up one of these critical squares which leads to immediate disaster.

5...♕xb6 6 ♖xa1+ ♕a7 7 ♖xa7+ ♔xa7 8 ♔c7

White wins the c-pawn and the h-pawn with an easy win.

273

Bukić – Marović
Yugoslavia 1968

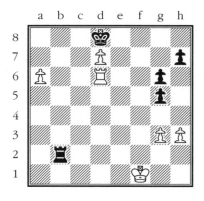

White to move

Here is an elementary example showing how to win Black's rook by sacrificing both pawns on their way to promotion.

58 a7!

58 ♖f6! wins in the same fashion as in the game after 58...♖a2 59 a7 ♔xd7 60 ♖f8!.

58...♖a2 59 ♖f6!

White is leaving both pawns to their fate. The key idea is the decisive control of the eighth and seventh ranks.

59...♔xd7

Or 59...♖xa7 60 ♖f8+ ♔xd7 61 ♖f7+.

60 ♖f8!

The dynamic rook has done its duty.

274

Bellon – Chekhov
Barcelona 1984

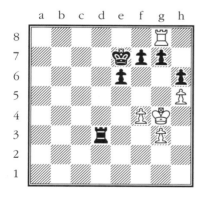

White to move

White would have had very good chances to draw, thanks to his space advantage on the kingside, if he had chosen a waiting policy. Instead he played too aggressively by wanting to apply pressure on the g-pawn and was most probably expecting

33...♔f6 when he would have continued a waiting game. This is what happened:

33...♖d8! White resigns.

White realised that 34 ♖xg7 (34 ♖xd8 leads to a clearly lost pawn ending.) didn't work due to 34...♔f8! (34...♖h8? gives White the possibility to evacuate the g4-square for the rook after 35 ♔f3) 35 ♖h7 ♔g8 36 ♖xh6 ♔g7 and the rook is trapped as 37 ♔g5 is met by 37...♖d5+.

275

Capablanca – Schiffman
Simultaneous exhibition, Detroit 1909

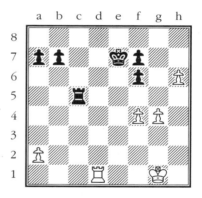

White to move

36 ♖d8? Black resigns.

After this natural move it's actually more difficult to win and it will not work at all after best play. Capablanca played several games simultaneously and he can obviously be forgiven for overlooking the finesse 36 ♖e1+!! ♔d7 37 ♖e8!! with the big difference that the black king is outside the square of the h6-pawn. 37...♖c1+ 38 ♔g2 ♖c2+ 39 ♔g3 ♖c3+ 40 ♔h4 ♖c2 41 ♖e3 ♖c8 (After 41...♖h2+ 42 ♖h3 ♖xh3+ 43 ♔xh3 the black king is unable to stop the h6-pawn from queening. This was the whole point of checking the black king.) 42 ♔h5 ♖h8 43 g5 fxg5 44 fxg5 followed by 45 g6 decides the game in White's favour.

Capablanca's opponent didn't realise that Black had a lot to play for after 36...♖c1+ 37 ♔g2 ♖c2+ 38 ♔g3 ♖c3+ 39 ♔h4 ♖c1 40 ♖d3 (The best chance to keep winning chances alive was either 40 ♖b8 ♖h1+ 41 ♔g3 ♖xh6 42 ♖xb7+ ♔f8 43 ♖xa7 or 40 ♖h8 ♔d7 41 a4 One winning plan is to transfer the king to f5 and then play for g5-g6.) 40...♖h1+ 41 ♖h3 ♖xh3+ 42 ♔xh3 ♔f8 White can play 43 g5 but after 43...f5! the pawn ending is surprisingly a draw as the following variation shows: 44 ♔g3 ♔g8 45 ♔f3 ♔h7 46 ♔e3 ♔g6 47 ♔d4 f6 48 gxf6 ♔xf6 49 h7 ♔g7 50 ♔e5 ♔xh7 51 ♔xf5 ♔g7 52 ♔e6

This position is extraordinarily tricky and like a study. Black can draw only by the hard-to-find moves 52...a6!! 53 ♔d6 ♔g6!! (The natural move 53...♔f6? loses to 54 ♔c7 a5 55 a4! b5 [or *55...♔f5*

56 ♔xb7 ♔xf4 57 ♔b6 ♔e5 58 ♔xa5] 56 axb5 a4 57 b6 a3 58 b7 a2 59 b8♕ a1♕ 60 ♕h8+ and Black has to give up his newborn queen.) 54 ♔c7 (Naturally 54 ♔e6 is met by 54...♔g7) 54...a5! 55 ♔xb7 (55 a4 b5!! works now that the king is on g6.) 55...a4! (55...♔f5? loses to 56 a4) 56 ♔b6 ♔f5 57 ♔b5 a3! Black gains a decisive tempo for the third time! 58 ♔b4 ♔xf4 59 ♔xa3 ♔e5 and thanks to the hard-working a-pawn the king reaches the critical zone in time.

What a pity that Schiffman prematurely resigned in such an incredible endgame!

276

Kaiszauri – Niklasson
German Junior International 1975

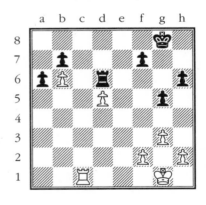

White to move

Black threatens two pawns, but White has a tactical resource to save the position.

31 ♖c6!

Konstantin Kaiszauri exploits the far advanced b6-pawn to secure the draw.

31...♖xd5

Of course not 31...bxc6? 32 b7
♖d8 33 dxc6 and White queens the
c-pawn.

32 ♖c7 ♖b5 33 ♖xb7

The position is an elementary
draw as the queenside pawns are
doomed to disappear from the
board.

**33...♖b2 34 ♖b8+ ♔g7 35 b7
♖b1+ 36 ♔g2 a5 37 ♖a8 Draw.**

277

Hašek
Československý šach 1937

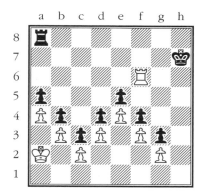

White to move

This position is incomprehensible
for Stockfish. It only calculates
variations and fails to see that
White's position is an impregnable
fortress.

1 ♔b1! ♔g7

1...♖h8 is answered by the
amazing 2 ♖f8!! (2 ♖h6+? ♔xh6
3 ♔c1 ♔g5 4 ♔d1 ♖h2 and White
needs the move ♔f1, which doesn't
exist, to draw.) 2...♖xf8 3 ♔c1 ♔g6

4 ♔d1 ♖h8 5 ♔e1 leads to the same
thing as in the main variation.

**2 ♖h6!! ♔xh6 3 ♔c1 ♔g5 4 ♔d1
♖h8 5 ♔e1**

White is just in time to create
stalemate or to defend the g2-pawn.

5...♖h1+ 6 ♔e2 ♖h2

The rook has to avoid the first rank
to avoid stalemate but the sacrifice
on g2 leads to a draw as well.

7 ♔f1 ♖xg2

It's only after this move Stockfish
is with us. Otherwise White's king
goes back and forth between f1 and
g1.

**8 ♔xg2 ♔h4 9 ♔g1 ♔h3 10 ♔h1
g2+ 11 ♔g1 ♔g3 stalemate.**

278

Ciocaltea – Pachman
Prague 1954

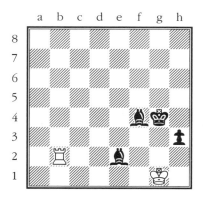

White to move

The following endgame, which
arose in a real game, shows how
important it is to be familiar with a
zugzwang idea.

91...h2+?

Black missed an important zugzwang possibility in the variation 91...♗f3! 92 ♖f2 ♗d5 (92...♗e3 93 ♔h2) 93 ♖c2 ♔g3 94 ♖c3+ (94 ♖g2+ ♔f3) 94...♔h4 95 ♖c2 ♔g4 96 ♖b2 ♔g3 97 ♖g2+ ♔f3 98 ♖c2 (98 ♖e2 ♗e3+ 99 ♔f1 ♗c4 100 ♔e1 ♗f4) 98...♔e4!. This idea to force White into a zugzwang was discovered by the famous study composer Johann Berger (1845-1933).

After the further 99 ♖e2+ (99 ♖b2 ♔d3 100 ♖e2 ♔c3 would not help either. There are no safe moves for the rook along the second rank so White is in zugzwang after 99...♔d3 100 ♖b2 ♔c3 101 ♖e2 ♔b3 and the elementary endgame two bishops versus a lonely king will arise by force after 102 ♖f2 ♗e3 103 ♔h2 ♗xf2 104 ♔xh3. Black mates in eight moves after 104...♗f3.

92 ♔h1 ♗f3+ 93 ♖g2+ Draw.

Unfortunately the long-time standard endgame book *Theorie und Praxis der Endspiele* (1891, 1922) (*Theory and practice of the Endgame*) by Berger is not easily obtainable.

279

Topcheev
64 1927

White to move

This study is tricky to solve because apart from all the stalemate tricks inherent in the position White must calculate rather deeply while seeing the correct knight manoeuvre.

1 ♖h8+ ♔d7 2 ♖h7+ ♔d6! 3 ♘f7+

3 ♖xa7 is an unusual stalemate pattern.

3...♔c7 4 ♘e5+

The trap in the study is that 4 ♘d6+? fails to 4...♔d8! which might lead to a more familiar stalemate.

4...♔b6 5 ♘c4+ ♔a6 6 ♖h6+ ♔b7

6...♔b5 is answered by 7 ♖b6+ ♔a4 8 ♔c3 and now the stalemate trick 8...♖b7 doesn't work due to 9 ♘b2+ followed by a capture of the rook.

7 ♘d6+ ♚b8 8 ♖h8+ ♚c7 9 ♘b5+

The fork decides.

A perfect exercise to practice calculation, stalemates and forks! The knight was the hero. The king was perfectly placed, while the rook was pretty static, mainly performing checks on the h-file.

280

Hildebrand
1984

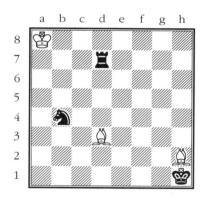

White to move

Both White's bishops are hanging so the question is how to save them by tactical means.

1 ♗f5! ♖d8+

1...♖f7 2 ♗d6! ♖xf5 3 ♗xb4 is an easy draw. White can just play the bishop to b8 or a7 and let Black come closer, as it's still an easy draw.

2 ♗b8 ♘a6 3 ♔b7!

The point is to force the knight to a bad square where the bishop and king can surround it.

3...♘xb8 4 ♔c7 ♖f8 5 ♗c8! ♘c6 6 ♗b7 Draw.

The white-squared bishop was the key piece which dominated events. The bishop manoeuvre ♗d3-f5-c8-b7, eventually forcing a draw with a pin on the long diagonal, was cunning.

281

Karpov – Sveshnikov
Match 2015

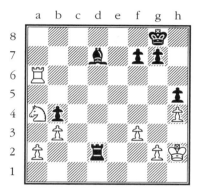

White to move

Karpov misses an easy win by pinning and winning the black bishop.

33 ♖a8+

In the game the inferior 33 ♘c5? was played when Sveshnikov would have had drawing chances if he had played 33...♗f5! targeting the a2-pawn. However instead he targeted the g2-pawn with 33...♗b5? and eventually lost after 34 ♖a8+ ♚h7 35 ♘e4 ♖b2 36 ♘g5+ ♚g6 37 ♘h3! etc. Sveshnikov resigned on move 48.

33...♚h7 34 ♖d8

Black has no defence against either 25 ♘b6 or 25 ♘c5. And if Black tries to counter-pin White's knight with...

34...g6

it's still an easy win after...

35 ♘c5

35 ♘b6 also works as White can go for a rook ending with two passed pawns on the queenside after 35...♖d6 36 ♘xd7 ♔g7 37 ♖b8 ♖xd7 38 ♖xb4.

35...♖d5 36 ♘xd7 ♔g7 37 ♖g8+!

The knight is released so White remains a piece up.

282

Réti/Mandler/Rinck
Kölnische Volkszeitung 1928/1935

White to move

Garry Kasparov was especially fond of solving studies when he was focused on tackling chess problems. The reason was that the time he put in on studies told him if he was in good shape or not, and many of the ideas actually turned up in practical play. In addition to these arguments for solving studies, it also develops one's imagination and creativity to greater heights. There are some really good out-of-print books like *Test Tube Chess* (Stackpole Books 1972) by John Roycroft and *Endgame Magic* (Batsford 1996) by John Beasley and Timothy Whitworth. The three writers are well-known experts in the world of studies. All serious chess players should own at least one of these books since, apart from Kasparov's reflections, there is also an aesthetic and entertaining aspect to solve well-chosen studies. The present study is mainly composed by Richard Réti in 1928, and seven years later Arthur Mandler and Henri Rinck improved it a little. It's a position which certainly wouldn't occur in a real game. However this study isn't only about finding White's best moves but also Black's and after these have been found we have to find an incredibly delicate winning continuation. It may take some time to solve it but if you succeed I can guarantee that you will feel completely satisfied, since it will not only increase your self-confidence when it comes to solving chess problems, but also give you a deeper feeling for chess as an art form. This in itself will most probably have the effect that you continue to solve studies of the likes of Réti and other great study composers.

1 ♗f5+!

The continuation 1 ♗c6+ ♔d6 2 ♖d4+ ♔e5 3 ♖e4+ ♔d6 4 ♖xe3 e1♕ 5 ♖xe1 leads to stalemate.

1...♔d8 2 ♖d4+ ♔e7 3 ♖e4+ ♔d8 4 ♗d7!!

The key move to the study. Of course not 4 ♖xe3 e1♕ 5 ♖xe1 stalemate.

4...e1♕

4...♔xd7 5 ♖xe3 wins.

5 ♗b5

Black has no check and cannot control the critical e8 square so White wins the queen or mates next move.

Black is in a fatal zugzwang and cannot prevent the loss of his rook. Such ideas are very useful to know even though they will perhaps not happen in your game. The main thing here is to develop the fantasy and the tactical alertness regarding zugzwang situations which can appear in other positions and with other pieces. Here both of Black's pieces are passive and the principal question is whether or not there is an immediate solution to take advantage of this.

283

G. Abrahams
Technique in Chess 1961

White to move

In this position it's not a matter of grinding the opponent down in 50 moves and testing the different defences available to Black like Szen, Cochrane, second-rank or third-rank. Here you can win in two moves if you are tactically alert or familiar with the idea, maybe from frequent study-solving.

1 ♗g6+ ♔d8 2 ♗f7!!

284

Hašek
1929

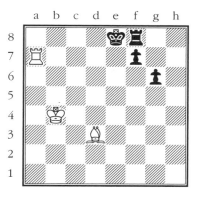

White to move

As always when the opponent's pieces are passively placed it's important to be alert for a tactical solution to exploit them.

1 ♗f5!!

This key move removes Black's main opportunity to liberate his rook. 1 ♔c5? would give Black the chance to breathe with 1...f5 2 ♔d6

♜f6+! 3 ♔e5 ♜b6 and Black's rook is fit to fight. If Black has an active rook like this the draw is secured.

1...gxf5

After 1...f6 the fastest win is 2 ♗xg6+ ♔d8 3 ♔c5 f5 4 ♗f7! f4 5 ♔d6.

2 ♔c5

The main mantra of rook endings is activity and it's difficult to find more convincing proof than this position where the contrast is striking.

2...f6 3 ♔d6 ♜g8

3...♜f7 4 ♜a8 mate.

4 ♔e6 ♔f8 5 ♔xf6

White mates or wins the rook.

285

P. Cramling – E. Berg
Swedish Championship,
Stockholm 2007

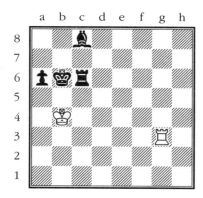

White to move

This endgame is normally a win as was demonstrated in the classic game Capablanca – Tarrasch, St Petersburg 1914. However the actual position is like a study because White has a forced draw due to stalemate. Black's last move was the blunder 72...♔c7-b6??. Emanuel Berg explained what happened in the Swedish magazine *Tidskrift för Schack*: "After just over six hours hard work I make a careless move and lost half a point. Besides that, I was ahead on time and under no time pressure whatsoever. The only explanation I can give is fatigue due to playing a long tournament with many hard-fought games. Obviously I had seen White's next move but I missed the main point. Simplest is to start with 72...♜h6! to get the rook out of the way. Then Black can quietly improve the king and advance the pawn."

73 ♜c3 a5+

Black obviously wants to keep the rooks on the board to avoid an elementary draw. After Berg had delivered the pawn check he was struck by lightning and understood what was going to happen.

74 ♔a4!!

This is the key move which was overlooked by Berg, who had only reckoned on 74 ♔b3? which would have been wrong since Black gets time to move the bishop with tempo. After 74...♗e6+ 75 ♔a4 Berg had planned to avoid the rook trade with 75...♜d6.

74...♜xc3 Draw.

"After a couple of minutes I accepted the inevitable and completed the stalemate combination. A very bitter draw in an otherwise well played game. Luckily it didn't have any influence on my tournament placing but it was still very annoying."

Pia Cramling was lucky to get this opportunity but at the same time she was alert to the tactical slip by her opponent.

286

S. Koslowski
1931

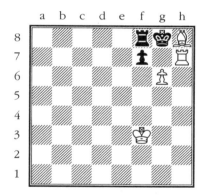

White to move

This study made a great impression on me the first time I saw it and it still does. The key is the bishop in the corner. First White uses the bishop to play...

1 ♖g7+!!

There is no win after 1 g7 ♖a8 2 ♖h1 even though White can win the f-pawn by force. White brings

the king to b7 and the rook to d7. If Black has his rook on e8 and is to move he is in zugzwang and loses the f-pawn. A plausible variation is 2...♖e8 3 ♖a1 ♖b8 4 ♔e4 ♖d8 5 ♖a7 ♖b8 6 ♔d5 ♖c8 7 ♖d7 ♖a8 8 ♔c6 ♖b8 9 ♔c7 ♖e8 10 ♔b7

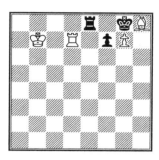

Black is in zugzwang and loses the f-pawn by force. However, it doesn't matter because it's still a draw after 10...♔h7 11 ♖xf7 ♖e1 12 ♖f8 ♖g1 etc. The only way to effectively use the bishop is to play g8♕+ when the rook isn't placed on the eighth rank and then try to win the drawn ending rook + bishop versus rook.

1...♔xh8

Now that the corner is empty White goes back with the rook and after...

2 ♖h7+ ♔g8

...he exploits the empty corner with...

3 g7!.

Of course it's necessary that Black doesn't have any available check so if Black moves the rook White wins after 4 ♖h8+.

287

Goryachkina – Kosteniuk
Women's World Cup 2021

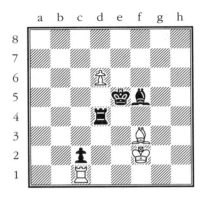

White to move

53 ♔e3?

The simplest way to draw was to reach the notorious ending rook and bishop versus rook. Correct was therefore 53 d7! ♖xd7. Note that even if Black doesn't take the pawn at once White can reply 54 ♗g4!! since both Black's pieces are overloaded. 54 ♗g4! White's exploits the fact that Black's bishop is overloaded as it protects both the rook and the pawn. 54...♗xg4 55 ♖xc2 White is ready for the second-rank-defence which is the easiest way to hold the draw in this position.

Another way to draw was 53 ♔e1 ♖xd6 54 ♗d1! cxd1♕+ 55 ♖xd1 ♗d3. White can play according to the second-rank-defence by continuing 56 ♖d2 and waiting for the inevitable stalemate occurring on e2 when the black king reaches e3.

53...♖d3+ 54 ♔e2

54 ♔f2 fails to 54...♔f4.

54...♖xd6

White is completely lost since Black just marches with her king to the b2-square. It's impossible to sacrifice the bishop for the pawn under reasonable conditions.

55 ♔e1 ♔d4

55...♔f4! was more precise.

56 ♗d1

56 ♗g4! ♗e4 57 ♗d1! was the best defence but it wouldn't help in the long term on account of 57...♖h6! (57...♔e3? 58 ♗xc2) 58 ♔d2 (58 ♗xc2 ♖h1+ 59 ♔d2 ♖h2+ 60 ♔d1 [60 ♔e1 ♗xc2] 60...♗d3 61 ♗b1 ♔e3 62 ♗xd3 ♔xd3) 58...♖h2+ 59 ♗e2 ♗d3 60 ♖e1 ♖f2 61 ♔c1 ♗xe2 62 ♔xc2

The ending rook and bishop versus. rook is won for Black since White cannot construct any effective defence.

The main variation is 62...♗c4+ 63 ♔d1 ♔d3 64 ♖g1 ♗d5 65 ♔e1 ♖e2+ 66 ♔f1 ♔e3 67 ♖g5 ♗e4 68 ♔g1 ♖a2 69 ♖g4 ♗c2 70 ♖g5 ♖c8 71 ♔h2 ♔f4 72 ♖h5 ♖c2+ 73 ♔g1 ♖g2+ 74 ♔f1 ♔e3 75 ♖h3+ ♗f3 76 ♖h8 ♖g5 77 ♖e8+ ♗e4 78 ♖e7 ♖h5 79 ♖g7 ♖a5 80 ♔g1 ♖a1+ 81 ♔h2 ♖h1+ 82 ♔g3 ♖g1+ and Black wins.

56...♔e3! 57 ♖xc2

The English GM Nigel Short, who commented on this game live, mentioned the pretty variation 57 ♗xc2 ♖g6! 58 ♔f1 ♗h3+ 59 ♔e1 ♖g1 mate.

57...♗xc2 58 ♗xc2

58...♖d2

Kosteniuk missed the instant win 58...♖a6! but in this position it doesn't matter since White cannot avert the loss of the bishop anyway.

59 ♗f5 ♖f2 60 ♗e6 ♖f6 61 ♗d5 ♖d6 62 ♗b3 ♖b6 63 ♗c2 ♖a6! White resigns.

288

Wotawa
1955

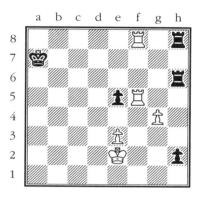

White to move

1 ♖5f7+ ♔a6 2 ♖f6+ ♔a5

After 2...♖xf6? 3 ♖xh8 it is Black who must fight for a draw.

3 ♖a8+! ♔b5 4 ♖b8+! ♔c5 5 ♖c8+! ♔d5 6 ♖d8+! ♔e4

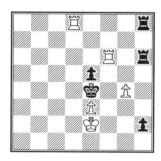

7 ♖e6!!

The most beautiful move of the whole study. White threatens 8 ♖d4 mate. Such tactical ideas are the reason double rook endings have to be studied. They can not only be played for mate, they can also create tensions between the four rooks.

7...♖xe6 8 ♖xh8 ♖a6 9 ♔f2!

Of course not 9 ♖xh2? ♖a2+.

9...♖a2+ 10 ♔g3 ♔xe3 11 ♖xh2 ♖xh2 12 ♔xh2 ♔f4 13 g5

Actually all moves hold the draw except 13 ♔g2? ♔xg4 14 ♔f2 ♔f4 15 ♔e2 ♔e4 when Black has the opposition. If White plays for example 13 ♔g1 ♔xg4 14 ♔g2 ♔f4 15 ♔f2 ♔e4 16 ♔e2 it's White who has the opposition with a clear draw.

13...♔xg5 14 ♔g3 ♔f5 15 ♔f3

It's an elementary draw.

289

Evreinov
1975

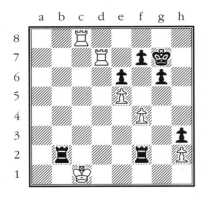

White to move

1 ♖dd8! g5

Forced, so the king can flee via g6 and f5. Not 1...♖xh2? 2 ♖g8+ ♔h6 3 ♖h8+ ♔g7 4 ♖cg8 mate.

2 f5!! g4

Black frees g5 for his king. Not 2...exf5 3 ♖g8+ ♔h6 4 ♖h8+ ♔g6 5 ♖cg8 mate.

3 ♖g8+ ♔h6 4 ♖xg4 ♔h7

Black must defend against the mate threat on h8.

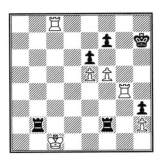

5 ♖c3!! ♖xh2 6 ♖h4+

6 ♖cg3? doesn't win on account of 6...♖hc2+ 7 ♔d1 ♖d2+ 8 ♔e1 ♖e2+ 9 ♔f1 ♖f2+ and now 10 ♔g1?? is unplayable because of 10...h2+ and Black mates White.

6...♔g7

7 ♖g3+

Note how the white rooks coordinate: first they use their power on the back rank, then on the side and then again on the back rank. This technique how to play with the rooks is very important to know since the rooks show what they really are capable of.

7...♔f8 8 ♖h8+! ♔e7 9 ♖d3! exf5

The only way to prevent the deadly 10 f6+.

10 ♖dd8 f6

The only defence against 11 ♖he8 mate.

11 ♖he8+ ♔f7 12 e6+

Now White has a devastating passed pawn which will decide the game with the combined efforts of the rooks.

12...♔g6 13 ♖g8+ ♔h6 14 e7 ♖bc2+ 15 ♔d1 ♖a2

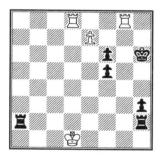

Black threatens two different mates.

16 ♖g6+! ♔h7 17 ♖h8+!

A beautiful study that shows what stuff rooks are really made of when the circumstances are as ideal as here.

It's particularly impressive that while White was trying to checkmate the black king, at the same time he always controlled the strong black rooks on the second rank.

290

Blomqvist – Wiedenkeller
Swedish Championship,
Eskilstuna 2014

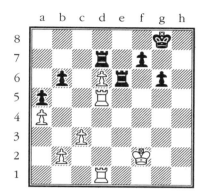

White to move

39 b4?

Now it's not possible to get two passed pawns. The problem move to be played was 39 c4!!. White threatens 40 b4 axb4 41 a5 bxa5 42 c5 followed by c6. A plausible continuation is 39...♖e8! 40 b4 axb4 41.♖b5! (Stronger than 41 a5 bxa5 42 c5 ♖c8 43 ♖a1) 41...♖c8 42 ♖xb6 ♖xc4 43 a5 with good winning chances.

39...axb4 40 cxb4

Note that the ambitious idea 40 c4 with the idea 41 a5 doesn't work on account of 40...♖f6+ 41 ♔g3 ♖e6 42 a5 bxa5 43 c5 ♖e3+ 44 ♔f4 ♖c3.

40...♔f8

More active is 40...f5.

41 a5 bxa5 42 bxa5 ♔e8??

Black plays too passively with his rooks and king and lays the foundations for a defeat. 42...♖e8 followed by ...♖a8, ...f6 and ...♔f7 was in accord with Black's passive strategy and would secure a draw.

43 a6 ♖d8 44 a7 ♔d7 45 ♖b5 ♖a8 46 ♖b7+ ♔c6 47 ♖c7+ ♔b6 48 ♖b1+ ♔a6 49 ♖c2 ♖f6+ 50 ♔g3 ♖xd6 51 ♖a2 mate.

Black was kind enough to let White play the so-called ladder mate, also known as a lawnmower mate. It's one of the main checkmating methods that a beginner should know.

291

Sahović – Korchnoi
Biel 1979

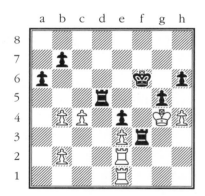

Black to move

When the opponent's king is close to the edge of the board it sometimes pays to look for the ladder mate or other mates in rook endings with two rooks each. A typical case is the following:

39...h5+! 40 ♔xh5 ♖d8!!

Black threatens mate in two moves.

41 hxg5+

41 ♔g4 gxh4 42 ♖c2 ♖g8+ 43 ♔xh4 (43 ♔h5 ♖f5+ 44 ♔xh4 ♖fg5 45 ♖f2+ ♔g6 and White cannot prevent mate on h8.) 43...♔f5! and mate next move.

41...♔f5

When the king is in opposition, one rook is even enough to mate so White must side-step the king.

42 ♔h6 ♖h3+ 43 ♔g7 ♖d7+ 44 ♔g8 ♔g6 45 ♖f2 ♖g7+ 46 ♔f8 ♖h8 mate.

Note what was required to reach this ladder mate: a pawn sacrifice, a trianglular manoeuvre with the king (f6-f5-g6) and last but not least manoeuvres with both rooks, both on a rank and a file. So intricate for a very primitive mate! This is the reason why even the best sometimes fall victim to "silly" mates.

292

Svidler – Vitiugov
World Cup 2021

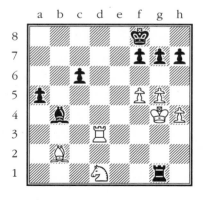

White to move

Perhaps inspired by Short's immortal king manoeuvre ♔h2-g3-f4-g5 against Timman (Tilburg 1991) Svidler tries a similar geometrical manoeuvre ♔g2-f3-g4-h5. It's every chessplayer's dream to cross the opponent's danger-zone and with the help of his majesty checkmate the king. However, one must make sure that the opponent cannot efficiently attack it!

38 ♔h5!!

Interestingly this is also Stockfish 11's first choice which makes the move even more impressive, because it proves that a human has found an "impossible" computer move.

38...♔g8

The human move. Black plays for mate. 38...g6+ would only have helped White to penetrate deeper into enemy territory with 39 ♔h6. If Black tries to mate the bold king with 39...♔g8 White counters with 40 ♖d8+ ♗f8+ 41 ♔g7! and Black mates next move.

39 ♖d8+ ♗f8

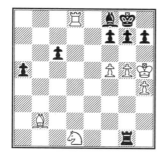

40 ♗xg7!!

This is actually the only move to win but also the only move not to

lose which must have been foreseen by Svidler before he fulfilled his dream sequence of moves.

40...♔xg7 41 f6+ ♔g8 42 ♘e3!

And here we go. The apparently passive knight is on its way to cross the "equator" (the f5-square) to use Bronstein's terminology, and prepares a mate either on e7 or on h6. A very beautiful knight manoeuvre. There is nothing Black can do to disturb the perfect coordination of White's pieces.

42...h6 43 ♘f5 hxg5 44 ♘e7+ ♔h7 45 ♖xf8 Black resigns.

Svidler has joined the club, together with Short, by delivering this unforgettable king manoeuvre!

293

Horwitz and Kling

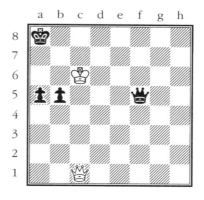

White to move

1 ♕h1!

This idea is the same as was used by Neumann against an unknown opponent in Vienna 1887. It can also be found in Euwe's *Das Endspiel*

(Das Schach-Archiv 1957-1960). This is an important tactical device to remember, where White puts the queen on the long diagonal, behind its own king, and weaves a mating net around the enemy king situated in the corner by threatening a deadly discovered check either by 2 ♔c7+ or 2 ♔b6+.

Black's two extra pawns count for nothing with such a cornered king and Black needs a saving move like 1...♕d8, which doesn't exist, to prevent the white king from penetrating the black squares near its counterpart.

The main variation is:

1...♕c8+

1...♔a7 2 ♕g1+ ♔a8 (2...♔b8 3 ♕b6+!) 3 ♕g8+ ♔a7 4 ♕g7+ and mate follows on b7.

1...♔b8 2 ♕h2+! It doesn't help to cover the mating square b7 due to the weakness on the eighth rank which is clearly visible after 1...♕f7 2 ♔b6+ ♔b8 3 ♕h8+.

2 ♔b6+ ♔b8

White now needs to carry out a staircase manoeuvre to finally mate on a7.

3 ♕h2+ ♔a8 4 ♕g2+ ♔b8 5 ♕g3+ ♔a8 6 ♕f3+ ♔b8 7 ♕f4+ ♔a8 8 ♕e4+ ♔b8 9 ♕e7!

White wins. Black cannot prevent mate on a7 next move without giving up the queen.

294

Moravec
1961

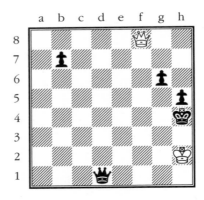

White to move

Black is three pawns up but they are of no help if the king is badly placed. White wins by placing Black in zugzwang.

1 ♕f4+ ♕g4 2 ♕e3!

This is the key idea to exploit Black's vulnerable king on the edge of the board and in close contact with White's queen and king.

2...b6

Black's queen must cover g3 and 2...♕g5 loses instantly to 3 ♕h3 mate.

3 ♕e7+ ♕g5 4 ♕e4+ ♕g4 5 ♕e3!

White repeats the pattern until the pawn can be taken with check on b4.

5...b5 6 ♕e7+ ♕g5 7 ♕e4+ ♕g4 8 ♕e3 b4 9 ♕e7+ ♕g5 10 ♕xb4+ ♕g4 11 ♕e7+ ♕g5 12 ♕e4+ ♕g4 13 ♕e3

408

Black is completely helpless and must either succumb to a quick mate or desperately sacrifice the queen to prolong his suffering.

295

Smajović – Babić
Yugoslavia 1949

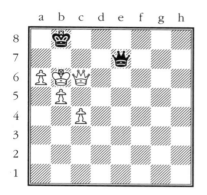

White to move

Incredibly, White cannot prevent perpetual check despite the fact that he's three pawns up and it's his turn to move.

1 ♕c5

The only reasonable move in view of 1 ♕b7+ ♕xb7+ 2 axb7 stalemate.

1...♕d8+ 2 ♔c6 ♕c8+ 3 ♔d6 ♕f8+ 4 ♔d5 ♕f5+ 5 ♔d4 ♕f2+

What one can learn from such an ending is to think twice before penetrating the opponent's position. Sometimes the defender can get this remarkable cooperation between his king and queen and work miracles.

296

Zvonitsky – Khelmnitsky
USSR 1988

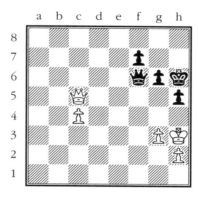

Black to move

White loses due to his badly placed king, but Black must play accurately to achieve victory.

1...♕f3!

Black prevents the king from escaping to g2 and places White in a state of zugzwang. Note that 1...♕f1+? looks better than it is. After 2 ♔h4 Black is forced to repeat the position following 2...♕f6+ 3 ♔h3 and then play 3...♕f3 transposing to the game.

2 ♕f8+

(a) 2 ♕d5 ♕f1+ (Transferring to a pawn ending is the wrong path. After 2...♕xd5? 3 cxd5 ♔g5 [*3...♔g7 4 g4 hxg4+ 5 ♔xg4 f6 6 h4 ♔f7 7 h5 gxh5+ 8 ♔xh5 is a draw.*] 4 d6 ♔f6 5 ♔h4 ♔e6 6 ♔g5 h4! and Black maintains the balance.) 3 ♕g2 (3 ♔h4 f6 Black exploits the fact that White no longer has a queen check on f8 to mate him: 4 g4 g5+

5 ♔g3 h4 mate.) 3...♕f5+ 4 g4 ♕d3+ 5 ♔g3 ♕f1+ 6 ♔g2 hxg4+ 7 ♔g3 ♕xg2+ This is the moment to exchange queens and win the pawn ending. 8 ♔xg2 ♔g7! 9 c5 ♔f8! 10 ♔g3 f5.

(b) 2 ♕d6 to keep the queen on the a3-f8 diagonal leads to mate after 2...♕f1+ 3 ♔h4 ♕f5!.

(c) 2 ♕g1 is answered by 2...g5 3 ♕a1 f6 4 ♕c1 ♕e2! 5 c5 f5 6 c6 ♔g6 7 c7 g4+ 8 ♔h4 ♕xh2 mate.

2...♔h7 3 ♕c5 ♕f1+ 4 ♔h4

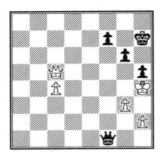

4...♕g2?

Simpler was the forced variation 4...♕e2 5 ♔h3 ♔g7 6 ♕d4+ f6 7 ♕d7+ ♔h6 8 ♕c6 ♕f1+ 9 ♔g2 ♕f5+ 10 g4 ♕d3+ 11 ♔g3 ♕f1+ 12 ♔g2 hxg4+. Black wins the pawn ending after 13 ♔g3 ♕xg2+ 14 ♔xg2 ♔g5 15 c5 ♔f5 16 ♔g3 ♔e5 17 ♔xg4 ♔d5 18 h4 ♔xc5 19 h5 gxh5+ 20 ♔xh5 ♔d5.

5 h3?

The best defensive continuation was 5 ♕c7! ♕xh2+ 6 ♔g5 ♕f2 7 ♕f4 ♕c5+ 8 ♔h4 (8 ♔f6 ♔g8! 9 ♕b8+ ♕f8) 8...♔g7 and it's not easy for Black to exploit his three-to-one majority on the kingside.

5...♕e4+ 6 g4

After 6 ♔g5 ♔g7 7 ♕d6 ♕e3+ 8 ♔h4 f6 White cannot prevent mate in four moves.

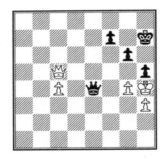

6...♕f4! 7 ♕e7

The alternatives also lead to disaster: 7 ♕d5 ♕f2+ 8 ♔g5 f6 mate or 7 ♕c6 ♕f2+ 8 ♔g5 ♔g7 followed by 9...f6+.

7...hxg4 8 hxg4 ♕h2+ 9 ♔g5 ♕h6+ 10 ♔f6 ♕f4 mate.

297

Radulov – Osmanović
Sarajevo 1978

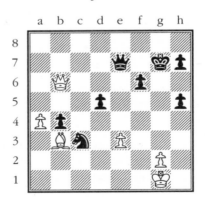

Black to move

Black exploits his more active pieces and the strong combination of queen and knight versus queen and bishop with a beautiful tactical breakthrough in the centre.

42...d4!!

Undoubtedly the strongest move.

43 e4

The pawn is taboo due to 43 ♕xd4 ♘e2+ or 43 exd4 ♕e1+ 44 ♔h2 ♘e2 45 ♕c7+ ♔h6. The f4-square is covered so White has to flee with his king. After 46 ♔h3 there are several wins but the simplest and most beautiful is 46...♕h1+ 47 ♕h2 ♘f4+ 48 ♔g3

48...h4+!! 49 ♕xh4+ ♘h5+ 50 ♔g4 f5+. After the two checks White's queen is lost.

43...♕xe4 44 ♕c7+ ♔h6 45 ♕f7 ♘e2+! 46 ♔f1 ♘g3+ 47 ♔g1

Note that the hero, the d4-pawn, even participates in constructing the mate after 47 ♔f2 ♕e3 mate.

47...♕e1+ 48 ♔h2 ♘f1+ 49 ♔g1 ♘e3+ 50 ♔h2 ♘g4+ 51 ♔h3 ♕h1+ 52 ♔g3 ♕h2+ White resigns.

Because of the fork on e5 next move.

298

Harabadze – Volkov
USSR 1986

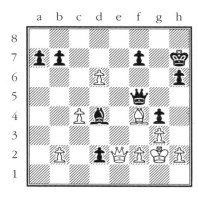

Black to move

When in possession of a dangerous passed pawn one must always look carefully if there is a combination available.

Here it looks as if Black's passer is doomed.

1...♗e3!!

An incredible move which highlights the important white squares f3, e4 and c2.

2 d7

(a) 2 fxe3 is answered by 2...♕e4+ (or 2...♕c2) 3 ♔f2 ♕f3+! 4 ♕xf3 gxf3 and a beautiful cooperation of the pawns has been achieved!

(b) 2 ♗xe3 ♕f3+ loses in the same way.

2...♕e4+ 3 ♔g1 ♕b1+ 4 ♔g2 d1♕ White resigns.

299

Alburt
Chess Training Pocket Book III
2010

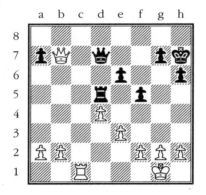

Black to move

When analysing such a position it's easy to go for the move...

1 ♕xd7

But the trap in this position is to think that there is a more effective candidate move. It might seem that 1 ♖c7?? is such a move but Black has the devilish trap 1...♖c5!! which exploits the double pin of the c7-rook and the d4-pawn. 2 ♖xc5 (2 ♖xd7 ♖c1 mate and 2 dxc5 ♕d1 mate lead to back rank mates.) 2...♕xb7 loses the queen.

1...♖xd7 2 ♖c5 leading to an easily winning rook endgame.

300

Bacso – Szalabey
Hungary 1983

Our final position features an original queen ending where common

sense suggests that whoever is to move will win.

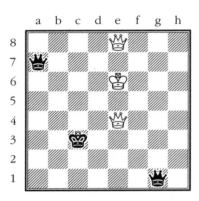

White to move

Black to move can play 1...♕a2+ but if it's a win is up to the reader to decide. A fun variation though with four queens on the board is 2 ♕d5 ♕e3+ 3 ♔f6! It's not that easy to win for White because Black's queens are placed on good squares where they are protecting each other. However, it works with slightly unusual methods. The main tactical device when playing with several queens on the board is to use the pin.

1 ♕h8+! ♕ad4

1...♕gd4 2 ♕h3+ ♔c4 (2...♔d2 3 ♕hg2+ ♕f2 4 ♕b4+ ♔e2 5 ♕b2+ ♔d3 6 ♕g6+ ♔c4 7 ♕c1+ ♔d4 8 ♕g4+) 3 ♕c2+! (Of course White can exploit the fact that the d4-queen is pinned by 3 ♕hd3+ but the main variation is more effective.) 3...♔b5 4 ♕hb3+ ♕b4 5 ♕cc4+ and mate next move. White exploited the pin at a better moment.

2 ♕c8+! ♕c5 3 ♕e5+ ♔b4 4 ♕b2+ ♔a5 5 ♕a8+ ♕a7 6 ♕d5+ Black resigns.

Because of 7 ♕da2+ next move.